JOHN WYCLIF

A STUDY OF THE

ENGLISH MEDIEVAL CHURCH

From the mezzotint by R. Houston in Rolt's Lives of the Reformers, 1759

JOHN WYCLIF

A STUDY OF THE ENGLISH MEDIEVAL CHURCH

BY

HERBERT B. WORKMAN, D.Lit., D.D.
PRINCIPAL OF WESTMINSTER COLLEGE
SENATOR OF LONDON UNIVERSITY

VOL. I

Wipf & Stock
PUBLISHERS
Eugene, Oregon

ΠΟΛΥΜΕΡΩΣ ΚΑΙ ΠΟΛΥΤΡΟΠΩΣ

ΠΑΛΑΙ

Ο ΘΕΟΣ ΛΑΛΗΣΑΣ

Wipf and Stock Publishers
199 West 8th Avenue, Suite 3
Eugene, Oregon 97401

John Wyclif, A Study of the English Medieval Church, 2 volumes
By Workman, Herbert B.
ISBN: 1-57910-606-4
Publication date 3/6/2001
Previously published by Oxford at the Clarendon Press, 1926

A. M. D. G.

ET

IN MEMORIAM

ALVMNORVM COLLEGII WESTMINSTERIENSIS

QUI PRO PATRIA BELLIGERANTES CECIDERE

MCMXIV–MCMXVIII

'*In tentatione inventi fideles*'

PREFACE

WITH much thankfulness I write the concluding words of a work that has occupied the scanty leisure of the last twelve years. But with gratitude there is mingled regret. For twelve years I have lived in Wyclif's presence until his words and person alike have become strangely real. Parting from an old friend is always difficult.

My thanks are due to the Delegates of the Oxford Press for the generous and ready response with which they consented to publish, and for the care with which the work has been carried out. To my daughter also, who has corrected the proofs, I owe much. In a work of this size involving so many transcriptions of notes it is impossible but that errors should arise. For these the author alone must be held responsible.

For the numerous references I make no apology. Any work on Wyclif that is without references is of little value. The subject-matter is far too controversial and difficult for opinions to be accepted without proof. Should the critic insist that the references to Wyclif's writings might have been reduced, I answer that only by a wide survey can the student estimate the degree to which any idea gripped Wyclif's mind, or the precise part it played in his development. The weakness of much writing on Wyclif has lain in an insufficient knowledge of his Latin writings, studied chronologically, and an uncritical acceptance of the

English works, to which must be added the frequent disregard of their late date. Nor do I apologize for the space I have devoted to the description of Wyclif's environment, whether as an Oxford schoolman, a politician, or a reformer. Lack of such study was the weakness of Lechler's biography. Abstraction from environment is the defect of much theological writing, and presupposes that there is a sort of constant, invariable truth, independent of the age, the measure of which in any man it is the biographer's task to discover.

To those who have walked the road before me I acknowledge my obligations. I may especially single out Lewis, Shirley, Lechler, Loserth, Matthew, Denifle, Rashdall, Wylie, and Miss Deanesly. Nor would I overlook the labours of the *Wyclif Society*. May I add that I have accepted nothing second-hand, but have sought by direct study, especially of Wyclif's Latin writings, to ascertain the facts and to form my own conclusions; I have tried also to be fair and impartial, remembering that in every controversy there is always the other side.

The student will notice the great use I have made of the various *Calendars*. They have proved a gold mine of information. The same is true of the bishops' *Registers*. It is a profound pity that the registers of Lincoln for the most part are still unprinted. The *Canterbury and York Society* deserves all encouragement. The county of Lincoln also lacks good local histories. I have spent days in the British Museum in a vain endeavour to discover anything of value about Fillingham.

One difficulty in any life of Wyclif is to know at what point to conclude. To end with Wyclif's death were absurd; no biographer has attempted it. So far as Oxford was concerned I have brought down the story to Arundel's crushing out of lollard teaching in the university in 1411. For the political movements after Wyclif's death that owed their rise to his influence I have fixed upon the events of 1395 as the terminus. I have left over the story of the fortunes of Wyclif's teaching among the townsmen and peasants of England in the fourteenth and fifteenth centuries. This will form the subject-matter of another volume, entitled *The Origins of Nonconformity*.

The reader should note that quotations from original or contemporary writings are always indicated by single inverted commas; quotations from authors who cannot be regarded as sources, by double inverted commas. As a rule I have modernized the spelling of Wyclif's English and Latin quotations, in order not to add to the reader's difficulties.

*Written at Westminster College on or about the
Sixth Centenary of the Birth of Wyclif.*

H. B. W.

CONTENTS

VOLUME I

ABBREVIATIONS AND EDITIONS . . . xxvii

BOOK I. THE SCHOOLMAN

I

THE IMPORTANCE OF WYCLIF   3–20

§ 1. Obscurity of details of Wyclif's life; His middle position; Revolution and medievalism; Importance as a schoolman; Thorpe, Knighton, and Arundel on his pre-eminence; The development of his teaching; Contrast with other reformers; Complex combinations; A Nonconformist of Nonconformists 3–7

§ 2. Wyclif's influence in other lands; Hus and Bohemia; Luther's discovery of Hus; Scotland; Paul Krawer, Reseby, and Folkhyrd; Lollards of Kyle; Murdoch Nisbet 7–12

§ 3 Biographies of Wyclif; Foxe, Bale, Lewis, Vaughan, Lechler; Publication of his works; Todd, Shirley, Arnold, Matthew, the Wyclif Society; The manuscripts and their homes; The marriage of Anne and its results; The Thirty Years' War; Prague, Vienna, and Stockholm 12–20

II

EARLY YEARS   21–51

§ 1. Date of Wyclif's birth; Birthplace; Spresswell, Hipswell, and other claimants; Manor of Wycliffe; The church of Wycliffe; Tunstalls and Constables; The isolation of Wycliffe; Coal mining 21–28

§ 2. Richmond; The archdeaconry and its privileges; Honour of Richmond; The Scots invasions; Desolation of the North; Richmond and John of Gaunt . 28–37

§ 3. The Wyclif family; His parents; Rectors of Wycliffe; John de Clervaux; Wyclif's later connexion with the estates; A Roman Catholic enclave; Robert Wyclif; Bishops of Durham; Lewis Beaumont; Portraits of Wyclif; Thorpe's character of Wyclif . . . 37–51

III

GRADUATE DAYS AT OXFORD   52–102

§ 1. Date of entering Oxford; A blunder of Bulaeus; Journey to Oxford; England on the road; Sharpers; Vagabond clergy   52–55

§ 2. Oxford city; Its military strength; Bocardo; St. Martin's; Hoary fictions; Alfred the Great; Cambridge also; Remains of medieval Oxford; Oxford economics; Weavers and Jews; Carfax; Touting masters; The Opening Mass   55–63

§ 3. What College was Wyclif at?; Queen's; Wyclif and Queen's; The almonry boy; The claims of Merton; Robert's catalogue; Wyclif or Whitclif?; Mr. Cronin's theory   63–70

§ 4. Balliol's claim, Story of the foundation; Dervorgilla; Franciscan procurators; Complex government; Burnel's inn; Limitation to artists; Somervile's endowment; Other extensions; Wyclif as Master; Abbotsley; Appointed to Fillingham; Delay in choice of successor; Changes at Balliol   70–81

§ 5. Inner life of the University; Meaningless oaths; Henry Simon; Ingram and Wylliott; Black Death; Oxford dirt; The Great Slaughter; Dispute with John Gynwell; Emancipation of the Chancellor; Oxford numbers; Moral conditions; Brewsters; Sports; Oxford expenses; Struggle of seculars and regulars; Friars at Oxford; Wax doctors; Stealing children   81–94

§ 6. Oxford studies; Length of course; Responsions; Quodlibeta; Vespers; Theological course; The *Sentences*; Aulatio; Resumpta; Books in use; Mathematics; John Holywood; Arabic notation; John of Basing; Bradwardine; Squaring the circle; Wyclif's love of optics; Vitellio; Greek and Hebrew at Oxford; Adam Easton; Wyclif's knowledge of law; Hostiensis and Lyndwood   94–102

IV

WYCLIF'S PLACE AMONG THE SCHOOLMEN 103–50

§ 1. The authority of Aristotle and of Plato; Avicenna and Averrhoës; Thomas Aquinas; Kilwardby and Peckham; William de la Mare; The life and work of Duns; The Reformation and Duns; The philosophy of Duns; Influence on Wyclif; William Ockham; Nominalism; Nominalism and the Church; *Odium Philosophicum*; Wyclif, Hus, and the Nominalists . 103–14

2. Wyclif's list of Oxford scholars; Bacon; Wyclif's debt to Grosseteste; Walter Burley; Canon, Cowton, and Holcot; Richard Bury; Wyclif and St. Augustine; The life and influence of Bradwardine; Nicholas de Autrecourt; Fitzralph; Influence on Wyclif; The Poverty of Christ; Fitzralph and Conway; Fitzralph's *de Pauperie Salvatoris*; Marsiglio of Padua . . 114–34

§ 3. Wyclif's early Oxford Writings; His quotations; Obscure authors; His knowledge of history; Wyclif's realism; Effect on his views; Wyclif's *de Benedicta Incarnacione*; Wyclif and the Humanity of Christ; Wyclif and the annihilation of the real; Realism and Sin; The nature of the Individual; Wyclif the last of the schoolmen; Discussions on angels; Christopher Binder; Scholasticism and freedom of thought; Minor heretics; Trivet; Tremur; Drayton; Paris heretics; Ludovic of Padua; Foullechat . . . 134–50

V

FROM MASTER OF BALLIOL TO DOCTOR OF THEOLOGY 151–206

§ 1. Fillingham; the Plague of 1361; Prebend in Westbury; Leave of Absence; Bishop John Buckingham; Rooms at Queen's 151–56

§ 2. Westbury-on-Trym—Godfrey Giffard; John Carpenter; Canynges; Wittlesey's visitation; 'John Wynkele'; a Canon's duties; Wyclif and Aust; Urban V and the bull *Horribilis*; Wyclif's excuse for absenteeism; Wyclif's fellow-delinquents; Bryan, Hyndele, and Ottery; John Trevisa; Wyclif and Bristol; Robert de Farrington; Length of Wyclif's tenure of Westbury . 156–71

§ 3. Queen's once more; Warden of Canterbury hall; History of the hall; Islip's Statutes; His endowments; Islip's intentions; Islip appoints Wyclif; Wyclif's secular colleagues; Struggle of regulars and seculars; Simon Langham; His suit against Wyclif; Wyclif appeals to Urban V; Southam and Freton; Result of the Appeal; Illegality all round . . 171–84

§ 4. Wyclif or Whitclif?; Testimony of Woodford; Of the *Chronicon Angliae*; Arguments for Wyclif; Counter-claims for Whitclif; Wyclif's reference in his *de Ecclesia*; Wyclif and Chaucer 185–94

§ 5. Renewed licence for absence; Ludgershall; Stir and tumult; Still at Canterbury hall; Middleworth and Selby; Wyclif's financial difficulties; William Askeby; Wyclif his executor; Doctor of divinity at last; A Prebend in Lincoln; Did Wyclif receive it?; Refusal to pay firstfruits; Philip Thornbury . . . 194–206

BOOK II. THE POLITICIAN

I

THE MISSION TO BRUGES   209–56

§ 1. Wyclif enters the Service of the Crown; Reasons for so doing; Rector of Lutterworth; The Parliament of 1371; Bankyn and Ashbourne; Richard le Scrope; Political Movements; Decay of England; The French Wars; Disasters at home; John of Gaunt; Belling the cat 209–17

§ 2. Peter's Pence and Tribute; Urban V's demands; Unfortunate chronology; Arnold Garnier; The Mission in 1373 to Avignon; The members of the mission; Gilbert, Uhtred, Sheppey, and Burton; Falling among thieves; Gregory XI and the Visconti; Gregory's demands on England; Benefices held by aliens; The Council of May 1374; Uhtred, Mardisley, and Ashbourne; Verdict of the barons 217–30

§ 3. Wyclif and the Tribute; Wyclif, Uhtred, and Binham; Wyclif's *Determinatio*; The speeches of the Seven Lords; 'Peculiaris regis clericus'; Wyclif's relation to parliament 231–39

CONTENTS

§ 4. The Mission to Bruges; Wyclif's colleagues; Guttierez and Moulton; Wyclif's expenses; Wyclif, Strode, and Benger; Gregory's nuncios; Procurations; Bruges and its trade; Wyclif comes back; Queen's once more; A second conference at Bruges; Wyclif left out; Adam Houghton and Erghum; Proposed Concordat; Gregory's rewards; Wyclif and the bishopric of Worcester; Victory of Gregory; Small part played by Wyclif at Bruges; John of Gaunt at Bruges 240–56

II

THE GOOD PARLIAMENT   257–74

§ 1. A disillusioned man; Queen's again; *Divine and Civil Dominion*; Wyclif's theory; 'Lordship', 'dominion' and 'use'; 'Merit' and 'grace'; The nature of Civil Lordship; Kingship and grace; Mortal sin and lordship; Sigismund and Hus; the Ownership of church property; Limits of a just war; Defence of Simon de Montfort; Wyclif's vision of a 'happy England'; Wyclif sides with the friars; Lordship and the grace of illness 257–66

§ 2. The actual background of these ideal reconstructions; The Good Parliament; Peter de la Mare; Alice Perrers; the King's misgovernment; 'The sinful city of Avenon'; The pope's collector; Death of the Black Prince; John of Gaunt's triumph . . . 266–74

III

THE SUMMIT OF INFLUENCE   275–324

§ 1. Lancaster and Wyclif; Contrast between the two; Cause of the alliance; The alliance a mistake; Anachronistic thinking; Alliance with friars; Lancaster's packed parliament; Reactionary proceedings . . 275–84

§ 2. Convocation and Wykeham; Career of Courtenay; Wyclif cited to St. Paul's; Lancaster and the London citizens; The friars come to Wyclif's help; Fitzwalter; The riot at the Savoy; Struggle of the City and the Crown. 284–93

§ 3. Gregory XI issues his bulls ; Gregory's claims ; A papal inquisition ; Gregory and the Waldenses ; The accusers of Wyclif ; Wyclif's errors and heresies ; Death of Edward III 293–300

§ 4. Richard's first parliament ; Critical conditions ; Wyclif and the export of gold ; Wyclif on the papal bulls ; A 'motley doctor' ; Oxford and the papal bulls ; Use of the incident by the Crown ; Wyclif at Lambeth ; Death of Gregory ; Gregory's citation of Wyclif ; Wyclif's reply to Urban VI ; Wyclif's *Protestatio* ; Wyclif's *XXXIII Conclusions* ; The movement withers away . 300–13

§ 5. Haulay and Shakyl ; Invasion of sanctuary ; Lancaster is blamed ; Parliament summoned to Gloucester ; Gloucester abbey ; Wyclif at Gloucester ; Long litigation ; Wyclif on the rights of sanctuary . . . 313–24

APPENDIXES TO VOLUME I

A. The Meaning of 'Lollard'	327
B. Luther and Hus	327
C. Wyclif's English Works	329
D. Wyclif's Philosophical and Early Theological Writings	332
E. Wyclif's Quotations from Rare Writers . .	335
F. Peter's Pence	337
G. John's Tribute and its Payment	338
H. John Sheppey	339
I. Was Wyclif a Member of Parliament ? . .	340
J. The Fitzwalters	341
K. Wyclif's Debt to William of Pérault . . .	342

VOLUME II
BOOK III. THE REFORMER

I

WYCLIF'S CONCEPTS OF CHURCH AND STATE	3–45
§ 1. From politician to reformer; *de Veritate Sacrae Scripturae*; Its date and contents	3–6
§ 2. Wyclif's *de Ecclesia*; Its influence in Bohemia; The three parts of the Church; Predestinarian basis; Wyclif's difficulties; Universal priesthood of the predestinate; Character as the test of function; Privilege and poverty; Absolution and indulgences; Saints, relics, and pilgrimages; Purgatory and hell; Wyclif's individualism	6–20
3. Wyclif's *de Officio Regis*; The Dignity of the king; Honour of office and honour of merit; Duties of the king; Kings and the law; Kings and episcopal jurisdiction; Wyclif on Canon and Civil Law; Excommunication; Writ *significavit*; 'Cursing for muck'; Wyclif on War; Summary of the treatise; Wyclif and Henry VIII; Divine Right of kings	20–30
§ 4. Wyclif on the sacraments; Transubstantiation; The theories of Aquinas and Duns Scotus; Wyclif's realism; Consubstantiation; Wyclif's *Wycket*; Hair-splitting distinctions; Wyclif's real aim; Fasting Communion; Sacraments and character; Confession; Confirmation; Wyclif and his antagonists; *de Apostasia* and *de Eucharistia*; Wyclif on marriage	30–45

II

WYCLIF AND THE PAPACY	46–82
§ 1. The Captivity; Urban V returns to Rome; His journey; Bridget's prophecy; Gregory XI and St. Catherine; Disorder in Italy; Hawkwood; Gregory's promise to return; His death in Rome	46–52
2. The French cardinals unprepared; Election of Urban VI; Character of Urban; Wyclif's support; Urban's folly; The French elect Clement; Clement's character; Europe split into two; Pope by act of parliament; Schism in the religious orders; Rival bishops; Wyclif on the 'general strife'	52–64

§ 3. Spenser's Crusade; Spenser's character; Mixed motives in the Crusade; Spenser's defeat and disgrace; Urban and Clement; Urban's tyrannies; Adam Easton; Urban's death; Extraordinary epitaph . 64–73

§ 4. Wyclif and the papacy; His early views; Causes of change; *de Potestate Papae*; Analysis of the book; Papal pretensions; The temporal power; Rome the capital of heathendom; *de Ordine Christiano*; Wyclif's later views; Antichrist; Contrast between Christ and His vicar; Wyclif welcomes the Schism . . . 73–82

III

THE ABUSES IN THE CHURCH 83–118

§ 1. The silence of goodness; Wyclif and Avignon; Record of the Avignon popes; Scanty justice; Corruption of the city; Europe gropes for a lost centre; Contrast between the plans of Dante, Marsiglio, Wyclif, and Gerson; Wyclif and Avignon finance; Provisions, Firstfruits, and Procurations; Venality of papal courts 83–89

§ 2. Wyclif on Monasticism; Monks at Oxford; Osney and Rewley; St. Frideswyde's and its scandals; Oxford friars; Wyclif's root objection to monasticism; 'The Order of Christ'; 'Private religions'; The Faults of Possessioners; Monastic appropriations; Decay of monastic hospitality; Wyclif's invective spares none . 89–97

§ 3. Wyclif and the Spiritual Franciscans; *The Introduction to the Eternal Gospel*; John XXII; Michael of Cesena and Ockham; The lollards and the friars; Wyclif changes his views; Wyclif and St. Amour; Wyclif attacks the friars; 'The order of Caim'; The crimes of the friars; Reducing confession to a farce; Letters of fraternity; Burial in a friar's robe . . . 97–108

§ 4. Evils in the secular Church; Invectives against bishops; 'Caesarean clergy'; Pluralists and absentees; Boy pluralists; Wyclif on the excessive number of the clergy; Figures for various dioceses; Chantries; Wyclif on the wealth of the Church; Estimate of income; Glaring inequalities; Collegiate churches; Grandisson's descriptions of disorders in his diocese; Clerical immorality; An age of violence . . . 108–118

CONTENTS

IV

FRIENDS AND FOES AT OXFORD   119–48

§ 1. Oxford controversialists ; Cunningham ; William Remington ; Nicholas of Durham ; John Wells ; John Sharp ; Wyclif and Ralph Strode ; Cooling friendships ; Strode's plea for the peace of the Church ; Nameless opponents   119–29

§ 2. Oxford friends ; Repingdon ; Nicholas Hereford ; His early history ; His appeal to Rome ; His imprisonment in St. Angelo ; Hereford's return ; Hereford's English tracts ; *On the Seven Deadly Sins* ; Imprisoned at Nottingham ; His relapse ; John Purvey ; Early life ; John Aston ; John Ashwardby ; Lawrence Bedeman ; Robert Alington   130–40

§ 3. Chancellor Berton ; His attack on Wyclif ; The Council of Twelve ; Robert Rigg ; John Landreyn and John Loney ; Wyclif's condemnation ; Wyclif appeals to the king ; Wyclif's *Confessio* ; Winterton replies in his *Absolutio* ; Wyclif's illness ; Wyclif leaves Oxford .   140–48

V

WYCLIF AND THE BIBLE   149–200

§ 1. The authority of Scripture ; Wyclif's claims ; Right of every man to examine for himself ; Medieval exegesis ; 'God's Law' ; Extent of medieval knowledge of the Bible   149–55

§ 2. Anglo-Saxon translations ; Wyclif's first purpose ; Wyclif and *The Lay Folks' Catechism* ; The first translation ; The part taken by Hereford ; Purvey's revision ; Purvey and Lavenham ; *XXXVII Conclusions* ; Purvey's later life ; Purvey and Palmer   .   .   .   155–70

§ 3. Rolle and Wyclif ; Rolle's *Psalter* ; Lollard interpolations ; Other English versions ; *Pauline Epistles* ; *Northern Homily Collection* ; Wyclif's translation in his *Sermons*   170–77

§ 4. The two Wycliffite versions ; Purvey's difficulties ; Influence of Purvey's version ; Effect on English ; Decline of French language in England ; An Age of Translations ; John Trevisa   177–85

§ 5. Sir Thomas More and Wyclif's Bible; 'The angle not the angel speech'; Arundel's verdict; Lyndwood's interpretations; Was Wyclif's the first version?; Evidence of More; Cardinal Gasquet's "authorized version"; The Church and vernacular scriptures; The Constitutions of Oxford; Licences for bibles; Persecution of the non-licenced; *The Chastising of God's Children*; William Butler and the burning of English bibles; Wyclif, Tindale, and Wesley . . . 185–200

VI

THE POOR PREACHERS   201–20

§ 1. Wyclif's Poor Preachers; Their title; They were not Laymen; Wyclif's intentions; Persecution by bishops and friars; Use of the writ *significavit*; Wyclif's indignation 201–5

§ 2. Wyclif's Oxford sermons; How some can be dated; Wyclif's insistence on preaching; Function of the bishops; Vernacular preaching no novelty; Texts or postillizations; Wyclif on the defects of preaching in his age; Wyclif's own claims 206–13

§ 3. Medieval preaching; St. Francis; Medieval anecdotes; Outline books of sermons; *Dormi secure*; *Exempla*; Odo of Cheriton; Fables; Bozon; Bestiaries; Properties; Legends of saints; Wyclif's attitude to medieval methods; Consequent neglect 213–20

VII

THE PEASANTS' REVOLT   221–45

§ 1. Causes of the Revolt; Widespread character; Poll-tax; Economic ignorance; Astonishing blunder of the parliament of 1371; Contrast between the taxes in 1379 and 1381; Unfair incidence; Discontent among the clergy; Parsons who were rebels; The real causes of revolt; Corvées and Opera; Thorold Rogers' mistake; Villeinage; Statute of Labourers; Depreciation of coinage; Flight to the towns; System of fines; The Great Society; Disaffection in the towns; St. Albans and Bury; Narrow oligarchies; Rival guilds; Close connexion of town and country . . 221–36

CONTENTS

§ 2. Effect of the Rising on Wyclif's fortunes; Confessions of Ball and Straw; Wyclif's Poor Priests and the Rising; Story of Ball; Spiritual Franciscans and the Rising; Effect of Wyclif's attacks on the friars; Popular interpretation of Wyclif's theory of dominion; Wyclif's views on serfdom; After the Rising Wyclif defends the serfs; *Servants and Lords*; Contrast between Wyclif and Luther 236–45

VIII

THE BLACKFRIARS SYNOD   246–93

§ 1. Renewed struggle at Oxford; The friars appeal to Lancaster; Stephen Patrington; Richard Maidstone; Appeal to Courtenay; Wyclif's *de Blasphemia*; Wyclif appeals to parliament; Wyclif's *Complaint*; Hereford back in Oxford 246–53

§ 2. Courtenay summons the Blackfriars Council; The character of the Council; Tale of Lawrence of St. Martin; Bishops Brunton, Braybroke, Fordham, and Brantingham; 'Nanatensis'—a curious puzzle; Diss, Waldby, Bankyn, and Pickworth; Noted pluralists, Appleby and Waltham; Ralph Tregrisiow and others   253–66

§ 3. The Earthquake; Courtenay's happy inspiration; Wyclif's counter version; The *Twenty Four Conclusions*; Courtenay's pretended Statute; Antagonism of the Commons; Courtenay strikes at the lollards; What happened to Cornelius de Clone? . . . 266–73

§ 4. Courtenay and Oxford; Repingdon in St. Frideswyde's; Rigg and Stokes; Courtenay and Rigg; John Bromyard; Rigg capitulates; James and Brightwell; Crump calls the seculars 'lollards'; Richard protects Crump 273–82

5. Rigg suspends Hereford and Repingdon; A second gathering at the Blackfriars; Aston's daring; Courtenay excommunicates Hereford and Repingdon; They appeal to Rome; Bedeman's recantation; Courtenay visits Oxford; Convocation in St. Frideswyde's; Repingdon and Aston recant; Courtenay crushes the Oxford lollards; Rigg gets back his own by imprisoning prior Dodford; Trial of Crump 282–93

IX

THE LAST YEARS — 294–324

§ 1. Courtenay leaves Wyclif alone ; Explanation of this clemency ; Wyclif's supposed recantation at Oxford ; Wyclif and Lancaster ; Wyclif's yearning for Oxford . 294–97

§ 2. Lutterworth ; Its hospital and fairs ; The Feildings ; Lutterworth Church ; Relics of Wyclif . . . 298–302

§ 3. Stress and strain ; French invasions ; The rise of de Vere ; Friar Latimer and Lancaster ; Wyclif defends Lancaster ; Wyclif at Lutterworth ; His last writings ; Incredible activity ; *Trialogus* ; Increasing bitterness ; Effects of his stroke ; Wyclif and university studies ; *Opus Evangelicum* 302–14

§ 4. Gregory's citation again ; Wyclif's letter to Urban ; Wyclif's death ; John Horn's testimony ; Wyclif on Thomas Becket ; Slanders of his enemies ; The Council of Constance, Martin V, and Wyclif's body ; Fleming throws Wyclif's ashes into the Swift ; Character of Wyclif ; Causes of the failure of his reformation . . 314–24

X

BROKEN REEDS — 325–404

§ 1. Wyclif's followers ; Their tracts ; *Fifty Heresies and Errors of Friars* ; *Of Prelates* ; *Of Clerks Possessioners* ; *The Office of Curates* ; *de Officio Pastorali* ; Their appeal to the people 325–30

§ 2. The Oxford lollards ; Repingdon's career ; Bishop and cardinal ; Resigns his bishopric ; Aston revokes his recantation ; Hereford recants ; His rewards ; Enters the Charterhouse at Coventry ; Recantation of the lesser lollards ; William James 330–40

§ 3. Death of Courtenay ; Thomas Arundel ; Arundel attacks Oxford ; The bull of Boniface IX ; Commission to examine the *Trialogus* ; Arundel's disgrace ; Archbishop Roger Walden ; Arundel returns from the Grand Tour ; Arundel and Cambridge ; The forged certificate ; Who was its author ? ; Career of Peter Payne ; Payne and Partridge ; Payne in Bohemia and at Basel ; Convocation meets at Oxford ; The Constitutions of Oxford ; Arundel's attack on preaching . 340–59

CONTENTS

§ 4. The Committee of Twelve; Delay in its report; Richard Fleming; He appeals to Convocation; Fleming's supposed lollardy; Fleming receives his reward; Wyclif's works are burned; Oxford lollards write to Arundel; Curious exaggerations; Arundel determines to visit Oxford; Chancellor Richard Courtenay; Arundel's grandiloquence; Oriel fellows fortify St. Mary's; Arundel's victory; Oxford surrenders its bull; The lollards are crushed; The Council at St. Peter's and the works of Wyclif; The downfall of lollardy and the decline of Oxford . . 359–76

§ 5. Prevailing discontent; Statutes of *Provisors* and *Premunire*; Boniface IX attempts their repeal; Lollard gentry; Latimer, Clifford, and Stury; Sir John Montague; Herefordshire lollards; John Cheyne and John Greyndor; Lollard outbreak in 1388; *Twenty Five Points* 376–90

§ 6. The lollard outbreak in 1395; Petition to parliament; Origin of this petition; *XII Conclusions*; *XXXVII Conclusions*; Purvey's *Ecclesiae Regimen*; Relation of the three; Later lollard doctrine; Purvey's scheme of disendowment; Curious verses; Convocation petitions Richard; Richard returns from Ireland; Collapse of political lollardy; Recantation of Stury, Clifford, Montague; Montague's last days . . . 390–404

APPENDIXES TO VOLUME II

L.	Vicarious Pilgrimages	407
M.	The Date of Wyclif's Raising of the Eucharistic Controversy	408
N.	The Great Schism	409
O.	Appropriated Churches and Vicars	410
P.	The Four John Wells	412
Q.	Ralph Strode	412
R.	Broadgates Hall	414
S.	The Peasants' Rising	415
T.	The Twenty Four Conclusions	416
U.	The Constitutions of Oxford	417
W.	Richard Fleming	419
Y.	Chancellor Thomas Pressbury	420
Z.	Purvey's Scheme of Disendowment	420
	ADDENDA ET CORRIGENDA	422
	INDEX.	425

LIST OF ILLUSTRATIONS

VOLUME I

John Wyclif. From the mezzotint by R. Houston (in Rolt, *Lives of the Reformers*, 1759) from the portrait in King's College, Cambridge . . . . *Frontispiece*

Richmond Castle, Yorkshire. From the painting by J. M. W. Turner, engraved by J. Archer in Whitaker, *County of York*, 1821 . . . . *facing* 30

The Keep of Richmond Castle. From the painting by J. Buckler, engraved by J. Le Keux, in Whitaker, *County of York*, 1821 . . . . *facing* 34

South-east view of the Greyfriars' Tower, Richmond. From the painting by J. Buckler, engraved by J. Pye in Whitaker, *County of York*, 1821 . . . . . *facing* 34

Wycliffe Church, Yorkshire. Exterior and Interior views. Reproduced by permission from photographs in the *Victoria County History* . . . . . . *facing* 42

St. Mary's Church, Oxford. From the engraving by Loggan, 1675 . . . . *facing* 60

The Old Congregation House in St. Mary's . . *facing* 62

The Catherine Wheel before 1828. Reproduced by permission from a drawing in the house of the Master of Balliol *facing* 74

Ludgershall: the Church of St. Mary. Exterior (from a photograph in the Report of the Royal Commission on Historical Monuments; by permission of the Controller of His Majesty's Stationery Office); Interior (from a photograph supplied by the Rev. T. Appleton) . . . . . *facing* 196

John of Gaunt. From the window in the Chapel of All Souls College, Oxford . . . . . . *facing* 216

Lady Chapel in Old St. Paul's. From the engraving by Hollar
facing 286

VOLUME II

John Wyclif. From the portrait by Basire in Nichols, *Leicester*
Frontispiece

Ruins of Osney Abbey. From the engraving by Hollar *facing* 90

The interrupted translation of the Bible by Nicholas de Hereford. (*a*) The last folio of the original corrected copy of the translator (MS. Bodl. 959, f. 332 r); (*b*) A folio from a copy transcribed from the preceding before its correction, with a note assigning the translation to Hereford (MS. Douce 369, f. 250 r) . . . . . . *between* 148 *and* 149

xxvi　　LIST OF ILLUSTRATIONS

Preaching at St. Paul's Cross. From an engraving after the picture in the possession of the Society of Antiquaries of London . . . . *facing* 210
The Peasants' Revolt; showing John Ball and Wat Tyler. From MS. Royal 18 E. i. 165 v (Br. Mus.) . . . *facing* 236
Old Lutterworth Church, 1792. From Nichols, *Leicester* *facing* 300
The river Swift at Lutterworth. The modern bridge marks the place from which Wyclif's ashes were thrown into the river. *facing* 320
A University Lecture, early 15th century. From MS. Royal 17 E. iii. 209 (Br. Mus.) . . . . . . *facing* 342
Archbishop Arundel in the pulpit[1] . . . *facing* 342
Richard II.[1] (a) with Earl Percy; (b) Delivered to the citizens of London . . . . *facing* 400

[1] NOTE.—These illustrations are reproduced from a fifteenth-century manuscript of a contemporary chronicle, written in French by Jehan Creton, of the Fall of Richard II (British Museum, MS. Harley 1319). Creton was an eye-witness of the events he describes. There is a full account of the Chronicle and its miniatures by Sir Edward Maunde Thompson in *The Burlington Magazine* for May and June 1904.

ARUNDEL IN THE PULPIT.—The deposed Archbishop Arundel, returned from exile, preaching and reciting a papal bull of indulgence (possibly forged) to arouse the people in favour of Henry Bolingbroke.

RICHARD II AND EARL PERCY.—The interview between Richard II (in the dark hooded cloak) and Sir Henry Percy, Earl of Northumberland (the figure on the left, with pointed beard) at Conway Castle in 1399. Other figures in the picture are the reputed lollard John Montague, Earl of Salisbury, and the Bishop of Carlisle.

RICHARD II DELIVERED TO THE CITIZENS OF LONDON.—After Richard had been delivered into the hands of Henry Bolingbroke he was taken to London, and within a few miles of the capital the mayor and citizens met him. Before entering the city Bolingbroke handed over Richard to their charge. He was then interned in the Tower.

ABBREVIATIONS AND EDITIONS

[N.B. Works whose titles are fully quoted in the notes or whose use is restricted to one section are not given in this list. It should be noted that all references are made by volume and page. The abbreviation R.S. is for the Rolls Series; E.E.T.S. is Early English Text Society; O.H.S. is Oxford Historical Society; D.N.B. is *Dict. National Biography*; N.E.D. is *New English Dictionary*; P.R.O. is Public Record Office.]

Amundesham.	*Annales Mon. S. Albani*, ed. H. T. Riley, 2 vols. (R.S.).
Ang. Sac.	*Anglia Sacra*, ed. H. Wharton, 2 vols., 1691.
Ann. Mon.	*Annales Monastici*, ed. H. R. Luard (R.S.), 3 vols., 1864.
Anstey, H.	*Munimenta Academica Oxon.*, 2 vols. (R.S.), 1868.
„	*Epistolae Academicae Oxon.* (O.H.S.), 1898.
Archaeol.	*Archaeologia*.
Arch. Camb.	*Archaeologia Cambrensis*.
Arch. Cant.	*Archaeologia Cantiana*.
Archiv.	*Archiv für Literatur und Kirchengeschichte des Mittelalters*, ed. P. H. Denifle and F. Ehrle (Freiburg, 5 vols.).
Arch. Jour.	*Archaeological Journal*.
Armitage-Smith, S.	*John of Gaunt*, 1904.
Arnold, R.	*The Customs of London, otherwise called Arnold's Chronicle*, ed. F. Douce, 1811.
Arnold, T.	*Memorials of St. Edmund's Abbey, Bury*, 3 vols. (R.S.), 1890.
„	*Select Eng. Works of Wyclif*, 3 vols., 1869.
Ashley, W. J.	*Economic History*, 3rd ed., 1894.
Ayliffe, J.	*Ancient and Present State of the Univ. of Oxford*, 2 vols., 1714.
Bacon, J.	*Liber Regis vel Thesaurus*, 1786.
Bacon, R.	*Opera Inedita*, ed. J. S. Brewer (R.S.), 1859.
Baldwin, J. F.	*The King's Council in England during the Middle Ages*, 1914.
Bale, J.	*Illustrium majoris Brit. Script. Catalogus*, 2 vols., Basel, 1557, 1559.
„	*Index Script.*, i.e. *Index Britanniae Scriptorum*, ed. R. L. Poole and M. Bateson in *Anecdota Oxoniensia*, 1902.
„	*Brief Chronicle of Sir John Oldcastle* (Parker Soc., vol. xxxvi.).
Baluze.	*Vitae Paparum Avenionensium.* See Mollat-Baluze.
Barnes, Joshua.	*History of Edward III*, 1688.
Bekynton, T.	*Official Correspondence of Thomas Bekynton*, ed. G. Williams, (R.S.), 2 vols., 1872.
Blomefield, F.	*Topographical History of Norfolk*, 5 vols., 1739–75.
Boase, C. W.	*Register of Exeter Coll.* (O.H.S.), 1894. N.B. The 1st ed. in Latin occasionally has documents not in this edition.
Brewer, J. S.	*Calendar of Letters and Papers of Henry VIII*, 1862 f.
Brodrick, G. C.	*Memorials of Merton* (O.H.S.), 1885.
Brown, E.	*Fasciculus rerum Expetendarum et Fugiendarum*, 2 vols., 1690.
Brut.	*The Brut or the Chronicle of England*, ed. F. W. D. Brie (E.E.T.S.), 1908.

Cal. Docs. Scots.	*Calendar of Documents relating to Scotland*, 4 vols., 1881 f.
Cal. Pap. Let.	*Calendar of Entries in the Papal Registers relating to Gt. Britain and Ireland. Papal Letters*, 1902 f.
,, Pet.	—— *Petitions to the Pope*, 1896. (Vol. i. only published.)
Cal. Pat.	*Calendar of Patent Rolls.* N.B. The number of the King is only given where there can be any doubt of the reference. Quoted by volume and page except for the early volumes.
Camb. Lit.	*Cambridge History of English Literature.*
Cantor, M.	*Vorlesungen über Geschichte der Mathematik*, 4 vols., 2nd ed., Leipzig, 1900.
Carm. Burana.	*Carmina Burana*, ed. J. A. Schmeller, Stuttgart, 1847 (v. 16 in *Bibliothek des Lit. Vereins*).
Capes, W. W.	*Charters and Records of Hereford Cathedral*, 1908.
Capgrave.	*The Chronicle of England*, F. C. Hingeston (R.S.), 1858.
,,	*de Illustribus Henricis*, ib., 1858.
Cart. Frid.	*The Chartulary of the Monastery of St. Frideswyde's* (O.H.S.), 2 vols., 1895.
Cat Anc. Deeds.	*Catalogue of Ancient Deeds in the Public Record Office.*
Chanter, J. B.	*Barnstaple Records*, 2 vols., 1900.
Charter Rolls.	*Calendar of Charter Rolls.*
Chart. Par.	*Chartularium Univ. Paris*, ed. H. Denifle, 4 vols., 1889–97.
Chron. Ang.	*Chronicon Angliae*, ed. E. M. Thompson (R.S.), 1876.
Chron. Lan.	*Chronicon de Lanercost*, ed. 1839 (vol. 46 of Maitland Club).
Chron. Maj.	See *Paris, Matthew of*.
Ciaconius, A.	*Vitae Pontificum Rom. et Cardinalium*, 1677.
Clark, A.	*Colleges of Oxford*, 1891.
Clay, R. M.	*The Medieval Hospitals of England*, 1909.
Close Rolls.	*Calendar of Close Rolls.* See remarks under *Cal. Pat.*
Collect.	*Collectanea* (O.H.S.), 4 vols., 1885 f.
Collect. Top.	*Collectanea Topographica et Genealogica*, 1838.
Cont. Murimuth.	*Adami Murimuthensis Chronica cum Continuatione*, ed. T. Story, 1846. [To be distinguished from Murimuth *Cont. Chron.*]
Cooke, W. H.	*Continuation of Duncombe's Herefordshire*, 1892 f.
Cooper, C. H.	*Annals of Cambridge*, 5 vols., 1842 f.
Copinger, W. A.	*Supplement to Hain*, 3 vols., 1895–1902.
Cotton, H.	*Fasti Eccles. Hibernicae*, 5 vols., 1848–78.
Coulton, G. G.	*A Medieval Garner*, 1910.
,,	*Five Centuries of Religion*, 1923 (vol. i. only published).
Coxe, H. O.	*Catal. MSS. in Coll. Aulisque Oxon.*, 1852.
Crane, T. F.	*The Exempla or Illustrative Stories from the Sermones Vulgares of Jacques de Vitry*, 1890.
Creighton, M.	*The History of the Papacy*, ed. 6 vols., 1897.
Davies, J. S.	*An English Chronicle* (Camden Soc.), 1856.
Deanesly, M.	*The Lollard Bible*, 1920.
Deiser, G. F.	*Year Book of 12 Richard II*, 1914.
Delachenal, R.	*Hist. de Charles V*, 3 vols., 1909.
Dempster, T.	*Hist. Ecclesiastica Gentis Scotorum*, 2 vols., 1829.
Devon, F.	*The Issues of the Exchequer*, 1837.
Dig. Peer.	See *Report Dig. Peer.*
Dugdale, W.	*Monasticon Anglicanum*, ed. J. Caley, 6 vols., 1817–30.
,,	*Summons of the Nobility to the Great Councils and Parliaments*, 1685.
Duncombe, J.	*Collections towards the Hist. and Antiquities of the County of Hereford*, 4 vols., 1804–92.

ABBREVIATIONS AND EDITIONS

Eng. Hist. Rev.	*English Historical Review.*
Eng. Works.	See Matthew.
Ep. Grosseteste.	*Epistolae,* ed. H. R. Luard (R.S.), 1861.
Eubel, C.	*Hierarchia Catholica Med. Aevi,* 2 vols., 1898.
Eulog. Cont.	i.e., vol. 3 of *Eulogium* (R.S.), 1863.
Fabyan, R.	*The New Chronicle of England and France,* ed. H. Ellis, 1811.
Feudal Aids.	*Inquisitions and Assessments Relating to Feudal Aids* (P.R.O.), 1900 f.
Finchale.	*The Priory of Finchale* (Surtees Soc.), 1837.
Flenley, S.	*Six Town Chronicles of England,* 1911.
F. and M.	*The Holy Bible: made from the Latin Vulgate by John Wycliffe,* ed. J. Forshall and J. Madden, 4 vols., 1850.
Flete.	*Hist. of Westminster Abbey,* ed. J. A. Robinson, 1909.
Flores Hist.	*Flores Historiarum* (R.S.), ed. H. R. Luard, 3 vols., 1890.
Forshall, J.	*Remonstrance against Romish Corruptions,* 1851.
Foxe, J.	*The Acts and Monuments,* ed. J. Pratt, 8 vols., 1877 f.
Froissart.	Quoted by book and chapter. Various eds.: see Gross.
Fuller, T.	*The Worthies of England,* ed. J. Nichols, 2 vols., 1811.
Furnivall, F. J.	*The Fifty Earliest English Wills* (E.E.T.S.), 1882.
Gairdner, J.	*Three Fifteenth-Century Chronicles* (Camden Soc.), 1880.
"	*Lollardy and the Reformation in England,* 4 vols., 1908 f.
Gale, R.	*Registrum honoris de Richmond,* 1722.
Gascoigne, T.	*Loci e libro veritatum,* ed. J. E. T. Rogers, 1881.
Gasquet, F. A.	*The Great Pestilence,* 1893.
"	*Old English Bible,* 2nd ed., 1908.
Gayet.	*Le grand Schisme d'Occident,* 2 vols., 1889, with *Pièces Justificatives.*
G. E. C.	*The Complete Peerage.* (There is a new ed. in progress. I have quoted from this where it was available. If not, from the old.)
Geneal.	*Genealogist.*
Gibbons, A.	*Early Lincoln Wills,* 1888.
Girald. Cambrensis.	*Opera* (R.S.), 8 vols., ed. J. S. Brewer, 1861–91.
Godwin, F.	*de Praesulibus Angliae,* ed. W. Richmond, 1743.
Goldast.	*Monarchia S. Romani Imp.,* 3 vols., 1611–14.
Gough, R.	*Sepulchral Monuments of Great Britain,* 2 vols., 1796.
Gregorovius, F.	*The Hist. of the City of Rome in the Middle Ages,* Eng. Trans. by A. Hamilton, 8 vols., 1894 f.
Gross, C.	*The Sources and Literature of English History,* 2nd ed., 1915.
Hain, L.	*Repertorium bibliographicum,* 2 vols., 1826–38.
Hardt, H.	*Mag. Constanciense Concilium,* 7 vols., 1697–1742.
Harnack, A.	*History of Dogma,* Eng. Trans., 7 vols., 1894–9.
Harpsfield, N.	*Historia Anglicana Ecclesiastica,* ed. R. Gibbons, 1662.
Hasted, E.	*The Hist. and Topographical Survey of Kent,* 4 vols., 1778–99.
Hennessy, G.	*Novum Repertorium Eccl. Parochiale Londiniense,* 1898.
"	*Chichester Diocesan Clergy Lists,* 1900.
Higden, R.	*Polychronicon* (R.S.), ed. C. Babington and J. R. Lumby, 9 vols., 1865–86. It contains Trevisa's translation, and also in vol. ix. Malvern's Continuation.
Hist. MSS. Com.	*Reports of the Historical Manuscripts Commission.*
Hook, W. F.	*Lives of the Archbishops of Canterbury,* 12 vols., 1860–94.
Horstmann, C.	*Yorkshire Writers,* 2 vols., 1895–6.

ABBREVIATIONS AND EDITIONS

Hurst, H.	*Oxford Topography* (O.H.S.), 1899.
Hutchins, J.	*The County of Dorset*, 3rd ed. by W. Shipp and J. W. Hodson, 4 vols., 1873.
Inquis.	*Calendar of Inquisitiones post Mortem* (R.S.). (A new ed. in progress, from which I have quoted where possible; otherwise the old ed.)
Isaacson, R. F.	*Episcopal Registers of St. Davids*, 2 vols., 1917.
James, M. R.	*Manuscripts in St. John's Coll., Camb.*, 1913.
,,	—— *Peterhouse*, 1899.
,,	—— *Gonville and Caius*, 2 vols., 1907.
,,	—— *Trinity*, 3 vols., 1902.
,,	—— *Corpus*, 2 vols., 1912.
Jour. Brit. Arch. Soc.	*Journal of the British Archaeological Association.*
Jusserand, J. J.	*English Wayfaring Life in the Middle Ages*, 5th ed., 1897.
Kingsford, C. L.	*The Greyfriars of London*, 1915.
,,	*Chronicles of London*, 1905.
Kirkby's Quest.	See Gross *Sources*, pp. 482, 490. Also Surtees Soc., 1867.
Knighton, H.	*Chronicon Hen. Knighton*, ed. J. R. Lumby (R.S.), 2 vols., 1889.
Lantern.	*The Lantern of Light* (E.E.T.S.), 1917.
Lawton, G.	*Collectio rerum ecclesiasticarum in Diocesi Eboracensi*, 2 vols., 1840.
Lay Folks' Cat.	*Lay Folks' Catechism* (E.E.T.S.), ed. T. F. Simmons and H. E. Nolloth, 1901.
Lea, H.	*The Inquisition of the Middle Ages*, New York, 3 vols., 1887.
Leach, A. F.	*Schools of Medieval England*, 1915.
,,	*Educational Charters*, 1911.
Lechler, G. V.	*John Wycliffe and his English Precursors*: trans. P. Lorimer, 2nd ed., 1884.
Leclercq-Hefele.	*Histoire des Conciles*, by C. J. Hefele. French Trans. in 16 vols., with valuable notes by H. Leclercq.
Leland, J.	*Commentarii de Scriptoribus Britannicis*, ed. A. Hall, 1709.
,,	*Collectanea de rebus Brit.*, ed. T. Hearne, 6 vols., 1774.
,,	*The Itinerary of John Leland*, ed. T. Hearne, 2nd ed., 1744.
Le Neve, J.	*Fasti Eccles. Ang.*, 3 vols., ed. T. D. Hardy, 1854.
Levett, A. E.	*The Black Death* (Oxford Studies in Social Hist.), 1916.
Lewis, J.	*The History of the Life and Sufferings of the Rev. John Wicliffe*, 1720.
Liber Albus.	Ed. T. R. Riley (R.S.), 1859-62.
Lipscomb, G.	*The History of Buckingham*, 4 vols., 1847.
Lit. Cant.	See Sheppard.
Little, A. G.	*The Grey Friars in Oxford* (O.H.S.), 1892.
Loserth, J.	*Wiclif and Hus*, trans. M. J. Evans, 1884.
Lowth, R.	*William of Wykeham*, 3rd ed., 1777.
Lützow, F. H.	*The Life and Times of Master John Hus*, 1909.
Lyndwood, W.	*Provinciale*, Oxford, 1679.
Lyte, C. M.	*History of the Univ. of Oxford*, 1886.
Macleane, D.	*Pembroke College* (O.H.S.), 1897.
Madan, F.	*Oxford Books* (O.H.S.), 2 vols., 1895-1912.
Magrath, J. R.	*The Queen's College*, 2 vols., 1921.

ABBREVIATIONS AND EDITIONS xxxi

Maitland, F. W.   *Canon Law in the Church of England*, 1896.
   ,,   *Memoranda de Parliamento* (R.S.), 1893.
Major, J.   *Hist. Maj. Britanniae*, ed. 1740.
Makower, F.   *The Constitutional Hist. of the Church of England*, Eng. Trans., 1895.
Mallet, C. E.   *History of the University of Oxford*, 2 vols., 1924.
Manning, B. L.   *The People's Faith in the time of Wyclif*, 1919.
Mansi, J. D.   *Sacrorum Conciliorum nova Collectio*, Venice, 1782.
Markham, C. A.   *Records of the Borough of Northampton*, ed. C. A. Markham and J. C. Cox, 2 vols., 1898.
Matthew, F. D.   *The English Works of Wyclif hitherto Unprinted* (E.E.T.S.), 1880.
Members.   *Return of Members of Parliament* (P.R.O.), 1878.
Mem. Lond.   *Memorials of London and London Life*, ed. H. T. Riley (R.S.), 1868.
Milman, H. H.   *History of Latin Christianity*, ed. 9 vols., 1883.
Mirbt, D. C.   *Quellen zur Geschichte des Papsttums*, 3rd ed., 1911.
Mollat-Baluze,   i.e. the new ed. of Baluze so far as it is printed.
Mollat, G.   *Les Papes d'Avignon*, 2nd ed., 1912.
Mon. Franc.   *Monumenta Franciscana* (R.S.), vol. i., ed. J. S. Brewer, 1858; vol. ii., ed. R. Howlett, 1882.
Mon. Hus.   *Hist. et Monumenta J. Hussii*, 2 vols., Nuremberg, 1558.
Mullinger, J. B.   *The University of Cambridge*, 3 vols., 1873 f.
Mun. Ac.   See Anstey.

Netter, T.   *Doctrinale Antiquitatum Fidei Eccles. Cath.*, ed. F. B. Blanciotti, 3 vols., Venice, 1757.
Newcourt, R.   *Repertorium Eccles. Paroch. Londin.*, 2 vols., 1708–10.
Nicolas, N. H.   *Chronicle of London*, 1827.
   ,,   *Testamenta Vetusta*, 2 vols., 1826.
Niem, T.   *Theoderici de Nyem de Scismate*, ed. G. Erler, 1890.

Ogle, O.   *Royal Letters addressed to Oxford*, 1892.
Oman, C. W.   *The Great Revolt of 1381* (1906).
Owst, G. R.   *Medieval Preaching in England*, 1926.

Page, T. W.   *End of Villeinage in England*, New York, 1900.
Palacký, F.   *Documenta Mag. Johannis Hus*, Prague, 1869.
Panzer, G. W.   *Annales Typographici*, 11 vols., 1793–1803.
Pap. Let ; Pap. Pet.   See *Calendar Pap Let.*, *Pet.*
Paris, Matthew of.   *Chronica Majora*, ed. H. R. Luard (R.S.), 7 vols., 1872–83.
Parker, J.   *Early History of Oxford*, (O.H.S.), 1885.
Parker, M.   *de Antiquitate Brit. Eccles.*, ed. S. Drake, 1729.
Pastor, L.   *History of the Popes*, ed. R. I. Antrobus, 1899 f.
Paues, A. C.   *A Fourteenth-Century English Biblical Version* (1902).
Pecock.   *The Repressor of Over Much Blaming of the Clergy* (R.S.), ed. C. Babington, 2 vols., 1860.
Petit-Dutaillis, C.   *Studies Supplementary to Stubbs*, 2 vols., 1908, 1914.
Pits, J.   *Relatio Historicarum de rebus Anglicis*, Paris, 1619.
Pollard, A. F.   *The Evolution of Parliament*, 1st ed., 1920.
Pollard, A. W.   *Fifteenth-Century Prose and Verse*, 1903. (A new ed. of vol. 6 of Arber's *English Garner*.)
Pollock, F. and Maitland, F. W.   *History of English Law*, 2 vols., 2nd ed., 1898.
Pol. Poems.   *Political Poems and Songs*, ed. T. Wright (R.S.), 2 vols., 1859.

ABBREVIATIONS AND EDITIONS

Pol. Songs.	*Political Songs of England*, ed. T. Wright (Camden Soc.), 1839.
Poole, R. L.	*Illustrations of the History of Medieval Thought*, 1st ed., 1884.
"	*Wyclif and Movements for Reform*, 1889.
Powell, E.	*The Peasants' Rising and the Lollards*, E. Powell and G. M. Trevelyan, 1899.
"	*The Rising in East Anglia in 1381* (1896).
Power, E.	*English Medieval Nunneries*, 1923.
P. Plow.	*Piers Plowman*, ed. W. Skeat (E.E.T.S.), 4 vols., 1867–85.
Prince, J.	*Worthies of Devon*, 1701.
Privy Counc.	*Proceedings of the Privy Council*, ed. H. Nicolas, 1834, 7 vols.
Prynne, W.	*Brief Register of all kinds of Parliamentary Writs*, 4 vols., 1659–64.
Purvey, J.	*Remonstrance*, see Forshall.
Putnam, B. H.	*Enforcement of the Statute of Labourers*, New York, 1908.
Quétif, J.	*Scriptores Ordinis Praedicatorum*, J. Quétif and J. Echard, 1719–21.
Ragusa, J.	*Initium et Prosecutio Basil. Conc.* (In the Vienna Akad. Wissen., Mon. Conc. Gen. Saec. xv, vol. i., 1857.)
Raine, J.	*Historical Letters and Papers from Northern Registers* (R.S.), 1873.
"	*Historians of the Church of York* (R.S.), 3 vols., 1894.
Ramsay, J. K.	*Genesis of Lancaster*, 2 vols., 1913.
Rashdall, H.	*Universities of Europe in the Middle Ages*, 2 vols. in 3, 1895.
Raynaldi.	*Annales Ecclesiastici*, 15 vols., 1747–56.
Reading, J.	*Chronica Johannis de Reading et Anonymi Cantuariensis*, ed. J. Tait, 1914.
Reg. Buck.	[N. B. Registers of bishops which have not yet been printed are not cited in the notes in italics, but in ordinary type; e.g. Reg. Buckingham.]
Reg. Brant.	*The Register of Thomas de Brantingham*, ed. F. C. Hingeston-Randolph, 2 vols., 1901.
Reg. Charlton.	*Registrum Ludovici de Charlton*, ed. J. H. Parry, 1914.
Reg. Gaunt.	*John of Gaunt's Register*, ed. S. Armitage-Smith (R.H.S.), 2 vols., 1911.
Reg. Giffard.	*Register of Bp. Godfrey Giffard*, ed. J. W. Willis Bund (Worc. Hist. Soc.), 2 vols., 1902.
Reg. Gilbert.	*The Register of John Gilbert*, J. H. Parry, 1913.
Reg. Grand.	*The Register of John de Grandisson*, ed. F. C. Hingeston-Randolph, 3 vols., 1897.
Reg. Lacy.	*The Register of Edmund de Lacy* (1417–20), ed. J. H. Parry.
Reg. Pal. Dunelm.	*Registrum Palatinum Dunelmense*, ed. T. D. Hardy (R.S.), 4 vols., 1873–8.
Reg. Peckham.	*Registrum Epistolarum J. Peckham*, ed. C. T. Martin (R.S.), 3 vols., 1882–5.
Reg. Rede.	*The Episcopal Registers of Robert Rede*, ed. C. Deedes, 2 vols., 1908, 1911.
Reg. Stafford.	*The Register of Edmund Stafford*, ed. F. C. Hingeston-Randolph, 1886.
Reg. Tref.	*The Register of John Trefnant*, ed. W. W. Capes, 1914.
Reg. Wykeham.	*Wykeham's Register*, ed. T. F. Kirby, 2 vols., 1896, 1899.
Reichling, D.	*App. ad Hain-Copingeri Repertorium*, 6 vols., Munich, 1905–11.
Rep. Dig. Peer.	*Report on the Dignity of a Peer*, Lords' Reports, 6 vols., 1829.

ABBREVIATIONS AND EDITIONS xxxiii

Réville, A.	*Le Soulèvement des travailleurs d'Angleterre en 1381*, Paris, 1898.
Rogers, J. E. T.	*Oxford City Documents* (O.H.S.), 1891.
„	*History of Agriculture and Prices in England*, 7 vols., 1866–1902.
„	*Six Centuries of Work and Wages*, 1891.
Rot. Parl.	*Rotuli Parliamentorum*, 8 vols., 1767–1832.
Rous, J.	*Rossi Historia Regum Angliae*, ed. T. Hearne, 1716.
Rymer, T.	*Foedera*. (Quoted, when in existence, from the incomplete Rec. Com. ed.; otherwise from the Lond. 2nd. ed. 1727–9.)
Salter, H. E.	*Medieval Archives of the University of Oxford*, 1920.
„	*Munimenta Civitatis Oxonie* (O.H.S.), 1920.
„	*Oxford Deeds of Balliol College* (O.H.S.), 1913.
„	*Snappe's Formulary* (O.H.S.), 1924.
Sbaralea, J. S.	*Supplementum ad Script. trium Ord. S. Francisci*, Rome, 1806.
Scotichronicon.	i.e. John of Fordun *Chronica* with W. Bower's *Continuation*, ed. T. Hearne, 5 vols., 1722.
Sede Vac. Worc.	*Registrum Sede Vacante* (Worc. Hist. Soc.), ed. J. Bund, 1897.
Sel. Eng. Works.	See Arnold.
Sergeant, L.	*John Wyclif*, 1893.
Shadwell, L. L.	*Enactments in Parliament concerning Oxford and Cambridge* (O.H.S.), 4 vols., 1912.
Sharpe, R. R.	*Calendar of Wills Proved in the Court of Hustings, London*, 2 vols., 1890.
„	*Calendar of Letter Books of the City of London*, 1899 f. These are distinguished by the letters A, B, C, etc.
Sheppard, J. B.	*Literae Cantuarienses* (R.S.), 3 vols., 1887 f.
„	*Christ Church Letters* (Camden Soc.), 1877.
Shirley, W. W.	*Fasciculi Zizaniorum Magistri Joh. Wyclif* (R.S.), 1858.
„	*Catalogue of the Extant Latin Works of Wyclif.* Revised by J. Loserth, 1924.
Skelton, J.	*Oxonia Antiqua Restorata*, 2 vols., 1823.
Snappe.	See Salter.
Stubbs, W.	*Registrum Sacrum Anglicanum*, 2nd ed., 1897.
„	*The Constitutional History of England*, 3 vols., ed. 1913.
Stanley, A. P.	*Historical Memorials of Canterbury*, 6th ed., 1872.
„	*Historical Memorials of Westminster Abbey*, 4th ed., 1876.
Statutes.	*Statutes of the Realm*, ed. 1810.
Stevenson, F. S.	*Robert Grosseteste*, 1899.
Stothard, C. G.	*Monumental Effigies* (1817).
Stow, J.	*Survey of London*, ed. C. L. Kingsford, 2 vols., 1908.
„	*The Annales of England*, ed. Howes, 1631.
Summers, W. H.	*The Lollards of the Chiltern Hills*, 1916.
Tanner, T.	*Bibliotheca Britannica Hibernica*, 1748.
Taylor, H. O.	*The Medieval Mind*, 2 vols., 2nd. ed., 1914.
Taxatio.	*Taxatio Ecclesiastica*, Record Com., 1802.
Test. Ebor.	*Testamenta Eboracensia*, 6 vols., Surtees Soc., 1836–1902.
Theiner, A.	*Vetera Monumenta Hib. et Scot. historiam illustrantia*, Rome, 1864.
Thorpe, J.	*Registrum Roffense*, 1769.
Traïson.	*Chronique de la traïson et mort de Richard II*, ed. B. Williams, 1846.
Trans. Hist. Soc.	*Transactions of the Royal Historical Society*.
Trevelyan, G. M.	*England in the Age of Wyclif*, 2nd. ed., 1899.

Tritheim, J.	*Carmelitana Bibliotheca*, ed. 1593.
Tucker, E. C.	*The Later Version of the W. Epistle to the Romans; a Study of Wycliffite English*, 1914.
Ueberweg, F.	*History of Philosophy*, trans. G. S. Morris, 2 vols., 1872.
Usk, A.	*Chronicon Adae de Usk*, 2nd ed., E. M. Thompson, 1904.
Val. Eccl.	*Valor Ecclesiasticus*, 5 vols., 1825.
Valois, N.	*La France et la grande Schisme d'Occident*, 1896–1902.
Vaughan, R.	*John de Wycliffe, A Monograph*, 1853.
Vict. Co.	The various volumes of the *Victoria County History*.
Villiers, C.	*Bibliotheca Carmelitana*, ed. Cosmo Villiers, 2 vols., Orleans, 1752.
Wadding, L.	*Annales Minorum*, 19 vols., ed. Rome, 1731–45.
Wake, W.	*The State of the Church . . . in their Councils, Convocations*, etc., 1703.
Walsingham, T.	*Historia Anglicana*, ed. H. T. Riley (R.S.), 2 vols., 1863.
,,	*Gesta Abbatum S. Albani*, ed. H. T. Riley in *Chron. Mon. S. Albani*, vols. iv.–vii. (R.S.).
Ware, J.	*de Scriptoribus Hiberniae*, 1639.
Weever, J.	*Ancient Funeral Monuments*, 1631.
Wells, J. E.	*A Manual of the Writings in Middle English*, Yale; 2nd ed., 1920.
Wilkins, D.	*Concilia mag. Britanniae et Hiberniae*, 4 vols., 1737.
Wilkins, H. J.	*Was Wyclif a Negligent Pluralist?* 1915.
,,	*Westbury College*, 1917.
Willis, Browne.	*Survey of the Cathedrals*, 3 vols. in 2, 1727–30.
Willis, R., and Clarke, J. W.	*The Architectural Hist. of the Univ. of Cambridge*, 4 vols., 1886.
Wills, Durham.	*Wills and Inventories from the Registry at Durham* (Surtees Soc.), 3 vols., 1906.
Wood, A.	*Fasti Oxonienses*, ed. J. Gutch, 1790.
,,	*Hist. and Antiquities of the Colleges and Halls in the Univ. of Oxford*, ed. J. Gutch, 1786.
,,	*History and Antiquities of the Univ. of Oxford*, ed. J. Gutch, 2 vols., 1792.
,,	*Survey of the Antiquities of the City of Oxford*, ed. A. Clark, 3 vols. (O.H.S.), 1889.
Worcester.	*Itinerarium W. Botoner dict. de Worcestre*, ed. J. Nasmyth, 1778.
Workman, H. B.	*The Age of Hus* (vol. 2 of *The Dawn of the Reformation*).
,,	*The Letters of John Hus*, Eng. Trans., 1904.
Wylie, J. K.	*History of England in the Reign of Henry IV*, 4 vols., 1884 f.
,,	*Henry Fifth*, 2 vols., 1914, 1919.
Zatacensis, P.	*Liber Diurnus.* (In Akad. der Wissenschaften, *Mon. Concil. General. Saec. xv*, vol. i., Vienna, 1857.)
Ziz.	See Shirley.

EDITIONS OF WYCLIF'S WORKS

(a) Published by the Wyclif Society. All in Latin.
    de Apostasia, ed. M. H. Dziewicki, 1889.
    de Benedicta Incarnacione, ed. H. Harris, 1886.
    de Blasphemia, ed. M. H. Dziewicki, 1893.
    de Civili Dominio, ed. R. L. Poole, 1885, and J. Loserth, vols. 2–4, 1900–4.
    de Compositione Hominis, ed. R. Beer, 1884.
    de Dominio Divino, ed. R. L. Poole, 1890.
    de Ecclesia, ed. J. Loserth, 1886.
    de Ente, ed. M. H. Dziewicki, 1909.
    de Ente Praedicamentali, ed. R. Beer, 1891.
    de Eucharistia, ed. J. Loserth, 1892.
    de Logica, ed. M. H. Dziewicki, 3 vols., 1899.
    de Mandatis Divinis et de Statu Innocencie, ed. F. D. Matthew and J. Loserth, 1922.
    de Officio Regis, ed. A. W. Pollard and C. Sayle, 1887.
    de Potestate Papae, ed. J. Loserth, 1907.
    de Simonia, ed. Herzberg-Fränkel, 1898.
    de Veritate Sacrae Scripturae, ed. R. Buddensieg, 3 vols., 1905–7.
    Dialogus sive Speculum Ecclesiae Militantis, ed. A. W. Pollard, 1886.
    Miscellanea Philosophica, ed. M. H. Dziewicki, 3 vols., 1902–5.
    Opera Minora, ed. J. Loserth, 1913.
    Opus Evangelicum, ed. J. Loserth, 2 vols., 1895.
    Polemical Works in Latin, ed. R. Buddensieg, 2 vols., 1883.
    Sermones, ed. J. Loserth, 4 vols., 1887 f.
(b) *de Officio Pastorali*, ed. G. Lechler, Leipzig, 1863.
    Tractatus de Christo et suo adversario Antichristo, ed. R. Buddensieg, Gotha, 1880.
    Trialogus, ed. G. Lechler, Oxford, 1869.
(c) For Wyclif's English Works, see Arnold, Matthew, Forshall and Madden, and the critical study, *infra*, vol. i, Appendix C.

CHRONOLOGY OF WYCLIF'S LIFE

		VOLUME AND PAGE
1319	Marriage of Wyclif's parents	i. 38
? c. 1328	Birth of Wyclif	i. 21
20 Sept. 1342	Transference of the honour of Richmond to John of Gaunt	i. 36
? 1345	Wyclif goes to Oxford	i. 52
1349	The Black Death causes much interruption to Wyclif's studies	i. 82
1350	Fitzralph publishes his *de Pauperie Salvatoris*	i. 127 n.
1353	Full resumption of work by the University	i. 83
After Jan. 1353	Death of Wyclif's father. Wyclif becomes lord of the manor of Wycliffe and patron of the living. Further interruption of studies. *Cal. Fine Rolls*, vi. 375	i. 40
10 Feb. 1355	St. Scolastica riots. Further interruption of studies	i. 85–6
? 1358	Wyclif becomes Master of Balliol. The first draft of his philosophical works begun	i. 78
23 March 1361	John of Gaunt becomes duke of Lancaster	i. 152
Spring 1361	Great outbreak of pestilence in Oxford	i. 152
7 April 1361	As Master of Balliol Wyclif appropriates the living of Abbotsley	i. 79
Spring 1361	Wyclif takes his degree as Master of Arts	i. 77
14 May 1361	Wyclif instituted as rector of Fillingham	i. 79
July 1361	Wyclif leaves Balliol	i. 80
24 Nov. 1362	Oxford petitions Urban V for a prebend for Wyclif. Wyclif obtains Aust in Westbury	i. 153
7 Aug. 1363	John Wyclif presents William de Wycliffe to the living of Wycliffe	i. 40
29 Aug. 1363	Wyclif is granted leave of absence to study at Oxford for his degree in theology	i. 153
8 Oct. 1363	Wyclif hires rooms at Queen's College	i. 156
6 June 1365	Urban V demands payment of the Tribute	i. 218
9 Dec. 1365	Wyclif appointed by Islip the Warden of Canterbury hall	i. 177
27 June 1366	Wyclif reported as an absentee at Westbury	i. 160
30 March 1367	Wyclif deposed from the wardenship by Langham. Wyclif appeals to Urban V	i. 180–1
17 May 1367	Wyclif in Yorkshire	i. 44
13 April 1368	Wyclif obtains a further licence to study at Oxford	i. 195
20 & 30 May 1368	Wyclif undertakes mainprise for sundry persons in Yorkshire	ii. 422
12 Nov. 1368	Wyclif, by exchange, instituted rector of Ludgershall	i. 195
March 1369	Wyclif takes his B.D. degree	i. 97, 201 n.
After 7 Oct. 1369	Death of Wyclif's mother	i. 40
15 May 1370	Wyclif's appeal to Urban dismissed	i. 182–3
Oct. 1370	Wyclif begins his 'Sententiary' lectures. Writes the *de Benedicta Incarnacione*	i. 97

xxxviii CHRONOLOGY OF WYCLIF'S LIFE

		VOLUME AND PAGE
Autumn 1370	Wyclif's doubts on the Eucharist begin	i. 97 & ii. 34
Nov. 1371	Wyclif left a legacy by William de Askeby	i. 201
1372	Wyclif enters the service of the Crown	i. 209
1372	Controversy with Cunningham, Woodford &c. at Oxford. On 28 Aug. Wyclif preaches at Oxford	ii. 206 n.
Autumn 1372	Wyclif takes his D.D. degree	i. 203
26 Dec. 1373	Gregory XI renews the promise to Wyclif of a prebend in Lincoln	i. 203
7 April 1374	Wyclif presented by the Crown to Lutterworth	i. 209
April 1374	Gregory XI makes demand for the Tribute	i. 228
26 July 1374	Wyclif appointed on the deputation to Bruges	i. 240
26 July 1374	Wyclif and R. Strode undertake mainprise for Benger	i. 242
14 Sept. 1374	Wyclif returns from Bruges and retires to Oxford	i. 242, 245
Oct. 1374	Wyclif begins the publication of his *Summa*. Publishes his *de Mandatis* and *Determinatio de Dominio*	i. 257
23 Nov. 1374	Wyclif preaches before the University	i. 245
6 Nov. 1375	Wyclif's prebend of Aust confirmed	i. 169
18 Nov. 1375	Wyclif's prebend of Aust taken away	i. 169
1375–6	Wyclif publishes his *Divine and Civil Dominion*	i. 258
22 Sept. 1376	Wyclif sent for by the Council. He preaches in London (autumn) and on 23 Nov. in Oxford	i. 279
22 Dec. 1376	Wyclif's prebend of Aust restored	i. 170
19 Feb. 1377	Wyclif's trial in St. Paul's	i. 286
22 May 1377	Gregory XI issues his bulls against Wyclif, and cites Wyclif to Rome	i. 295
6 Dec. 1377	Wyclif preaches in Oxford	ii. 206 n.
18 Dec. 1377	The bulls published in England. Wyclif formally imprisoned in Blackhall, Oxford	i. 305–6
? 1377	Wyclif begins sending out his Poor Priests, and writing English tracts for them	ii. 201
March 1378	Wyclif tried at Lambeth	i. 308
24 March 1378	Wyclif is writing his *de Veritate Scripturae*	ii. 4
Summer 1378	Wyclif publishes his *Protestatio, Libellus, XXXIII Conclusiones*, and his *Letter of Excuse to Urban*	i. 310, 312
11 Aug. 1378	The Haulay and Shakyl breach of sanctuary	i. 316
30 Sept. 1378	The Great Schism begins. Pope and anti-pope send deputations to the parliament at Gloucester	ii. 57
20 Oct. 1378	Parliament meets at Gloucester. Wyclif appears before it in defence of the breach of sanctuary	i. 321
Winter 1378	Wyclif publishes his *de Ecclesia* and *de Officio Regis*	ii. 6, 20
Spring 1379	Wyclif publishes his *de Potestate Papae* and *de Ordine Christiano*. Breach with the papacy	ii. 74, 78
Summer 1379	Wyclif begins the Eucharistic controversy. Breach with the friars. Controversy with Rimington	ii. 30, 408
Autumn 1379	Wyclif publishes his *de Apostasia* and *de Eucharistia*	ii. 43–4
? Spring 1380	Wyclif begins the translation of the Bible	ii. 148

CHRONOLOGY OF WYCLIF'S LIFE

		VOLUME AND PAGE
? Spring 1380	Berton appoints at Oxford the Council of Twelve. Wyclif is condemned	ii. 141
10 May 1381	Wyclif publishes his *Confessio*. Controversy with Winterton, Wells, Uhtred and others	ii. 146
30 May 1381	The Peasants' Revolt begins	ii. 221
Summer 1381	? Wyclif is ill. Leaves Oxford for Lutterworth	ii. 147
Autumn 1381	Wyclif defends the Peasants in his *Servants and Lords*	ii. 243
March 1382	Publishes his *de Blasphemia*	ii. 249 n.
Spring 1382	Activity of Hereford, Ashton, Bedeman	ii. 252
7 May 1382	Wyclif appeals to parliament. Publishes his *Complaint*	ii. 250 f.
15 May 1382	Hereford defends Wyclif at Oxford	ii. 252
17–21 May 1382	The Blackfriars Synod condemns Wyclif	ii. 253 f.
22 May 1382	Courtenay's 'pretended statute' against lollards and preachers. Breach between Wyclif and the Crown complete	ii. 269
5 June 1382	Repingdon's lollard sermon at St. Frideswyde's. Great strife at Oxford	ii. 274
12 & 13 June 1382	The Blackfriars synod and the Privy Council deal with Rigg and the Oxford supporters of Wyclif	ii. 279
15 June 1382	Repingdon and Hereford suspended at Oxford	ii. 282
18 June 1382	Repingdon and Hereford condemned at the third Blackfriars synod	ii. 282
26 June 1382	Letters Patent against lollard preachers	ii. 269
1 July 1382	Repingdon and Hereford appear before Courtenay at Canterbury. Hereford escapes to Rome	ii. 284
? Autumn 1382	Publication of the first Wyclif Version	ii. 162
Nov. 1382	Recantation of Repingdon, Bedeman, Aston	ii. 287
Nov. 1382	Wyclif has a first stroke	ii. 316
Autumn 1382	Wyclif publishes his *Trialogus*	ii. 309
21 Dec. 1382	Spenser formally opens his Crusade	ii. 66
Spring 1383	Wyclif bitterly attacks the Crusade	ii. 308
17 May 1383	The Crusade sets out, and returns (Sept.)	ii. 68
1383–4	Wyclif writes many English and Latin Works, including his *Opus Evangelicum* and *de Citationibus Frivolis*	ii. 309
May 1384	Alleged plot of Lancaster. Wyclif defends him	ii. 303
After 17 Aug. 1384	Writes his *de Quattuor Sectis Novellis*	ii. 93 n.
28 Dec. 1384	Wyclif's second stroke	ii. 316
31 Dec. 1384	Wyclif's death at Lutterworth	ii. 316
1388	Great lollard activity. Special repressive measures. *XXV Points*	ii. 387 f.
Jan. 1395	Lollard activity in parliament, Purvey's *XII Conclusions*, *XXXVII Conclusions*, and *Ecclesiae Regimen*	ii. 390 f.
Summer 1395	Purvey publishes the second version of the English Bible	ii. 165
28 Nov. 1407	The Oxford Constitutions	ii. 417
20 Dec. 1409	Alexander V orders Wyclif's works in Bohemia 'a fidelium oculis amovendi'	ii. 366 n.
Jan. 1409	The Oxford Constitutions reaffirmed at St. Paul's. A Committee of twelve censors of Wyclif's works appointed	ii. 358

CHRONOLOGY OF WYCLIF'S LIFE

		VOLUME AND PAGE
16 July 1410	Wyclif's works burnt at Prague. Palacký, Doc. 734	
Summer 1410	Wyclif's works burnt at Carfax	ii. 366
17 March 1411	Convocation condemns 267 errors and heresies of Wyclif	ii. 366
2 Feb. 1413	Wyclif's *Dialogus* and *Trialogus* condemned at the council in St. Peter's	ii. 373
10 Feb. 1413	Wyclif's *Dialogus* and *Trialogus* burnt before the door of St. Peter's	ii. 374
4 May 1415	The Council of Constance orders Wyclif's bones to be dug up, and condemns his writings	ii. 319
6 July 1415	Hus burnt at Constance	ii. 320
9 Dec. 1427	Peremptory orders from Martin V that the exhumation of Wyclif be carried out	ii. 320
Spring 1428	Wyclif's bones dug up by Fleming and burnt	ii. 320

KINGS, POPES, AND ARCHBISHOPS

Kings.	Popes.	Archbishops of Canterbury.
Edward III (27 Jan. 1327)	Clement V (*de Goth*) (5 June 1305–20 Apr. 1314)	—
	John XXII (*Duèse*) (7 Aug. 1316–4 Dec. 1334)	—
	Benedict XII (*Fournier*) (20 Dec. 1334–25 Apr. 1342)	Thomas Bradwardine 19 July 1349–26 Aug. 1349
	Clement VI (*Roger*) (7 May 1342–6 Dec. 1352)	Simon Islip (20 Dec. 1349–26 Apr. 1366)
	Innocent VI (*Aubert*) (18 Dec. 1352–12 Sept. 1362)	
	Urban V (*Grimoard*) (6 Nov. 1362–19 Dec. 1370)	Simon Langham (24 July 1366–11 Oct. 1368)
Richard II (21 June 1377)	Gregory XI (*Roger*) (30 Dec. 1370–27 March 1378)	William Wittlesey (11 Oct. 1368–5 June 1374)
	Urban VI (*Prignano*) (8 Apr. 1378–15 Oct. 1389)	Simon Sudbury (12 May 1375–14 June 1381)
Henry IV (30 Sept. 1399)	Boniface IX (*Tomacelli*) (2 Nov. 1389–1 Oct. 1404)	William Courtenay (9 Sept. 1381–31 July 1396)
		Thomas Arundel (25 Sept. 1396–19 Feb. 1414)

BOOK I
THE SCHOOLMAN

IN PRAISE OF OXFORD

Cum enim presens universitas Oxoniensis que propter multiplices effectus vinea Domini non inmerito nuncupatur, a sanctis patribus fuerat fundata et loco congruo situata, fontibus et fluviis irrigata, pratis et pascuis circumdata, planiciebus et saltibus protensa, montibus et collibus ad pellendum procellarum spiritus circumvallata, arbustis virentibus et locis nemorosis vicina et ut verbo uno singula concludam : Locus amenus fertilis et optimus et habitacioni deorum convenientissimus domus Dei et porta celi congrue vocitata.

WYCLIF. *Opera Minora*, p. 18.

I

THE IMPORTANCE OF WYCLIF

§ 1

"On most of us the dim image of Wyclif looks down like the portrait of the first of a long line of kings, without personality or expression—he is the first of the reformers."[1] This judgement of the Oxford professor, Walter Shirley, is unfortunately still too true, despite the efforts of recent years to make up for the neglect and "windy declamation"[2] of centuries. Almost every particular in the life of Wyclif is the occasion of controversy; over his earlier years there hangs a more than medieval obscurity; while the vague chronology of his life is in marked contrast to our exact knowledge of his teaching. In the following pages we shall try to disentangle from the mass of fiction and misstatements such facts about Wyclif's life as seem probable. Nevertheless we must confess, in spite of the industry of many workers, that the harvest of certainty reaped is but small. Oftentimes we are reduced to conjecture in supplying the missing evidence, or in attempting an adequate explanation of Wyclif's actions.

If the details of the life of Wyclif are obscure, his influence is beyond dispute. The source of this influence is clear. As a schoolman he was the acknowledged leader among his contemporaries at Oxford. As a politician he voiced for some years the national aspirations or rather the national dissatisfaction. As a reformer he promulgated ideas that would have destroyed the medieval Church. But extreme as his views became in his last days, he obtained a hearing because he expressed in clear, logical form what many were feeling but had not thought out. This triple combination gives the secret of the strength as well as of the weakness of Wyclif's revolt. Nor should we forget that Wyclif stands half in and half out of the Middle

---

[1] *Ziz.*, p. xlvi. [2] Arnold in *Sel. Eng. Works*, i. p. xvi.

Ages. The century in which he lived was a transition age. The old order was breaking up in spite of the efforts of politicians and churchmen to keep all things as they were. Medievalism was sick unto death, but she was dying hard, with leeches many seeking by their nostrums to prevent her decease. Wyclif was one of the few men who realized the issue. Nevertheless his theological and political ideas, his schemes of reform in Church and State, though hopelessly in advance of his age, are clothed in full medieval dress. As we listen to his theories the voice is the voice of revolution, but the hands are the hands of a vanished past. And the same double character is seen throughout his life. He is a master of English—a language only just claiming with hesitation its place as a literary organ—as well as of Latin, the historic language of Church and State. As he abandons Latin for English the academic disputant whose style and matter is medieval passes with ease into the pamphleteer whose outlook and appeal are to a new world, in essence an English world, no longer divided as in the countless charters of the previous generation into French and English. As a politician he is eager for reform, yet allies himself with John of Gaunt whose whole attitude is reactionary. He appeals by his democratic conceptions to the growing towns; at the same time he wraps up these conceptions in the terms of a decaying feudalism.

Wyclif as a schoolman has not always received the recognition he deserves. Yet without such recognition his work as a reformer cannot be rightly appraised. For the importance of Wyclif's attack upon the medieval Church lay in the fact that the assault was conducted not by an obscure fanatic but by the foremost schoolman of his age—'the flower', as his enemies owned, ' of Oxford '[1]—at a time when the decay of Paris had left Oxford without a rival. The first of the reformers was, in fact, the last of the schoolmen, according to the judgement of an uncompromising opponent: ' the most eminent doctor of theology of his times, in philosophy second to none, in the training of the schools without a rival '.[2] ' Sir,'

---

[1] *Eulog. Cont.* iii. 345. The date when this was written is uncertain, see *op. cit.* iii, p. 1.   [2] Knighton, ii. 151.

said the lollard[1] Thorpe, in his defence before archbishop Arundel,

'Master John Wyclif was holden of full many men the greatest clerk that they knew then living; and therewith he was named a passing ruely man and an innocent in his living, and therefore great many communed oft with him and they loved so much his learning that they writ it and busily enforced them to rule themselves thereafter. Therefore, Sir, this foresaid learning of Master John Wyclif is yet holden of full many men and women the most agreeable learning unto the living and teaching of Christ and his Apostles.'

Arundel acknowledged in reply: 'Wyclif, your author (*founder*), was a great clerk, and many men held him a perfect liver.'[2] An unrevised note-book of some of his lectures at Oxford, evidently taken down by one of his pupils, has come down to us, and amazes the reader by its "accumulated stores of learning from every field of human knowledge, and the mastery displayed of the entire Bible".[3] That we discover the knowledge to be largely copious extracts from medieval text-books, Gratian's *Decretum* and the like, may lessen our estimate of Wyclif's scholarship but should not detract from our conception of his influence. To the medieval mind it was precisely in such knowledge of text-books and in the ability to bring to bear their authority in debate that true wisdom consisted.

Equally clear with the source of Wyclif's influence is the general development of his teaching. Religious teachers as a rule have owed their influence in politics to their reputation as saints or reformers. We may instance St. Bernard, Savonarola, Luther, and Calvin. With Wyclif the development was otherwise. From subtle disputations at Oxford Wyclif passed, like William of Ockham, into politics, bringing thereto the methods and, we may add, the impracticability of a great schoolman. He was the brains of the party who sought in Parliament and elsewhere to resist papal claims. Hitherto reformers, e. g. Hildebrand, St. Bernard, had attempted to accomplish their reforms from within, and would have resisted interference from the State. Wyclif introduced a new idea by calling upon the State to reform an unwilling Church. Throughout the

---

[1] For the meaning of 'lollard' see Appendix A.
[2] *Examination of William Thorpe*, in Pollard, *Garner*, 118–20.
[3] Beer, *de Comp. Hom.*, p. xvii, the note-book in question. See its indices.

fourteenth century the student will discern two movements in England, both tending in the same direction, both temporarily defeated, both preparing the way for future triumphs. The one attack, the more popular and influential, was directed against the temporal and political power of the clergy ; the other attack, enterprised by the few, was set against the dogmas and superstitions of the Church. On all sides we discern signs of revolt : in some a fear lest the Church should become too strong for the State ; in others a desire to deliver religion from a degrading materialism or to give its government and theology a new content. The two movements, though finally they became separate and even opposed, for a short time were united under one leader. This leader was John Wyclif.

From political movements Wyclif passed in the last years of his life to the special work which has given him his place in history. He attacked in no halting manner the whole medieval conception of the Church, and lashed with his scorn its characteristic institutions. He felt that the souls of men were being sacrificed to an overgrown sacramental system, at the roots of which he struck by his attack on the fundamental doctrine of transubstantiation. Next Wyclif laboured to effect the revival of religious life, especially among the lower classes, by the restoration of simple preaching, and by the distribution to the people of the Word of God in their mother-tongue. In all these aspects—Schoolman, Politician, Preacher, Reformer—Wyclif was the foremost man of his age, the range of whose activities was not less remarkable than the energy with which he pursued his aims. Even if we limit our survey to the centuries immediate to Wyclif we may admit that there were schoolmen more profound, political thinkers more discerning, preachers more soul-reaching, reformers more successful, saints more attractive. As a schoolman he is far inferior to Thomas Aquinas or Ockham ; as a political thinker he is secondary to Marsiglio ; as a preacher he cannot be put on the same level as St. Bernard ; as a saint we miss in him the sweetness and light so characteristic of St. Francis ; as a reformer he is not comparable in the permanence of his work either with Hildebrand at the one extreme or with Luther at the other. Nevertheless in the combination of many qualities

Wyclif stands almost alone, at any rate in England. To this we must add the interest always felt in one who lived before his time. For Wyclif was the harbinger of a premature spring, and the reform which he sought to bring about was then impossible. He tried to accomplish in a few months what the Puritans failed to work out in a century. But whatever view may be taken of their teaching, the world cannot afford to forget the men who faced their generation with the proclamation of new principles.

In this complex combination lies the difficulty of the biographer's task. Wyclif unites in himself so many diverse forces that the study of his career becomes of necessity the study of the later Middle Ages. On some sides in the daring of his concepts he is a Nonconformist of Nonconformists, a Modernist of the Moderns; but in the main he is a medievalist. To understand him at all, even in his reforming ideas, we must understand the times of which he was in many respects the characteristic man, in others the most revolutionary force. For Wyclif's life cannot be treated as if built up in watertight compartments. To isolate his work as a reformer from his career at Oxford is to obscure the meaning of both. To understand Wyclif's importance at Oxford we must reconstruct the medieval university, and learn the secret of its scholasticism. To give due weight to Wyclif's political ideals we must realize the political and social ideas of the England of his day. But to appraise his theological and ecclesiastical judgements is, perhaps, the most arduous task of all. This involves not merely sympathy with the Reformer but also an impartial estimate of the qualities and defects of the medieval Church; in other words, sympathy with the attacked as well as with the attacker.

§ 2

The right understanding of the life of Wyclif becomes of added importance when we remember that his influence in England was by no means limited to the men of his own generation. His movement, it is true, failed to accomplish his purpose; nevertheless it lingered on right down to the Reformation itself. Moreover, Wyclif's influence outside England was even greater and more abiding than in his own country. Among the many fictions concerning Wyclif at one time accepted as history is the story, first set afloat, it would appear, by Polydore Vergilius, and adopted by bishop Bale,[1] that the Reformer in his last years ' sought a voluntarily exile rather than change his opinions '. So he came to Bohemia, ' already slightly infected with heresy ', and was ' received by that rude race with great honour '. In return he established them in the belief ' that little reverence was due to the priesthood, and no consideration at all to the Roman pontiff '. This fable is one of those guesses at truth which anticipate modern research. ' O good God,' added an indignant Czech scribe, condemned to copy the *de Christo et suo Adversario Antichristo* of Wyclif, ' do not let this man come into our beloved Bohemia.' [2] His prayer was not answered. Wyclif lived again in Bohemia ; Hus and Jerome of Prague continued the work which he had begun.

Buddensieg tells us that he had seen in a Bohemian Psalter of 1572, now in the university library at Prague, a remarkable picture. Wyclif is represented as striking a spark, Hus is kindling the coals, while Luther is brandishing the lighted torch.[3] The picture is correct in its belief in a close connexion between the reformers. For though Hus did not embrace all Wyclif's ideas, the doctrines for which he was condemned at Constance were copied by him almost verbatim from the works of Wyclif. The Englishman was right who tells us that as he listened to the guarded answers of Hus before the Council he detected the manner of Wyclif.[4] By a strange injustice the doctrine of the plagiarist, because Hus was linked with a national movement, came to be regarded as almost the original, while Wyclif, from whom he had borrowed, receded into obscurity. To a great extent this was due to the fact that while Wyclif's works slumbered undisturbed in Continental libraries, the works of Hus were printed at an early date. Moreover, the burning of Hus placed his relations to the English reformer in a somewhat false light. " The flames

---

[1] Vergil, *Hist. Anglica*, xix fin. ; Bale, i. 451. For the absurd idea that Wyclif's views infected Holland and Brabant as early as 1372, see *Eng. Hist. Rev.* vii. 351. [2] *Pol. Works*, ii. 685.
[3] *Ver. Script.* i. p. xliii *n.* [4] Palacký, *Doc.* 277.

which rose from the pile at Constance on the 6th of July 1415 displayed to posterity the form of Hus in clearer illumination than that of his English colleague. Only deep in the background has been discerned, since then, the shadow of that man for whose doctrine Hus went to the stake."[1] Hus in his turn handed on the torch to Luther. In 1525 Wyclif's *Trialogus* had been printed at Basel. Of this work Luther seems to have possessed or borrowed a manuscript copy. But he failed to recognize Wyclif's importance or his relation to Hus. For in February 1529, after pondering the matter over with Melanchthon, Luther wrote to Spalatin :

'I have hitherto taught and held all the opinions of Hus without knowing it. With a like unconsciousness has Staupitz taught them. We are all of us Hussites without knowing it. I do not know what to think for amazement.'

The reader must not assume that by this confession Luther intended to hint that he had become Luther by the help of Hus. His real meaning is expressed when in the same letter he goes on to explain that ' Paul and Augustine are Hussites to the letter '. He was feeling his way rather to a doctrine of evangelical continuity than hinting at any relation of cause and effect.[2] But the result of Luther's discovery of Hus and his ignorance of Wyclif [3] was the printing of several of the works of Hus, often with a preface or notes by Luther, and thus the emphasis once more of the importance of Hus at the expense of the English master.[4] Nearly four centuries elapsed before the right perspective was obtained of the theological output of the two reformers.[5]

[1] Loserth, *Wiclif and Hus*, 177.
[2] *Letters* (ed. De Wette), i. 425 ; quoted in C. Beard's *Reformation*, 30.
[3] In the Corpus Christi library at Cambridge (James, i. 199) there are 15½ lines written by Melanchthon to Myconius, called *Judicium Melanchthonis de Wiclevo*. The gist is seen in the sentence, 'Inspexi Wiclefum sed deprehendi in eo multa alia errata '. In his disputation with Eck at Leipzig (5 July 1519) Luther defended ' articulos Wyclif et Hus damnatos ', B. J. Kidd, *Documents Illustrative of the Continental Reformation* (1911), 49.
[4] See Appendix B.
[5] By the publication in 1883 of J. Loserth's *Wiclif and Hus*, Eng. trans. by M. J. Evans in 1884. For the correction of this work's exaggeration see my *Age of Hus*, pref. viii ; and D. S. Schaff on *Hus' Treatise of the Church* in Amer. Soc. of Church Hist., 2nd ser., vol. iv, p. 105 f. The publication by Dr. Flajshan of Hus's *Super iv Sententiarum* (1906) has led to greater appreciation of Hus's independence as a scholar ; see Lützow, *Hus*, 90–2.

Bohemia and Germany were not the only lands to which the influence of Wyclif penetrated. In 1407 a lollard preacher, 'celeberrimus predicatione', 'of the school of John Wyclif', James Reseby by name, fled into Scotland to escape his English persecutors, " probably the first Presbyterian to set foot on that kindly soil. Whether his eyes were delighted with angelic visions of future kirk assemblies, it is for poets to say ".[1] Reseby himself was soon burnt at the stake in Perth on the accusation of the inquisitor Lawrence Lindores.[2] But his teaching and that of other lollards who fled across the border carrying with them the writings of Wyclif could not be burnt out. Prominent among these was a certain Quintin Folkhyrd or Folkhart [3] of whose evangelistic labours we hear in certain letters written by him to Prague in 1410. Folkhyrd, who describes himself as a 'poor servant of God', tells us that 'for the fear which he had of eternal damnation' he 'had started in the cause of God to ride through the land and to preach in the mother tongue to all who reached a hand to him'. In August 1407 Folkhyrd obtained a safe conduct to journey to London, and in September a like permission to return to Scotland with his three servants. It was stated that he would return before Christmas, bringing with him 'certain animals to sell for his necessary expenses'. Nothing further is known of this interesting Scots cattle-drover and evangelist. But we are not surprised to learn that according to his own account he suffered much persecution from the clergy whom he upbraided for their slackness in teaching the people, and that he fell into a bitter controversy with the bishop of Glasgow.[4] As a result of the preaching of Reseby and Folkhyrd, Gerson, the opponent of Hus at Constance, complained in 1415 of the influence of lollardy in Scotland. Heretics

'who claim that their sayings are founded on holy Scripture and on its literal sense and who say that they follow and recognise

---

[1] Trevelyan, 353.

[2] *Scottish Hist. Rev.* i. 260–73. Bower, *Continuation of Fordun*, gives the date as 1408 (see *Scotichron*, iv. 1168). Reseby was not burned under statute law, for the act *de Heretico Comburendo* did not apply to Scotland, but under canon law.

[3] For Folkhyrd see Loserth, *Mittheilungen*, xii. 261–2 ; *Eng. Hist. Rev.* vii. 310 ; *Cal. Pat. Hen.* iii. 362 ; *Cal. Doc. Scots*, iv. 144.

[4] I have interpreted 'Glatonensi' as Glasgow.

Scripture only are present in England, have destroyed the university of Prague, and have even reached Scotland '.[1]

Reseby and Folkhyrd were not alone. ' In the scrolls of Glasgow ', writes Knox,[2] ' is found mention of one, whose name is not expressed, that in the year of God 1422 was burned for heresy ' ; while on the 23rd July 1432, under the same inquisitor Lindores, ' Paul Craw (Krawer), a Bohemian, was committed to the secular judge (for our bishops follow Pilate, who both did condemn and wash his hands) ' and ' was consumed in the said city of St. Andrews '. Krawer not only denied transubstantiation but administered the cup to the laity, after the manner of the followers of Hus.[3] Krawer practised as a physician, ' sent ' under this guise ' by the heretical people of Prague to infect the realm of Scotland '. But, in spite of these measures, Scotch lollards seem to have survived among the mountains and moss hags of Galloway until the coming of Knox, much as they survived in Norfolk or Buckinghamshire until the coming of the Reformation. For in 1494 we read of ' thirty persons remaining, some in Kyle Stewart, some in King's Kyle, and some in Cunninghame ', among whom we notice the Lady of Pokely and the Lady of Stairs. ' These were called the Lollards of Kyle,' and, judging from the thirty-four articles of their faith which were condemned in the archbishop of Glasgow's court, they had not departed widely from Wyclif's teaching. The strength of lollardy in Scotland is further evidenced by the translation about 1520 of Purvey's revision of Wyclif's version of the New Testament, together with sundry lessons from the Old Testament ' read in the kirk upon certain days of the year ', done into the Scots dialect, by Murdoch Nisbet.[4] Nisbet, of Hardhill in Ayrshire—one of whose descendants was executed as a Covenanter (4 Dec. 1685)—had joined the lollards about 1500. In 1513 he fled ' over seas ', probably to Germany, ' and took (i. e. made for himself) a copy of the New Testament

---

[1] Gerson, *de Sensu Litterali sacrae Scripturae* in *Opera* (ed. du Pin).
[2] John Knox, *Hist. Ref. Scotland* (ed. W. McGavin, 1831), 3–6.
[3] Workman, *Age of Hus*, 308 f. For Krawer see *Scotichron*, iv. 1298–9.
[4] Edited from the unique manuscript in the possession of lord Amherst of Hackney by T. G. Law and Joseph Hall (Scottish Text Soc., 3 vols., 1901–5), with an excellent introduction on Nisbet and his family.

in writ' to which he added, when he had finished his text, a translation of Luther's *Prologue* first printed in 1522. On his return home two of his companions were burnt at Glasgow (1539), but 'Murdoch, being in the same danger, digged and built a vault at the bottom of his own house, to which he retired himself, serving God and reading his new book'. But this Scots version was made so shortly before Tindale's New Testament, copies of which in 1525 were imported into Scotland, that it never passed into circulation, but remained in a solitary manuscript. Thus in Scotland, as well as in England and Bohemia, Wyclif's life-work was linked on with the larger reformation of which he was in popular opinion the " Morning Star ". Wyclif's revolt was not the " isolated movement " without lasting effect which some historians have represented it to be.[1] By its emphasis of an extreme protestantism it has passed into the life of the nation itself as one of the factors in our rough island story.[2]

§ 3

At this point it were well to give some account of the biographies of Wyclif and of the sources of our knowledge of his life and teaching. 'Lives' of Wyclif abound, but for the most part they are valueless. The majority derive such basis of fact as they possess from the full treatment of Wyclif by Foxe in his well-known *Acts and Monuments*. Foxe's account, though the work of a partisan, is still of value for its many documents, especially extracts from bishops' registers and other official sources. From Foxe also Milton would derive the information which led him in a well-known passage to salute Wyclif as the true herald[3] of the Reformation. There were, however, other ' Lives ' to which Milton could have had access. But the accounts of Wyclif by Bale, James,[4] and Fuller, are dependent either on Foxe or on extracts from the important

---

[1] e.g. H. O. Wakeman's popular *Hist. English Church* (1898), 152.
[2] The emphasis of this in a hostile sense is the *raison d'être* of Gairdner's *Lollardy and the Reformation in England*, in four volumes (1908 f.).
[3] *Areopagitica* (ed. Bohn), ii. 91.
[4] *An Apologie for John Wickliffe, showing his conformitie with the new Church of England*, 4to, Oxford, 1608, by T. James, in answer to Robert Parsons and others.

Fasciculi Zizaniorum, of which the only existing manuscript, bearing date 1439, was freely annotated by Bale. From Bale this manuscript was borrowed by Foxe, who used it in his account of the lollard Purvey. Of the works of Wyclif Milton could have had little knowledge, for the Latin manuscripts for the most part were not in England, and only four had been printed: the *Trialogus* at Basel in 1525,[1] the little English tract *The Wycket* at Nuremberg in 1546[2] as also at Oxford in 1612, and *Two Short Treatises against the Begging Friars* published at Oxford in 1608 by Dr. Thomas James, Bodley's first librarian. To Wyclif's English writings, it is true, Milton might have had access in Cambridge.[3]

The above lives of Wyclif were all of the same school and origin. Of very different character was a work called *The Pretended Reformers*, published in 1717 by ' Matthias Earbery, Presbyter of the Church of England ', who had recently become a nonjuror and an advocate of the usage of the first prayer book of Edward VI with its mixed chalice and prayers for the dead.[4] This scurrilous work[5] was really a translation from the French of Varillas.[6] Its only importance, apart from its incidence as a weapon against the jurors, lay in its leading an Oxford scholar, John Lewis, ' Minister of Margate ',[7] to write in 1720 his *History of the Life and Sufferings of the Reverend and Learned John Wicliffe*[8] as an answer to Earbery and a rebuke to the

---

[1] Probably by Frobenius, on 7 March 1525. For the lengthy title see Lechler, *Trial.* 11–12, and for the faultiness of the edition, *ib.* 11–18.

[2] *Infra*, ii. 39 *n.*, for my doubts as to its genuineness.

[3] See James, *MSS. Corpus*, ii. 74–5, 166, 344.

[4] For Earbery (†1740) see J. H. Overton, *The Nonjurors* (1902), 211–13, 290 f. He was noted for the violence of his writings, the full list of which is in Hearne, *Reliquae Anglicanae*, ii. 143–4.

[5] See especially pp. vii, xi, xxxiii, xxxv.

[6] Varillas wrote *Hist. de Wicklefianisme avec celle des Guerres de Bohème* (1682); also *Hist. des Revolutions dans l'Europe de religion*, 6 vols., 1686–8, in the sixth of which he dealt with Wyclif. The book brought bishop Burnet into the field against him in 1686, Burnet's reply being translated into French.

[7] For Lewis see *D. N. B.* At the publication of his *Wyclif* Lewis was vicar of Minster (10 March 1709 until his death 16 Jan. 1747). He was buried at Minster. It is interesting to note that he was for a short time rector of Saltwood (see *infra*, ii. 167). For his edition of Wyclif's New Testament see *infra*, ii. 199 n. He wrote in 1738 *A Brief History of the Rise and Progress of Anabaptism in England; to which is prefixed some account of Dr. John Wicliffe, with a Defence of him from the false Charge of his denying Infant Baptism.*

[8] A reprint was brought out in 1723, also with some of Lewis's own corrections in 1820, both at Oxford.

bias of Wood. The importance of Lewis cannot be exaggerated. As a general life of Wyclif it is still of value, though deficient in its knowledge of Wyclif's writings and teaching. A more thorough understanding of Wyclif's position at Oxford was made possible by the well-known writings of Anthony à Wood. Wood's account of Wyclif himself is far from friendly, as is seen in his endorsement of the judgement of Dr. Fell:

'John Wyclif was a great dissembler, a man of little conscience, and what he did for religion was more out of vain glory and to obtain him a name than out of honesty.'[1]

After the issue of the work of Lewis nothing further of value was published for over a century. But we should not overlook the first German biography of Wyclif[2] by P. W. Wirth in 1754. Wirth had shown his interest in the Reformer by the republication in the previous year of the Basel edition of the *Trialogus*.[3] The reprint in 1820 of Lewis's work marks the absence of new material and of any fresh attempt to understand Wyclif's position. In 1828 Robert Vaughan, a well-known Congregational divine, brought out his *Life and Opinions of John de Wycliffe*,[4] a work superseded in 1853 by the same writer's more mature *John de Wycliffe, a Monograph*. Vaughan's works suffered both from his bias and his limited acquaintance with Wyclif's writings, in spite of the "two thousand miles which he travelled in those old stage-coach days to acquaint himself with the contents of manuscripts". By a stroke of ill-luck the first so-called work of Wyclif to be published in the nineteenth century was a fanatical tract written in 1356 entitled *The Last Age of the Church*,[5] the work, really, of some Spiritual Franciscan.[6] This deceived many and did not conduce to a higher estimate of the Reformer. But in 1851 Dr. J. H. Todd atoned for this unfortunate step by printing at Dublin *Three Treatises by John Wyclif*, namely *The Church and Her Members*—undoubtedly by Wyclif—*The Apostasy of*

---

[1] *Univ.* i. 484.
[2] *D. Johannes* (sic) *Wiclefi wahrhafte und gegründete Nachrichten von seinem Leben, Lehrsaetzen und Schriften.*
[3] Published by J. G. Vierling, Frankfort and Leipzig, in 1753. No author given, but without doubt Wirth. See Lechler, *Trial.* 19.
[4] Second ed. 1831.
[5] Dublin, 1841. It was republished by Wilmot Marsh, *Biblical Versions of Divine Hymns* (1845), 121 ff.   [6] See *infra*, ii. 100.

the Church, and *Antichrist and his Meynee*. In 1845 Wilmot Marsh published *A Postil of the Annunciation*.[1] In the middle of the century the first serious steps towards the introduction of Wyclif to the modern world were taken. Wyclif's reputed translations of the Bible were printed in their entirety in the superb edition of Forshall and Madden (1850). Almost equally important was the publication in 1853 by Professor W. Shirley of Oxford in the newly instituted ' Rolls Series ' of the celebrated work of Wyclif's opponent Thomas Netter of Walden, entitled *Fasciculi Zizaniorum*, with a valuable introduction on the life of Wyclif. The quickened interest in Wyclif[2] was further shown when in 1863 Dr. G. V. Lechler—name ever illustrious among students of Wyclif—published Wyclif's *de Officio Pastorali*—the first important work of Wyclif to be printed since the Reformation. This was followed by the publication in 1865 by Professor Shirley of a valuable *Catalogue of the Original Works of John Wyclif*. Four years later (1869-71) Thomas Arnold edited for the Clarendon Press *The Select English Works of John Wyclif*, a work of prime importance for all students. In 1869 Lechler brought out at Oxford the first accurate edition of the *Trialogus*, and in 1873 gave to the world the first scholarly life of Wyclif.[3] Lechler's knowledge of the conditions of English medieval life is often imperfect, and many sources of information have been opened since his day. But no student will ever surpass Lechler in his intimate acquaintance with the Reformer's writings, the result of his exhaustive study of then unpublished manuscripts. In 1880 Mr. F. D. Matthew brought out for the Early English Text

---

[1] Marsh, *op. cit.* 91 f.
[2] I pass over as now of no account : Ruever Gronemann, *Diatribe in J. W. reformationis prodromi vitam, ingenium, scripta* (Utrecht, 1837) ; O. Jäger, *J. W.* (Halle, 1854) ; A. Jepp, *Gerson, Wiclif, Huss inter se et cum reformatoribus comparati* (Göttingen, 1857) ; C. W. Le Bas, *Life of Wiclif* (1832). Of more recent works on Wyclif I mention the following : R. Buddensieg, *J. W. und seine Zeit* (Gotha, 1885) ; M. Burrows, *Wiclif's Place in History* (1881, 1884) ; A. R. Pennington, *John Wiclif* (1884) ; R. L. Poole, *Wycliffe and Movements for Reform* ; H. B. Workman, *The Age of Wyclif* (1901) ; J. C. Carrick, *Wycliffe and the Lollards* (1908).
[3] G. V. Lechler, *Johann von Wiclif und die Vorgeschichte der Reformation*, 2 vols., Leipzig, 1873. Translated (and abridged) by Peter Lorimer, *John Wyclif and his English Precursors*, 2 vols., 1878 ; new eds., 1 vol., 1881, 1884. As early as 1858 Lechler had given an inauguration thesis at Leipzig, *Wiclif als Vorlaüfer der Reformation*.

Society *The English Works of Wyclif hitherto Unpublished*. But many of the writings here ascribed to Wyclif were probably by his disciples rather than by the master himself, a criticism also true to some extent of the earlier work by Arnold.[1] In the same year R. Buddensieg published at Gotha Wyclif's *Tractatus de Christo et suo adversario Antichristo*. The approach of the fifth centenary of Wyclif's death brought home to English students the disgrace of their continued neglect of Wyclif's Latin treatises. The result was the formation of a Wyclif Society. With but indifferent support from the public this society has edited over thirty volumes of his works, some by English scholars of renown, the major part by Germans and Austrians.[2]

The neglect of Wyclif's Latin works by English students must not be wholly attributed to lack of interest. By a curious fortune the greater number of the manuscripts of Wyclif are found at Prague and Vienna, usually the work of Czech scribes, oftentimes copying from a Czech rather than an English source.[3] One Czech, Paul de Slawikowicz, who took his bachelor's degree at Prague in 1395,[4] alone possessed at least fifteen works of Wyclif. For their presence at Prague there is an explanation of considerable importance for the student of Wyclif's influence abroad. Wyclif's works had been introduced into Bohemia within a few years of his death. Almost from its foundation there had existed links closely connecting the university of Prague with Oxford. We have an illustration of this in the scholarships for Czech students at the English university founded on the 4th March 1388 by that warm supporter of the Czech national movement, Adalbert Ranco.[5] The growing intercourse received a powerful stimulus by the marriage on

---

[1] For the difficulties of deciding the genuine English works of Wyclif see Appendix C.   [2] For a list see *Introduction*.
[3] See Buddensieg in Wyclif's *Pol. Works*, i, p. xcii.
[4] *de Off. Reg.*, pp. xxix–xxx.
[5] See Loserth, *Wiclif and Hus*, 38–41 ; for Adalbert Ranco or Rankow see Loserth, *Beiträge zur Geschichte der Hussitischen Bewegung* (Vienna, 1880), vol. ii, with large extracts from Adalbert's *Apology*. See also Lützow, *op. cit.* 43 f., based on the Czech work of Dr. Tadra, *Mistr. Vojtech Ranknv* (1879). Loserth in his *Ueber die Beziehungen zwischen englischen und böhmischen Wiclifen* in *Mittheilungen*, xii. 254–69, thinks (p. 255) that Ranco was possibly at Oxford himself. For Bohemian students at Oxford see also *Eng. Hist. Rev.* xxxix. 72–84.

the 14th January 1382 in the chapel of St. Stephen at Westminster of Richard II of England with Anne the sister of Wenzel, king of Bohemia. The alliance was the work of Urban VI, who dreaded lest Bohemia should ally itself with France and thus acknowledge his rival at Avignon.[1] By the irony of fate this papal marriage was destined to work much harm to the papacy. The Bohemian attendants of Anne, the many Czech courtiers whom Richard 'retained to stay with him for life',[2] as well as the travelling students, carried home to Prague the writings of Wyclif. The precise year in which these were introduced cannot now be determined. Following the authority of Aeneas Sylvius, the introduction has usually been attributed to 1407.[3] But this year is too late, for in 1411, in his controversy with the Englishman Stokes, Hus informs us that 'members of this university and myself have possessed and read those works for twenty years now, and more'. Hus's date is as vague as the reference, which, however, probably denotes only Wyclif's philosophical works. Of these, five tractates, written out, with enthusiastic marginal comments in Czech, by Hus himself in 1398, are now in the Royal Library at Stockholm.[4] In the autumn of 1401 Jerome of Prague, who in 1398 had obtained his licentiate and permission to go abroad, came back from Oxford, bringing with him a painting which he hung in his rooms representing Wyclif as the prince of philosophers,[5] as well as copies of Wyclif's *Dialogus* and *Trialogus*,[6]

[1] Walsingham, i. 452. Hence a loan of £1,114 3s. 10d. made by Richard to Wenzel on 9 Dec. 1381 is said to be 'for the urgent affairs of the state of the Holy Church of Rome' (Devon, *Issues*, 218). One result of the marriage was the introduction into England and into the west generally of the cult of St. Anne as a sort of compliment. See Wilkins, iii. 178; *Reg. Wykeham*, ii. 348; and *Eng. Hist. Rev.* xviii. 107 f.

[2] See the list in *Cal. Pat.* ii. 4 of those who received considerable pensions on 1 May 1381. The marriage was settled on 2 May and 20,000 florins lent to Wenzel (Rymer, iv. 113).

[3] Aeneas Sylvius, *Hist. Boh.*, c. 35. See also *infra*.

[4] See Wyclif, *Misc. Phil.* i. introd., pp. 47 ff. They were long considered to be the works of Hus himself. For the authorship of one of the five, the *Replicacio de universalibus*, see *infra*, App. D. The manuscript is very hastily and indistinctly written (*ib.*, p. lii). These treatises exist also in Vienna, Cambridge (Trin. Coll.), and Dublin (*ib.*, p. lix).

[5] Hardt, iv. 654, 751. Jerome was charged with putting a halo round Wyclif's head. This he denied.

[6] Hardt, iv. 634, 651. On this matter of dates see *Mon. Hus.* i. 108a; Palacký, *Doc.* 280. I can find no authority for Creighton's statement that "the writings of Wyclif were brought to Prague as early as 1385 by Jerome of

together with some other lesser works whose names are given. All these Jerome had written out with his own hand. ' Young men and students ', he said in a public disputation, ' who did not study the books of Wyclif would never find the true root of knowledge.' In this conviction he introduced the works to two noted leaders of Czech reform, John Christan of Prachaticz and John Hus.[1] Between 1403 and 1407 Hus translated the *Trialogus* into Czech, probably with the assistance of Jerome of Prague.[2] Soon the Wyclifists, as the contemporary writer Stephen Dolein complained, swarmed everywhere ' in state apartments of princes, the schools of the students, the lonely chambers of the monks and the cells of the Carthusians '.[3] Large sums were given for manuscripts of the English doctor, and corrected copies were constantly brought from England.[4] The manuscript of the *de Ecclesia* in Vienna was partly written at Kemerton[5] in Gloucestershire by a German-Bohemian student, Nicholas Faulfiss, assisted by his Czech friend George de Knychnicz[6] and ' corrected ' at Oxford in February 1407 or 1408.[7] One of the four manuscripts at Vienna of the

---

Prague " (*Hist. Papacy*, i. 360). This seems impossible. Neander, x. 348, speaks of Prague as possessing the works for "thirty years ", i. e. from 1381. He has misread *Mon. Hus.* i. 108, which refers to Oxford, as is clear from the context, and *ib.* i. 109*b*, 110*a*. His " Count " Faulfisch is a further confusion, due to Aeneas Sylvius, *Hist. Boh.*, c. 35. For other variations of the same tale, see Loserth, *Wiclif and Hus*, 72-3. A fairly contemporary writer is Ludolph of Sagan, in his *Tractatus de longevo Schismate* [ed. Loserth, in the *Archiv. für Oesterreichische Gesch.*, vol. lx (Vienna, 1880), pp. 345-561, with life and introduction. Also reprinted, with pagination altered, in *Beiträge zur Geschichte der Husitischen Bewegung*, vol. iii (Vienna, 1880). I have used this last]. Sagan says (iii. 84) ' Nescio quo portante'. That Jerome was home in 1401, see Palacký, *Doc.* 175. Additional evidence of date as 1401 is given in Hardt, iv. 651, where, in the official charges against Jerome, the first year of his teaching Wyclifism is put as 1401. On the whole subject, see Höfler, *Abzug der deutschen Prof. v. Student aus Prag.* (1864), 138-66, especially 158-9 ; Palacký, *Die Verläufer Hussitenthums* (Leipzig, 1845), 113-16 ; *Eng. Hist. Rev.* vii. 306-11. For the date (1404-5) of Czech copies of Wyclif's *de Eucharistia*, see *Euch.* p. 54.

[1] Hardt, iv. 650, 652.   [2] Lützow, *op. cit.* 89.
[3] Stephen of Dola, *In Medullam Tritici*, 158 (in Pez. *Thesaurus*, iv, pt. ii).
[4] Palacký, *Doc.* 389 ; *Dom. Div.*, p. x.
[5] *Eccles.* 47 *n*.
[6] One of the Czech barons who on 2 Sept. 1415 protested against the condemnation of Hus (Palacký, *Doc.* 589).
[7] *Ver. Script.* iii. 310 *n*. Not " Whitsuntide 1407 " as Loserth, *Eccles.*, p. xvii. The exact year is uncertain ; see Poole's note in *Dom. Div.*, p. xii. The first manuscript of this group, *Ver. Script.*, had progressed up to ii. 154 by 24 July.

de Dominio Divino was written or corrected in the same year by the same two students partly at Oxford and partly at Braybroke[1] not far from Lutterworth. The late lord of Braybroke, Sir Thomas Latimer, had at one time been a lollard, but had now repented. His rector, Robert Hoke, still continued to be a follower of Wyclif, and no doubt showed his hospitality and loaned his copy of Wyclif's treatise to these travelling students. How early the works came to Bohemia is seen in the fact that one manuscript of the *de Eucharistia* was written as early as 1405 by Andreas of Kourím, a small town in Bohemia.[2] Of the *Trialogus* a copy written about 1400 was read by Martin Luther.[3]

The presence of a few Wyclif manuscripts at Stockholm, and of a large number at Vienna, must not be attributed to any love for these writings by Swede or Austrian. For two centuries after his death Wyclif, as far as we have any evidence, was totally unknown both in the Swedish and Austrian Church. But as a result of the Thirty Years War, and of the invasion of Germany by Gustavus Adolphus, the Swedish king brought back to Upsala as plunder of war some of the manuscripts of Bohemia. Other manuscripts of Wyclif were also taken as spoils to Vienna by the noted Waldstein.[4] To these vicissitudes we owe it that until the recent publications of the Wyclif Society it was almost impossible for English scholars to obtain first-hand knowledge of the writings and theology of Wyclif, unless prepared to spend long months in Prague or Vienna. English manuscripts of the Latin works of Wyclif were few and, except for the *Opus Evangelicum*, of secondary value.[5]

[1] *Dom. Div.* 249 n., also *ib.*, p. x; Loserth, *Wiclif and Hus*, 101 n. As this work is not among the list of books condemned in Prague in 1410 (Palacký, *Doc.* 380), it evidently had not circulated in Bohemia by that date.
[2] *Euch.*, pp. lxii–lxiv.
[3] *Trial.* 21.
[4] Illustrations of the number at Vienna and Prague are as follows: *Dialogus*, 8 Vienna, 1 Prague; *Comp. Hom.*, 3 V., 2 P.; *Ben. Incarn.*, 3 V.; *Polem. Works*, 10 V., 4 P.; *Blas*, 4 V., 2 P.; *Euch.*, 3 V., 2 P.; *Trialogus*, 4 V. not elsewhere; *Off. Reg.*, 2 V., 1 P.; *Dom. Div.*, 4 V. only; *Civ. Dom.*, 1 V. only; *Pot. Pap.*, 4 P. only.
[5] See James, *MSS. Trin.* i. 513–14; *MSS. Caius*, 380–1 (where Wyclif's name nowhere appears), for the Latin works at Cambridge. There is a manuscript of *de Blasphemia* at Trin. Coll. Dublin, also an imperfect manuscript of *de Apostasia*. The only English manuscript of the *Trialogus* at Trin. Coll. Camb. has long been lost. In lord Ashburnham's collection is a manuscript of

the *Dialogus* and one of the *Polemical Works*. Of the *de Benedicta Incarnatione* there is a manuscript in the Brit. Mus. bound up with the works of Wyclif's opponents Woodford and Winterton (*infra*, ii. 146). But this is rather a summary than a manuscript. There is another manuscript at Oriel. Wyclif's *de Veritate Sacrae Scripturae* is remarkable in that of the four manuscripts one only is at Vienna, the others are in the Bodleian, Queens', Cambridge, and Trinity Coll. Dublin. Of these only the Vienna MS. is really trustworthy. Of Wyclif's *Latin Sermons* there is a splendidly embellished copy, evidently written for some one of high rank, at Trin. Coll. Cambridge. Its faults are so many that its editor doubts whether the scribe knew Latin (*op. cit.* iii. p. iv). But for some of the sermons it is the only source, as also of Wyclif's *de Ente*. Of the *Op. Evang.*, the only sources are at Trin. Coll. Cambridge and Trin. Coll. Dublin. There are no MSS. of his English works on the Continent. Of the *De Mandatis*, which is wholly non-polemical, there are two MSS. at Cambridge, two at Oxford, two at Vienna, and eight at Prague.

II

EARLY YEARS

§ 1

THE year of Wyclif's birth cannot be fixed. The data for decision are few, the most important the marriage of his parents in 1319. The guess of Lewis that he was born in 1324 has been widely accepted,[1] and inasmuch as Wyclif was not the eldest son there is much to be said for it. The date would also fit in with Wyclif's description of himself in 1383 as being ' in fine dierum nostrorum ',[2] though we must remember that when Wyclif thus wrote he was already suffering from a stroke of paralysis. The chief argument against this date is the late age, if so, at which Wyclif took his doctorate, a year now fixed as in or about 1372. A later year of birth than 1324 will also fit in better with the revised chronology of his life based on materials unknown to both Lewis and Shirley. A later date will also better explain the remarkable mobility of Wyclif's mind after 1374. Men over fifty do not as a rule make right-about turns, or proceed from the moderate to the extreme with an accelerating pace. The extraordinary work which Wyclif accomplished, especially between 1374 and his death in 1384, will account sufficiently for the notes of tiredness and age which we may detect in his writings. Men who have seen the failure of their hopes are inclined to exaggerate the length of their life. We are confirmed in our impression that Wyclif was under sixty at his death when we find that his

---

[1] Shirley, *Ziz.*, p. xii, followed by Lechler, 84 (who makes him " well on towards seventy at the time of his death ", whereas the earliest date of his birth would only allow of his being sixty-four, and that only if we assume against the evidence that he was the eldest son) argues for an earlier date than 1324. But Shirley's arguments rest upon a wrong date for Wyclif's doctorate. He refers also to a passage in Wyclif's *de Compositione hominis*, p. 67, in which Wyclif speaks of certain views that he once held as now deemed by him ' deliramenta juvenilia '. Cf. *Serm.* ii. 384, ' Quando fui junior '. The *Comp. hom.* is certainly one of his earlier writings (*infra*, p. 142), but the idea that Oxford men at thirty never change their views is contrary to experience.

[2] *Serm.* i. Pref. p. xxx.

Oxford opponent, Cunningham, who according to Netter was Wyclif's senior in years, as he certainly was in his doctorate, was actively engaged in 1398 in certain negotiations with reference to the Great Schism, and only died in the following May.¹

The little lad was given the baptismal name of John, then as now the most common. As illustrations of its extensive use we may mention that at the Blackfriars Synod of 1382, which condemned Wyclif, twenty-five out of the sixty-six who took part were called John, while of the twelve Oxford doctors who in 1381 sat in judgement upon his theses no fewer than nine bore this name. That the Reformer was thus baptized roused the indignation of a monk of St. Albans who moaned :

'This fellow was called John, though he did not deserve to be. For he cast away the grace which God gave him, turning from the truth which is in God and giving himself up to fables'.²

One of the few certainties of Wyclif's life is that he was a Yorkshireman of the North Riding. Three places—Wycliffe-on-Tees,³ Hipswell, and Spresswell—have claimed the honour of his birth. The last may be dismissed as a clerical blunder for Ipswell or Hipswell, first making its appearance in Hearne's printed copy of Leland's *Itinerary*.⁴ Whitaker is emphatic that " there neither is nor ever was in the neighbourhood of Richmond a village of the name of Spresswell ".⁵

Of direct evidence of Wyclif's birthplace there is little or none apart from his name. Walsingham records that he came from the north ;⁶ others do not even mention this. The first definite statement was made by John Leland, who lends his authority to both claimants, Wycliffe-on-Tees and Hipswell.

---

¹ See *Ziz.* 3, ' canitiem reverendam etc.' ; Wood, *Univ.* i. 534.
² *Chron. Ang.* 115.
³ The first syllable is Wy ' water ', not wick or wic. The German form ' Wiclif ' should therefore be avoided. By medieval writers Wyclif's name was spelt in over thirty ways, Walsingham alone giving eight forms. The name gave itself to malicious puns, e. g. ' Wyclyff sive Wikkebeleve ' (Walsingham, i. 451), ' Wicked life ' (cf. Gascoigne, 141, ' Wiclyffe nequam vita ', reading *vita* for *rita*). It is of importance to note that Wyclif lived in a period of transition as to proper names. At the beginning of his life names were usually local. By the end they were rapidly passing into true proper names, with the ' de ' dropped.
⁴ Poole, *Med. Thought*, 285 *n*.   ⁵ Whitaker, *Richmond.* ii. 41.
⁶ ' quidam borealis ' (i. 324).

For while in his *Collectanea* he says that Wyclif 'drew his origin' from Wycliffe-on-Tees, in his *Itinerary*[1] he tells us: 'They say that John Wyclif Haereticus was born at Spreswell (Ipreswell) a poor village, a good mile from Richemont.' The words seem definite enough, and on the rules of evidence Hipswell, restoring the right name in place of Hearne's clerical blunder, would seem to have the better claim. For while the surmise that Wyclif was born at the village from whose name he is invariably called is obvious, his birth at Hipswell would hardly have been conjectured, unless there had been some warrant. But there are many difficulties that prevent us from accepting this.[2]

The form of Leland's statement shows that he is recording local tradition, and that in his opinion it needed verification. In fact the Hipswell hypothesis becomes more untenable the more it is studied. If Wyclif's mother lived permanently at Hipswell—a village about eight miles south-east of Wycliffe-on-Tees, in the parish of Catterick, with no connexion with the Wyclif family,[3]—it is hard to explain, as surnames then went, why the Reformer should be called John de Wycliffe. If on the other hand she was but on a passing visit, as the mother of Luther in Eisleben under similar circumstances, it is difficult to understand how this one straw of tradition should have survived where all the more valuable has perished. So great is this difficulty that some writers,[4] misled by Hearne's blunder, have conjectured a village, now non-existent, of Spresswell or Hipswell within the manor of Wycliffe, or have suggested that "Spresswell is a corruption of Thorpeswell. There is a manor house in the township of Thorpe and there are ruins of a village close to it."[5] It is true that half the vill of Thorpe belonged to the Wyclifs from about 1270 onwards, but there is no evidence that it was ever called Thorpeswell. Moreover, it was sublet by the Wyclifs to others, the most

---

[1] *Coll.* i (ii), 329; *Itin.* v. 112.
[2] Still accepted by many, e. g. Wells, 465; *Vict. Co. Yorks N. R.*, i. 302.
[3] The manor was granted in 1318 to Roger de Fulthorpe (*Vict. Co. Hist.* i. 306).
[4] e. g. Lechler, 81.
[5] For these valueless conjectures see R. Vaughan in *Athenaeum*, 1861, p. 529; L. Sergeant, *ib.* 1892, pp. 344, 405; or Sergeant, *Wyclif*, 79 f.

important tenants being the Siggiswick family.[1] On the other hand, tradition connecting Wyclif with the village of his name has been uninterrupted. In 1634 Simon Birckbeck 'minister of God's word at Gilling in Richmondshire', in a book entitled *The Protestant Evidence*, records that this tradition was unquestioned.[2]

Another conjecture is, perhaps, the most doubtful of all. With the idea that Leland's 'good mile from Richemont' could not possibly be an error, some writers have invented an Old Richmond, on the Tees, three or four miles below Wycliffe.[3] True enough in modern maps such a name may be found. The map-makers have copied it, after the manner of their tribe, from that source of much map-making, Carey's *Atlas*. But Old Richmond, if it ever existed,[4] was certainly not the 'Richemont', the only town of the name at that time in England— for the town named after it in Surrey was then called Sheen— whose magnificent castle, of which Leland gave so complete a description, dominated the district. Leland's miles may be wrong—others besides Leland's informants have mistaken distance—and his name of the hamlet or manor may be corrupt or obscure; but we can scarcely conceive that Leland would have confused the famous Richmond with an obscure and doubtful place, some six miles away.

The manor of Wycliffe[5] was but small, 720 acres in all. Its value would depend upon whether it were arable or pasture, if the former at from 4d. to 8d. an acre, if the latter at about 4s., and if woodland at 1s.[6] In addition there would be the fines which, however, in Yorkshire, where there were few villeins, would be of little value. From about the middle of

---

[1] *Kirkby's Quest*, 168. [2] *op. cit.* ii. 71. [3] Lechler, 80.

[4] In Domesday the town round the castle at Richmond is called 'Neutone'. Hence possibly the origin of the story of an Old Richmond. Cf. the myth of 'Old Rome' in the Campagna, and of 'Old Oxford' (*infra*, p. 64).

[5] This parish in the Wapentake of West Gilling, 2,229 acres in extent, contained 185 inhabitants in 1871, which number had dropped in 1901 to 120 (*Vict. Co. Hist.* iii. 511), probably much the same as in Wyclif's day. It is one of the few civil parishes in Yorkshire out of which no ecclesiastical parish seems to have been carved.

[6] J. Cullum, *Hist. Hawstead* (2nd ed. 1813), 212–24, enters at length into the matter of the relative value of pasture and arable land. See also Levett, *Black Death*, 22 f. Everything, however, depended on the quality. In Yorkshire in 1300 we find some arable land valued at 18d. an acre; and meadow in demesne at 5s. 2d., but some only worth 8d. (*Eng. Hist. Rev.* viii. 557).

the thirteenth century until after the Reformation it belonged to the family of Wyclif of Wycliffe. ' Wyclif, a mean (*poor*) gentelman ', writes Leland,[1] ' dwelleth in a little village called Wyclif ', though there is ground for doubting whether even this Wyclif was connected by blood with the family of the Reformer.[2] In 1611 the estate passed by the marriage of Katherine Wyclif to the family of Tunstall, and from the Tunstalls[3] in 1790 to that of Constable, in whose possession it still lies. A collateral branch carried on the name at Thorpe, until the death of its last male representative Francis Wyclif. The last of the Wyclifs, according to some writers, was a poor gardener who dined every Sunday at Thorpe Hall as the guest of Sir Marmaduke Tunstall, on the strength of his reputed descent.[4] But according to the prosaic investigations of genealogists the last male heir was Thomas Wyclif, who died on the 3rd November 1821 and is buried in the chancel of Kirkby Ravensworth church, where several others of the family were buried before him.[5] His sister, Mrs. Katherine Wade, was buried in 1838 at Whitkirk, Yorkshire, claiming on her tomb to be the last of the line.[6] But though family and name are now extinct, the branches seem at one time to have been numerous. As we shall see later, no less than three different Wyclifs were at Oxford at the same time. The extinction of the family may be attributed to the number of priests it supplied in days when there was no other refuge for poor younger sons.

The village of Wycliffe lies in the midst of some of the most beautiful scenery of England, familiar from the drawings of Turner[7] and the songs of poets. The next manor to Wycliffe is that of Rokeby, to which the genius of Sir Walter Scott has

---

[1] *Itin.* v. 112.   [2] See *infra*, p. 48.
[3] The last was Marmaduke Tunstall (*D. N. B.* lvii. 316), whose museum passed in 1822 to the Lit. and Phil. Soc. of Newcastle (*Vict. Co. Yorks. N. R.* i. 139). For the genealogy of the later Wyclifs see *Geneal.* xx. 133–6, xxi. 95–9 ; and for the Constables and Tunstalls, J. Foster, *Pedigrees of Yorkshire Families*, v. 2. Cf. also *Visitations of Yorkshire in 1563* (Harl. Soc. 1881), 352.
[4] Sergeant, *Wyclif*, 82 ; *Athenaeum*, 1892, p. 345. See also Vaughan, 6. At Colnbrook a family named ' Weekly ' used to claim a collateral descent from Wyclif ; probably a fable based on similarity of name (Summers, 32).
[5] For the connexion of Kirkby Ravensworth with the Wyclifs see *infra*, p. 45.
[6] *Notes and Queries* (ser. 5), ix. 343 ; *Geneal.* xxi. 99.
[7] These give the great value to Whitaker's *Richmondshire* (1823).

given celebrity. But the instinct for the beautiful in nature is of modern growth ; and the picturesque valley with its thickly wooded, undulating hills, its vistas of rock and water, its vast ancient British earthworks and considerable Saxon remains,[1] would have no influence upon the character of the Reformer. The times were too wild, the ways too rough, accommodation on the moors too scanty for men to care for scenes that are to-day the delight of the traveller. Even the churches of the district bear witness to the former insecurity. Their towers were usually constructed to serve as temporary defences.[2] We are on surer ground when we remember that the loneliness of life in these northern parts, the constant need for the strong man armed, and for watchfulness against marauding Scots, the rough and tumble of a feudalism which found no place for the weakling, had produced in Yorkshire a type of character singularly tenacious and stout-hearted, equally energetic whether in the maintenance of conservative habits or in the propagation of radical opinions. As research has shown, at the time of the Domesday survey there were few serfs in Yorkshire or northern Lincolnshire, and this absence of the servile spirit has ever been a note of the county.[3] Unless we are mistaken, all the characteristics of the Yorkshireman, not forgetting a certain angularity, will be found fully developed in Wyclif. Like most of his countrymen he would pride himself on his undoubted independence of outlook. His life at the university did little towards toning down a northern bluntness which at times became barbarous in its violence.

The little church [4] of Wycliffe without spire or tower, with its porch on either side, its pavement beneath the level of the soil, and its Gothic windows almost hidden by the ivy, shows externally little change. The oldest parts that now remain date from about 1240. When Wyclif was a boy it was a small building with a nave about 30 feet long and a small chancel, but between 1340 and 1350 it was rebuilt and enlarged, no doubt with the help of Wyclif's parents, by extending both the nave and chancel. The piscina with broken basin still

---

[1] *Vict. Co. Yorks.* ii. 5, 6, 128.   [2] Whitaker, *op. cit.* i. 15.
[3] *Vict. Co. Yorks.* ii. 148 exaggerates this into "no serfs". We may detect Danish influence in this freedom.
[4] *Vict. Co. Yorks. N. R.* i. 138–42.

dates from his days, as do also the three windows in the south wall and the priest's doorway between the second and third windows. The ancient font has disappeared, but the church is still rich in remains of early stained glass. In one of the windows of the chancel is a representation of the Trinity, the Father with a dove on His shoulder holding His Son on the cross. In one of the windows of the nave is St. James with his pilgrim's staff, wallet, and scallop, carrying a book. In two of the windows there are representations of the Virgin and Child. Stained glass windows in churches in later life fell under Wyclif's Puritan lash.

Life at Wycliffe must have been singularly lonely and rough. Even in these days of travel that portion of Teesdale, lying off both the Great North Road and the railway, is but rarely visited. The noise and rush of the world do not penetrate these glens; still less would it reach six hundred years ago the little village, not above one hundred souls in all, which lay at the foot of a steep slope crowned with a manor-house that has long since been modernized out of touch with the past. Occasionally, however, a traveller—knight or pedlar—might stray for the night from the old Watling Street which cuts through the parish in its south-west corner. A water-mill—doubtless on the site of what is now a saw-mill [1]—supplied the local needs of flour, while the villagers would spin their own rough clothes. Beyond this most things were regarded as the luxuries of the few.

Rude as was the northern world in which Wyclif was born, the eye of a prophet might have seen the beginnings of the industrial movement which in modern times has turned the county palatine of Durham into a hive of industry. Coal was already mined and beginning to compete with wood. In December 1229 John Balliol tried to prevent the 'king's miners' from going to their work in Teesdale.[2] In 1357 the citizens of Newcastle obtained the right to have 'mines of coal and stones' in the Town Moor, 'in aid of the farm of the town'.[3] In July 1373 the town obtained the right to levy for five years a penny on every chaldron of coal sent by water,

[1] *Vict. Co. Yorks. N. R.* i. 138. Mentioned in 1348 in *Cal. Pat.* vii. 453.
[2] *Cal. Docs. Scots*, i. 193.   [3] *Chart. Rolls*, v. 154-5.

for the repair of its walls and bridges.[1] On the 5th March 1378 certain citizens were granted a licence to transport to London by sea 3,000 chaldrons of coal and 300 grindstones, and tried to escape from this penny rate. It is interesting to note that they gave bail that they would not export the coal to foreign parts.[2] In 1383 John Fordham, bishop of Durham, secured from Richard II that there should be no interference on the part of the men of Newcastle with the shipping of his coal ' whither he will '.[3] The quarrel was continued into the following year when the bishop obtained a commission to destroy all coal ' keels of greater measure than they ought to be '.[4] In the year that Wyclif died we read of ' 300 keels of sea-coal granted to the king ' from the bishop's ' mine at Gateshead ', sold for the king's benefit by the mayor of Newcastle.[5] Iron also was beginning to be worked in Weardale and Teesdale, though deemed inferior to Spanish, and was already adding its quota to the princely revenue of the bishops of Durham.[6] But for the most part all this was still in the womb of time.

§ 2

In Domesday the manor of Wycliffe with all Richmondshire,[7] once belonging to earl Edwin, forms part of the vast domain of count Alan le Roux (†1089)—one of three contemporary counts Alan of Brittany—to whom it had been transferred in 1069 through the influence of Queen Maud, after the failure of earl Edwin's insurrection. The centre of this extensive fief was a height eleven miles south of Wycliffe. There count Alan, or more probably one of his successors, earl Conan (1148–71), built one of the stateliest of Norman keeps whose fine masonry indicates a somewhat late date. Round the castle there had gathered in place of some destroyed village

---

[1] *Cal. Pat. Ed.* xv. 326.   [2] *Cal. Pat. Ric.* i. 141, 155.
[3] *Chart. Rolls*, v. 290–1 (28 Dec. 1383).
[4] 28 July 1384, *Cal. Pat. Ric.* ii. 499.   [5] *Close Rolls Ric.* ii. 355.
[6] Bishop Langley tried the experiment of working and smelting his own iron. For his account books, see *Eng. Hist. Rev.* xiv. 509–29.
[7] For Richmondshire and Richmond see Whitaker, *op. cit.*; *Vict. Co. Yorks.* and *Vict. Co. Yorks. N. R.* For its castle see also *Eng. Hist. Rev.* xix. 422–44. The documents *re* Richmondshire are in R. Gale, *Registrum honoris de Richmond* (1722).

a hamlet, in Domesday called 'Neutone', to which afterwards was given the French name of Richmond, 'the rich mount'—probably an indication of the value set upon its strength. Slowly the hamlet grew into a town with a fine parish church built in the twelfth century, the advowson of which belonged to the abbey of St. Mary, York. The bells of the church date back to Wyclif's days. In 1279 the town received the rights of a fair, and in the reign of Edward III was deemed of sufficient importance to be enclosed with a wall, certain houses being pulled down for the purpose. But, as Leland remarks, the walls—two of whose gates still remain, hoary now with age but in Wyclif's youth newly built—enclosed little more than the market-place. To the boy Wyclif, Richmond would be the largest town he had seen, for practical purposes his county town, the owner of rights in the pastures of his native village,[1] the centre of an honor, as also of an archdeaconry that possessed many privileges usually associated with an independent diocese. When the boy visited its fairs or its Saturday market in grain, he would note the number of strangers, if indeed we may trust the boast of its citizens that it was attended by 'foreign merchants' as well as by farmers from Lancashire and Cumberland. Nor would the boy marvel, as later writers and tourists marvel still, at the difficulties of access to this castle-town. "Generation after generation were content to plunge headlong into Richmond down a steep ascent from the north and to ascend an equal precipice into the market-place." But to Wyclif this would seem as much part of the fitness of things as the gallows in the Gallowgate, or the fact that the sewer was turned into the brook with whose waters the townsmen brewed their beer.

The importance of Richmond was seen in its religious houses. In addition to a small Benedictine priory for ten monks, a cell of St. Mary's at York dedicated to St. Martin, there was also at Easby, close by Richmond, a large Premonstratensian abbey dedicated to St. Agatha. This abbey, originally endowed in 1152 by Roald the constable of the castle, had been refounded

---

[1] These were granted in 1268. See Gale, App. 209, 213 f.; *Cal. Pat. Hen. VI*, iii. 452, 509–10, where the status of the town and its rights are set out in full. In 1441 it is stated that the grass of 'Wytteklyf' has been destroyed by the growth of furze, &c.

by Sir Henry le Scrope, chief justice of the king's bench, who was buried there in 1336. In Wyclif's day the canons were few, but Scrope's son, Richard, first lord of Bolton, whose tomb was in its precincts, about 1393 increased their number by twelve to pray for himself and his family, building for them also a fine refectory. A weather-beaten shield in stone over the doorway of the adjoining parish church, charged with the bend so famed in the annals of medieval lawsuits,[1] is now the only existing memorial of this connexion. Wyclif may have noted that the two mills on the Swale, of which the town boasted, were both in the hands of an alien priory. In addition to the older institutions there was also a Franciscan friary, founded in 1258, which at the Dissolution had a warden and fourteen brethren. The tower of this friary, standing in a field northward of the town, is to-day one of the features of the view. The importance of the friary was evidenced by the extent of its close, sixteen acres in all. The seal of the friary represented St. Francis preaching to the birds, and the adventures of one of the friars with a savage sow have taken a place in our ballad literature.[2] There was also a hospital of St. Nicholas outside the town. This existed as early as the reign of Henry II, and at the Dissolution had a revenue of £13 12s.[3] Traces of this hospital still survive in a private house. It is interesting to note also that there was an anchoress in Richmond whose cell[4] was close to the walls, 'a little beyond the end of Frenchgate street', writes Leland. She received a rent charge of 21s. a year paid by the cell of St. Martin, as also a quarter and a half of corn from the hospital of St. Nicholas. From a legacy of two shillings left to the anchoress in the reign of Henry I we see how early was the foundation of this anchorage. The nomination to any vacancy was in the hands of the bailiff and burgesses of Richmond.[5]

[1] The curious may dip into the *de Controversia in curia militari inter Ric. le Scrope et Rob. Grosvenor, 1385–90*, ed. H. N. Nicholas, 2 vols. 1832.
[2] See the ballad of the 'Felon Sow of Rokeby', printed by Sir Walter Scott in *Rokeby* (ed. 1847). Scott is said to have lost the manuscript. A corrected version is in C. J. D. Ingledew, *Ballads and Songs of Yorks.* (1860), 93.
[3] *Val. Eccl.* v. 238.
[4] Still marked in Speed's plan of 1610. This seems to have been a second anchorage, the more important being on the site of the hall of the Masons (W. H. Longstaffe, *Richmondshire*, 1852, p. 24).
[5] See the interesting lawsuit in *Test. Ebor.* ii. 114 *n*.

RICHMOND CASTLE, YORKSHIRE, ABOUT 1821

Wyclif's boyhood recollections of Richmond would strengthen the conviction of his later life that the regulars were in many places far too numerous for the financial resources of the country.

The importance of Richmond was evidenced most of all in the status of its archdeaconry. When Wyclif was still a child an agreement was made between the then archdeacon, Robert de Woodhouse,[1] then chancellor of the exchequer, and archbishop William de Melton, who had recently taken over from Woodhouse the treasurership of England. By this there were handed over to the archdeacon certain privileges usually associated with a bishop, e.g. the custody of vacant benefices, the sequestration of livings, the confirmation of elections to benefices, the institution of incumbents, the visitation of hospitals, lazar houses, anchorites and hermits, licences for non-residence in benefices, excommunications,[2] and the like, the archbishop reserving little more than the right of visitation.[3] The archdeaconry itself was of vast extent, embracing not only Richmondshire in Yorkshire but the parts of Lancashire north of the Ribble, the greater portion of Westmorland and certain parishes of Cumberland.[4] When in 1541 the archdeaconry of Richmond was separated from the diocese of York and made part of the new bishopric of Chester, the privileges of the archdeacon were suppressed. But if Wyclif, while a boy at home, took note of these matters, he must have formed a curious idea of the value and meaning of a bishop. Wyclif also would not fail to note that his native archdeaconry was always either held by an alien, for archdeaconries were the common hunting-ground of cardinals, or else became the perquisite of the king's favoured servants; whether one or the other alike absentees.

[1] For Woodhouse see *D. N. B.*

[2] The issue of writs *significavit* (see *infra*, ii. 26) was especially granted to John Waltham on 19 Feb. 1385 (*Cal. Pat. Ric.* ii. 536).

[3] For this document, dated July 1331, see Raine, *Hist. Church York*, iii. 248–50. As early as 10 March 1331 the Crown recognized some arrangement of this sort, see *Cal. Pat.* ii. 82.

[4] These parts of Westmorland and Cumberland were formerly in Yorkshire, or rather in Deira, though not reckoned as part of its ridings. The see of Carlisle, on its formation in 1092, was made coterminous with the old county of Carlisle (not called Cumberland till 1177) and not with Henry I's enlargement of Cumberland by the addition of the Yorkshire parishes. Not until 1856 did the see include the whole of the modern county.

As later views are often the result rather of concrete fact than abstract theory, we give illustrations. During Wyclif's early years the archdeaconry [1] was held by Elias Talayrand, papally provided on the 16th August 1322.[2] On his elevation to the see of Auxerre [3] Talayrand was succeeded by the king's servant Robert de Woodhouse (14 Sept. 1328). On the decease of Woodhouse in the winter of 1345 [4] the archdeaconry was given to John Raymond de Comminges, cardinal-bishop of Porto.[5] The archdeaconry was farmed out, and in November 1347 the profits were seized by Edward III with other alien benefices.[6] The work was done by John Gynwell, of whom more anon. On the death of Raymond in 1348 Clement VI provided (23 Apr. 1349) [7] Henry de Walton, rector of the rich living of Preston. During Wyclif's last days the archdeacon was the pluralist courtier John de Waltham, who was installed on the 11th January 1384.[8]

Richmond was also the centre of an important 'honor', whose boundaries were very different from those of the archdeaconry.[9] The object of the Conqueror in thus erecting this strong fief was twofold—to prevent insurrection and to serve as a bulwark against the Scot.[10] The first was scarcely necessary, for all Yorkshire had been reduced to a 'waste'—so it is entered in Domesday—by William's remorseless

---

[1] For a list of the archdeacons see Gale, *Registrum*, App. 78–9; Whitaker, *op. cit.* i. 35 f.; Le Neve, iii. 135 f. All need considerable corrections.

[2] Rymer, ii. 495. Talayrand's absence from England was officially recognized (*Cal. Pat. Ed. II.* iv. 365, v. 12).

[3] 4 Jan. 1328 (Eubel, i. 122). Talayrand was made a cardinal 24 May 1331, d. at Avignon 17 Jan. 1364 (*op. cit.* i. 15).

[4] His will was proved 3 Feb. 1346 (Le Neve, iii. 138).

[5] Comminges was made a cardinal 18 Dec. 1327 (Eubel, *H. C.* i. 15). For his provision to the archdeaconry, installed 19 Jan. 1345, see *Pap. Pet.* i. 151, 152. He is mentioned as archdeacon on 20 Nov. 1346 (*Cal. Pat.* vii. 209), which shows that Eubel's date for his decease, 20 Nov. 1344 (Eubel, i. 15) must be altered to 1348 (Ciaconius, ii. 519; cf. Eubel, i. 35). Comminges is not in Gale, Whitaker, or Le Neve, who by mistake call the then archdeacon 'John Gynswell', following Hutton. This curious mistake arose from Gynwell acting as vicar-general. As such his register records institutions to the churches of Goldsborough and Preston (see *Arch. Journ.* lviii. 306). For Gynwell see *infra*, p. 87.

[6] *Cal. Pat.* vii. 425.   [7] *Pap. Let.* iii. 290.

[8] For Wyclif's protest against the profits of a cure being sent to an absentee cardinal, see *Serm.* ii. 312.

[9] Its extent in 18 and 19 Ed. I is set out in Gale, App. 28 f.

[10] See the charters of its earls, e.g. Gale, App. 151.

harrying in 1068, followed by the raid of Malcolm Canmore. The wapentake of E. and W. Gilling, of which the village of Wycliffe formed part, had been worth in the time of the Confessor £205 a year; its rental in Domesday was not more than £44 10s.,[1] while the whole population of Yorkshire— York excluded—scarcely reached 7,000.[2] Only very slowly had Yorkshire recovered from this great desolation, largely, it would appear, through the continuous immigration of Flemish weavers,[3] though these foreigners, with their culture and wealth, were probably restricted to the great plain. Nor was the harrying by the Conqueror the only cause of the backward condition of the country. The Scots took care that its progress should not be rapid.

Wyclif would be brought up with a bitter hatred of these invaders. Their raids in the years after Bannockburn were too close for the memory of their devastations lightly to pass. Tales of the raids would be handed down, and these would lose nothing in the telling.[4] The inhabitants in their fear had taken refuge, some in church towers,[5] others in the castles or fortified towns. In one raid (May 1318) Northallerton had been burnt and Richmondshire devastated, though the village of Wycliffe seems to have escaped. According to a letter from pope John XXII 'the towns, manors and other places had been stripped of inhabitants'.[6] The monks of Durham had bought off ruin by a payment of 800 marks.[7] Nevertheless in May 1319 bishop Lewis Beaumont of Durham was forced to raise a loan of £6,000 with which to meet the losses caused by the Scots.[8] In another raid, 3,000 Yorkshiremen, including a

---

[1] *Vict. Co. Yorks.* ii. 160.

[2] Dr. Beddoe (*Yorks. Arch. Jour.* xix. [2]) calculated that in 1086 the total population of the West Riding was 3,143; East Riding, 2,300; and North Riding, 1,311.

[3] For proofs see Cunningham, i. App. E; *Eng. Hist. Rev.* xxi. 510–13; *Vict. Co. Yorks.* iii. 437–40.

[4] There are official reports of these raids and their horrors, from the English side, in Raine, *North Registers*, 222, 238. See also J. Bain, *On the Sufferings of the Northern Counties of England between 1314 and 1319* (1874); *Cal. Docs. Scots*, iii. 119, 127, 163. A list of the towns burnt and of the taxes reduced in 1319 in consequence is in Rymer, ii. 409; Gale, *op. cit.*, App. 156 f.

[5] e. g. John Sayer at Houghton-le-Spring, who was killed in descending (Raine, *op. cit.* 250).

[6] *Pap. Let.* ii. 188; cf. *Chron. Lan.* 235–6.

[7] Raine, *op. cit.* 232 (7 Oct. 1314).   [8] *Pap. Let.* ii. 187; cf. 192.

number of clergy, had been slain at Myton near Boroughbridge (Sept. 1319).[1] In a third, Edward II was only rescued with difficulty. In 1321 the Scots ravaged the northern part of Lancaster, burning Preston, and exacting ransom from the abbey of Furness.[2] The hands of the invaders had fallen with special heaviness upon the Church. Byland had been plundered;[3] the abbey of Eccleston, near Wyclif's home, almost destroyed.[4] At Fountains the Cistercians were unable either to pay taxation or to maintain themselves.[5] Ripon had bought off the Scots with 1,000 marks and six wives of burgesses as the hostages for payment;[6] Tadcaster and Pannal churches were destroyed, the canons of Bolton in destitution, the smaller monasteries and nunneries deserted. "It is difficult to realize in what a state of terror the inhabitants of the scattered farm-houses and homesteads must have lived. . . . But the enthusiasm evoked by the defeat of the Scots at Neville's Cross in 1346, the blow which freed the county from the yoke under which she had groaned helpless for more than fifty years, bears witness to what had been endured. The presence of the archbishop, William de la Zouch, in the thickest of the fight testifies to the resentment of the Church against the persecutors."[7] As a result of the losses and expenses thus incurred many of the Yorkshire churches obtained in 1318 a 'nova taxatio', or reduced scale of rating, which continued as the basis until the Reformation.[8] The manors also would be heavily burdened in finding the ransoms of captive knights.[9] The wrongs that northern England suffered would be brought home to Wyclif, for the living of Wycliffe, in the gift of his

---

[1] *Chron. Lan.* 239. For this battle with the device of firing the haystacks by which it was won see A. D. H. Leadman, *Battles fought in Yorkshire* (1891), 26-31. In consequence of the number of the clergy in it, it was called 'The Chapter of Myton'. A chantry to their memory was erected on the field in 1325 (*Cal. Docs. Scots*, iii. 159). Archbishop Melton lost in it most of his plate, &c. (Raine, *op. cit.* 295).
[2] *Chron. Lan.* 246.   [3] *Pap. Pet.* i. 18.
[4] *Cal. Doc. Scots*, iii. 117.   [5] Raine, *op. cit.* 282.
[6] *Cal. Doc. Scots*, iii. 157; Raine, *op. cit.* 274.
[7] *Vict. Co. Yorks.* iii. 442; cf. *ib.* 403 and *Chron. Melsa*, ii. 333 f.
[8] In *Eng. Hist. Rev.* xxiii. 437 there is a different explanation given of the 'antiqua taxatio' dating it back at least a century earlier. According to *Pap. Let.* ii. 509, 568, the 'nova taxatio' in Durham, Carlisle, and part of York dioceses, worked out at £2,000 less values.
[9] See the payments of archbishop Greenfield in 1315, Raine, *op. cit.* 248.

THE KEEP OF RICHMOND CASTLE

GREYFRIARS' TOWER, RICHMOND

From *Whitaker's* County of York, *1821*

family, had been halved in value—or at any rate in assessment —by the invasions.¹ He would hear also how on an autumn Sunday in 1322 'Scots rebels' had entered the nunnery of Ellerton in Swaledale and carried off seven charters granted by one of his ancestors, Robert de Wyclif, in favour of the priory.² In the same raid they had captured John of Brittany,³ earl of Richmond. The pastures of Wycliffe and other parts of Richmondshire had been filled with the stock led off by the frightened farmers.⁴ Of the device adopted in one of these raids by the Scots to surprise the English we have an interesting reminiscence in a lollard tract written by a disciple who may well have heard it from Wyclif's own lips.⁵

Of the desolation round Wyclif's home caused by these Scots raids, we have a very full record made in 1342 on the death of the earl of Richmond, John, duke of Brittany. The castle of Richmond, we are told, was dilapidated and worth nothing; the pigeon-house, at one time worth 12*d*., was now valueless. The rents of the houses adjoining the wall and ditch had also vanished. A tannery and limekiln that once produced 40s. a year now brought in nothing ' on account of the poverty and weakness of the country '. For the same reason the court leet was worth no more than 20s. There was also a profit called ' overfoot ' from the impounding of beasts; but there were now no animals to stray. A toll for travelling through the forest of Bainbridge brought in but 40s. for the same cause. The pastures, the chief wealth of the district, paid but little ' because of the poverty of the tenants and their want of stock '. At Moulton an oxgang (about ten acres) which used to pay 16s. was now lying waste. At Gilling, where rents were higher (about 2s. an acre), three oxgangs were vacant. Cottages also which should have been worth 6s. 11*d*. a year were lying empty or destroyed. The common oven, a feudal right which had already largely lapsed, still brought

¹ See *infra*, p. 44.
² *Cal. Docs. Scots*, iii. 276. From an inquisition held at Richmond (8 Sept. 1347), we learn that Robert Wyclif had granted '6s 8*d*. out of his mill at Wycliffe' (*Cal. Pat. Ed.* vii. 453). Whether this Robert de Wyclif was John's grandfather or great-grandfather is uncertain; see *infra*, p. 39.
³ Rymer, ii. 498, iii. 978; Gale, App. 161 f.; cf. *Pap. Let.* ii. 460.
⁴ Rymer, ii. 490.
⁵ *Eng. Works*, 99. See *infra*, ii. 327.

in 5s. a year at Gilling. At Bowes the castle was ruinous and untenable, and the six hens a year which the inhabitants should have paid for the right of gathering firewood in the forest were not forthcoming.[1]

While Wyclif was still a youth an event occurred of more than local interest. In 1342 the fief of Richmond was transferred from its former lords to John of Gaunt, a lad then in his third year, who was duly invested by the girding on of the sword.[2] Thus Richmond became one of the titles of the house that afterwards bore the more famous name of Lancaster. The severance of the honor from its long connexion with the counts and dukes of Brittany and its passing into English hands was one of the many illustrations of the growth in the fourteenth century of English self-consciousness. No part of England could now be regarded as the fief of alien lords, while alien priories, though more difficult to deal with, were under constant suspicion and danger of confiscation. In 1372, it is true, Richmond was temporarily restored, for political reasons, to John de Montfort, duke of Brittany,[3] who was wavering in his choice between England and France. Montfort's adhesion to the French ten years later led to a second forfeiture in 1384.[4] For this surrender in 1372 John of Gaunt was adequately rewarded by receiving the castle of Pevensey, the castle, honor, and manor of Tickhill and of Knaresborough, the castle and manor of the High Peak and other manors and advowsons.[5] For thirty years, however, John of Gaunt was

---

[1] Whitaker, *op. cit.* i. 54–64 ; *Inquis.* (n.s.), viii. 231.

[2] In *Dig. Peer*, v. 42 ; *Chart. Rolls*, v. 12 ; Gale, App. 187–8 ; the date is given as 20 Sept. 1342. In Rymer, ii. 1214, as 20 Nov. 1342. For the descent of the counts of Richmond see Gale, i. 106, and for the history of the honor and its change of masters, *Vict. Co. Yorks. N. R.* i. 2 f.

[3] Indenture made between Gaunt and the king on 25 June 1372 (*Cal. Pat. Ed.* xv. 184 ; Rymer, iii. 948 ; *Cal. Pat. Ric.* i. 79–80). The earldom was delivered 20 July 1372 (Rymer, iii. 956 ; Gale, App. 192 f. ; *Cal. Pat.* xv. 183) ; the castle and town surrendered 2 Dec. 1372 (*Close Rolls*, xiii. 484) ; the muniments, measures, and standards on 18 Feb. 1373, after a diligent search, begun on 30 Aug. 1372, for stray rolls (*Reg. Gaunt*, ii. 130 ; Armitage-Smith, 203 n.).

[4] *Vict. Co. Yorks. N. R.* i. 9. But the connexion of Brittany and Richmond was not finally broken until Oct. 1399.

[5] 25 June 1372. Set out in full in *Reg. Gaunt*, i. 10–14 ; *Cal. Pat. Ric.* i. 24 ; W. Hardy, *Charters of the Duchy of Lancaster* (1845), 26 f. On 4 June 1377 he secured a larger interpretation of this grant (*Chart. Rolls*, v. 233–4 ; Hardy, *op. cit.* 49 f.).

Wyclif's overlord,[1] a fact not without its results, as we shall see later, on the Reformer's life. As a tenant of the honor of Richmond Wyclif would be free of all tolls throughout England, though as an ecclesiastic this prescriptive right would not benefit him greatly.[2]

§ 3

Some writers have spoken of the Wyclifs as of Norman origin and have dwelt upon their long possession of the manor. In reality the family had not been lords of Wycliffe for more than about fifty years when the Reformer was born. In Domesday book 'Witcliffe' is entered as among the places 'altogether waste',[3] but this refers to oxen and live stock, and does not mean that there were no inhabitants. Whether the Wyclifs were of native Saxon stock or whether they had come from other parts to fill up the desert places after the Conqueror's harrying of Yorkshire we cannot say. In either event the Wyclifs at first were only under-tenants. At what date they obtained the enfeoffment of the manor is not recorded; it cannot have been before 1286–7, in which year we find William de Kirkton mesne lord of Wycliffe, Girlington, and half the vill of Thorpe, from whom Robert de Wyclif held seven carucates[4] in the same townships, 'which make a knight's fee'.[5] This Robert de Wyclif was possibly the same Robert to whom had been granted in 1253 a messuage and rent in Wycliffe,[6] and who on the 6th May 1263 obtained from Roger, prior of Markeby, 'for himself and his heirs for ever' the advowson of the church.[7] At Thorp Robert Wyclif had a sub-tenant, Felicia de Houghton, and at Girlington he sublet three carucates to a certain Thomas. These additional five

---

[1] *Inquis.* (n. s.), viii. 401, 'the tenements in Wycliffe are held of the said John of Gaunt by knight's service'.
[2] *Vict. Co. Yorks. N. R.* i. 12; Rymer, iv. 65.
[3] *Vict. Co. Yorks.* ii. 190, 231.
[4] The carucate, or plough-land, divided into eight bovates or oxgangs, was the northern writ of assessment, due to Danish influences, as the hide was the southern (*Eng. Hist. Rev.* xi. 219).
[5] Gale, 50; *Feudal Aids*, vi. 95; *Kirkby's Inquest*, 167–8. The inquisition for Richmondshire was made about 1287, see *ib.* p. viii.
[6] Feet of Fines Mich. 37, Hen. III, no. 6; in *Vict. Co. Yorks. N. R.* i. 139.
[7] *Final Concords of the Co. of Lincoln*, ii. 289 (ed. C. W. Foster for Lincoln Rec. Soc. v. 17, 1920). Robert's daughter was named Alice, *ib.* ii. 152.

carucates Robert Wyclif held from Mary of Middleham, a tenant of the count. For these Robert rendered the due services.[1] He also bought certain tenements at Gayles near Kirkby Ravensworth, possibly for a younger son, for descendants of the Wyclif family lived on there to the early years of the nineteenth century.[2] In the inquisition made in 1280-1 into the estate of Peter of Savoy, among the knights who ' owe guard at the castle of Richmond ' there is mention of a ' fee for the same for which Robert de Wyclif renders one half mark '.[3] Robert seems to have been a pushing, successful man, the founder of a family of small country gentlemen.

In Whitaker's *Richmondshire* three generations of the family in the fourteenth century are given in the following form :

Robert de Wycliffe (6 Ed. I, by *Kirkby's Inquest*).
|
Roger Wycliffe, lord of Wycliffe, etc., buried at Wycliffe. Maried in 1319 Catherine his wife, buried at Wycliffe.
|
William Wyclif of Wycliffe, esq., *m.* Frances, d. of Sir Robert Bellasis of ——, Kt.

John Wyclif (*Hereticus*).

The significance of the dotted line must not be overlooked. The genealogy of the Wyclifs, preserved so fully in their family records, makes no mention whatever of John Wyclif. His name seems to have been deliberately erased by this devout family of Romanists.

Modern research enables us to correct Whitaker's pedigree. Of the Robert de Wycliffe who heads it we have already spoken. If we identify him with the Robert who obtained a rent in Wycliffe in 1253 he lived to be an old man, for he was alive in 1300[4] but died before 1303 when his heir, Roger, paid the

---

[1] Gale, 50, 71. For the fiefs of Mary of Middleham see Gale, 70 f. She married Robert Neville, lord of Raby. For the inquisition at her death before April 1320 see *Inquis.* (n. s.), vi. 137.

[2] *Vict. Co. Yorks. N. R.* i. 92-3 ; also *supra*, p. 25.

[3] *Inquis.* (n. s.), ii. 214.

[4] Feet of Fines Yorks., Trin. 28 Ed. I, no. 29, from *Vict. Co. Yorks. N. R.* i. 139.

subsidy.¹ Possibly Robert I was Roger's grandfather; if Roger's father, he must have been over 70 at his decease. Robert's son Roger cannot, however, have been the Roger Wyclif who figures as second in Whitaker's pedigree, and who was, as we take it, the father of the Reformer, for in 1316 it would appear that another Robert de Wyclif was lord of the manor.² We must therefore interpose in Whitaker's pedigree a Roger de Wycliffe, lord of the manor in 1303, who died before 1316, and a Robert de Wycliffe, lord of the manor in 1316. Whether this Roger was the father or elder brother of this Robert we cannot tell, but assuming the long life of the founder of the family, they may well have been father and son. At what date Robert de Wyclif, lord of the manor in 1316, died we do not know. All that is certain is that the Reformer's father, Roger de Wyclif, paid a relief of 25s. for three carucates that he held at Thorp in 1319,³ and for Wycliffe paid the subsidy in 1332–3.⁴ In July 1345 he held Wycliffe, Thorpe, and Girlington by service of a knight's fee from William le Scrope.⁵ He was still alive in 1347–9.⁶ In his old age he was exempted by the king from civic duties, the liability to serve at assize, on jury, or as mayor, sheriff, coroner, or bailiff against his will.⁷ As he married in 1319 Katherine, the Reformer's mother, we may assume that he was born about the year 1300. The fact that he was not at the time of his marriage the lord of the manor may account for the uncertainty as regards Wyclif's birthplace. The Reformer's father may have dwelt after his marriage in one of the smaller houses on the estate, very possibly at Thorp, of which, as we have seen, he paid the relief in 1319. This would be the more likely if the Robert de Wyclif, the lord at that time, was Roger's uncle and not his father. When the Reformer's father died is not known, except that it was before 1362,⁸ for unfortunately the black letter inscription in the church at Wycliffe over the tomb

---

¹ *Lay Subs. R.*, 30 Ed. I (Yorks. Arch. Soc. v. 21, 1897), p. 24. *Vict. Co. Yorks. N. R.* i. 139 seems inaccurate in the name of this son.
² *Kirkby's Quest*, 334; *Feudal Aids*, vi. 182.
³ Gale, 73.
⁴ *Lay Subs. R.* 211, no. 7a in *Vict. Co. Yorks. N. R.* i. 139.
⁵ *Inquis.* (n. s.), viii. 404.
⁶ *Lay Subsidy* no. 23; also *Feudal Aids*, vi. 239 for 1346.
⁷ Assize R. 1127, m. 16 in *Vict. Co. Yorks. N. R.*   ⁸ See *infra*, p. 40.

of Roger and Katherine his wife gives no date. 'Hic jacet Rogerus de Wyclif quondam dominus istius ville et Katerina uxor ejus quorum animabus propicietur Dominus. Amen.'[1] Below the inscription are the arms of the family.

We have assumed that Roger de Wyclif and Katherine were the parents of the Reformer. If so, Wyclif's father, Roger, was alive in 1349. In order to make room for William Wyclif we must assume that Roger died a few years later, for by August 1362 the lordship of the manor had passed both from Roger Wyclif and William Wyclif to another, and in 1363, as we shall see, was definitely in the hands of John de Wycliffe. So William Wyclif, who succeeded Roger in the estates, and who, presumably, was the eldest son, died childless at some date before August 1362. Probably his wife Frances Bellasis was dead also. For in James Torre's invaluable collections, in the catalogues of the rectors of Wycliffe,[2] we note the following institutions:

Date.	Rector.	Patron.
—	John de Clervaulx	
2 Aug. 1362	Dns. Robert de Wycliffe, *cl.*	Kath. relicta Rogi Wiclefi.
7 Aug. 1363	Dns. William de Wycliffe	John de Wycliffe.
7 Oct. 1369	Dns. Henr. Hugate, *Cap.*	*iidem.*

This list, taken along with the preceding, supplies many points of interest, especially if used with a little conjecture. In the first place it gives proof of the death of William Wyclif— we allude to the layman of that name—before August 1362. It further shows that Katherine, Wyclif's mother, was still alive —'*iidem*'—in October 1369, when she was associated with her son 'John de Wycliffe' in the presentation to the living. At this date she must have been at least 65 years of age. We further note the names of two other members of the family, parson Robert and parson William Wyclif.[3] Of the former we

---

[1] Whitaker, *op. cit.* i. 198.

[2] Whitaker, *op. cit.* i. 200, from Torre, *op. cit.* f. 1697. The five folio manuscript vols. of James Torre (†1699) on the archdeaconries of York are in the York Chapter library. See *D. N. B.* The registers for the archdeaconry of Richmond, unfortunately, do not now exist save in Torre and in Mat. Hutton. Harl. MS. 6978, pp. 5 ff. For a copy of the old *Ledger or Voucher of the Archdeaconry of Richmond*, giving its Peter's pence, synodals, &c., see Gale, 62 f.

[3] See *infra*, p. 42. *Vict. Co. Yorks. N. R.* i. 139 identifies the two.

know little, for he cannot be the same as the Robert Wyclif, rector of Rudby,[1] who died in 1423, of whom more anon, for that would make him nearly 90 at his decease. We have reason to believe, however, that Robert Wyclif's retirement from the living of Wycliffe in August 1363 was due to exchange or preferment, not to death.[2] For on the 22nd June 1382 orders were issued to restore to John, son of Thomas, lord de Roos of Hamlake in the North Riding of Yorkshire, and Mary his wife, certain estates belonging to the said Mary which had been hitherto in the king's hands because of her minority. Among these estates was the manor of Dronfield, which Mary's grandfather, Sir John de Orby of Toft by Witham, Lincolnshire, 'long before his death' had granted 'for life to Robert de Wycliff'. But 'on the said Robert's death the late king (Edward III) seized it into his hand'. From this we learn that Robert Wyclif was dead before 1377, but cannot have died before 1368, inasmuch as Mary's father, Henry, third baron de Percy, did not die until the 16th June 1368,[3] and therefore Mary was not a minor at law until after that date. Probably Robert Wyclif died a year or two after 1368. What the bond was between Robert de Wyclif—if indeed he be the parson of 1362—and Sir John de Orby we know not.

We may further assume that John de Wycliffe in the second list is the John Wyclif 'hereticus' of the first list. For otherwise we are driven to the position that the Reformer was a cadet of a junior branch of whose genealogy we have no trace whatever. Conjecture is turned into proof when we discover among the fellows of Balliol[4] a certain John de Hugate, who succeeded Wyclif as master,[5] one of whose relatives might well have been 'Henry Hugate, chaplain',[6] presented by John

---

[1] *Cal. Pat. Ric.* ii. 144–5.

[2] In Torre's list the vacancy is not entered as caused by death. This Robert Wyclif in question cannot be the ancestor Robert. Orby seems to have died in 1354 (*Inquis.* ii. 182). He granted the estate, therefore, to Robert Wyclif, say, in 1334.

[3] G. E. C. vi. 230.   [4] In April 1361, see *Hist. MSS. Com.* iv. 447.

[5] The duration of his mastership is not known. He vacated before 1371, when Thomas Tyrwhit was master (Wood, *Coll.* 82).

[6] Hugate, however, is a fairly common name. Cf. *Vict. Co. Yorks.* iii. 349. Another Hugate was provost of Beverley in 1331 (*ib.* iii. 357), and William de Hugate in 1355 a prebendary of Lincoln, Southwell, Penkridge, Dalton, Bishop Auckland, Bridgenorth, and of Houghton in Durham (*Pap. Let.* iii. 575).

Wyclif to the living on the death[1] of 'William de Wycliffe'. This William, whom we identify with the William Wyclif who was a fellow of Balliol in 1361[2] when John was the master, was appointed by John the rector of Wyclif on the 7th August 1363, a benefice that he held for six years. His position as 'cl.', i. e. *clericus*, prevents us from identifying him with squire William Wyclif, who was 'married'. He was therefore in all probability a cousin of John Wyclif, who would naturally enter the college of which his namesake was master. On the 5th August 1365 this William Wyclif was granted by archbishop Thoresby a licence for non-residence for two years to study at Oxford,[3] probably in theology. But it is not likely that he returned to Balliol.[4] Another Wyclif, probably a cousin of Wyclif, whether once or twice removed we cannot say, was John, son of Symon de Wyclif, who at the Whitsuntide of 1351 was ordained deacon at St. Mary's abbey, York, and priest in York Minster 'on the Saturday after St. Matthew's day',[5] but of whose after career we know nothing. The number of priests that came at this time from this one family is remarkable, and argues either its zeal, or, more probably, the narrow circumstances of a country gentleman with no future for his younger sons save in the church.

We further notice that John Wyclif, though, presumably, the legal patron of the living by the death of his elder brother, took no part in the presentation of 1362.[6] Wyclif at that time was rector of Fillingham in Lincolnshire, and as the vacancy occurred in the Long Vacation may have been at his country living. He seems to have left the management of the estate to his widowed mother. At a later vacancy the Reformer interposed to secure the presentation of two fellows of Balliol, taking care to associate his mother with him, a tribute of respect doubtless very gratifying to the old lady and not without credit to the son.

A word may be added on 'John de Clervaulx', who according

---

[1] See Thompson in *Arch. Jour.* lxxi. 148.
[2] *Hist. MSS. Com.*, loc. cit.
[3] *Lay Folks' Cat.*, p. xxiv. [4] See *infra*, p. 81.
[5] i. e. 27 Sept., for in 1351 St. Matthew's Day took place on Sunday.
[6] The idea in *Vict. Co. Yorks. N. R.* i. 139 that Wyclif did not present in 1362 because he had not attained his majority is untenable.

INTERIOR

WYCLIFFE CHURCH, YORKSHIRE

to this list was rector until his death in 1362,[1] and who may have been the rector in Wyclif's childhood, and as such the first parson with whom Wyclif would be acquainted, from whom, probably, he would learn his letters. Possibly he was the John de Clervaux of whom we hear as holding a small fee in Great Cowton at a rent of half a mark,[2] and who held lands at Croft and Joleby from the lords of Bolton at a rental of 2s. 8d. a year and ' a pound of cinnamon ', or, in default, an extra fourpence.[3] The rector was thus a man of some small means, a scion of the family who held several estates near Croft, both then and now. The founder of the family was a Robert Clervaux, a rich citizen of York—did he derive his name from service to the Cistercian foundations in that city ?— who in 1254 bought the mills of Croft.[4] Shortly after Wyclif's day the Clervaux married into the family of the Nevilles, thus bringing into their strain royal blood.[5]

The living of Wycliffe, returned in the *Taxatio* of 1291 as £13 6s. 8d.,[6] was of fair value. But its worth—in the money values of pre-war days between £200 and £250 a year [7]—had

[1] In Torre the vacancy is expressly stated as due to death. For the Clervaux family, see W. H. Longstaffe, *The House of Clervaux* (1852) or the more readable article in W. H. Longstaffe, *Darlington* (new ed. 1909), 448–71. See also *Vict. Co. Yorks. N. R.* i. 164 f. [3] Gale, 34.

[2] Gale, 81 ; Longstaffe, *Clervaux*, 3. But there are several Johns at this time in the Clervaux family. See Addenda.

[4] Longstaffe, *Darlington*, 450–1. Confirmed 8 Sept. 1255 (not 1254 as Longstaffe), *Cal. Pat. Hen.* s.a. 424.

[5] Longstaffe, *Clervaux*, 4, § 3, where the royal descent is given in full. The present owner of the estates, Chaytor of Croft (J. Foster, *Pedigrees of Yorkshire Families*, v. 2), traces his descent from the old family.

[6] *Taxatio*, 306, 308, 327. In 1428 it was taxed at 10 marks, subsidy 13s. 4d. (*Feudal Aids*, vi). In the *Val. Eccl.* v. 239 ; Bacon, *Thesaurus*, 1250, it is £14 12s. 1d. See also Lawton, *Coll.* i. 584. In the old Ledger of the archdeaconry it is returned as giving 10s. ' procurations ', 4s. Peter's pence, and 4s. ' synodals ' (Gale, 74). In the list of the possessions of St. Mary's abbey, York (*Pap. Let.* v. 3, Nov. 1396), we find ' Withffl ', i. e. Wycliffe, pays ' two parts of the tithe of sheaves '. The priory of St. Martin's, Richmond, also possessed tithes in Wycliffe worth 15s. a year (*Taxatio*, 308). *Vict. Co. Yorks. N. R.* i. 142, *n.* 73 seems to me founded on an error. I find no reference in the *Taxatio* to its appropriation by St. Leonard's hospital, York.

[7] As I shall not, as a rule, translate medieval values into modern equivalents, I may add that I consider that sums in Wyclif's day should be multiplied by between 15 and 20 as compared with 1912 (*sic*). Some writers, however, consider this too high. See the note of Tait in Reading, *Chron.* 285. The Great War has rendered all calculations out of date. Readers should bear this in mind, and should multiply the figure of 15 or 20 by the varying money values of post-war years.

been halved by the invasion of the Scots.[1] Fourteen pounds a year—paid chiefly in kind, for money-exchange had not yet established itself in Yorkshire [2]—was a competence quite as good, considering its lesser obligation, as the revenue of the manor of Wycliffe, more especially when we remember that the values in the *Taxatio* are always under-estimated.

The Reformer's connexion in later years with the family estates, apart from his exercise of patronage, was probably but slight. Among the flotsam and jetsam of time we find, however, one interesting item. On the 17th May 1367 a commission ' for the waters of Humbre, Ouse, Derwent, Ayre, Done, Querf (Wharfe), Tese, Gore, Nydde and Swale ' was issued to seven Yorkshire gentlemen to see to the keeping of the statute recently passed against taking salmon in certain seasons. Among the commissioners is John de Wyclif.[3] The reader may make of the commission what he likes. If it pleases him to draw pictures of parson Wyclif as a sportsman coming up from Oxford or Fillingham to have a throw for salmon he may do so; but the picture would be modern rather than medieval, let alone that at this time Wyclif was so deeply involved in a struggle over Canterbury hall at Oxford that he would have no time for a visit to Yorkshire.[4] A more certain deduction is that among Yorkshire gentlemen Wyclif's name was already known in London in 1367, possibly through John of Gaunt. Indirectly it gives confirmation of our claim that from about 1360 the Reformer was the lord of the manor of Wycliffe. He seems also to have been returned as lord of the manor in 1375.[5]

With such slight links between John Wyclif and his family we must rest content. That so little has been preserved is due, no doubt, to the complete lack of all sympathy with him in the home circle, as we see in the elimination of all mention of his name from their records. In the years of the triumph of Wyclif's faith his family, as also other families in the neighbour-

[1] In the ' nova taxatio ' in 1318 it is given as £6 13s. 4d. (*Taxatio*, 306, 327).
[2] The canons of St. Paul's were paid in kind in the fifteenth century. Ashley, *Econ. Hist.* i. 44 f.
[3] *Cal. Pat.* xiii. 439.   [4] But see Addenda.
[5] *Chanc. Inquis. Post-mort.*, 49 Ed. III, no. 1, 20, quoted in *Vict. Co. Yorks. N. R.* i. 139.

hood,[1] with Yorkshire tenacity remained devoted adherents of Rome, carrying with them the majority of the inhabitants of the tiny village. During the time of the penal laws mass was celebrated in secret at their manor house of Girlington. At Wycliffe the family built a chapel of the old faith close to their house, in its turn superseded by a chapel at some little distance.[2] This lack of sympathy is seen especially in one Robert Wyclif, probably his nephew. This energetic ecclesiastic, who showed much of John Wyclif's mental powers, according to some writers began his clerical career as rector of Wycliffe from August 1362 to August 1363. But we have shown cause for regarding this as extremely unlikely. Our earliest mention of Robert would appear to be a letter from John of Gaunt to his forester at Knaresborough ordering him to deliver a grey doe to 'sire Robert de Wyclif' (21 June 1373).[3] In May 1378 Robert was parson of Holy Cross, York.[4] Like the Reformer, possibly through his assistance, Robert entered the king's service before 1378 when he signed as one of the witnesses of a grant to Robert Alington of an acre of land at Radclif-on-Trent.[5] In July 1379 Robert, described as 'the king's clerk', was appointed a member of a commission to ascertain the yearly values of the alien priories in the counties of Northumberland, Westmorland, and Cumberland.[6] As 'king's clerk' he secured (20 Sept. 1380) the promise of 'the second vacant canonry in Dublin'.[7] From the poor living of Holy Cross Robert went to Kirkby Ravensworth[8] in the dales of North Yorkshire, a parish in which the Wyclifs owned some tenements. This living he exchanged with Richard Middleham on the 7th May 1382[9] for that of St. Ronald Kirk.[10] Both these

[1] *Vict. Co. Yorks.* iii. 59.   [2] *Vict. Co. Yorks. N. R.* i. 138.
[3] *Reg. Gaunt.* ii. 198.
[4] *Cal. Pat. Ric.* i. 216. Worth in the *Valor*, v. 23, £5 0s. 10d.; in *Taxatio*, 298, £5.
[5] *Cat. Anc. Deeds*, vi. 108.   [6] *Cal. Pat. Ric.* i. 417.
[7] *ib.* i. 538.
[8] Worth in 1291, £40; in the 'nova taxatio' of 1318, £13 6s. 8d. (*Taxatio*, 306); in the *Val. Eccl.* v. 238, £25 5s. 2d. For Ravensworth, then the property of the Fitzhughs, lords of the neighbouring castle, see Whitaker, i. 118 f.; *Vict. Co. Yorks. N. R.* i. 88 f. It was at this time in the gift of the Crown as custos of Henry Fitzhugh (Whitaker, 133).
[9] *Cal. Pat. Ric.* ii. 132, 155.
[10] For this ancient church see Whitaker, i. 130; *Vict. Co. Yorks. N. R.* i. 123 f.

livings had at one time been rich—the second living was worth in 1291 the large sum of £73 6s. 8d.[1]—but they had suffered much from the Scots. Robert's last cure of souls, for he resigned St. Ronald Kirk on the 1st January 1392,[2] was at Hutton Rudby in Cleveland, a district in which he had negotiated many business transactions. This wealthy living[3] he held till his death. From 1390 to 1405 Robert acted as chancellor and receiver-general of his friend Walter Skirlaw, bishop of Durham.[4] As chancellor he took a leading part in the trial at Bishop Auckland of a famous lollard, Richard Wyche. During the same period Robert was also constable of Durham castle.[5]

Robert Wyclif was a trusted man of affairs, who was frequently employed in splitting up tenancies in chief in Yorkshire into demesne tenancies.[6] But other legal business was not refused. In 1386 he acted as agent in raising money for Sir Ralph Neville.[7] In June 1388 he became bail in London in a will case for one of his clients, Alice Cotterell.[8] In the same year he brought a writ under the Statute of Labourers against one M. B., with whom he had made a covenant:

[1] *Taxatio*, 306. It was worth only £20 in 1318 (*ib.*); in the *Val. Eccl.* v. 238, £58 14s.   [2] Whitaker, 133.
[3] In *Taxatio*, 324, it is £80, new taxation £45 p. a. In the *Valor*, v. 89, it is returned as a vicarage worth £30 net, appropriated to Wolsey's new college at Oxford. For its later changes, see *Vict. Co. Yorks. N. R.* ii. 284. It seems to have varied between rectory and vicarage.
[4] W. Hutchinson, *Durham*, i. 324 n.
[5] *Wills Durham*, i. 66 n.; Hutchinson, *op. cit.*
[6] The earliest I have noticed is one in Yorkshire, 26 Nov. 1383 (*Close Rolls*, ii. 413). On 8 May 1391 he is one of the parties for enfeoffing the manor of Harewood 'held in chief' (*Cal. Pat.* iv. 405). On 7 Dec. 1401 he is party to an involved deal between Henry Percy, Thomas Percy, Sir Thomas Fauconberge (cf. *Cal. Pat. Ric.* ii. 303), Sir William Hilton with reference to the castle of Skelton in Cleveland, Marske in Cleveland, the advowson of the priory of Gisburn in Cleveland, &c. (*Cal. Pat. Hen.* ii. 24). On 24 Apr. 1398 Robert de Wyclif, parson of Rudby, acted in a similar transaction with reference to Henry Percy and the manor of Hunmanby (*Cal. Pat.* vi. 334). On 6 Aug. 1400 Sir Peter de Manley, one of the commissioners for the peace of both East and North Riding (*Cal. Pat.* i. 486-7)—the eighth Peter in succession from the founder of the family, the reputed murderer of Arthur of Brittany—enters into a complicated arrangement in which Robert Wyclif is one party for enfeoffing Mulgrave and other Yorkshire manors held in chief from the Crown (*Cal. Pat.* i. 325), and on 6 June 1412 he became enfeoffed with a third of the manor of Baynton in Yorkshire (*Cal. Pat.* iv. 422).
[7] *Close Rolls*, iii. 251, 18 July.
[8] Sharpe, *Letter-Book H*. 326. In Feb. 1386 he was also the chief adviser or agent in another settlement of a will (*Close Rolls Ric.* iii. 125).

'M.', he said, 'was in his service and lived with him at his house and afterwards departed out of his service in Holburn within the term without reason and against the statute.'

'M.' was taken by the sheriff of London, but pleaded that he had made no covenant with Wyclif. Finally he was committed to the Fleet prison, 'but afterwards found mainprise'.[1] From this record it is evident that Robert had lodgings in London near the lawyers of the Temple, with whom, virtually, he should be classed. On the 22nd October 1392 Wyclif acted as attorney for Sir Philip Darcy who was 'going to Ireland',[2] for whom also, six years later, he served as executor.[3] As such he was responsible for seeing that 'five wax lights each of 8 lb., and 24 torches' were burnt at the funeral and that £10 were spent 'for a marble stone to be laid on my grave with the image of myself and of Elizabeth my wife fixed thereon'. But there were few noble families in the north of England, including the Percies, with whom Robert Wyclif had not legal dealings, often as an executor, sometimes as legatee. He was more than a lawyer priest; from the death of John Wyclif he was the recognized head of his family.[4] He was proud of his family. Even the curtains of his bed, as we see in his will, were embroidered with their arms. He placed also the Wyclif armorial bearings—argent, a chevron sable between three crosslets gules [5]—in the cloisters of Durham cathedral. The building of these was begun by bishop Skirlaw, Robert Wyclif's patron, and finished by Skirlaw's executors, of whom Robert was one.[6]

In 1412 Robert Wyclif settled the manor and advowson of Wycliffe on himself with remainder first to Sir John Pykeworth, knight, and the children of Ellen, his late wife, and then to John, son of John de Ellerton and his heirs male who were to assume the cognomen of Wyclif and bear the ancient arms.[7] Probably John Ellerton thus became the John de Wyclif who

---

[1] G. F. Deiser, *Year Book of 12 Richard II* (1914), 4–5.
[2] *Cal. Pat. Ric.* v. 188.
[3] Gibbons, 98 (16 Apr. 1398); Nicolas, *Test. Vet.* i. 146.
[4] *Vict. Co. Yorks. N. R.* i. 139. In 1392 he pays a fine of 20*d*. twice a year to the lords of Middleham for the ville of Thorpe (Gale, 78).
[5] For a copy of these arms see *Vict. Co. Yorks, N. R.* i. 139.
[6] *Wills Durham,* i i. 66 *n.*   [7] *Vict. Co. Yorks. N. R.* i. 139.

was lord of the manor in 1423[1] and 1428[2] and from whom the future lords until Marmaduke Tunstall descended.[3] If so Robert Wyclif was the last blood descendant of the Wyclifs of whom we have any knowledge, the further lords of Wyclif being of a new stock.[4] On the 8th September 1423 Robert made his will[5] at Kepier hospital, a mile from Durham, of which before 1405[6] he had become master, though still retaining his living at Rudby, a lucrative post worth about £60 a year.[7] There also he died a few days later. He left numerous cups of silver and gilt to various friends, and his chief books to the hospital of Kepier. To his senior curate, John de Middleton, he left the worsted coverlet in which he used to sleep. He bequeathed considerable legacies to various local churches including 40s. for the repair of Wycliffe church, and 40s. for 'the restoration of the ornaments in the chancel', and '40s. for the poor of Wycliffe', as well as 40s. to each of the parishes of which he had been rector or vicar. Few stranger contrasts can be drawn than that between the careers of John and Robert Wyclif; the one was the embodiment of all that the other hated.

The part played by early impressions in the formation of later opinion cannot be exaggerated. Possibly Wyclif's hatred of 'Caesarean' clergy and of political bishops may have arisen from his neighbourhood to the see of Durham. Across the river men were under the jurisdiction of the earl-bishop[8]

---

[1] For a debt of 16s. paid to him as such in that year see *Finchale*, p. clxxxii, and for his other financial transactions in 1418–20, *ib.*, pp. clxxvi–ix.

[2] *Feudal Aids*, vi. 296. Evidently the family was already impoverished, for John held only 'a fourth part of that which Roger once held in Wycliffe, Thorpe, and Girlington'.

[3] Hence future Wyclifs quartered the three harts' heads of the shield of Ellerton (*Test. Ebor.* i. 405 n.).

[4] Of the later Wyclifs the will of John Wyclif of St. Nicholas, Richmond, in 1562 has an interesting inventory. See J. Raine, *Wills and Inventories of Richmond* (Surtees Soc. 1853), pp. 156–64.

[5] First printed in Vaughan, *Mon.* 545–6 from Reg. Langley, f. 115. It has since been printed in *Wills Durham*, i. 66–8. The roll of legacies was not appended to the Durham probate, but is printed in *Test. Ebor.* i. 403–5. The legacy in it to 'John Wyclif' must be to John de Ellerton who had now taken the name of Wyclif.

[6] *Wills Durham*, i. 66 n. For this hospital, founded in 1122 by the notorious bishop Flambard, see *Vict. Co. Durham*, ii. 111 f.; Hutchinson, *Durham*, ii. 299 f.; Dugdale, *Mon.* vi. 731. Nothing now remains but the gateway. In 1574 it became a school (*Arch. Jour.* lxvi. 67–76).

[7] *Pap. Let.* v. 78. In *Val. Eccl.* v. 308 the hospital is worth clear £167 2s. 11d.

[8] 'although the bishop is earl-palatine', *Close Rolls Ed.* xiv. 428.

of a palatine county. Nor did the county of Durham with castles and palatine rights exhaust the bishop's estates. In addition he owned Lindisfarne, Norham, and Bedlington, and other possessions beyond the Tyne—all of which were reckoned as part of the county of Durham until recent legislation—Howden, the liberty of Allertonshire,[1] and other manors in the counties of York and Lincoln, together with coal mines and iron mines ' and the mooring, loading and unloading of ships and vessels ' on the Durham side of the Tyne.[2] Few nobles were so great or so rich as the prince-bishop, while his jurisdiction as a count-palatine gave him rights that belonged to no other save John of Gaunt. What with alien archdeacons of the semi-see of Richmondshire, and prince-bishops of Durham, rich beyond the dreams of avarice, Wyclif would grow up with a conception of a bishop against which his life was a long protest. One of the bishops of his boyhood was the notorious Lewis de Beaumont. The exploit whereby this court bishop was kidnapped on his way to his enthroning was long told in the villages of the north.[3] In one of his works the Reformer instances Durham as a proof of his proposition that where the clergy wax ' insolent ' with pride and power there tumult abounds and religion diminishes,[4] and relates at length a scandalous tale concerning bishop Thomas Hatfield.[5] Wyclif also would form early impressions of what he afterwards deemed to be useless endowments from the six chaplains that in 1275 had been established by John of Brittany in the castle of Richmond to pray for his soul and that of his wife Beatrice. The six chaplains were found by the abbot of Ecclestone. One of Wyclif's ancestors, Robert, had been a witness to the deed, whereby property in Moulton bringing in £25 a year had been left for their benefit.[6]

Before we leave the home of Wyclif some notice should be taken of the fine portrait in the rectory with its inscription :

' Thomas Zouch A.M., formerly fellow of Trinity College Cambridge

[1] *Vict. Co. Yorks. N. R.* i. 397. Granted by William Rufus with return of writs, jail delivery, assize of bread and ale, &c.
[2] For the estates and rights of the bishops of Durham in 1383 see *Cal. Pat.* ii. 362.
[3] See *infra*, p. 324. Wyclif refers to it in *Eccl.* 217 very inaccurately.
[4] *Pot. Pap.* 379.   [5] *ib.* 231.   [6] Gale, 95-6

and rector of Wycliffe, gave this original picture of the great John Wyclif, a native of this parish, to his successors the rectors of Wycliffe 27 April 1796.'[1]

The reputed painter, a Flemish artist, Anthonis Mor, generally known as Antonio Moro or Sir Anthony More,[2] ranks among the great painters, and executed some commissions in England in the reigns of Edward VI and Mary, including the fine portrait of Mary for Philip of Spain, now at Madrid. But few of the English portraits attributed to him are genuine, save those of Gresham and Lee, for his residence in England was but short. There appears therefore to be no sufficient authority for attributing this portrait to him, nor is the subject one that would appeal to a painter who enjoyed the patronage of Philip and Mary. Apart from this we have no reason to believe that it was other than a fancy portrait, worked up, possibly from the half-length woodcut which Bale prefixed in 1548 to his *Summary of the Famous Writers of Great Britain*.[3] In this woodcut Wyclif appears to be about fifty years of age and is represented as preaching from a stone pulpit, with his right hand raised in front of him and his left hand on a closed book. The age is almost correct, as we judge, whereas in the Denbigh portrait, copies of which are at Lutterworth and Balliol College, Wyclif is represented as a very old man. But neither the Denbigh portrait, nor the Dorset portrait, now kept at Knole park and frequently engraved and reproduced, have any claim to antiquity; the Dorset portrait, in fact, does not date from earlier than the eighteenth century. The portrait which most satisfies our conceptions is R. Houston's[4] mezzotint prepared in 1759 for Richard Rolt's *Lives of the Reformers*,[5] purporting to be 'a tabula in Coll. Reg. Cantab'. The portrait combines strength, dignity, and gravity with the face that we should associate with a scholar.

[1] For this Moro portrait see Whittaker, *Rich.* i. 197 f.; Sergeant, 18-19. It was engraved by Edward Finden for John Murray in 1827 and published by him. It is reproduced in Sergeant, 258.
[2] For Mor see *D. N. B.*
[3] For reproductions of Wyclif portraits see Sergeant, 1, 12, 22.
[4] *D. N. B.* Houston's forte was the making subject plates after old masters, especially Rembrandt.
[5] For Rolt see *D. N. B.* As a Jacobite he lost his place in the customs and took to hack-work of all sorts.

We miss in it, however, the note of passion and temper. One feature in all the portraits is that Wyclif is represented with a long beard and full moustache. The beard probably represents tradition, but we are inclined to believe that the moustache is a Reformation addition. Priests who partook of the Cup in the fourteenth century avoided moustaches for fear of the sacrilege, as it was held, of the wine adhering thereto.[1] If Wyclif had thus run contrary to current opinion we should probably have heard of it from his opponents.

Fortunately, in the absence of any authentic portrait, we have a description of Wyclif by a contemporary. In 1407 the lollard Thorpe, in his examination before archbishop Arundel, spoke of Wyclif with a warmth of feeling which would indicate personal knowledge, probably at Oxford whither Thorpe had betaken himself in 1377.[2] He described Wyclif as of 'spare, frail, emaciated frame, in conversation[3] most innocent'. According to Thorpe the extraordinary hold he possessed over his generation was due not only to his learning, but in part to his charm—'eum dulciter amabant'[4]—as well as to the example of his asceticism, though, with the usual humility of the saint, in one of his later works Wyclif admitted that he had not always lived a self-denying life as regards food and raiment.[5] One of his Oxford opponents accused Wyclif of hiding, like Arius, his false doctrine under the cloak of a simple life.[6] According to his own confession Wyclif had a quick temper, which he tried to control, not always successfully, and which thus led 'all our life' into seeming 'arrogance' and lack of 'charity'.[7] And this we can well believe, for his words are often the words of one who has let his indignation make shipwreck of his judgement. Yet even archbishop Arundel confessed that he was 'a great clerk and a perfect liver'.[8]

---

[1] See Andrew Brod in *Hardt*, iii. 392–415, especially 406–9; Lea, ii. 472 f.
[2] Pollard, Garner, 116.   [3] i.e. habit of life.
[4] See the original Latin in Bale, Bodl. MS. E. Mus. 86 f. 100, quoted in *Ziz.*, p. xlv *n*. This is only loosely paraphrased in Bale's version of Thorpe, Pollard, *Garner*, 119.
[5] *Ver. Script.* i. 363, quoted with wrong reference in *Ziz.*, p. xlvi *n*.
[6] *Ver. Script.* i. 360.
[7] *ib.* 366; *Civ. Dom.* iv. 538; *Op. Min.* 197; *Eng. Works*, 312.
[8] Pollard, 120. Cf. the remarks of Cunningham, *infra*, ii. 121.

III

GRADUATE DAYS AT OXFORD

§ 1

OF Wyclif's life in Oxford we know little except by inference, for in this as in all else his writings are singularly lacking the human note. A few brief remarks exhaust his reference to the university apart from its disputations.[1] But Wyclif's career at Oxford is so important that if we would realize the man as a whole we must reconstruct the events which would befall him there. An initial difficulty is that of chronology.[2] But if he was born shortly before the year 1330 Wyclif would probably go to Oxford about 1345, at the age of sixteen, unless indeed—but this is pure conjecture—he had been an inmate of the school for boys recently founded (1341) at Queen's college, a supposition which has this in its favour that thirty years later a John Wyclif, presumably from the same district, was a lad at the school. Fifteen was the usual age for a lad to enter the university, except in the great law university of Bologna, where students were largely beneficed ecclesiastics. At Oxford early entrance was the rule; the more necessary because of the length of the course.[3]

---

[1] The most interesting is in *Eccl.* 15, ' pueri vocant Oxonie Romam monticulum Belli Montis '. Cf. Wood, *Univ.* i. 20, " Rome, a piece of ground so called in the middle almost of Beaumont fields." In Wood, *City,* i. 344, ' Rome ' is ' a little hill sometimes containing a cave underneath, and on the top thereof a cross '. It stood at the north-west corner of the University Park. See its position on the map, *ib.* i. 660. It was one of the boundaries of the liberty of Holiwell (Wood, *City,* i. 380 ; *Cal. Pat. Ric.* ii. 340). The name still survives for a " fancy-garden place " (Hurst, 113).

[2] The chronology of Wyclif's university course has the inevitable puzzles. If he entered Oxford in say 1345 he would normally have finished his doctorate in 1361. But instead he had only just completed his master's degree in arts (*infra,* p. 79). We may assume considerable breaks, due to the Black Death, the Great Slaughter, &c. There is in fact a gap here which we have now no means of filling, for to shift the date of entrance to Oxford till later only leaves the gap at the Wycliffe end. For the chronology of his doctorate see *infra,* p. 203.

[3] We have a number of ages at Paris in *Chart. Par.* iii. 368-89 (1385). Cf. also *Pap. Let.* v. 91. These show a range of from 15 to 36 (doctorate). By Paris statutes a master was required to be ' over the 21st year of his age '

Wyclif's journey to Oxford would be the first of any length which the boy had taken, and the reader may imagine the interest with which the lad would look out on a world strange and new. Term invariably began on the feast of St. Denis (9 Oct.), and as the journey took nine or ten days [1] Wyclif would set out towards the end of September. Of part of his route we may be reasonably certain. Not far from Wycliffe there runs the road which the Romans built from London to the Wall. Along this the lad would travel in charge either of some monk of Durham on his way to his hall at Oxford, or else of some 'fetcher' or 'bringer' [2] who had certain fixed routes for gathering pupils. The latter part of the route is uncertain. Maybe Wyclif caught his first glimpse of Oxford from Shotover, in whose woods, as he would learn from his escort, some undergraduates had recently been poaching.[3] More likely he came in by the north road, past the cross in Godstow village in memory of the fair Rosamund.[4] By whatever road he came he would note the long causeways on stone arches, from the foot of Hinksey hill to South Gate more than forty in number, whereby the traveller escaped the floods of Thames and Cherwell. For Oxford, as its name shows, was the city of waters.[5]

On his way to the University Wyclif would be struck by the immunities and privileges he already enjoyed. He had suddenly become hedged round with sanctities. To kill him would have been a very serious matter indeed, as the 'offspring of swine-breeders in the town of St. Quentin' found to their

and to have completed ' at least ' six years (*Chart. Par.* i. 78, ii. 678). Bulaeus, iii. 81, misprinted the 21 as 12, and this blunder has been widely copied. A statute of the English nation required a determining bachelor to be 20 (*Chart. Par.* i. 227). Wykeham's statutes of New College required a boy not of the founder's kin to be not less than 15 nor more than 20 (Rashdall, ii. 501 ; Leach, *Charters*, 360). The skit in *Carmina Burana*, 40, has too often been treated as fact.

[1] Rogers, *Prices*, i. 139–40 ; ii. 610, 635–42, for route and expenses. For expenses of a student from Oxford to Barnstaple, 1 shilling, see Chanter, ii. 45–6.

[2] *Mun. Ac.* 346 (1459). Fetchers were paid 5*d.* per day per boy (Boase, p. xxxv).

[3] *Mun. Ac.* 670 ; *Collect.* iii. 154 (1421). [4] Hurst, 118.

[5] Hurst, 13 f. For 'Ox' = Usk, cf. Osney = Ousen-eye, the river Ock near Abingdon. For the three spots which claim to be the ford, Wood, *City*, i. 46 *n.*

cost when in 1296 they were condemned to pay 1,000 livres for killing a master of arts. In France the persons, goods, and horses of all students on their way to Paris were free from all tolls, even when landing at Wissant from England.[1] As they drew near to Oxford the company would need to be on their guard against robbers lying in wait for students coming into residence with purses filled for the year's needs. But sometimes the robbers were students themselves in need of replenished pockets.[2] To guard against these marauders students coming into or going out of Oxford were allowed to carry weapons, otherwise strictly forbidden.[3] Wyclif's opponent William Woodford, 'going from London to Oxford to incept in Theology fell among robbers, who took from him £40'—such small respect had these miscreants for sacred persons.[4] When we arrive at Oxford we must forget to surrender our weapons; they will come in useful in any brawl with " Town ".[5]

Whatever his route Wyclif could not fail to note how all England seemed to be on the move. The roads were thronged by a motley group; pedlars laden with their wares, minstrels and jugglers, villeins who sought freedom and work by flight to the town, sturdy beggars ' with their bellies and their bags, of bread full crammed ', of whom Wyclif enumerates several types;[6] they evidently made a great impression upon him. There were also pilgrims combining a holiday with worship, some of them begging the means for their journey. Possibly his pity would be aroused as he saw a man ' who made a horrible noise ' and pretended to be deaf and dumb, carrying about with him ' part of a tongue edged with silver, and with writing around it to this effect : This is the tongue of John Ward '. By the side of the supposed tongue were ' iron hooks and pincers ', and a legend that with these hooks robbers had

[1] *Chart. Par.* ii. 71, 159, 507 (cf. 79, 114).
[2] *Cal. Pat. Ed.* v. 363 ; *Mun. Ac.* 531 ; Wood, *Univ.* i. 438 (1341).
[3] *Mun. Ac.* 91, 355. [4] Little, 246.
[5] For a student at Cambridge in 1398 who took his arms with him on a walk, and the consequent brawl, see *Pap. Let.* v. 266. In 1320 the university of Oxford petitioned that as no clerks were allowed arms they should be forbidden to the laity. This was done except for town officials (*Rot. Parl.* i. 373 ; *Collect.* iii. 119). For Peckham's ordinance in 1279 sequestrating the benefices of clerks at the university who bore arms see *Mun. Ac.* 40.
[6] *P. Plow.* Prol. 41 ; Wyclif, *Serm.* ii. 339–44, including ' Robertini ', i. e. ' Robardesmen ' (*Rot. Parl.* iii. 332). See also Jusserand, 262 f.

torn it out. But when Wyclif was about to give a coin his more experienced companions would tell him that the man was a fraud. They would warn the lad also against the rogues with ' false chequer-boards, called *queeks* in which all the white squares were lower than the black squares', so that the gamester would always win.[1] Fellow scholars, too, he would meet, some of riper age coming from a brief visit to their cures of souls ; Scots too among them in spite of Bannockburn, for there is as yet no university north of the Tweed. Here, too, is a great ecclesiastic on his way to Avignon, and other ' Rome-seekers '[2] of lesser status, begging their way to the seat of patronage. Here, too, is the knight of the shire, or the representative of the town, the latter creeping like a snail to Westminster, ready to jump at any excuse to secure release from this irksome duty.[3]

Wyclif would marvel greatly at the number of wandering clergy. Some were broken down vagabonds who complained that they could neither study nor find employment, and were in consequence destitute. Here is the pardoner selling relics of the saints, his bulls commonly forged and always useless.[4] He would note also the friars, carrying little portable altars, with which they entered into competition with the secular clergy. But the lad could not fail to see how the crowds listened to their homely if sometimes vulgar preaching. And when all the wanderers foregathered at night in the inn the rustics or townsfolk would come to hear the news, for the friars and pedlars were the postal service and newspaper of the age. They bound the country into one and broke down an exclusive localism. They were the channels through which flowed the popular movements, peasants' revolts, lollard teaching, and the like.[5]

§ 2

On arriving at Oxford Wyclif would find a walled city of remarkable natural strength, surrounded on three sides with

---

[1] Riley, *Mem. Lon.* 395, 445, 455 ; Wyclif, *Serm.* ii. 342.
[2] Wyclif, *Serm.* ii. 341, ' spolacio Romipetarum '.
[3] Cf. for Colchester *Cal. Pat. Ric.* ii. 214 ; *Rot. Parl.* iii. 395.
[4] Wyclif, *Serm.* ii. 342, 343 ; Chaucer, Pardoner's Prologue ; *P. Plow.* (C.), i. 66–77, 96–102.   [5] Jusserand, 29–32.

water.¹ To its position at the head of navigable waters Oxford owed its commercial and military importance, first as a border town between Wessex and Mercia, and then incorporated in Wessex and made the head of a county. The dedication of its churches pointed back to days before the Conquest. Its stockaded, artificial mound—whose site shows that it was thrown up as a protection against enemies from the west rather than foes coming up the river—had been a residence for Saxon kings. In one of its apartments king Eadmund had been foully murdered. Beneath its shadow in 1018 Cnut had held a Gemot, and there in 1036 another Gemot had chosen his successor. But now that mound was dominated by a ten-sided Norman keep. The old earth fortifications round the town had been replaced by an embattled wall with a few towers. Close to the castle was a little eminence, still discernible though almost levelled, the Jews' Mount, i.e. mont de juis, where criminals were executed. Wyclif would note the new appearance of the castle. This had recently undergone repair, twelve trees for the purpose being furnished from the forest of Shotover.² Outside the castle was the castellan's ballium or bailey, a name which survives in the existing church of St. Peter-le-Bailey.³ To Wyclif, familiar with Richmond, the castle would not be a matter of great interest. But he may have noted that the city walls were not in good repair, owing to insecure foundation on the old earthworks, while in places the moat was filled in ⁴—signs of a general security which in the north the Scots did not allow.

Wyclif would enter Oxford by the North Gate or Bocardo with its two bulky towers, the main gate of the town and the strongest, for it lacked the defence of the river. But even before Wyclif's day the Bocardo had become the University prison,⁵ where in later days were confined Cranmer, Latimer,

---

¹ For this section the student may consult J. Parker, *Early History of Oxford* (Ox. Hist. Soc. 1885); H. Hurst, *Oxford Topography* (ib. 1899); and Wood, *City*.
² In 1331, Wood, *City*, i. 274–5.
³ Hurst, 85.
⁴ Wood, *City*, i. 242, 262; *Close Rolls Ric.* i. 51 (1378); Rymer, iv. 30.
⁵ The earliest mention as a prison is in 1217, for scholars in 1317 (Wood, *City*, i. 256 n.). Bocardo was also the name of a part of Newgate prison, Riley, *Mem. London*, 474; Sharpe, *Letter Book* (*H*), 204.

and Ridley.¹ The gate had been recently repaired, at a cost of eighteenpence, with stout beams and bolts, the bolts for the ' maiden's chamber ', as the prison for whores was called.² Close to the gate within the walls was St. Michael's, whose tower was " standing as visible to the inhabitants of Oxford at the time the Domesday survey was compiled as it is to the inhabitants of Oxford now ".³ Just outside the gate on the south side of Magdalen parish church⁴ Wyclif would note a large stone cross erected a few years previously (1339) to commemorate the assertion by the university of certain rights in the northern suburbs.⁵ It was the sign that Oxford was a city in which mayor and commonalty played but a subordinate part.

Wyclif might establish himself for the night in some inn, possibly the Mitre—a well-known surviving relic of ancient days ⁶—possibly in the Cardinal's Hat, just outside the North Gate and close to Balliol ; an alluring signpost this for youths with dreams of the future. Outside the door would be a great bush projecting from a pole ; this last in London was not allowed to be more than seven feet long.⁷ Wyclif's bill would not be dear, but the inn-keeper, who is not above stealing a horse,⁸ tries to persuade the ' yellow-beak ' that he had better sell him his nag, as horse-bread is dear, at least a penny a day. Oxford in the early days of October must have had more horses than men. But the medieval horse had learned to stow himself away—were there not according to the worthy burgher Ulrich von Reichental 30,000 horses in Constance at the time of the Council ?⁹ In Oxford there was a good market for

---

¹ Hurst, 70. For a drawing of this gate and cell see Skelton. The gate was taken down in 1771 (*Gent's Mag.* xxxxi. 376).
² Hurst, 120. Now part of the site of the United Methodist chapel. Wood, *City*, i. 255 *n*.
³ Parker, *op. cit.* 258 ; Hurst, 68–70.
⁴ It was customary to have a church just outside the main gate, as a rule dedicated to St. Giles (Parker, 209). For St. Mary Magdalen see Hurst, 102–3.
⁵ Wood, *City*, i. 341. A pillar-box now marks the site (Hurst, 109).
⁶ For its existence in Wyclif's day see Wood, *City*, i. 79, who, as usual, makes every inn a hall ; Hurst, 171.
⁷ Riley, *op. cit.* 387 in 1375.
⁸ *Mun. Ac.* 685.
⁹ Reichental's vivid journal with these details (pp. 154–215) has been printed by M. R. Buck (Tübingen, 1882).

horses; Balliol itself was situated in the Horsemonger.[1] Horse-thieves also did a roaring trade with the raw lads.[2]

On looking out through the window of the inn the lad would see a sight that would cause his heart to swell with pride—the masons hard at work at St. Martin's. The landlord would reluctantly tell him the reason. St. Martin's was the town church, and in times of combat Town " would retire up there as their castle and from thence gall and annoy (gown) with arrows and stones ". So in 1340, Edward III gave orders for the said tower to be lowered;[3] at any rate that is the tale that is believed. As a matter of fact it was not the tower that was the cause of trouble, but an aisle which it was alleged the citizens were crenellating with a view to future struggles.[4] There were other fictions which would minister to the pride of the undergraduate. He would hear of the thousand years of Oxford's history as a university;[5] how the Greek philosophers who accompanied Brutus the Trojan founded their schools at Greeklade (Cricklade), and how they were afterwards transferred—whether by Britons, Saxons, or king Alfred, was a matter of dispute—to Bellositum, now corrupted into Beaumont. Had not the Latins established themselves at the same time at Latinlade (Lechlade)? Were there not found on the city walls three Greek coins, proof beyond all doubt?[6] Was not St. Giles in Beaumont the old university church?[7] In the old house of the Congregation at the north-east corner of St. Mary's is there not a figure of Alfred, ' Academiae Oxon. Conditor ', " which neither utters nor listens to arguments "?[8] That

---

[1] The title Horsemonger is a century earlier than Canditch, which first occurs in 1361 (Hurst, 120). The importance of the horse trade is shown by there being in 1447 six bakers of horse-bread at Oxford (*Mun. Ac.* 577).

[2] For an interesting record in 1373 see *Cal. Pat.* xv. 297–8. For two Welsh students who steal a horse at the Cardinal's Hat in 1461 and ride off home, see *Mun. Ac.* 684.   [3] Wood, *City*, ii. 86.

[4] Hurst, 60; a commission of inquiry was appointed 20 Jan. 1321, Salter, *Univ. Archives*, i. 104.

[5] For this myth and its variants see Parker, 5–62. For its existence in Wyclif's time see *Mun. Ac.* 367; also in Walter Burley's *Problems of Aristotle* (Wood, *Univ.* i. 18; Parker, 27).

[6] *Gent's Mag.* xxxx. 423.

[7] Rous, 21, took it from *Lib. Mon. de Hyda* (R.S.), 412, where the change is attributed to St. Scholastica's riots! Wood, *Univ.* i. 15–20; *City*, 14, 65 *n.*, copied it from Rous.

[8] F. Madan, *Oxford Books*, i. 251–2. The Alfred variant, for which see

Beaumont lay outside the city walls troubled not an uncritical age. But possibly the pride of Balliol would lead Wyclif to reject the claim presented to parliament with forged charters in 1379, repeated in 1427, wherein University college ascribed its foundation 'for twenty-six perpetual divines' to king Alfred, maintaining also that 'John of Beverley and Bede' were 'formerly scholars in that college'.[1] Wyclif, it is true, would hear with horror of the claims of Cambridge, established as a small *studium generale* a few years before Wyclif's birth.[2] Not to be outdistanced in imagination, Cambridge boasted an earlier papal foundation, substituting charters of Arthur for those of Alfred.[3] Wyclif would show no surprise when told that Bocardo was standing in the year 700, and had been used in Saxon times, as its name proved, as a library for the university at Bellositum.[4] But as all these tales were firmly believed by Twyne and Wood, and printed in the official *University Calendar* at the close of the nineteenth century, we can scarcely blame Wyclif for not being wiser than his generation. Historical criticism was a thing unknown, contrary indeed to the laws of God and of the Church.

For all save a few years Oxford henceforth was Wyclif's home. Let not the reader picture to himself the Reformer pacing the streets of the city of palaces of to-day. Of the then Oxford, a huddled mass of mean houses, nearly all has vanished. A few fragments of the six older colleges—the beautiful chapel of Merton is the best of these, though two windows and a patched doorway still survive from an older Merton building, the Warden's Great Hall—the old Congregation house, St. Frideswyde's and three or four of the older but lesser churches, for the most part sadly " restored ", still however survive. Of the six existing colleges not one possessed a

Rous (†1491), *Hist.* 76, owed its vitality to its insertion by Henry Savile of Bank in Camden's ed. of Asser, printed at Frankfort in 1603 (Parker, 40 f.).

[1] Higden, vi. 354 ; *Rot. Parl.* iii. 69a ; *Collect.* iii. 144–6. The fiction of Wood, *Univ.* i. 43, that this was first found in William of Malmesbury is due to an interpolation by John of Glastonbury (*c.* 1400), elaborated by Rous, *op. cit.* 76. The forgery was exposed by W. Smith, *Univ. Coll.* (1728) 107–45.

[2] Bull of John, xxii, 9 June 1318 (*Pap. Let.* ii. 172 ; at length, T. Fuller, *Hist. Camb.* 80).

[3] Parker, 20 f., 38. See also *infra*, ii. 350.

[4] Wood, *Univ.* i. 20, derives it from A.S. *boc*, a book, a myth accepted in *Gent's Mag.* xxxxi. 376.

gateway-tower, a feature first introduced by Wykeham.¹ St. Mary's is new, the chancel rebuilt in 1462, the church in 1482. But the tower of St. Mary's, with the spire added at the close of the thirteenth century, still survives, though in Wyclif's day the tower stood clear of the body of the church.² Nor must we forget stretches of the old city wall, with part of the Norman keep. Even the level of the streets has changed. The old Carfax of Wyclif's day was twelve feet below the present surface.³ Unlike most medieval cities, Oxford was largely built of ragged stone from Chilswell quarry, the use of which had become common since the great fire of 1190. But the poor "that could not be at the charge to build in that manner" had to be content with erecting a stone wall between every four or six of their wooden houses, to break the flames.⁴ Every householder also must keep for the same purpose a tun of water before his doors. The streets of the city were dark and filthy tunnels, through the midst of which there ran an open kennel or sewer. Instead of the famous High, Wyclif would find a narrow lane blocked on market days with stalls and carts, with overhanging buildings from whose doors would issue smoke, for chimneys there were none. Broad Street was then the town ditch, separating Balliol from the walls and city. St. Mary's was surrounded with dark lanes that rendered a journey there at night an unsafe adventure.⁵ Here and there you will find glazed windows, but for the most part lattices only. The doors, too, have not always staples, only "latch and catch".

At Oxford Wyclif would find himself in a city that from the economic standpoint was almost unique. In medieval towns the citizens were all producers; there were no men living on their dividends. In Oxford alone was there a large body of residents, numbering as many as the citizens themselves, who were solely consumers, the majority living on incomes derived

---

¹ Willis and Clark, iii. 284.
² The statues in the Congregation house are said to be mostly modern, but a few may date from Wyclif's day. A few fragments survive of the old twelfth-century church.
³ For this section see Hurst, 46, 80–1, 204. Part of Pembroke is built on the wall (Macleane, 51). For St. George's Tower see engraving in *Gent's Mag.* v. 102, p. 401.
⁴ Wood, *Univ.* i. 171–2; Hurst, 36.   ⁵ Boase, p. xiii.

ST. MARY'S CHURCH, OXFORD
From the engraving by David Loggan, 1675

from elsewhere. Hence at Oxford, and to a lesser degree at Cambridge, there was that conflict between producer and consumer so characteristic of modern times. This conflict was more sharply defined as the consumers, who also owned the greater part of the real estate of the town, were all more or less a part of the Church. This state of things was new. Originally Oxford had been made by its commerce, or rather by the famous river on which that commerce depended. The free navigation of the Thames to its navigable head at Oxford, without let from dams or the nets of fishers, was always a matter of vital concern, as we see from the many petitions of its anxious citizens.[1] The former commercial importance of Oxford was also attested by its fair of St. Frideswyde's,[2] one of the oldest and most important in the country. At one time also it had boasted a Great and Little Jewry, true signs of business activity. The Jews had been banished in July 1290.[3] They had left behind them a heavy silver cross carried by the university in processions, as well as a marble cross erected near Merton, memorials of an outrage committed on Ascension Day, 1268.[4] With the departure of the Jews few signs remained of Oxford's former commercial importance; its civic population, in fact, was probably not much larger than before the Conquest.[5] At one time Oxford had been a centre of weaving, but long before Wyclif's day the industry had decayed. Few weavers were now left, though the guild still survived in name and paid a yearly tax of 42 shillings.[6] The narrow spirit of the Oxford guilds, by prohibiting strangers from carrying on their trade in the city, had also assisted to drive away commerce.[7] Such trade as survived was retail, the market in the High and in the other streets that opened on Carfax. There is Cook Row, for stalls in which cooks paid two shillings per annum. So numerous are the cooks that they have a guild and chapel of their own in St. Mary's. For white

---

[1] Hurst, 24–5; *Rot. Parl.* ii. 240 (1351).   [2] Wood, *City*, i. 499–503.
[3] Rymer, i. 736, for safe-conduct.
[4] *Mun. Ac.* 36–7; *Collect.* ii. 286. For Jews in Oxford, *ib.* ii. 277–316.
[5] See *infra*, p. 89.
[6] For the weaving industry, which in John's time employed 60, see Ogle, 14, 49; *Rot. Parl.* i. 50; *Collect.* iii. 123; Salter, *Civ. Ox.* 108 (Rogers, *City Docs.* 6, states that there were 23 weavers in 1381 against all other evidence).
[7] Ogle, 15, 28–9.

bread we go to Carfax ; for horse-bread to the Northgate near Cheyney Street, close by the stalls of the cutlers and fletchers or bow-makers. In case of riot the seizure of these stalls will be our first object, as Robert of Gloucester noted long ago.[1]

The night of his arrival Wyclif would be hunted up by some scholar who would endeavour to book him for a touting master. He might even receive a call from the master himself who would point out 'with prayers, promises and threats' the advantages of his hall, or even claim that he had already enrolled himself among his scholars.[2] For by the time of Wyclif the halls had ceased to be self-governing communities and had become commercial speculations. Every year on the 9th September the masters appeared before the chancellor at St. Mary's and before the bell ceased to toll deposited their pledges for due payment of rent. Touting naturally abounded, though expressly forbidden at Paris. As Wyclif was entering Balliol he would resist all blandishments, even though offered a day's trial of the lectures free of all fees. But the country lad would be impressed by the master's dress ; his powdered hair hanging down his shoulders, his long beard like that of a soldier.[3] Nor were touting masters the only visitors Wyclif received that night. There are friars on the look-out for promising lads, for whose benefit they have stuffed their gowns with apples and other dainties that boys love. Perhaps Wyclif, who is a little in dread that his north-country scholarship be found lacking, half envies the youths that have joined the friars, for he hears that the Austins have the best teachers of grammar in the town, a fact which may account even better than the 'apples' for their success in capturing lads.[4]

The next day, 10th October, term opens with a mass of the Holy Ghost at St. Mary's. Wyclif may have noticed the tower of the church with its abundant decoration of lilies as emblematic of the Virgin, of which one only is now left. But it is within we see the glory. All the masters are there in their

---

[1] Wood, *City*, i. 486–7, 496 ; *Collect.* ii. 13 f. (gives the arrangement of the market in Wyclif's day), 108, 109, 138 ; Robert of Gloucester (R.S.), ii. 743.
[2] *Chart. Par.* ii. 46 ; Wood, *City*, i. 60.
[3] *Mun. Ac.* 15, 521–2 ; Rashdall, ii. 606 ; *Ann. Camb.* i. 94 in 1342 ; Wilkins, ii. 703.
[4] *Mun. Ac.* 363. There is no evidence of a Franciscan school at Oxford (Little, 43).

THE OLD CONGREGATION HOUSE IN ST. MARY'S

robes, and the young student would look for the first time on chancellor, proctors, and regents. Three days later there would be another solemn procession and a mass 'for the king and queen, their children, the peace of the University, and benefactors, living and dead'.[1] After this masters and students settled down to their work, sorely interrupted, however, by feast days and funerals, when no lectures could be given nor disputations held.

§ 3

We have assumed that Wyclif on coming to Oxford enrolled himself at Balliol, then governed by its first master, Hugh of Corbridge on Tyne.[2] Unfortunately Wyclif's life at Oxford is bound up with a puzzle in identity. For there were in the university at that time at least two other John Wyclifs. These doubles have naturally introduced much dispute into many details of his life. Three colleges, Queen's, Merton, and Balliol, have claimed Wyclif as a member—half in fact of the colleges then existing, more than half if we remember that until 1355 Exeter, then known as Stapeldon hall, was restricted to natives of the founder's diocese, with the exception of the chaplain,[3] and that Oriel, though an unrestricted college, was only open to those who had taken their bachelor's degree.[4] Curious to say, the one college specially linked with the neighbourhood of Durham, University, has made no claim to Wyclif's presence.[5] In addition a college and a hall have each claimed a Wyclif as their head. What college Wyclif entered, who were the other Wyclifs then in Oxford, whether Wyclif the master of Balliol was also Wyclif the warden of Canterbury hall, are questions closely connected. Taken by themselves, apart from the matter of the warden of Canterbury, the questions are not of much importance, but taken together they throw light on Wyclif's career, and give insight into the Oxford of Wyclif's day.

The first claimant for Wyclif's name is Queen's, then called

---

[1] *Mun. Ac.*, p. cxlviii. 419, 448; Hurst, 179.
[2] Wood, *Coll.* 81. See *infra*, p. 75.
[3] Wood, *Coll.* 105; Boase, p. xxxi. [4] Wood, *op. cit.* 122–3.
[5] *Mun. Ac.* 88. As the fellows could study theology Wyclif might have found this useful.

Queen hall.[1] Queen's was a northern college founded in 1341 by Robert of Eglesfield, rector of Brough under Stainmore in Westmorland, chaplain of Queen Philippa, after whom the college was named. The object of the founder was the revival of the Church in the wild district in which he lived. Its fellows were chosen from Westmorland and Cumberland, though others were not excluded. In the first list we find six malcontents from Merton, including the famous mathematician William of Heytisbury, and John of Polmorva, a future chancellor, from Exeter. But these were appointed probably to give the place a start. The fellows—on paper twelve in number, though in Wyclif's day never more than six or seven—sat with their provost on three sides of the high table 'with backs against the wall or wainscot', in memory of the Last Supper, though some have given the more prosaic reason that a former fellow was 'killed by a stab in the back'. They were summoned to dine by a trumpet. Fellows were allowed 18d. to 2s. a week, as well as provisions for servants, including a watchman who made night hideous with his whistling at fixed hours. The fellows were allowed to converse at table in French instead of Latin, possibly a graceful flattery of the Queen. The right of visitation was lodged with the archbishop of York, a source of constant dispute until settled on the 18th November 1376 in the archbishop's favour. Attached to Queen's there was a grammar school for its 'poor boys' or choristers, chosen from places where the college had property. These 'poor boys', dressed in tabards, for whose instruction an artist and grammarian were provided,[2] were commanded to kneel opposite the fellows while they dined, and to be 'opposed' in dialectics by such of the fellows as could break off from their meal for the purpose. After this the 'poor boys' dined on the fellows'

---

[1] In view of the exhaustive account of *The Queen's College* published in 1922 by J. R. Magrath, I have curtailed my original narrative and references. For Eglesfield see Poole in *D. N. B.* For his appropriations for Queen's see *Pap. Let.* iii. 88, 224; *Pap. Pet.* i. 122. For his reputed brass, really that of Robert Langton, Gough, i. 102. The list of original fellows in Rogers, *Prices*, ii. 670-4, differs from that in Magrath, i. 87, 91, by giving only three to Merton.

[2] Both Merton and Queen's possessed grammar schools, the grammar school at Queen's being the last school at which boys were forced to converse in French. See *infra*, ii. 181. For these schools see Leach, *Winchester*, 83; *Schools*, 195; *Charters*, 210-22; Wood, *City*, i. 183; Magrath, i. 45 f.

leavings.¹ Among these 'poor boys' in 1371 was one called Wyclif, for whom the college in 1371 spent 8*d*. in the purchase of a Latin grammar,² also ' 8*d*. for making a new gown ' as well as ' 3*d*. for a knife'.³ The shadowy form of this almonry boy, tonsured like a cleric, has led many astray. Probably he was some kinsman of the Reformer's—for Westmorland and the larger part of Cumberland were then in the archdeaconry of Richmond—who had come to Oxford for his schooling, to be under the guardianship of his renowned namesake.

Vaughan and others tell us that Wyclif entered Queen's " in 1340 " as a " commoner ". " The testimony of history ", he adds, " is unquestioned and decisive." ⁴ This rash verdict must be rejected.⁵ The name of Wyclif is not found among the first fellows, and " commoners " did not then exist.⁶ The mistake has arisen either from confusion with the almonry boy, or, more probably, from the fact that among those to whom Queen's was driven in its poverty⁷ to let rooms was John Wyclif, ex-fellow and ex-master of Balliol ; for owing to the plagues in 1349 and 1361 the rents from Southampton were in arrears and students were scarce. These rooms which Wyclif hired at varying dates from October 1363 onward were out of repair, and three shillings were spent on making them habitable.⁸

¹ Wood, *Coll.* 140.
² Probably the *Doctrinale* of Alexander de Ville Dieu which had been recently introduced into Oxford in place of the old *Donatus* (1361).
³ *Hist. MSS. Com.* ii. App. 141 ; Magrath, i. 114 *n*. There is no proof that his name was John.
⁴ Vaughan, *Mon.* 26. So Leland, *Comment.* 378 *n*. ; Tanner, 767 *n*. ; Wood, *Coll.* 82 ; and C. W. Le Bas, *Life of Wyclif* (1832), 92.
⁵ Birckbeck in his *Protestant Evidence*, ii. 71, though a fellow of Queen's, assigns Wyclif only to Merton and Balliol. As Birckbeck devoted considerable attention to Wyclif his negative evidence is of value.
⁶ Rashdall, ii. 488 *n*. They were first provided for by Waynflete at Magdalen in 1448.
⁷ This poverty was so great that on 16 May 1384 Queen's was handed over to the chancellor of England and others with ' protection, with clause *nolumus* ' for the provost and scholars for three years (*Cal. Pat.* ii. 401). On 18 Nov. 1347 Queen's was granted the hospital of St. Julian at Southampton called *Domus Dei*. For this hospital and its existing ruins see Clay, 78 ; Magrath, i. 20 f.
⁸ For these accounts see *Hist. MSS. Com.* ii, App. 141–2 ; Foxe, ii. 941 ; *Ziz.* 515 ; Wilkins, *Westbury*, 88–9. The latrine in 1374 gave trouble : ' For straw for covering the latrine of Wyclif 2*s*. '. ' More straw 15*d*.' ' To the woman carrying the same 4*d*.' ' For the tile work over the latrine of Wyclif 10*d*.' A door-fastener ('nouschyn'? ; Magrath, i. 112 *n*., takes it as ' nuncheon ', i.e. luncheon for the tiler) cost 1*d*. and a key 6*d*.

The rent was 20s. per annum. In these rooms, as we shall see, Wyclif, unable to return to Balliol, read as a lodger for his doctorate in theology.[1] But any earlier connexion with Queen's is extremely improbable. It is interesting to note that Wyclif took up his residence at Queen's in the year in which the college commenced the building of their chapel. The need of money for this enterprise was one of the causes which led the fellows to let to outsiders.

The second college to claim Wyclif is Merton,[2] by some writers as a fellow, by others as a steward of the fellows' table.[3] Here again there is a possible double. It is true that in Wyclif's time " Balliol and Merton formed the opposite poles of the academical world ", the head-quarters of northern and southern nations respectively,[4] and that Merton refused to elect northern scholars unless they came from dioceses in which the college had estates.[5] But there is no rule without exception, and Wyclif may have been one of the few so elected.[6] As regards 'steward' it is difficult to know exactly what is meant. If a mere servant it is hard to believe that this was the son of the squire of Wycliffe. Others have claimed that by 'steward' we should understand "portionist", a term now corrupted into postmasters, a poorer class—twelve in all, nominated by the senior fellows—who had no share nor prospect of rising to a share in the government of the college, who waited in hall and dined on the broken meats, singing also in the college choir.[7] But 'portionists' do not seem to have been grafted into the foundation until about 1370 at the earliest[8] (or ten years after Wyclif had become master of Balliol) as the result of a bequest by John Wylliot, the foe of

[1] *Infra*, p. 156. The rooms were popular with ecclesiastics (Magrath, i. 131).
[2] For Merton, transferred by its founder, bishop Walter de Merton, from its first home at Malden in 1274, marking the real beginning in England of the college system, see Brodrick; Mallet, i. 112 f.; Hobhouse, *Life of Walter de Merton*; E. F. Percival, *Foundation Statutes of Merton* (1847).
[3] Brodrick, 36, 215.
[4] Poole, *Med. Thought*, 286 *n.*; Brodrick, 18.
[5] Brodrick, 18, 157. Fellows of Merton were by preference from the diocese of Winchester (*ib.* 7).
[6] In 1317 there was one from Durham, and one from Pontefract (*Pap. Let.* ii. 159, 160).
[7] Rashdall, ii. 488; Brodrick, 20.
[8] Brodrick, 19, 217. Wood, *Coll.* 5, dates about 1380 and is more correct. See Hurst, 56; *Collect.* iii. 147; *Cal. Pat. Ric.* i. 550.

the northern nation. Even if without evidence an earlier date for their establishment be assumed, it is hard to believe that Wyclif filled a position whose status is illustrated by a resolution of 1498 forbidding the fellows to supply them with bread and meat out of hall.

The existence of a fellow of Merton called John Wyclif or Whitclif seems more certain. For in a catalogue of fellows of Merton made in 1395 by Thomas Robert his name occurs with the remark :

'Doctor in Theologia qui cum nimium in proprio ingenio confidebat ut primum erat Socius istius Domus unum annum probationis habuit plenarie in eadem.'

The date is added ' a° xxx Edw. Ter ' i. e. 1356, the only name in the list to which a date is attached.[1] But in 1356 Wyclif showed no signs of heretical or aggressive thought. Moreover, it may be doubted whether we have here Robert's original, for the entry is now but a reproduction in modern ink of the original as read by Astry in 1700. Moreover, it is cited by Leland, from whom Wood copies,[2] in precisely the opposite sense, that Wyclif was never a fellow, but only on probation, a junior position which he resigned before the year was out, whether because he was of "turbulent spirit" and "the college was weary of him" we cannot say. Some writers who hold that Robert's entry without the negative is correct maintain that this fellow of Merton who was also seneschal for the week[3] was a certain John Whitclyve or Whitclif of Mayfield, who is also put forward by the same writers as the warden of Canterbury. This Whitclif—whose name suggests that he came from a part of the parish of Sevenoaks that belonged at this time to the see of Canterbury[4]—was appointed by Islip

---

[1] Brodrick, p. vii f., 215–16. Robert left Merton 1422, d. 1446 (*ib.* 36). Robert's list is copied by Bale, *Index Script.* App. vi, without remark. In Wyclif's day there were on the average 13 senior and 17 junior fellows (Brodrick, 27).

[2] Leland, *Coll.* iv. 55, '*nec* erat socius, *nec* annum probationis', &c. ; Wood, *Coll.* 82 ; Tanner, 767. Shirley, *Ziz.* 517 *n.*, looks upon the negative as "the zeal" of a "college antiquary before Leland's time to vindicate his foundation from the charge of having fostered the heretic". But as Leland had direct access to Robert's catalogue (Brodrick, ix), the negative was inserted at an early date or was in the original.

[3] Shirley in *Ziz.* 513 *n.*, who adds to difficulties by adding "and therefore a fellow of some standing"

[4] Hasted, *Kent*, i. 341, 342.

the vicar of Mayfield in July 1361, in succession to another Sevenoaks man, Ralph Baker. On the 18th December 1380 he exchanged for Horsted Keynes in Sussex.[1] At a date unknown he was given the prebend of Heathfield,[2] and died suddenly about a year before the Reformer.[3] Whitclif, it is true, is never called a fellow of Merton nor does he seem to have completed his master's degree. But the indirect arguments in favour of this identification are of weight. The vicarage of Mayfield was in the presentation of Islip,[4] himself a Merton fellow, as also was Rede, bishop of Chichester, to whom Whitclif owed his prebend.

The arguments against the identification of this fellow of Merton, if indeed Robert and not Leland be correct, with the Reformer must also be weighed. The southern character of Merton, as we have seen, is not absolutely conclusive. But we may ask, Why did Wyclif leave Merton? At Merton every fellow received ' fifty shillings a year ' as well as ' a robe yearly if there be means enow and the Warden consent thereto ', to say nothing of the extras for ' delicate living ' of which Peckham complained in 1284, but which in March 1385 received the sanction of Innocent VI since ' 50s. in modern times is hardly enough for their food '.[5] Balliol on the contrary was a poor college whose master even was only allowed 40s. a year, as compared with the ninety marks, five servants, and two post-horses ' to assist him to go his rounds and visit all the manors which belonged to the house ' which were given the warden of

---

[1] Foxe, ii. 943, quoting Reg. Sudbury, f. 134a; Hennessy, *Clergy Lists*, 86, 106. In Nov. 1402 the rectory was appropriated to the Cluniac priory of Lewes. It was worth 26 marks, the income of the priory 'not exceeding 3,000 ' (*Pap. Let.* v. 548).

[2] So expressly stated in the will of Michael Northburgh, canon of Chichester, of which on 5 Mar. 1382 Whitclif was one of the executors (Gibbons, 63-4). There is no mention of this prebend in Hennessy, *op. cit.* 9, though the date of the next prebendary, 1383-4, will fit in with Whitclif's tenure. The registers of Chichester before 1396 are lost. From *Close Rolls Ric.* i. 91, we learn that in Oct. 1377 he was not yet a prebendary.

[3] Whitclif's will was made 12 Nov. 1383, proved 21 Nov., and is in Reg. Courtenay, f. 207. It was discovered and printed by W. Courthope, *Gent. Mag.* (1842), ii. 146-8; by Pratt in Foxe, ii. 943. Whitclif directed that he should be buried in the hospital of St. Peter and St. Paul, Maidstone. In Sept. 1368 Whitclif received a legacy of five marks from a neighbouring vicar, John Watford of Snargate, Dover, to pray for his soul (Foxe, ii. 943).

[4] The church of Mayfield had been annexed by Peckham to his *mensa* (*Reg. Peckham*, iii. 910).   [5] *Cal. Pap.* iii. 561.

Merton.[1] Wyclif, if a fellow of Merton, was not bound to leave, unless promoted to 'too liberal a benefice'[2] or expelled for misconduct. Some fellows found their position so comfortable that they stayed on for thirty years without proceeding to their degree in divinity.[3] Migrations to Merton were common,[4] but from Merton to another college, where a fellow must leave when his degree in arts was obtained, almost unknown. To Wyclif the library of Merton with its 250 volumes would have been a great magnet.[5]

A recent writer[6] has posited an ingenious theory to explain the tradition of Wyclif's fellowship at Merton College. He considers that possibly Wyclif had "been worked into Merton to pacify the Northerners".[7] The Reformer had then tried as a "*borealis militans*" to "capture Merton for the North". This led to his expulsion at the close of a year, in 1356, during part of which he had been seneschal of the week. In defence of this theory Mr. Cronin points to the excessive number of fellows of Merton, nine in all, who disappeared at the end of 1355 and to Islip's visitation of Merton by instruction of the pope.[8] The theory, apart from making this junior fellow a seneschal, is possible, though not probable. It assumes that Wyclif, previously a fellow of Balliol—for to assume that in 1356 Wyclif had only just come to Oxford would make havoc of the chronology of his life—after his expulsion from Merton returned once more to Balliol, of which college he was shortly afterwards elected the master. On a review of the whole argument we are of opinion, failing further

---

[1] Brodrick, 333-4. The dogs and horses kept by fellows of Merton made a scandal as early as 1338. See Rogers, *Prices*, ii. 670-4.

[2] 'uberius beneficium', an ambiguous phrase which led to many appeals to the Visitor (Brodrick, 324). In 1317 there were three appeals to John XXII (*Pap. Let.* ii. 159, 160, 164).

[3] Complaints of Arundel in 1401, Brodrick, 27.

[4] Brodrick, 174, 176, 202. From Exeter there were constant migrations, e.g. Rede, Rigg (*ib.* 211-12).

[5] On this library and its catalogue see Mallet, i. 130 *n*. As Wyclif may have used it, it is of interest to note that it contained 43 volumes with glosses on parts of the Bible, 42 volumes of Augustine, Aquinas, Duns, as also a Josephus (see *infra*, p. 136). Of all these only 24 now remain.

[6] H. S. Cronin in *Trans. Hist. Soc.* (1914), 73 *n*.

[7] Presumably after the Wylliot riots. See *infra*, p. 82.

[8] *Pap. Let.* iii. 561 (Mar. 1355), on petition of the scholars' to increase their emoluments.

evidence, that Wyclif was never a fellow of Merton, in spite of the portrait claiming him as such which hangs in the hall of that college.

§ 4

The third college to claim the Reformer is Balliol,[1] the oldest in date of actual foundation of the colleges of Oxford, though its right in early days to be called a college might be disputed. Balliol lay outside the city walls, near the Bocardo gate, in the Horsemonger or market for horses. Between the college and the walls was the Canditch, now Broad Street, a fosse sixteen feet wide and sixteen feet deep, which seems to have been made by joining a chain of older pools.[2] Balliol owed its origin to a penance. About the middle of the thirteenth century John de Balliol, lord of Barnard Castle and of vast possessions in Scotland, the north of England, and northern France,[3] knelt at the door of Durham cathedral and was there scourged by the bishop, Walter de Kirkham, for that he had 'unjustly vexed and enormously damnified' the Church at Tynemouth, and laid in wait for the bishop himself.[4] Moreover, according to another account, 'he had gotten himself exceedingly [5] drunk, quite contrary to the fair esteem beseeming his rank'. When the bishop ' so sagaciously brought back his erring

---

[1] For the early history of Balliol see *Hist. MSS. Com.* iv. 442 ff. (often perfunctory); F. de Paravicini, *Early Hist. of Balliol* (1891)—useful, though not always accurate Eng. trans. of documents; Wood, *Coll.* 70-4; H. Savage, *Balliofergus* (1668), one of the earliest college histories by a former master of Balliol, still useful, in spite of its blunders; H. E. Salter, *Oxford Deeds of Balliol College* (1913), a model volume; Dr. Poole's sketch in A. Clark, *Colleges of Oxford* (1891), 24 f.; H. W. C. Davis, *Balliol Coll.* (1899).

[2] Hurst, 124-5. In Wood, *City*, i. 371, Canditch is derived from *candida* "because without doubt of the clear stream". But medieval fosses were not " clear " and it is more likely a corruption of camp-ditch, or canal-ditch (Hurst, 124; *Eng. Hist. Rev.* xv. 605).

[3] For the Balliols see B. J. Scott, *The Norman Balliols in England* (1914). The Great War made Bailleul-en-Vimeu in Picardy a well-known name in England. For the shield of the Balliols on the Town Hall see Scott, 80. There are several Bailleul chateaus, *ib.* 102, 103.

[4] Matt. Paris, *Chron. Maj.* v. 528, who dates in 1255 but says nothing of the scourging, the details of which we get from *Chron. Lan.* 69. The date is not certain, but as Walter de Kirkham died at Howden on 9 Aug. 1360 (*Ang. Sac.* i. 738) its limit is fixed. The author of the Lanercost Chronicle shows himself well acquainted with the inner history of Balliol. See *Eng. Hist. Rev.* xxxi. 275.

[5] MS. 'cervitese', i.e. 'cervicose', usually mistranslated 'with beer' (K. Sisam).

CH. III   GRADUATE DAYS   71

son to his bosom ', he added to the penance ' a sum of fixed maintenance to be continued for ever to scholars studying at Oxford '. The result was the foundation by that " stout obscurantist " [1] before June 1266 [2] of Balliol hall for sixteen poor students, probably on as meagre lines as were compatible with his oath. Two years later (1268) John of Balliol died,[3] and no doubt the students wondered how long his son Hugh would continue to pay the rent. The hall was saved by his widow, Dervorgilla, whose name as the real founder, rather than that of her rough husband, should by rights attach to the college. Dervorgilla of Galloway was a remarkable woman.[4]

> A better lady than she was nane
> In all the Yle of Mare Brettane.[5]

Related to the royal lines of both countries, a great heiress, Dervorgilla still lives in her foundations, the great bridge at Dumfries, the nearby abbey of Sweet Heart—whose ruins conceal the heart of her lord, as well as her own ashes—and in the college founded ' to the memory of lord John of Balliol, formerly our spouse '.[6]

Balliol's foundation differed but little from the many other halls of the university. At first the scholars were established in a hired house, probably the tenement known later as Old Balliol hall or Sparrow hall.[7] But in 1284 a beginning was made of a home of their own and of the establishment of a legal corporation under a ' keeper ' [8] or warden by the purchase for

[1] Davis, 10. He was one of the opponents of Simon de Montfort.
[2] See *Cal. Docs. Scots*, i. 476; *Lib. Rolls*, 50 Hen. III, m. 6.
[3] Writ issued on 27 Oct. 1368 (*Inquis.* n.s., i. 218–19).
[4] For a good life see W. Huyshe, *Dervorgilla, Lady of Galloway* (1913). Her ancestry was from the Conqueror on one side and on the other from David I of Scotland (Huyshe, 1–12). She married John de Balliol in 1233. Her youngest son, the future king, was born in 1249. She died 21 Jan. 1290 (*Chron. Lan.* 134).
[5] Andrew of Wyntoun, *Orygynale Cronykil*, ii. 321–3, in *Historians of Scotland* (1872), v. 3. ' Mare ', i.e. more, greater.
[6] Salter, 280.
[7] Salter, 29. In Savage, 7, the lease is dated in 1379. It was not acquired by Balliol until 1427 in exchange for the site of the Divinity School.
[8] So styled in 1288 in *Close Rolls*, s.a. 526, the said ' keeper ' being ' Master Walter de Fotheringhay ', who was ' keeper ' in 7 Jan. 1385 (*Cal. Docs. Scots*, ii. 76). Fotheringhay was one of the estates of Dervorgilla, and held by ' service of a sparrowhawk yearly ' (*Inquis.* n.s. ii. 467). Was this the origin of the name ' Sparrow hall ' ? On 8 July 1286 there was a suit between Dervorgilla and the warden and scholars (*Cal. Docs. Scots*, ii. 83).

the sum of eighty marks [1] of three tenements in Horsemonger Street, henceforth called New Balliol hall or Marey's hall.[2] Exemption from tithes was obtained for the house,[3] and ten years later further endowments were realized by the appropriation of St. Lawrence Jewry in London, purchased for 100 marks from Hugh de Vienne, a canon of St. Martin's le Grand, through another canon of the same house, Henry de Wichenbroke.[4] Nevertheless for some time still Balliol was rather a hall of the Paris type than a college. The scholars, who were solely artist undergraduates, were presided over as in other halls by a principal chosen by themselves, subject to the ratification of their nomination by the 'procurators'. They were governed by rules framed by themselves, provided they were not in conflict with the ordinances set forth by Dervorgilla [5]—a very hotbed, in fact, of university democracy. Exeter college, we may remark in passing, was of the same type, only more so, for there the rector or head was elected annually, nor until 1384 was he eligible for re-election.[6] Visitors at Balliol, in the strict sense of the term, apart from the diocesan, there were none. Their place was taken by two external officers called 'procurators'—later known also as 'rectors'—one of whom was a secular master of arts, the other a Franciscan. To these 'procurators' were assigned the duties usually discharged by a master—the control of finance, the payment of the weekly allowances, expulsion and election,

---

[1] Licence granted 12 Oct. 1285 (*Pat. Ed. I*, s.a. 196; cf. *Cal. Docs. Scots*, ii. 78, where it is dated 7 Oct. An inquisition had been held at Bristol on 29 Dec. 1284 (*Inquis.* 13 Ed. I, no. 127). For the position of these tenements where now is the front quad of Balliol see the map in Salter.

[2] For site see Salter, 4 *n.*; Hurst, 121-2. Riley, *op. cit.* iv. 447, and Rashdall, ii. 475 *n.*, state that the earliest site was St. Margaret's hall. But this was not acquired until 1342 (Salter, 19-26).

[3] *Hist. MSS. Com.* iv. 445.

[4] *Hist. MSS. Com.* iv. 449; Hennessy, *Nov. Rep.* 265; Savage, 33, dated 30 May 1294. Licence granted 18 Aug. 1295 (*Cal. Pat.*, s.a. 141). The vicar was given £5 a year. Savage wrongly identifies Henry and Hugh. There was a Hugh of Vienne, a Dominican, many manuscripts of whose writings still exist (James, *MSS. Caius*, i. 3, 295, 344; ii. 544-7, 552). Our Hugh died before 1296 (Salter, 360).

[5] For the intentions—they can hardly be called statutes—of Dervorgilla see Salter, 277-9; Savage, 15-17. They were dated 22 Aug. 1282 at 'Botel', i.e. Buittle in Galloway, not Bothal in Northumberland as Riley, *op. cit.* iv. 442. They assume existing 'statuta, consuetudines', &c.

[6] Wood, *Coll.* 107; Rashdall, ii. 491 *n.*

the redress of grievances. They were also given the care of the poorer students.

The close connexion of Balliol with the friars is important. Dervorgilla's so-called statutes took the form of a letter to ' friar Hugh of Hartlepool ' and ' Master William de Menyl '[1] —evidently the existing procurators or almoners of her dead lord's dole. When in 1284 she placed her foundation on a securer footing she sought the advice of friar ' Richard de Slikeburn ',[2] in whose ' discretion and devotion ' she had ' complete confidence '[3] and whom she urges to promote by all means in his power the perpetuation of ' our house of Balliol '.[4] In the same year we are told that many scholars from these poor lodgings had entered the religious life.[5] At Balliol from the first Wyclif would be brought into contact with Franciscan influences. At Balliol also Wyclif would come into close touch with poverty, for there was always on the foundation a poor scholar nominated by the procurators " to whom the scholars shall give every day the leavings or broken meats of their tables ".[6]

In the fourteenth century Balliol began to expand. In the first decade the college obtained Burnel's Inn,[7] as a legacy from the wealthy court ecclesiastic William Burnel, provost of Wells.[8] Burnel's Inn was part of the confiscated Jewry and

[1] Salter, 277.
[2] Sleekburn, near Bedlington, Northumberland.
[3] There is no evidence that he was her confessor (*Eng. Hist. Rev.* xxxi. 276).
[4] For the letter in full, dated 16 Apr. 1284, see Salter, 279–81 ; Paravicini, 72 f. On 28 Apr. 1285 Slikeburn demanded from the executors of Alan of Wigston 120 cows for debt due of £100 to executors of Balliol, evidently given by Dervorgilla to the college (Salter, 329, 331 ; *Cal. Docs. Scots*, ii. 76). Little (*Eng. Hist. Rev.* xxxii. 48) suggests that Slikeburn was the writer of the *Lanercost Chronicle* down to 1297.
[5] Reg. Sutton, f. 74, quoted by Rashdall, ii. 474 *n*.
[6] Wood, *Coll.* 72.
[7] For Burnel's Inn see Salter, 91–100. Difficulties were experienced in obtaining the legacy. But on 16 Jan. 1305 licence was granted for the alienation in mortmain of nine shops and a messuage (*Cal. Pat. Ed.* s.a. 310), for which see *Inquis.* (n.s.), iv. 193 ; Savage, 27–8. The order was repeated 5 Nov. 1305 (Rymer, i. 976). In 1307 Balliol obtained the Old Synagogue and the final ratification of the legacy 27 Aug. 1314 (Salter, 116–17).
[8] Brother of the noted chancellor Robert Burnel (*D. N. B.*). He was canon of Lichfield, Salisbury, Llandaff, St. Davids, St. Omer, and York, and provost of Wells (*Pap. Let.* i. 517, 530 ; Salter, 99, 105, 111), not dean, as Wood, *City*, i. 157, a mistake with another Burnel who died in 1295 (Le Neve, i. 150, 166). Our Burnel died before Nov. 1304 (*Inquis.*, n.s. iv. 192 ; Salter, 106 ; Le Neve, iii. 168).

included the old synagogue.¹ Steps were also taken to secure a chapel. At first the society had to content itself with the north aisle of the parish church of St. Mary Magdalene.² In 1293 the college obtained the right to have an oratory of their own, and plans were contemplated for its erection. About the year 1296 Hugh of Vienne left fifty marks for the purpose, stipulating that the new chapel should be built of stone and roofed with lead. The payment of the legacy was delayed,³ and the chapel, dedicated to St. Catherine,⁴ was only finished in 1328 by the help of a legacy of £20 left for the purpose by Adam Poleter, a citizen of Reading. To this Nicholas Quappelad, abbot of Reading, added ten marks, and 'a glass window worth ten pounds'.⁵ Before the chapel was completed provision was made in 1310 for a chaplain,⁶ further increased by a legacy in November 1320 of twelve acres of land in Steeple Aston.⁷ When Wyclif was master, though the chaplains had been increased to three, the college had no right to the administration of the Eucharist, at any rate on the greater feast days. This was first granted by Urban V by his permission to

'priests of the said House to celebrate in the aforesaid chapel mass and the other divine offices as well aloud as in a low voice even on the greater feasts'.⁸

[1] Full details, *Inquis.* (n.s.), iv. 192–3. Cf. also *Collect.* ii. 312. The Jewry granted to Burnel, 24 May 1291 (Salter, 99).   [2] Wood, *Coll.* 98.

[3] Salter, 336–8. For the site of this chapel, often identified with the dining-room of the master's house, see *ib.* 19, 360–1.

[4] Balliol was dedicated 'to the Undivided Trinity, the Glorious Virgin Mary, the Blessed Virgin and Martyr, Katherine' (Salter, 280 ; *Reg. Pal. Dunelm.* iii. 381). Hence the name of the inn belonging to Balliol called "The Katherine Wheel", which was destroyed in 1828; see opposite. The chapel is called 'St. Katherine' in *Cal. Pat. Ed. II*, i. 235. None of Wyclif's sermons, all delivered after he left Balliol, refer to St. Catherine.

[5] Salter, 315 ; Savage, 35.

[6] Wood, *Coll.* 99 ; Salter, 159 ; Savage, 33 ; licence in mortmain 16 May 1310, *Cal. Pat.* s.a. 235. The names of the donors are given by Wood as Hugh Warkenley (for which read Warkenby, a short form of Warkenethby, Salter, 139) and William de Gotham (Savage, 33, misreads Socham). Both these names constantly occur associated together in the transactions of Balliol (see index in Salter). William Gotham was the attorney of William Burnel (*ib.* 113) and a fellow of Balliol (*ib.* 141, 'consocio'). In Feb. 1314 he had left Balliol, for he was now 'parson of Hethere' (*ib.* 113). Warkenby was the second 'principal' of Balliol (1296–1303 ; Wood, *Coll.* 81). The two therefore may have been agents rather than donors.   [7] *Cal. Pat.* s.a. 407.

[8] 17 Apr. 1364. See Salter, 317 ; Paravicini, 137 ; Savage, 36 ; *Pap. Let.* iv. 41 ; *Pap. Pet.* i. 489. In Wood, *Coll.* 99, wrongly assigned to Urban VI.

THE CATHERINE WHEEL BEFORE 1828

See note on p. 74

In 1325 a doubt arose whether the members of the college might study other than arts. The procurators, of whom one was friar Robert of Leicester, decided that this was unlawful and contrary to the mind of the founder.[1] The decision was announced 'in the presence of the whole community', including the noted Richard Fitzralph. So down to 1340, or within a few years of Wyclif's entrance, the sixteen fellows of Balliol lost their places on completing their degree in arts. The effects of this were disastrous. Balliol lacked the stability that older students would have given it, nor could it be the avenue to a career in Church or State. The more ambitious of its students were driven elsewhere to obtain their higher degrees, Fitzralph, for instance, to University college.[2] Others, we are told, 'were compelled to leave their studies and seek a living as artisans'[3]—no doubt an exaggeration. The academic standing was low, nor could government by external procurators tend to the growth of college dignity. But in 1340 at the instance of Richard Bury, bishop of Durham,[4] who no doubt had heard of the dismal condition of Balliol from his chaplain Richard Fitzralph, Sir Philip Somervile, the tenth and last representative of an ancient Norman family, lord of Wichnor in Staffordshire and of many estates in Northumberland, founded six theological fellowships for regents in arts, with a master elected by the fellows, who does not, however, seem to have displaced altogether the principal or head of the artists, to say nothing of the procurators.[5] The master, whose position is of interest to us in view of Wyclif's tenure of the office, had 'a chamber assigned to him alone, and a boy or servitor to wait on him'. If strangers visited the college then the master was provided with 'a table in no way luxurious in

---

[1] *Hist. MSS. Com.* iv. 442–3. The decision (25 July 1325) is in Salter, 285.
[2] Wood, *Coll.* 54.
[3] Letter of Clement VI, 28 Apr. 1343 (Salter, 299 ; *Pap. Pet.* i. 16).
[4] Bury is one of the signatories to the statutes and in Dec. 1339 obtained the licence in mortmain (Salter, 297 ; *Cal. Pat.* s.a. 349).
[5] For instance Somervile provides that if the Master wastes the goods of the House 'he shall thrice be duly warned by the Principal' and if necessary deposed (Salter, 292). For the statutes of Somervile see *ib.* 286–99 ; inaccurately in Savage, 40–51 ; Paravicini, 184–209. Wood, *Coll.* 76, gives an abstract. There is a varying form in *Reg. Pal. Dunelm*, iii. 381 f. The original has disappeared, but the *inspeximus* made for Ed. Balliol, king of Scotland, before 1345 has survived.

his own chamber, at the common expense, but only for such an occasion '. In addition he received, should the revenues suffice, ' forty shillings annually for his necessary expenses '. If forced by illness to resign his post he had a pension for life ; scholars also, incurably sick, were granted ninepence a week. The votes in the election of the master were received and written down by the principal and two scrutators, who sat apart in the chapel, the fellows waiting outside and entering one by one, the practice followed, no doubt, in the election of Wyclif.

As endowment for this scheme Somervile granted the college the advowson of Mickle Benton in Northumberland, ' together with two carucates of arable land and twenty acres of meadow ' in the parish.[1] This bequest two months later (6 Feb. 1340) he enlarged into 224 acres in Mickle Benton.[2] The six theological fellows were to hail from the north, ' from those places nearest to the site of the aforesaid property given by me '. To ensure that this was carried out, the warden of Durham college was given certain vague rights in the election and removal of a master of Balliol.[3] The theological fellows were to receive ' elevenpence a week, and in the time of scarcity fifteen pence ' from their regency in arts to their inception in theology, an ampler allowance than that of the artist, who only received eightpence, i. e. a penny a day with twopence on Sundays. A list is given of the crimes for which a scholar might be excluded—murder, adultery, assault on master or scholar, and the like.[4]

In May 1342 the troubles of the alien priories led to Balliol securing further property. Thomas Cave, rector of Welwyck, Yorkshire, and William Brocklesby, two benefactors of Balliol,[5] secured from the alien priory of Lessay [6] in Normandy the

[1] Licence granted 6 Dec. 1339 (*Cal. Pat.* s.a. 349). For the bishop's licence in 1341 see *Reg. Pal. Dunelm*, iii. 397, 403–5.
[2] *Cal. Pat.* s.a. 416.   [3] Set out in *Collect.* iii. 28–9.
[4] Salter, 290, 292–3 ; *Reg. Pal. Dunelm*, iii. 389.
[5] Thomas de Cave and William de Brocklesby figure in the acquirement of Margaret hall, now the site of the master's dining-room (Salter, 19, 24–6). Licence granted 18 May 1342 (*Cal. Pat.* s.a. 433).
[6] Lessay (Exaquium) in Wood, *Coll.* 77, and *Cal. Pat. Ed.* v. 433. Savage, 52, mistranslates as Avranches. See also for deed Paravicini, 212. The other two livings are called by Wood Rysome (i. e. Riseholm near Lincoln) and Brocklesby (Savage, *op. cit.*, ' Bratleby ').

advowsons of three livings in Lincolnshire, one of which, Fillingham, is of interest for students of Wyclif. The money for the purpose seems to have been found out of a legacy by Cave of £100.[1] In November 1340 another northern noble, Sir William Felton, presented to the college ' the fruits, rents and revenues' of Abbotsley in Huntingdon,[2] value about ' forty marks'. This he purchased from the Crown, into whose hands it had fallen by forfeiture from the abbot of Jedburgh. But this endowment for the augmentation of the numbers and commons of the fellows as well as provision that they should have ' the books of the diverse faculties in common' did not become available until the death of the rector, William of Kingston, in 1361.

From this survey of the early history of Balliol we pass to Wyclif's relations to it. That he became master seems presumptive evidence that he had previously been an inmate, for that democratic college would scarcely elect the rejected of a southern college. The northern leanings of Balliol, the nearness of the Balliols of Barnard Castle to the home of Wyclif— fellowships were then obtained through personal influence— both point to Balliol as the Reformer's college. This is strengthened when we remember the links between another fellow of Balliol, Richard Fitzralph, and Wyclif. Nor must we forget that when John was master there was also among the fellows a certain William Wyclif, and that the living of Wycliffe was thrice given to members of Balliol. This membership in a college intimately associated with friars would also account for Wyclif's early alliance with friars. Finally, the restriction of the theological fellowships in Wyclif's time to six would explain how Wyclif came to leave Balliol before obtaining his doctorate. That the Reformer was the master of Balliol is not disputed. Let the reader beware lest he be deceived by modern terms. His allowance, as we have seen, was but a pittance. For a master's lodge you must wait two

---

[1] Savage, 52 f. For other bequests by Cave see *Cal. Pat. Ed.* 1332, p. 369. He died before the transaction with Lessay—licence of bishop of Coutances granted 3 Mar. 1344—could be completed (*Cal. Pat.* vi. 207).

[2] Consent of Clement VI on 28 Apr. 1343 (*Pap. Pet.* i. 16; *Pap. Let.* iii. 69; Salter, 299). For the gift see Wood, *Coll.* 76; *Hist. MSS. Com.* iv. 448; Savage, 38. Licence in mortmain granted 12 Apr. 1340 (*Cal. Pat.* s.a. 461).

centuries.¹ Common-rooms were unknown. Wyclif would be thankful that no longer was he forced to share his bedroom with two or three others, or even driven into the ' dorter '. His furniture would be limited to a chair, a bed, a trestle-table, a shelf for books, and a "mazer" for pledging toasts.² Chimneys were scarce; if he wanted a fire he must go to the kitchen, or do his best with a pan of charcoal, though on special feast days there is a brazier in the hall. To fight the cold the floor was strewed with rushes. The unglazed window of his room was closed with wooden shutters. Such money as he could spare would go in tallow candles; at twopence a pound they must be deemed a luxury.³ If these fail there is the hall which is lighted with torches. But as we dine at eleven and sup at five such extravagance is not always allowed. Meals as a rule were eaten in silence, broken only by the reading aloud of some holy book. The fellow who talked save in Latin was punished for a second offence by being served his meals in a corner by himself.⁴

In what year Wyclif was elected master is not known. Our earliest document, dating from 1360, tells us how :

' On Monday next after the Feast of our Lord's ascension, John de Wyclif master of the house of the scholars of the hall called Le Balliol halle in Oxford was attached to make answer to Nicholas Marchaunt in a plea of distresses taken.'

Wyclif as master had seized the property in Cat Street (now Gresham Street) of Nicholas, formerly the possession of ' the wife of Isaac of Southwark, a Jewess ',⁵ for Balliol was a large holder of the houses of expelled Jews both in Oxford and London. Wyclif gained his suit. In 1360 he was thus the third master, having succeeded at some date between 1356 and 1360 the second master, Robert Derby.⁶ To the method

¹ Willis and Clark, iii. 328 f., 378.
² For chambers see *ib*. iii. 296–327. The list of furniture is that in a master's lodge in Cambridge in 1451 (*ib*. iii. 351). For " mazers " see *Archaeol.*, vol. 50, pp. 129–93. The monks of Canterbury in 1328 possessed 182!
³ Boase, p. xl. Wax candles were 6*d*. to 8*d*. A provincial of the friars was restricted to twelve pounds a year (*Pap. Let.* v. 552).
⁴ Willis and Clark, iii. 365–7 ; Salter, 279.
⁵ *Hist. MSS. Com.* iv. 448 ; Stow, *Survey*, i. 271.
⁶ Not ' Serby ' as Wood, *Coll.* 81. Lechler, 101, following Shirley, *Ziz.* xiv *n*., says William Kingston, a mistake arising from Kingston being the vicar of Abbotsley from whom Wyclif took over the living (see *infra*). According to *Hist. MSS. Com.* iv. 448, Robert Derby was vicar of Abbotsley in 1365.

of election we have already referred, as also to the fact that he would have to secure the concurrence of the warden of Durham college, probably Uhtred Boldon, his opponent in later days.¹ By Somervile's statutes Wyclif, before entering upon his office, would have to present himself in person before the lord of Somervile's manor of Wichnor in Staffordshire with a letter certifying his election. He would also swear that

'every year on St. Margaret's day or at some time to be assigned by the society, he will give a faithful account of his administration, and of all goods belonging to the said House, before the whole community'.²

One other record of Wyclif as master has come down to us. In 1361 William of Kingston, the rector of Abbotsley, died, and the living fell in to the college as part of Somervile's purchase. To Wyclif thus came the duty of taking the necessary legal steps for its impropriation. So on the 7th April 'J. de Wyclif, Magister sive Custos Collegii Aulae de Balliolo, suburbio Oxoniae super Candych', was appointed by the college their proctor for the purpose. The document is still extant in which Wyclif reports on the 9th April 1361 that he has taken possession of the church and received oblations and 'young pigeons' from the parishioners.³ It is of interest to note the provision made for the vicar. He was to retain sixty acres of glebe land, an annual pension from Balliol of 'sixty pence sterling', the usual fees and lesser tithes, together with 'a suitable dwelling to be kept furnished containing a reception room, a sleeping chamber, a kitchen, a stable and a granary'. To all these provisions, as set forth by bishop John Gynwell of Lincoln, Wyclif would be a party.⁴ This act of impropriation must have been almost his last public act as master. For on the 14th May 1361 Wyclif was instituted at Holbeach in Lincolnshire, to which he must have journeyed for the purpose,

---

¹ See *infra*, p. 223. This would account for Wyclif calling Boldon ' magister specialis ' (*Op. Min.* 405).
² Salter, 289. The St. Margaret is probably of Scotland and the date therefore 20 July and not 10 June.
³ *Hist. MSS. Com.* iv. 447-8. Mullinger, i. 264, attributes this to Wyclif's care for the secular clergy. But the licence had been obtained long before.
⁴ Paravicini, 177 f.; Savage, 38.

to the college living of Fillingham ' value thirty marks '.[1] At Balliol the master was expected to resign on receiving a benefice of the clear value of £10, a provision not annulled until the 8th August 1433.[2] Some delay, possibly due to the then prevalence of plague and the consequent difficulty of electing a successor, occurred, for in the following July Wyclif still signed himself master of Balliol when forwarding to the bishop of Lincoln the bull sanctioning the transfer of Abbotsley to the college.[3] It is probable therefore that as master he would be called upon to give a receipt to the executors of Thomas Cheyner, mercer, buried in St. Lawrence Jewry, who on the 24th June 1361 left bequests to the scholars of ' le Baylolhall '.[4]

Somervile's statutes made the confusion of authorities worse confounded. Hitherto there had been a master, a principal, and the two procurators. Somervile reduced the powers of the procurators, and instituted a sort of visitorial board, with the power awkwardly divided between the chancellor, the bishop of Durham, the prior of Durham college, and the two procurators.[5] With Dr. Poole " one wonders how this elaborate scheme worked, and particularly how the society of Balliol liked the supervision of the prior of Durham college, just beyond their garden-wall ".[6] Wyclif, as master, would feel the pinch of this interference, and no doubt this added to the growing dislike which he felt for all regulars. But shortly after Wyclif left

---

[1] Reg. Gynwell, f. 123 (modern pagination, ix, f. 172), quoted in Vaughan, 50 n., wrongly dated as 16 May in *Ziz.*, p. xiv. As the living became vacant on 11 May by the death of John Reyner the college lost no time.

[2] *Hist. MSS. Com.* iv. 443 ; Salter, 302-3. Shirley, *Ziz.* 526, n. 4, attributes the resignation to scruples as to " perpetual eleemosynary endowments ". But medieval fellows were expected to take a living on completing their course. At Queen's the refusal to do so vacated the fellowship (Rashdall, ii. 486 n.). At University in 1311 every fellow ' elected to a benefice of 5 marks ' was compelled to resign (*Mun. Ac.* 89). At Exeter resignation was involved in acceptance of any benefice (Boase, p. xxxii), altered in 1405 to a benefice worth 10 marks (*Pap. Let.* vi. 48). For Merton see *supra*, p. 69.

[3] Shirley, *Ziz.*, p. xiv, quoting Reg. Gynwell, f. 367.

[4] Sharpe, *Wills*, ii. 37. Cf. *ib.* ii. 115, for a similar bequest of 20s. to Balliol in 1368 by another mercer buried in St. Lawrence Jewry.

[5] Somervile's statutes in Salter, 297-8 ; *Reg. Pal. Dunelm.* (R.S.), iii. 395. Though the prior of Durham college is meant, there is a slight ambiguity in the document. In Salter, 297, it is ' prior seu custos monachorum Dunelm. Oxonie studencium per priorem Dunelm. prefectus collegio sit '. But on p. 298 ' prior eccles. Dunelm. et ejusdem loci conventus ' seals the agreement. Probably the custos was regarded as the deputy of the prior.

[6] Poole in Clark, *Coll. Ox.* 29.

Balliol important changes took place. On the 11th February 1364 Urban V at the instance of the master and fellows instructed Sudbury, bishop of London, to revise the statutes.[1] A year later commissioners were appointed,[2] one of whom was Ralph Erghum. As a result the privilege of studying theology after regency in arts was extended to the original fellows, whose commons by the falling in of Abbotsley had been raised from eightpence to a shilling a week. The office of principal of the artists was abolished—how Wyclif had got on with him we have no records to show, but trouble was bound to arise. The powers of visitation were handed back to the procurators, except that they ceased to interfere with the management of the estates, and that an appeal lay from their decisions to the bishop of London.[3] They were also granted the right of control of the Somervile foundation. No wonder that there was constant friction until their abolition in the sixteenth century.[4] This restoration to the procurators of their old powers, coupled with their new control of the theological fellows, will explain why Wyclif when he returned to Oxford to read for his doctorate in theology engaged rooms at Queen's. A return to Balliol was blocked, for the Franciscan procurator had power of admission and expulsion, and would no doubt have used it against one whose doings at Canterbury hall had stirred up the anger of the regulars.

§ 5

We wish that our limits would allow us to depict at large the inner life of the university in Wyclif's day. But for this we must refer the reader to the many excellent works which have made this their theme.[5] In them, too, he may learn of the struggles of the nations, and in special of the riot between North and South, and the consequent secession to Stamford (Feb. 1334). Driven back after six months by the help of the Crown every master henceforth—Wyclif among them—

---

[1] Salter, 299–302.
[2] *Hist. MSS. Com.* iv. 443 (5 Feb. 1365). For Erghum see *infra*, p. 248.
[3] Davis, 33, 62.
[4] By Fox in his new statutes (Salter, 309–14).
[5] Wood, Lyte, Mullinger, Rashdall, and the new excellent Mallet.

when he took his degree was forced to swear that he would not lecture at Stamford.¹ In Wyclif's day this oath represented a real dread of secession. Another oath was also necessary, meaningless even then. All bachelors 'when they respond in vespers' swore that 'they would never consent to the reconciliation of Henry Simeon', who in 1264 had been guilty of the manslaughter of a student, one of the causes of the famous secession which came so near to making Northampton a university city. Simeon was dead and turned to clay, but Wyclif, Wesley, and Newman all alike took an oath to prevent his return.²

But however detached it is difficult to imagine that Wyclif's Yorkshire blood was not stirred by the outrage to the northern proctor, Robert Ingram, in 1349, and the attempt to prevent the election as chancellor of William Hawksworth, who at one time had been a fellow of Balliol.³ A faction of masters, chiefly from Merton, had bound themselves to secede from Oxford unless they secured the election as chancellor of their candidate John Wylliot. So " they entered rudely into St. Mary's church and there with clamours and shoutings cried him up to be their chancellor, and on those that did oppose him they laid violent hands, beat, kicked about and cudgelled till some were sorely wounded and others in a manner killed ". The university chest was broken open, and the money and university seal stolen, while Ingram was driven from Oxford. But on the 2nd April 1349 Edward III ordered Ingram to be restored and the seal replaced, though Wylliot's election on Hawksworth's death ⁴ was not quashed.⁵

The Reformer would also be in Oxford in 1349 when under

¹ For this riot and its consequences see Wood, *Univ.* i. 425–31 ; *Collect.* i. 3–16 ; Rymer, ii. 891–2, 898, 903 ; *Mun. Ac.* 375 ; Leach, *Charters*, 282–8 ; *Vict. Co. Linc.* ii. 468–74. The documents in Salter, *Univ. Archiv.* i. 123–7, appear to be connected with this.
² See Poole in *Eng. Hist. Rev.* xxvii. 515–17. Both repealed in 1827.
³ Magrath, i. 91, 94–5, 333–8 ; ii. 413.
⁴ 8 Apr. (Wood, *City*, iii. 114).
⁵ Wood, *Univ.* i. 448–9 (the date in Wood, *Fasti*, 24, should be 19 Mar. not 20 Apr.) ; *Close Rolls Ed.* ix. 74. Wylliott was chancellor until Whitsuntide 1350 (*Snappe*, 328). As chancellors play a great part in our story it is well to note that in Wyclif's day they were generally elected for two years, at the end of the Lent term, in St. Mary's by the Great Congregation of regent-masters (*Mun. Ac.* 106–7, 147 ; *Pap. Let.* iv. 83). Chancellors were expected to be doctors of divinity or canon law (*Mun. Ac.* 493).

the blazing July sun the Black Death reigned in the noisome alleys and crowded halls and even in the more sanitary colleges.¹ "The school doors were shut, colleges and halls relinquished, and none scarce left to keep possession or to make up a competent number to bury the dead. 'Tis reported that no less than sixteen bodies in one day were carried to one church and yard to be buried." ² The university did not fully settle down again until 1353, a break of which due account should be taken in any chronology of the life of Wyclif. The virtual cessation of Balliol for two or three years ³ may explain the somewhat late date at which Wyclif seems to have taken his master's degree. The marvel is that pestilences in Oxford were not annual events, though two other outbreaks while Wyclif was at Oxford witnessed to their virulence. For if, as Professor Sedgwick once remarked, the "dirt was sublime in former years", it was "sublimest", perhaps, in the university, too "sublime" even for the medieval nose. From a royal letter to the bailiffs and mayor of Oxford on the 18th March 1301 ⁴ we learn that 'the air is so corrupted and infected' by the filth in the streets and the broken condition of the kennel and pavements that 'an abominable loathing is diffused among the aforesaid masters and scholars'. But the frequent orders of king or chancellor ⁵ directing the inhabitants to clean and repair the pavements or remove the piggeries—there were piggeries in the streets of Oxford in 1331, and in Cambridge at a much later date ⁶—would seem to have been of little avail; while the kennel itself became so bad, in spite of frequent injunctions for its repair, that in 1380 Richard II had to 'compel all clerks and laymen to repair the pavements before their tenements'.⁷ But pavement and kennel were not the only sources of plague. At Oxford in 1293 brewers and bakers

¹ The statement that Merton lost its warden (Brodrick, 157) is a mistake. See Little, 101 ; Wood, *City*, ii. 73.
² Wood, *Univ.* i. 449.
³ In Clark, *Linc. Docs.* 27–9, we see that Lincoln in the pestilence of 1507-44 was constantly dispersing, leaving only two fellows to keep house.
⁴ Wood, *Univ.* i. 361–2 ; *Close Rolls*, iv. 484 ; Prynne, *Records*, iii. 909.
⁵ *Mun. Ac.* 174, 177 ; *Cal. Pat.* ii. 208 (1331) ; *Collect.* iii. 132 ; *Close Rolls*, iii. 661 ; Wood, *Univ.* i. 423, 435–6 ; Salter, *Univ. Archiv.* i. 120 ; *Civ. Ox.* 10, 98.
⁶ *Collect.* iii. 135 ; Cooper, i. 133, 141.
⁷ *Mun. Ac* 792 ; *Cal. Pat.* i. 427, 546 ; Salter, *Univ. Archiv.* i. 212.

were accustomed to use the foul waters of the Trillmill stream for making bread and ale, though over it, as Wood tells us, there were many "houses of easement".[1] So thick were the deposits of rubbish in the stream, especially butchers' bones, that at a later date the stream was reduced thereby in breadth from fifteen feet to about six; it was in fact blocked up with filth of all kinds which the mill-dams of the Blackfriars and the Greyfriars tended to accumulate, so that dry seasons were generally followed by plague.[2] In Wyclif's day the site of New College was not only the resort of thieves who congregated by day and night in its gravel pits, but was full of the corpses of dead animals flung into it.[3] Nor was it until July 1339 that butchers at Oxford were ordered to discontinue the slaughter of beasts at Carfax,[4] though the working of parchments and skins had been prohibited within the walls in 1305.[5]

All things considered, the marvel is not that there were frequent plagues, but that Wyclif or any other scholar survived. At Oxford, in 1349, the plague was especially severe. Between the 21st April and the 16th June the city had three mayors.[6] Between 1349 and 1351 All Saints lost its rector and two chantry priests. St. Ebbe's lost two vicars in succession, who died before their names were recorded. At St. Giles's one vicar was instituted on the 6th April; he was dead and succeeded by another by the 29th August. At St. Mary's death was equally busy, as also in four other churches in Oxford.[7] One striking instance of the fearful mortality is given in the details of the university chests. They were full of 'books and other pledges deposited before the pestilence' whose owners had perished. As no one came to redeem them the pledges rotted

---

[1] Wood, *Univ.* i. 345, a practice still continued in Wood's time. Cf. in 1305 Salter, *Civ. Ox.* 11–12. In 1341 the district was blocked with dung (Hurst, 34).

[2] Hurst, 35, 41. For filth in the town ditch in 1371 see Ogle, 72. When the ditch was cleaned Merton threw the dirt back (*ib.* 83).

[3] Hurst, 146. Cf. for a similar state of things in the yard of Hereford cathedral in 1389, *Cal. Pat.* iv. 160.

[4] *Collect.* ii. 27–30, iii. 135; *Cal. Pat.* (1339), 186, 306; Salter, *Univ. Archiv.* i. 136; *Civ. Ox.* 13. The slaughter-houses were then removed to Slaying Lane without the South gate (Lumbard Lane) which then became the general rubbish heap (Hurst, 34; Macleane, 52).

[5] Maitland, *Mem. Parl.* 47.

[6] Gasquet, 126–7. In Wood, *City*, iii. 15, John de Bereford (not 'Dereford' as Gasquet) is alone given as mayor in 1348, 1349, 1350, 1351.

[7] Wood, *City*, iii. 74, 82, 85, 90, 91, 93, 97, 98.

away until at last they were cleared out by a commission of eight masters appointed for the purpose.[1] Another illustration may be found in the Trinitarian friars. As every friar had perished their house fell by escheat to the king.[2] We could well sacrifice many pages of Wyclif's polemics for a few pictures from his pen of Oxford during the plague. But not a line is vouchsafed to us.

Wyclif would also be a student in Oxford at the time of the Great Slaughter of 1355, a riot which broke out in a tavern over the quality of the wine, but whose real cause was the vexation of the citizens over their lost rights. " On Tuesday February 10th "—we quote the lively narrative of Wood : [3]

' being the feast of S. Scolastica the Virgin, came Walter de Springheuse and other clerks to the tavern called Swyndlestock (being now the Mermaid tavern at Quatrevois),[4] and there, calling for wine, John de Croydon, the vintner, brought them some ; but they, disliking it, as it would seem, and he avouching it to be good, several snappish words passed between them. At length, the vintner giving them stubborn and saucy language, they threw the wine and vessel at his head. The vintner thereupon receding with great passion and aggravating the abuse to those of his family and neighbourhood, several came in, encouraged him not to put up the abuse, and withal told him that they would faithfully stand by him.'

Within a few hours the bell of St. Martin's was summoning " town ", while the bell of St. Mary's by the chancellor's orders called " gown " to arms. The leader of " town " seems to have been the owner of the Swyndlestock, John Bereford ' a viper ', now ' grown rich ', mayor also and five times member of parliament, who at one time had been a servant of the scholars. The first day's scrimmage was bloodless. The students averred that on the next day they were at work in the schools. But at dinner-time (11 a.m.), as " gown " was disporting itself

---

[1] *Mun. Ac.* 255. Some of the pledges were still ' incistatis ' (' in the chest ') in 1420 (*ib.* 275).

[2] Wood, *City*, ii. 481.

[3] The main sources are as follows : Wood, *Univ.* i. 455–70 (its wrong date, 1354, has misled most, including Rashdall, ii. 403 f., and led to much confusion) ; Salter, *Civ. Ox.* 127 f. ; *Univ. Archiv.* i. 148 f. ; Rogers, *City Docs.* 245–68 ; Ogle, 51 f. ; the poems printed by Hearne in Leland, *Itin.* vi. 141–6 ; *Collect.* iii. 165–87 ; and the important *Charter Rolls*, v. 143–6 (also in Salter, *Univ. Archiv.* i. 152 f.) for the University privileges. See also Rymer, iii. 300 f.

[4] i. e. Carfax, really derived from *furca*, not *voie* (Hurst, 58). The tavern in question is now a business house with curious old cellars.

in the fields of Beaumont, eighty men assembled at St. Giles', and began the attack with bows and arrows. " Gown " tried, but too late, to shut the gates of the city, for two thousand armed rustics, alleging a royal edict, were already pouring in by the West gate, " with a black dismal flag, erect and displayed ", and crying ' slay, slay ! havoc, havoc ! smite fast ! give good knocks ! ' By the close of the day " town " had won ; five halls had been pillaged and burnt. The next day while the chancellor, Thomas Brouweon,[1] was away at Woodstock seeking redress from the king the riot was renewed. Fourteen halls were broken open " with iron bars and other weapons ". When the friars, forgetting in the common danger their feud with the seculars, came to the rescue, not with carnal weapons, but bearing the host and chanting a litany for peace, their crucifix was dashed to the ground " by these confounded sons of Satan ". In the upshot "gown" was driven headlong from the city. Even those in the colleges fled, save only the students of Merton, safe behind their solid walls.[2] It is not without interest to note that of the sixty-three killed or mortally wounded many appear to have been Irish. The bodies of the slain were " scornfully cast into houses of easement ". That Wyclif took part in the fray we should doubt. He was probably among those who fled the city, though possibly Balliol, outside the walls, was sufficiently safe. He would, however, witness the subsequent triumph of Gown over the ' Canaanites and lepers of townsmen '. For retribution both from Church and State followed at once.[3] A cessation was proclaimed, which was not abolished until the 11th June, at the request of the Crown—Wyclif would fume probably at this interruption of his studies. An interdict by the bishop [4] was not finally removed until the 7th June 1357, after protracted negotiations with Bereford. The king within a month took the university under his protection and made the quarrel his own. Two hundred citizens were

[1] Salter, *Snappe*, 328. In Wood, *Fasti*, 25, given as Humphrey de Cherleton who succeeded. The help of the ' strong ' brothers Cherleton is invoked in *Collect.* iii. 185.
[2] Stow, *Annals*, 255.
[3] As a result of the mistake in date (1354) nearly all writers have spoken of the long delay of the Crown. It acted within three weeks, 5 Mar. 1355 (Salter, *Univ. Archiv.* i. 148 ; Ogle, 51–2).
[4] Imposed 14 Mar. 1355. See Reading, *Chron.* 267 *n*.

imprisoned, and a huge fine imposed of £250, in addition to the cost of damages.¹ Finally, on the 27th June 1355 Edward issued from the Tower a long charter in which he handed over to the university almost the whole of the privileges still remaining to the city. Henceforth the inhabitants were more than ever but hewers of wood and drawers of water for their enemies.² But of all this Wyclif tells us nothing.

Wyclif is equally uninterested in the other stirring events of his time. That riots should not appeal to him we can understand ; it is more difficult to explain why in thirty volumes he makes no reference to certain great academic issues, as for instance the dispute in 1350 between the university and its diocesan, John Gynwell. The question at issue was the position of the chancellor ; did the university elect or merely nominate subject to the bishop's approval and the appearance of the chancellor-designate before him in person ? For sixty years the custom of the chancellor-designate had been to send two or three members of the university to Lincoln with his excuses, danger to discipline if the chancellor were absent and the like, and these had been grudgingly accepted. Gynwell brought matters to a head by refusing in 1350 to confirm the election of William de Polmorva.³ Defeated on an appeal to Islip and Innocent VI, the dispute smouldered on until in 1367 the election of William Courtenay—Wyclif's future opponent—as chancellor and his refusal to appear at Lincoln led to the suppression by Urban V of the need of episcopal confirmation. A later attempt by bishop Buckingham on the 4th May 1369 to cite the new chancellor, Adam de Toneworth, before him on the ground of irregular election ended in Urban V once more putting the matter beyond all doubt.⁴ The joy of Oxford would not be lessened by the failure of Cambridge in 1374 to assert a similar independence against that masterful opponent of all

¹ 16 July 1355 (Rymer, iii. 309). On 1 July 1356 £50 was paid, whereupon the University gave an acquittance for £500 (Salter, *Civ. Ox.* 135).

² For the steps whereby the university secured control of the town see Rashdall, ii. 388–417. At one time Oxford possessed the same privileges as London (*Collect.* iii. 111, 131 ; Ogle, 35 f.).

³ Not ' Polmorna ' as Wilkins, iii. 3–9 ; Wood, *Univ.* i. 451 ; *Coll.* 139.

⁴ *Eng. Hist. Rev.* xxvi. 502–12 ; *Pap. Let.* iv. 66, 83 ; Wilkins, iii. 3–9, 75 ; Wood, *Univ.* i. 452–3, 481–2. The extracts from 1290 to 1367 from the Lincoln registers have been printed in full by Salter, *Snappe*, 40–89.

innovations, bishop Arundel of Ely.[1] Wyclif, possibly, was superior to such emotions.

There are some matters, however, connected with Oxford on which Wyclif has a word to say. He refers to the reputed fall in numbers: 'once there were 60,000 students whereas to-day there are but 3,000', and gives as the cause the appropriation of churches, which is even more absurd than its assignment by another writer to the effect of the St. Scholastica riots in 1355. This decline was a commonplace with all writers, and Wyclif was but repeating, with exaggeration, the statement of Fitzralph that Oxford had fallen from 30,000 to 6,000. The cause, said Fitzralph, was the fear of parents lest the friars should kidnap their lads! Gascoigne at a later date tells us that he had ascertained 'from the rolls of the ancient chancellors' that 'before the Great Plague there had been 30,000', which is double Rishanger's figure for the days of Henry III. Juggling with figures was a medieval weakness, and as arabic numerals were only slowly coming into common use [2] addition was difficult and imagination hard to check. We see this in the statement that in 1209 there were 3,000 students and masters in residence, whose migration, in part to Reading, in part to Cambridge, led to the foundation of a rival university. Fortunately we are able to check this wild guess, for only a few years earlier Gerald of Wales had entertained in two days the whole university in the small rooms of a medieval inn.[3] 'Twenty thousand' seems to have been a stock figure for universities, as we see in the Syrian account of Paris written in 1287 by the Nestorian monk, Rabban Çauma.[4] That the Black Death, which halved the population of England, had left its mark on the universities is doubtless correct, though decline had begun before, as we see from the complaint in 1346 of the unoccupied

---

[1] Cooper, i. 112. [2] See for proof, *Chart. Par.* ii. 673 in 1350.
[3] Gir. Cambrensis, *Typographica Hibernica* (*Opera*, i. 72–3).
[4] For these medieval estimates see Wyclif, *Eccles.* 374 ; Fitzralph, *Defensio Curatorum* in Brown, *Fascic.* ii. 473 ; *Flores Hist.* ii. 138 ; Matt. Paris, *Chron. Mag.* ii. 525–6, 569 ; Rishanger, *Chron.* 22 ; *Collect.* iii. 177 ; for Rabban Çauma, *Chart. Par.* iii, p. xvii ; Gascoigne, 202. For later figures and complaints see *Ep. Acad.* i. 155 f., or Wood, *Univ.* i. 589 (1438), and for Reformation times, *ib.* ii. 66, 85, 104, 113. For the exaggerations of medieval figures in general see *Eng. Hist. Rev.* xviii. 625–9. For the Leipzig exaggerations see *infra*, p. 114 *n.*

houses in Oxford. What the actual numbers were it is difficult to say; estimates vary between three hundred and fifteen hundred.[1] All we know is that the lay population of Oxford in 1377 of both sexes over fourteen years of age, apart from students, numbered 2,377.[2] As we never hear that 'gown' outnumbered 'town', it is probable that 'gown' was considerably under a thousand.

On the moral condition of Oxford Wyclif is silent, for the reference to the beneficed clerks 'who study with the cup and strumpets' is not from his pen.[3] We may attribute this silence either to his love of Oxford, or to a scholar's ignorance of the real facts. Drinking was the cause of many troubles. Half the householders of Oxford brewed and sold beer.[4] So many were the taverns round Carfax that the whole district was called the Vintry.[5] Another cause was the absence of all sports, using the word in its modern sense. Respectable amusements were few. Even chess was reprimanded, and at New College was classed with 'noxious, inordinate and unhonest games'.[6] 'Running in Beaumont' fields and walking on holidays to a cross 'on a bridge a mile from Oxford' were however recognized. In one of his rare personal touches Wyclif speaks of the value of walking for health.[7] The usual results of repression followed: 'throwing stones, balls or other things in chapel, cloister, stall or hall and also jumping, wrestling and other reckless and disorderly games in the same'. Beaumont

---

[1] Rashdall ii. 402 considers the numbers in 1315 were 1,500, and Rogers, *City Docs.* 7 agrees for 1380. Rashdall bases this upon the 1,500 psalters, i. e. prayers the Crown required from the university in 1315 (Salter, *Univ. Archiv.* i. 96). Salter, *ib.* ii. 275–6, puts the numbers at 300 undergraduates, 100 bachelors, 70 regents and 150 non-regents, a total which would agree with my estimate from the civil population. One cause of decline was the growing attraction of London as a school of law.

[2] Poll tax returns in Oman, *Great Revolt*, 164.

[3] *Eng. Works*, 156, probably Purvey's. Cf. Purvey's statement *re* sodomy in his Prologue to the Bible (Forshall and Madden, i. 51). For university morals see Bacon, *Op. Ined.* 412; *Chart. Par.* iii. 53–4, and the well-known indictment of Jacques de Vitry, *Hist. Occid.* (Douai, 1597), 278.

[4] Salter, *Univ. Archiv.* ii. 183.

[5] Hurst, 54. The digging out by the publicans of cellars was the cause of raising the level (*supra*, p. 60), for they threw the soil into the street (*ib.* 58).

[6] Workman, *Letters of Hus*, 151; Wyclif, *Sel. Eng. Works*, iii. 286; Rashdall, ii. 671.

[7] Wood, *City*, i. 440, ii. 346 *n.*; Wyclif, *Ente Praed.* 187.

became the battle-ground on more than one occasion of the two nations, ' with banners and flags to distinguish each division '.[1]

Wyclif also made his protest against the needless expenses which were cutting Oxford off from the life of the nation, and which would account for the fall in numbers. The cost of a university education had become as great as to-day. The chief difficulty in obtaining a degree was the financial outlay, the course of seven, ten, or sixteen years according to faculty; for a theologian almost half a lifetime and but uncertain benefices from the pope at the end. To crown all there were the feasts to all the regents on the night after inception, costing according to the rank of the candidate from ten marks to seventy pounds, not to mention suits of clothes for the stationers, paid to them ' from time immemorial ',[2] buckskin gloves and twenty shillings for each of the two bedels.[3] We would give much to know what Wyclif's own inception feast cost; his opponent, William Woodford, spent forty pounds. Or did Wyclif get some one to ' determine ' for him ? For a merciful university, unless indeed the proctors object, allows a Courtenay or Arundel when they determine ' to take under them ' a certain number of ' poor '[4] candidates whose expenses they paid, and who in return would form an appreciative claque for the great man's own determination.[5]

Wyclif flung himself with zeal, at any rate in later life, into the struggle at Oxford between the seculars and regulars; in reality—for the monks counted for little, either in numbers or intellectual contribution—between the seculars and friars.

---

[1] Rashdall, ii. 672 ; Wood, *Univ.* i. 257.
[2] *Mun. Ac.* 324–5 ; cf. *Chart. Par.* iii. 475.
[3] For Wyclif's protest see *Sel. Eng. Works*, iii. 376 ; *Op. Min.*, 333, 347. In *Blas.*, 246 he says friars spent ' 3,000 Toursgrossi '. This was the sum fixed at Vienna in 1311 as the maximum allowed (*Chart. Par.* ii. 169). For protests by friars themselves in 1331 and 1344 see *ib.*, ii. 344, 538. Benedict XII tried to reduce these expenses (*Chart. Par.* ii. 450, 464, 471, 481, 538, 679).
[4] i. e. not more than 40 marks a year (*Mun. Ac.* 431) which Wyclif would not have. In Paris fixed at 16*d.* a week in 1350 (*Chart. Par.* ii. 674), which leads me to doubt the reading in *Mun. Ac.*
[5] Rashdall, ii. 444 ; *Chart. Par.* ii. 674 ; *Mun. Ac.* 243. It was possible to compound for inception ; in 1428 a friar at £10 (Little, 258 ; cf. *Mun. Ac.* 565. For the determination feast of Richard Holland in 1395 see Rogers, *Prices*, ii. 643–5. Wyclif's opponent Wodehull (*infra*, p. 175) tried in vain to incept under William Wittlesey, afterwards archbishop. For this amusing case see *Mun. Ac.* 220–4.

The story of the friars at Oxford, apart from the Franciscans, yet awaits its historian. All the orders were there; they were in many ways the glory and pride of the university. They had contributed more than their share of great schoolmen. But between the seculars and the friars there was more than one matter of dispute, which jealousy and diversity of aim turned at times into burning questions. Both at Oxford and Paris there was the fight over the oath of obedience to the university.[1] This at Oxford, however, never became serious, for the university was founded upon arts whose masters, in theory, were supreme. The issue was different with the second claim of the friars. They tried to dispense with the course in arts, or a great portion of it, by means of graces. Their business, they said, was theology; they would spend more time on the Bible and less on Aristotle.[2] In spite of the pleading of Adam Marsh the university in 1253 decided that no one should be admitted to lecture in theology who had not taken his degree in arts, ' at least as bachelors '. Only thus, as Bacon contended, could theology meet the demands of ' human wisdom '. Any attempt to extort privileges ' by the power of any superior ' would involve expulsion. The measure was qualified by reserving to the chancellor and regents a dispensing power.[3] For fifty years this compromise worked smoothly. But at the commencement of the fourteenth century there was a great struggle, which ended, however, in the friars being forced to make an unconditional surrender (Dec. 1320). Henceforth they were forced to preach their examination sermons, no longer as heretofore in their own churches but in the ' noisy ' St. Mary's. A single master it was decided could veto a grace, and all the concession the friars could obtain was that the regent must swear that he had not 'refused a grace out of malice or rancour ' but only ' for the common utility and honour of the university '. Within ten days of his veto he must state his reasons, which must be satisfactory to the regent-masters in theology.

---

[1] Rashdall, i. 369–92; *Collect.* ii. 198–9; Lea, i. 280–8; *Chart. Par.* i. 242–4.

[2] The friars lectured on the Bible for two years, not the ' cursory ' one year of the seculars (*Chart. Par.* ii. 692).

[3] For this struggle see Rashdall in *Collect.* ii. 195–273; Bacon, *Op. Ined.* 425–6. Cf. also *Pap. Let.* ii. 111–12, 167, 199, 495; Rymer, ii. 178, 198, 305; *Close Rolls Ric.* iii. 378–9, 511.

Towards the end of Wyclif's career at Oxford trouble arose. On the 3rd February 1377 [1] at a congregation held at Oxford the usual 'graces, dispensations and reconciliations were granted according to custom'. But certain masters of arts who 'through malice or negligence were not present in the congregation' attempted to veto the grace. We do not suppose that Wyclif was among them; he had troubles of his own in London at this time, in which he needed the assistance of the friars.[2] But, no doubt, his friends, Hereford and Repingdon, would be active. The assistance of Edward was at once invoked, and on the 26th February 1377 a commission was appointed with power 'to impose silence on all who are contrarient'. The result was 'an agreement made in a solemn convocation held on the 26th March 1377', and the confirmation of the same on the 3rd January 1378 by letters patent, henceforth the charter to which distressed friars could turn. Thus in March 1384, and again in March 1388, Richard II came to the help of 'the men of religion' against the 'malice' of the chancellors and regent-masters of Oxford, and in the following August sent orders that the agreement should be strictly enforced.

Graces given by the Senate were bad enough; they were worse when obtained by letters from influential people. There was also a bitter argument between the university and the friars as to the age at which they might admit novices to their order. 'These are the names', ran a university proclamation of 1358,[3]

'of the wax-doctors. Doctors are so called who seek to extort graces from the university by means of letters of lords sealed with wax, or because they run from hard study as wax runs from the face of the fire. Be it known that such wax-doctors are always of the mendicant orders, the cause whereof we have found. For by apples and drink, as the people say, they draw boys to their religion, and do not instruct them after their profession as their age demands; but let them wander about begging, and so waste the time in which they could best learn, by gaining the favour of friends, ladies and lords to the peril of the lads and the detriment of the order. Such

---

[1] For the matter which follows see *Pat. Ed.* xvi. 491; *Pat. Ric.* i. 80, ii. 387, iii. 378–9, 511; Ayliffe, *Univ. Ox.* ii. App. lxxi–iii.

[2] *Infra*, p. 286 f.

[3] The cause seems to have been the attempt of a Franciscan from Sicily to obtain the B.D. by letters from Edward.

men when they come to preach are only reciters who imitate the ass of Balaam.'[1]

These two matters were the two chief subjects of dispute between the seculars and the friars in Wyclif's earlier career. The charge of stealing children had been openly made by Fitzralph at Avignon :

'An instance came to my knowledge this very day. As I came out of my inn an honest man from England, who has come to this court to obtain a remedy, told me that immediately after last Easter the friars at Oxford abducted in this manner his son, who was not yet 13 years of age, and when he went there he could not speak with him except under the supervision of a friar.'[2]

Accordingly the university in the same statute of 1358 had enacted that inasmuch as

'the nobles of this kingdom, nay very many of the vulgar, are afraid to send their sons to the University in tender years, the very time at which they would advance most in study, for fear lest the mendicants should entice such lads to their order. The said University, zealous in the bowels of piety both for the number of her sons and the quiet of her students enacts that if any mendicant friar shall induce, or cause to be induced, any member of the University under eighteen years of age to join the said friars or shall in any wise assist in his abduction, no graduate belonging to the community of which such a friar is a member shall be permitted for the coming year to give or attend lectures in the University or elsewhere when such exercises would count as a discharge of the statutable requirements in this University.'[3]

As for the 'wax-doctors', such sycophants were henceforth to be incapable of taking a degree. But this last evil still continued : 'What cursedness is this', said Wyclif, 'to get a cap of Masterdom by prayer of lords and great gifts, and making of huge feasts of a hundred and many hundred pounds.'[4]

---

[1] *Mun. Ac.* 207–8 ; cf. Denifle in *Chart. Par.* iii, p. x. For instances of 'wax-doctors', who abounded on the continent, see *Chart. Par.* ii. 551, 552, 557, iii. 61 *et passim* ; *Pap. Let.* iv. 161, 164, 166, &c.

[2] Brown, *Fascic.* ii. 473. See *infra*, ii. 103.

[3] *Mun. Ac.* 205–6. Wyclif and his followers refer to the matter in the following, all dating from after 1376. *Apost.* 28 ; *Op. Min.* 339 (written in 1383). *Polem. Works*, ii. 468 ; *Blas.* 212–13. *Eng. Works*, 9, 10, 68, 133, 223, 269, 278. *Sel. Eng. Works*, ii. 380, iii. 373. The same charge is made in *Pol. Poems*, ii. 22 ; *Lantern*, 13 ; Bacon, *Op. Ined.* 426. For actual cases see records in *Pap. Let.* iv. 352, vi. 223 (also *Reg. Stafford*, 376), vii. 77–8.

[4] *Sel. Eng. Works*, iii. 376 ; *Blas.* 245, 247. Friars themselves protested against the practice (*Pap. Let.* v. 19–20 ; *Pat. Ric.* iv. 330 ; Rymer, vii. 690, viii. 334).

The charge of 'stealing children' the friars did not deny. But they pleaded with friar Dan Topias that

To tille folks to Godward, I hold is no theft.[1]

Nor were there lacking friars to take up the cudgels in defence. In addition to Conway, the opponent of Fitzralph, William Woodford and William Folvyle of Cambridge entered the fray.[2] Meanwhile the friars sought the repeal of the statute. Urban V came to their help and ordered its removal from the books, first of Cambridge and then of Oxford.[3] The provincials of the four orders were instructed to lay their grievances before the king. They succeeded in May 1366 in obtaining its annulling on condition that they abandoned their suits against the two universities at Avignon or elsewhere. In spite of this, some of the friars would have resumed the struggle in 1367 ' by citing the Chancellor to Rome, had not the King sent his prohibition '.[4]

§ 6

From the life of Oxford we turn to its studies. Here again we must refer the reader for details to other writers. Nevertheless some knowledge is necessary if he would understand Wyclif's career at Oxford. In the first place there is the length of the course. At Oxford the full time required up to inception in arts was about seven or eight years. But this could be shortened by dispensations and graces, whether university or papal. Of neither of these would Wyclif avail himself. For the doctor's degree in theology the time was about the same; at Paris in 1366 sixteen years for the whole course including arts, and at Oxford it would not be different.[5] As we shall see later, between Wyclif's arts course and theology course there was a gap of some years.

The first great event in the artist's life was Responsions, a

---

[1] *Pol. Poems*, ii. 83.
[2] Little, 80 *n.*; Bale, *Index Script.* 124. But see *infra*, 185, n. 3.
[3] Nov. 1364, June 1365 (*Pap. Let.* iv. 52, 91).
[4] *Rot. Parl.* ii. 290; Wood, *Univ.* i. 480; *Collect.* iii. 139; Cooper, i. 108–9; *Pat. Ed.* xiii. 408.
[5] From *Pap. Let.* v. 20 we see the course for Carmelites in England was (1) Seven years arts; (2) Seven years theology; (3) Lectures on the *Sentences* two years; (4) Lectures on the Bible one year.

preliminary test to ascertain the candidate's fitness to 'determine'. This was held in the December of his fourth or fifth year, and consisted of disputes in grammar or logic with a master, the master sitting, the candidate standing, together with a formal examination before four regents, two australs and two boreals, chosen for the purpose before Ash Wednesday. Like every other event Responsions ended with a feast, with cost limited however to 'sixteen pence, under penalty of the prison, except by special licence of chancellor and proctors'. The candidate, no longer known as a 'sophist' but a 'questionist', now prepared for his 'determination' or tourney with the students of inferior status, held in the first week of Lent, in a 'school' hired by the candidate—as there were thirty-two schools in all [1] the supply was ample, and the cost not excessive.[2] If the candidates numbered under twenty they were all to determine in the same week, the event lasting seven days, from nine to twelve and one to five. The tourney began with the ringing of the bells at St. Mary's, and ended with the ringing of compline at St. Frideswyde's. While the candidate was preparing himself, his friends used every kind of bait in angling for a distinguished audience, providing wine, illuminating with wax candles his school, and the like. If all other devices failed the student would sally into the streets and drag in passers-by. Determination over, the student became a 'bachelor', originally a cant name for London apprentices with political leanings.[3] As such he lectured on certain books of Aristotle. After two or three years he was entitled to incept. This he did by disputing on a subject chosen by himself, a ceremony known as *Quodlibeta*. He then received from the chancellor a licence to incept as master, including the valued 'ius ubique docendi'. The 'licentiate', as he was called, took an oath 'that he purposes to incept within a year'. Six months later the crowning event of inception began with a disputation known as Vespers held on the evening before at St. Mildred's or at the Austin friars.[4] The next day in St. Mary's he delivered

---

[1] See lists in Wood, *City*, i. 570 f. Of these Osney owned fourteen.
[2] At Paris the price ranged from 6 sols. a week to 18 (*Chart. Par.* i. 531 ; ii. 673, 674, n. 5).
[3] See Tait in *Eng. Hist. Rev.* xvii. 89–95, and also *N. E. D.*
[4] Wood, *City*, ii. 96.

a formal lecture in the presence of the masters, and received the book, the ring, the biretta,[1] the kiss of fellowship of a regent master. Withdrawing to a crucifix in the choir he awaited the congratulations of his new brethren, whom he afterwards entertained at the costly inception feast.[2]

After a brief absence from Oxford Wyclif proceeded to take his doctorate in theology. Let us follow him in his course. In the age before Wyclif Oxford had supplied the world with great logicians, Duns, Ockham, and others, whose theological training was generally completed at Paris. But the monopoly in theology of Paris and Oxford was a thing of the past. At one time Paris or Oxford would have scorned to receive bachelors in theology of another university. Now at the bidding of popes men were licenced in Paris who had never studied there at all; in fact, such was the audacity of some candidates that they sought promotion at Paris though they had studied in towns where there was no ' studium generale ' but only ' mere stalls of pigs ', as the Curia in recording the petition contemptuously called them.[3] The great war had destroyed the old internationalism. Unlike his predecessors of renown, it was impossible in the days of Crecy and Poitiers for Wyclif to make Paris for any part of his career his spiritual home.

The first three years of the course were spent in attending lectures on the text of the Vulgate, without discussion of theology. There then followed two years' study of the great medieval text-book, Peter Lombard's *Sentences*. The libraries of Europe are full of the lectures on the *Sentences* of schoolmen, small and great. ' In the *Sentences* ', said abbot Henry of Cluny in 1309, ' the profound mysteries of all Scripture are contained '.[4] The book wielded a similar authority in theology

---

[1] Those interested in medieval academical costume may be referred to a series of articles by E. C. Clarke in *Arch. Jour.*, vols 50 and 61.

[2] I have not thought it needful to give the full references for the above, which is based on my own study of the badly edited *Mun. Ac.*, and the invaluable *Chart. Par.* It is needless to mention my constant obligation to Rashdall. In many details certainty is impossible, as regulations varied from time to time.

[3] *Chart. Par.* ii. 547.

[4] *Ib.* ii. 688; cf. Rashdall, i. 465, and the modern word " sententious ". Bacon, *Op. Ined.*, 81-2, 328-30, was almost alone in his refusal of exaggerated respect for the *Sentences*.

to that of Aristotle in logic, and the works of Wyclif are full of references to it. At the end of five years the candidate obtained his bachelor's degree. The 'cursor', as he was now called, entered upon his 'opponency' by a lecture called the 'principium'; then lectured for a whole year on one book of the Old and one of the New Testament, his lectures being limited to a chapter a time.[1] If a secular, such lectures were generally worthless—Wyclif would be a rare exception—often given by permission in the Long Vacation, hence the modern "cursory".[2] In his seventh year, Wyclif, now known as a 'sententiary', would himself begin to lecture on the *Sentences*, first swearing that he would put forth no proposition contrary to the Catholic faith.[3] He began lectures on each of the four books by a 'principium' before the doctors, the first delivered between the 14th September and the 9th October, the others about the first day of January, March, and May. At Paris these principia were always opened by Carmelites and closed by Dominicans.[4] In these lectures Wyclif would be 'opposed' by other sententiaries of the same year. As we shall see later, the 'opposition' to Wyclif was more than formal, for it was as a sententiary, about 1370, that he first put forward a debatable doctrine of the Eucharist. Wyclif would also be called upon to dispute with every regent doctor of divinity. That the principia had to be delivered without manuscript will account for so few surviving. Before the sententiary's treatise was handed to the stationers for publication [5] it had first to be examined by the chancellor and the masters of the faculty.[6]

After finishing the *Sentences* the candidate, now called a 'baccalarius formatus', was required within a year to preach a Latin sermon at St. Mary's—limited to not more than an hour and a half, or at most two hours—and to give a conference ('collatio') in the afternoon 'either by himself or another'.[7]

---

[1] *Chart Par.* ii. 692, 698, iii. 143. The 'principium' of D'Ailli on St. Mark is printed in Brown, *Fascic.* ii. 513-18, but has not much to do with St. Mark.
[2] On this neglect of the Bible for the *Sentences* see Rashdall, ii. 453 n., and cf. *Chart. Par.* ii. 588, 698; iii. 44, 144. In 1387 the faculty at Paris dispensed with the Bible altogether (*ib.* iii. 442). Cf. Bacon, *Op. Ined.*, 329.
[3] *Chart. Par.* ii. 675; iii. 121.   [4] *Ib.* ii. 692 n., 698, 700; iii. 144.
[5] Wyclif's sententiary treatise was the *de Benedicta Incarnatione*. See *infra*, p. 138.
[6] *Chart. Par.* ii. 698.   [7] *Mun. Ac.*, 392, 395-6; Rashdall, i. 468.

At last,[1] after all these toils the candidate received his reward. At Oxford all the doctors were required to testify as to his fitness, and a single adverse vote was fatal,[2] a proof that when Wyclif took his doctorate in 1372 the great quarrel had not yet begun. An elaborate and ceremonious disputation called 'Vespers' was held in St. Mary's on the eve of inception.[3] Eight days' notice to all regents and bachelors of the two questions to be discussed had to be given by the candidate, who was also expected to solicit attendance by a personal canvass. After the candidate and presiding master had finished, all the bachelors present brought forward their arguments in turn. Vespers ended with a speech of the president in praise of the inceptor—would that we possessed the speech given at the inception of Wyclif, or knew the name of the presiding master, very often a distinguished friend.[4] Vespers over, the candidate regaled his friends with cakes and wine, who then went round to the great and learned inviting their attendance at the final ceremony on the morrow.

The final ceremony or 'aulatio'[5] was held in St. Mary's, if possible in the middle of term. At Paris the candidate received on the previous day a letter, technically called the '*signetum*', from the chancellor. 'Honoured sir', it ran, 'come to-morrow to the bishop's court at the accustomed hour to receive your licence in sacred theology'. The bearer of this billet expected wine and spices, and took back 'secretly for the chancellor' 'ten gold denarii, at least of the value of ten francs', as well as from one to four florins for his servants. At Oxford you can distinguish the candidate, who is sitting on the left hand of the chancellor, from other Masters by his wearing boots, which came up, says Wood, " to the middle of the leg, with little or no tops to them ". The other Masters were

---

[1] At Paris four years at least after finishing the *Sentences, Chart. Par.* i. 79; ii. 697, 698, 700; iii. 479–80.

[2] *Mun. Ac.*, 204 (July 1357).

[3] For the ceremony of 'Vespers' I have followed Denifle in *Chart. Par.* ii, app. 693–4, altered here and there from *Mun. Ac.*, 393, 432–3.

[4] e.g. Grosseteste at Adam Marsh's (Bale, i. 306), archb. Kilwardby at Cantilupe's in 1273 (Wood, *City*, ii. 318).

[5] Or 'dies aulae', because held at Paris 'ad aulam episcopi'. On the 'aulatio' see *Chart. Par.* ii. 344 n., 683–4, 694, 704; iii. 405; *Mun. Ac.*, 392, 433. D'Ailli's *Resumpta* is in Brown, *Fascic.* ii. 525–40.

only allowed to wear "pynsons", which Wood explains as "pantables", "sandals", "slops", or "slippers", and states that these are "cut off from their shoes when they are made regents".[1] With the words 'Incipiatis in nomine Patris, Filii et Spiritus Sancti, Amen' the chancellor placed the doctor's biretta on the candidate's head, who thereupon mounted the cathedra and gave a short address in praise of the Scriptures, a theme that would be very congenial to Wyclif. 'Quickly finishing this' he maintained the two theses left over from the Vespers—the technical name for the first thesis was *Resumpta*—the chancellor himself entering the lists against him, as well as other masters of whom one must be an old man. Disputation over, they all walk back in procession to the high altar and escort the new doctor back to college or hall. 'Then the licentiates go round to the houses of the masters to thank them', and the day ends with a costly feast. Later on in the year the doctor entered on his regency by taking up in his first lecture the 'resumpta' of his 'aulatio'.

The books that Wyclif would read as a student, and the allotment of the same to their special years, is too technical a subject to be discussed in these pages.[2] Some indication of the width of his knowledge is given elsewhere. But there are one or two matters in this connexion which claim attention. It is impossible to turn over the pages of Wyclif's writings without discovering his bent for mathematics and physics. In Wyclif's day the arabic notation was only slowly driving out its cumberous predecessors; the symbol zero was still rarely used; a system devised by John of Basing—"a combination of a constant vertical with varying horizontal or vertical lines", multiplication indicated by reversing the sign, e.g. $\mathsf{J} = 8$, $\mathsf{L} = 80$—was not extinct. At Oxford the arithmetic of Boethius was still in use, though the mixture of arithmetic and algebra called 'algorism' was taking its place. But in spite of these difficulties Oxford in Wyclif's day was noted for its study of mathematics. The *tractatus de Sphaera* of the Yorkshireman, John of Holywood, a village near Halifax, had a

---

[1] Wood, *Univ.* i. 73–4; *Mun. Ac.*, 450.
[2] For the curriculum at Oxford in 1340, and Paris in 1366 see *Mun. Ac.*, 142–3 (cf. *ib.*, 34–6); *Chart. Par.* iii. 143–8 (cf. *ib.* ii. 691–708).

European reputation, as also the *Perspectiva Communis* of archbishop Peckham. Archbishop Bradwardine was as noted for his mathematical works as for his stern predestinarianism.[1] Of mathematicians at Merton among Wyclif's contemporaries, William Rede, John Ashingdon, Simon Bredon were specially noted.[2] There were also two friars of great repute, the Franciscan John Somer whose fame is recorded by Chaucer,[3] and the Carmelite Nicholas of Lynn who composed a calendar for the latitude and longitude of Oxford for the years 1386–1462.[4] From these men and others Wyclif picked up considerable mathematical lore. One of his many mathematical allusions is of interest. He rejoiced that the squaring of the circle could now be done ('scibilis') though 'not known in the time of Aristotle'.[5] In physics he was especially interested in the properties of light.[6] 'When I was still young', writes Wyclif, 'I made extensive collections from manuals on optics.'[7] He never refers, however, to Bacon—a fact significant of the little repute he held in England—but generally to the *Perspectiva* of the Pole, Vitellio or Witelo. Wyclif tells us that faith, like lenses properly arranged, will enable us to see things

[1] For Holywood (†1256) see Cantor, ii. c. 45. Thirty eds. of his *Sphaera* were printed before 1500. The reading of this work was obligatory at Oxford, *Mun. Ac.*, 243. For Bradwardine, *infra*, p. 120 f.
[2] For these see Brodrick, Bale, Tanner, and for Bredon (†1372) Cantor, ii. 111 f.; James, *MSS. Pet.*, 93, 356, 364; *MSS. Caius*, iii. 227.
[3] *Astrolabe* (ed. Skeat, iii. 177, cf. 353). See also Little, 245–6; James, *MSS. Johns*, 269, who shows that it was really an edition of the tables of Alphonso of Castile (1252). For the many astrolabes at Oxford in Wyclif's day see R. T. Gunther, *Early Science in Oxford* (1923), ii. 206 ff.
[4] Chaucer, *op. cit.* See also Little, 245, and in *D. N. B.*
[5] *Eccles.* 97, 100. In his earlier *Logica*, iii. 59, Wyclif is doubtful if it is 'scibilis'. Possibly Wyclif was alluding to the *Cognitio Circuli Quadraturae* of John de Muris, written about 1330, more probably to the work of John Campanus de Navara, often attributed to Bradwardine (Cantor, ii. 101, 114). In *Ente Praed.* 55–7 Wyclif refers to 'books of Euclid', and in *Apos.* 34 to the 'pons asinorum'.
[6] *Serm.* ii. 380 f.; iii. 244; iv. 210; *Op. Evang.* i. 52, 81 f.; *Civ. Dom.* i. 237.
[7] *Serm.* ii. 384. For Vitellio see Cantor, ii. 98–9, and for Wyclif's references *Dom. Div.* 188; *Civ. Dom.* i. 237; *Ent. Praed.* 97, 217; *Logica*, iii. 51, 61; *Misc. Phil.* i. 12; *Serm.* ii. 384–6; iii. 244. A copy of Vitellio, formerly at Peterhouse, is now in the Bodleian (James, *MSS. Pet.* 359). Vitellio was printed at Nuremberg in 1535 and Basel in 1572. His work was founded on Alhazen's *Perspectiva*, to which Wyclif refers in *Misc. Phil.* i. 12. See also James, *MSS. Pet.* 251. Wyclif also refers to 'Albunazar' (*Op. Evang.* i. 82; *Serm.* ii. 382), i. e. Abu Nasr Alfarabi, whose works had been translated by Gerard of Cremona, *c.* 1150 (Ball, *Hist. Maths.* 166; Cantor, i. 754 f.).

far off as if they were near, and 'to read minute letters like young men'[1]—we wonder if this is a bit of autobiography. He was also interested in astronomy, in the position of the sun, and in a solar eclipse that he expected to take place shortly, as well as in comets. He tells us that it is night at the antipodes when it is day in England.[2]

In view of his translation of the Bible, a word should be said about Wyclif's chances at Oxford of learning Greek and Hebrew. Unlike Grosseteste Wyclif made no effort to study Greek,[3] though he might easily have secured the assistance of a noted Greek then at Oxford, Peter Philargi, who afterwards became pope Alexander V.[4] But we must remember that the idea of translating the Bible only came to Wyclif when his Oxford days were over, and then only as a linear paraphrase of the Vulgate. Be that as it may, Wyclif's knowledge of Greek was limited to a few theological phrases, picked up from commonplace books. Hebrew at Oxford in Wyclif's day was less unknown than Greek, for the Jews had only recently been banished; Jewish manuscripts left from the sack of the Jewry abounded. An Oxford contemporary, Adam Easton,[5] was a Hebrew scholar, and Hebrew manuscripts of parts of the Bible, with interlinear Latin translation, written by an English hand, still exist.[6] Possibly from Easton Wyclif learned the derivations, mostly correct, that he gives of Hebrew names.[7]

There is one other matter that should be noted, for it shows the slow development of Wyclif's reforming zeal. In his later works Wyclif complained bitterly of the attention paid by the clergy to the study of law.[8] We are inclined to think that this

---

[1] *Serm.* iv. 485. This seems an unacknowledged reference to Bacon. See Gunther, *op. cit.* i. 270; ii. 288.

[2] *Ent. Praed.* 297-8; *Logica*, iii. 26, 29, 95, 206. The eclipse to which Wyclif refers (*Pol. Works*, i. 280) took place on 17 Aug. 1384 (*Chron. Ang.* 360) not 1383 as Buddensieg, *Pol. Works*, i. 236. Wyclif says he is no astrologer to know if the eclipse is propitious.

[3] For Grosseteste, see *infra*, p. 116. For Wyclif's ignorance of Greek see Lechler, 90, and for illustrations *Blas.* 1; *Apost.* 1. For his theological phrases see his early *Ben. Incarn.* 115, 135, 183.

[4] See Addenda.   [5] See Addenda.

[6] James, *MSS. Caius*, ii. 471; *MSS. Trin.* ii. 245.

[7] *Serm.* iv. 482; *Sel. Eng. Works*, i. 14, 30, 66. His Latin derivations are often worse than his Hebrew, e. g. 'lapis' equals 'ledens pedem', 'homo' from 'humo' (*Civ. Dom.* iv. 427).

[8] e. g. *Off. Reg.* 177 f.; *infra*, ii. 24.

was an afterthought, for Wyclif's early writings are so full of references to law books that we might suspect that at one time he contemplated taking his degree therein, possibly when he was preparing to enter the king's service. He quotes extensively, not merely from the recognized text-book of all canonists, Gratian's *Decretum*, but from the additional collections of decretals issued by Gregory IX, Boniface VIII, and John XXII. He had some knowledge also of Roman civil law, and more than once quotes from English statute law. He had not merely studied the master, ' Hostiensis ' ; [1] even the lesser lights of canon law, John Andreae of Bologna (†1348) and John ' Monachus ' do not escape his notice.[2] But Wyclif never mentions any English lawyers, neither Bracton nor William of Drogheda (*c.* 1239), nor John of Acton (*c.* 1345), though when appealing over Canterbury he would have found Drogheda's *Summa*, a recognized Oxford text-book, of value for its practical suggestions. The great English master of canon law, William Lyndwood, was but a lad of ten when Wyclif died. As might be expected, Wyclif's references to canon and civil law became fewer as he ceased to publish works on church government and turned to works on doctrine.

[1] Wyclif often quotes ' Archidiaconus ', i. e. Guido de Bayso of Bologna, as well as ' Hostiensis ', i.e. Henricus de Bartholomaeis, cardinal bishop of Ostia (1263-71). For Wyclif's law references see the index of *Eccles.* ; *Civ. Dom.* ; *Off. Reg.* ; *Apos.* and *Blas.* ; for statute law *Civ. Dom.* ii. 40–1. The quotation from John Andreae shows the speed with which foreign law books penetrated to England.

[2] *Civ. Dom.* ii. 269 ; *Pot. Pap.* 250 ; *Eccl.* 14 ; *Trial.* 251, 264. Jean le Moine became a cardinal in 1294.

IV

WYCLIF'S PLACE AMONG THE SCHOOLMEN

§ 1

For the understanding of Wyclif's work both at Oxford and as a "Reformer" it is needful that we glance at his place in the series of schoolmen, of whom it might be claimed with justice that he was the last. The reader will not expect any sketch, even in barest outline, of the fortunes of scholasticism, nor a survey of its divergent schools. For these he must have resort to the recognized text-books of philosophy.[1] We can only indicate the main features of medieval thought at Oxford in their relation to the movement of which Wyclif was the leader. Nor should the reader in his survey forget that there is much in scholasticism which cannot be translated into modern ways of thinking.

The reader would err greatly if he ascribed to Wyclif any revolt against current scholastic thought. He accepted almost unquestioned, as did all other thinkers of his age, the authority of Aristotle. He commonly calls him, without other designation, 'the philosopher'. The one matter which he expressly excludes is Aristotle's supposed belief in the 'eternity of creation',[2] though it must be owned his own doctrine became perilously similar. He acknowledges that Aristotle is a 'heretic', but leaves his ultimate fate 'to the Searcher of hearts'.[3] But Plato, he tells us, is to be preferred to Aristotle because he proceeds from the immutable to the fluctuating, while Aristotle reverses the process.[4] For the sake of Aristotle

---

[1] The reader may content himself with my *Christian Thought to the Reformation* (1911). H. O. Taylor's *The Medieval Mind* (2 vols., 2nd ed. 1914) is on a larger scale. There is an excellent summary in Rashdall, *Univ.*, vol. 1. Students of philosophy may consult Maurice de Wulf, *Hist. Medieval Philosophy* (3rd ed., Eng. trans., 1909); C. G. Harnack, *Hist. Dogma*, vi; Ueberweg; J. B. Hauréau, *Hist. de la Philosoph. scolastique* (1872–80).

[2] *Ver. Script.* i. 29, 30; iii. 280; *Misc. Phil.* i. 99. In *ib.* ii. 39 he objects to Aristotle's 'possible' denial of universals.

[3] *Ver. Script.* iii. 280. [4] *Ente Praed.* 276.

he also accepts his Arab interpreters Avicenna [1] of Bokhara, and Averrhoës of Cordova,[2] especially the latter, familiarly known as the ' Commentator '.[3] Of the anti-Christian elements in Averrhoës, especially the eternalness of matter, which threatened to sweep the Paris schoolmen into naturalistic pantheism,[4] Wyclif is strangely tolerant, possibly because of a sympathetic strain in his own thought, though careful to point out that Averrhoës is not a decisive voice in philosophy, much less in theology.[5] ' The error of Averrhoes ', he acknowledges, ' is that he posits that the soul of all men is one '. This led to the logical denial that the soul could remain individualized after the death of the body.[6] Nor is Wyclif conscious, any more than his contemporaries, of the impossibility of reconciling Aristotelian psychology with Christian dogma, though no doubt here and there he is driven by his attempt into contradictory positions. From these Wyclif's whole-hearted acceptance of Scripture as the ultimate authority made it impossible that he should escape, in spite of his clever dialectics.

Oxford in Wyclif's day was divided into the rival schools of Thomists and Scotists. If we classify Wyclif with the Thomists it would be because of his antagonism to the Scotists rather than by reason of any allegiance to Thomas Aquinas. Until his breach with the medieval Church, the synthesis that Thomas had made of Aristotle, Augustine, and the pseudo-Dionysius— as introduced and translated by John Scotus Eriugena—with the creed and practice of papal Rome, would appeal to Wyclif if only because of Aquinas's emphasis of the value of a sane mysticism based upon communion with God. We see the influence of Thomas also in Wyclif's movement back to Augus-

---

[1] For his life and influence see Carra de Vaux, *Avicenne* (Paris, 1900) and *Gazali* (Paris, 1902). For other Arabic writers quoted by Wyclif see Appendix E.

[2] E. Renan, *Averroës et l'Averroïsme* (4th ed., Paris, 1882).

[3] e. g. Wyclif, *Comp. Hom.* 55 ; *Logica*, iii. 75 ; *Ente Praed.* 127, *et passim*. Cf. *Chart. Par.* ii. 680.

[4] For Siger (Dante, *Par.* x. 136–8) condemned 1277, see P. F. Mandonnet, *Siger de Brabant* (2nd ed., Louvain, 1911) in vols. 6 and 7 of *Les Philosophes Belges*. For David of Dinant (condemned 1210, 1215), see *Chart. Par.* i. 71, 81.

[5] *Ben. Incarn.* 140.

[6] *Serm.* iv. 60. Ueberweg, i. 450. Wyclif drifts perilously near this in his *Comp. Hom.* See *infra*, p. 142.

tine.¹ He would also approve of the clear line which Thomas had laid down between philosophy and theology, between natural and revealed religion, and the province of reason as regards both, which has remained in force among thinkers ever since, though modified by the criticisms of Kant. Philosophy passes from the consideration of the creatures to God; theology from God to the creature. The doctrines of revelation are above but not contrary to reason, nor can they be demonstrated by reason. Hence the merit of faith as an act of confidence in the divine authority. To this the intellect assents in obedience to the will. But in his realism Wyclif goes far beyond the moderate doctrine of Thomas; nor would the Dominican, who assigns to free will a special range of action apart from grace,² have had any sympathy with Wyclif's extreme predestination creed. There are many indications in Wyclif's writings that though he would not have been a party to the condemnation of the doctrines of Thomas by the university of Paris ³ he would yet have favoured the old-fashioned Platonic-Augustinian party under the leadership of Henry of Ghent—'doctor solemnis'⁴—which resented the domination of Aquinas.

A similar protest was made in England and has received the criticism of Wyclif.⁵ At the council of Oxford archbishop Robert Kilwardby, himself a Dominican, condemned the Thomist doctrine of the 'unity of form', 'with the consent of all the masters, regent and non-regent' (18 Mar. 1277).⁶ In the letter to Pierre de Conflans, the archbishop of Corinth, in which Kilwardby defended his condemnation,⁷ Kilwardby laid down the distinction between the vegetable, sensitive, and intellectual 'souls' of men which he had derived from Augustine, but which Thomas had swept away by his insistence on the 'anima rationalis' which included all the vital functions.

¹ See *infra*, p. 119, and cf. Harnack, vi. 300; vii. 16. In *Euch.* 73. Wyclif calls Aquinas by the less usual title of 'doctor communis' (cf. *Apos.* 130, where Dziewicki's note is unfortunate).
² Harnack, vi. 296, 305.
³ In Dec. 1270 and on 7 March 1277. See *Chart. Par.* i. 487, 543–8; ii. 280. Mandonnet, *op. cit., cc.* 5 and 9.
⁴ *Misc. Phil.* i. 92.   ⁵ *Comp. Hom.* 74.   ⁶ Wood, *Univ.* i. 306.
⁷ Recently published by Ehrle in *Archiv.* v. 603 f. from the MS. at Merton. In 1287 Peckham wrote to the bishop of Lincoln to obtain a copy (*Reg.* iii. 944).

Seven years later there was a second condemnation, as Wyclif notes, by the first Franciscan archbishop of Canterbury, Peckham.[1] At one time Peckham had defended Thomas. When Aquinas's doctrine on the unity of form was submitted to the doctors of Paris, 'we alone', wrote Peckham, 'stood by him, defending him to the best of our power, saving the truth'.[2] But now

'we cannot and dare not fail to rescue our children, so far as we can, from the traps of error. . . . We by no means reprobate the studies of philosophers, so far as they serve the mysteries of theology, but the profane novelties which have been introduced in the last twenty years.'

Peckham was accused of being led astray by Franciscan jealousy. The impartial student looking through the propositions condemned will agree with the judgement of Ockham that Peckham curiously mixed up grammar, philosophy, and logic, and mistook the mixture for catholic truth.[3]

There were other attacks upon Aquinas that were equally futile, and that were reversed by Aquinas's canonization (18 July 1323).[4] The attack of Roger Bacon, if indeed Thomas and not Albertus Magnus were the subject, was both premature and tactless.[5] But in 1284 another Oxford Franciscan, William de la Mare, who seems directly inspired by Bacon, published a work *Correctorium fratris Thomae*, which won him the title of the standard-bearer of the anti-Thomists.[6] It was reserved for two other Oxford Franciscans to lead a more potent attack against Thomas with results that in the long run brought condemnation upon Wyclif, and led John Hus and Jerome to the stake. It came about in this wise. The triumph of Thomas had been the triumph of a moderate realism. Aquinas had rejected the Platonic theory that ideas can exist independently in things or in the divine mind. Nominalism seemed silenced,

---

[1] His name should be Pecham or Patcham from the village near Lewes. See Little, *Fr. J. Pecham Tractatus Tres* (1910), p. v. For complete bibliography of Peckham's works see *ib.* App.

[2] For this dispute see *Reg. Peckham*, iii. 852, 866, 896–901; Wilkins, ii. 107 f.; Wood, *Univ.* i. 318–24; Mandonnet, *op. cit.* 98 f.

[3] Ockham, *Dial.* ii, *c.* 24; Mandonnet, 235 *n.*; Wood, *Univ.* i. 320.

[4] *Chart. Par.* ii. 273 *n.*

[5] Bacon, *Op. Ined.* 327; Little, 73 *n.*; Mandonnet, 40 *n.*; Wood, *Univ.* i. 295.

[6] Charles, 240–1; Sbaralea, 323; Little, 215–16.

but in the next generation it recovered its strength. But more important than the victory of a philosophical creed was the powerful dissolvent of the Thomist conceptions of faith which the leaders in this reaction introduced into the schools. For nominalism, by denying objective reality to general notions, led, directly or indirectly, to the introduction of the experience of the senses as the only reality. The full consequences of this tendency were not felt until after the discredit of scholasticism in general. A prior result was an outburst of philosophic scepticism, the leader of which was the great opponent of Thomas, the famous John Duns Scotus.

Of the life of Duns,[1] the most ' subtle ' of the schoolmen, little is known save the memory of his greatness and the record of his incredible industry. Probably born at Duns in Berwickshire,[2] we have proof that in 1300 Duns was at Oxford where college patriotism has claimed him as a fellow of Merton,[3] in spite of his northern origin. On the 7th August of that year the Franciscan provincial minister, Hugh of Hartlepool, presented at Dorchester (Oxon) twenty-two friars to Dalderby bishop of Lincoln, with a request that he would licence them to hear confessions.[4] Dalderby inquired ' whether he was presenting them for all the friaries in the diocese of Lincoln '. On hearing that it was merely to deal with the crowds that thronged the Franciscan church at Oxford the bishop refused to licence more than four, a number he afterwards increased as a favour to eight. Among the rejected was a certain ' Johannes Douns '. The incident is of value as showing that Duns in 1300 must have been at least thirty by the rules of his order.[5] At Oxford he took his bachelor's degree in theology and delivered his lectures on the *Sentences*, or at any rate lectures afterwards expanded into the work called *Scriptum*

---

[1] *D. N. B.*; Little, 219–22; Wadding, vi. 107 f. or his *Vita Jo. Duns* (Mons, 1644); B. Landry, *Duns Scot* (Paris, 1922). For criticism of his writings, E. Pluzanski, *Essai sur la Philosophie de Duns Scot* (Paris, 1887), or Taylor, *op. cit.*, c. 43; Harnack, vi. 306 f; Seeberg, *Die Theologie des Duns Scotus* (Leipzig, 1900).

[2] Gascoigne, 3. Cf. Major, 74, and of course Dempster, 227 f.

[3] First found in a note to a Merton MS. of 1451 or 1455, bearing the signature of John Reynbold (Leland, *Comment*. 317; Bale, i. 362).

[4] Reg. Dalderby, f. 13, printed in Wood, *City*, ii. 386; *Univ.* (Lat. Ed.), 134.

[5] *Archiv*. vi. 128–9.

Oxoniense.¹ In November 1304 at Paris we find the minister of his order presenting for his licence in theology

' Johannem Scotum, de cuius vita laudibili, scientia excellenti, ingenioque subtilissimo aliisque insignibus conditionibus suis partim experientia longa, partim fama quae ubique divulgata est, informatus sum ad plenum '.²

The words seem to us to indicate that Duns had not been long at Paris, where, however, he probably remained until 1307. The date (8 Nov. 1308) and place of his death is one of the few certain facts in his life. In a list of the Minorites who died at Cologne we read :

' D. P. Frater Johannes Scotus, S.T.P. Doctor Subtilis nominatus, quondam lector Coloniae, qui obiit anno 1308, vi. Id. Nov.' ³

There he was buried in the Franciscan church, first in the sacristy and then translated to the middle of the choir. Later generations expanded these few facts into romances that they labelled memoirs, how all Cologne turned out to greet him, how he died of apoplexy, and the like. To these Bernardin of Siena, or rather the collector of his works, a certain Daniel de Purziliis,⁴ added the crowning embellishment that he was buried alive in a trance. The story that he died at the age of thirty-four is contradicted by what we have seen must have been his age in 1300. Nevertheless, even if we assume that he must have been at least thirty-eight—according to one version he was forty-four—the mere rapidity of his productiveness is one of the most marvellous feats of its kind in the intellectual history of our race.

The fates have dealt almost as hardly with the writings of this marvellous Scot as with those of Wyclif himself. Even Wyclif found his Latin to be difficult.⁵ His interminable length and spider-like logic concentrated upon him the wrath of the new learning which turned his name into the synonym for a stupid. Colet could not speak of him with patience, and caused Erasmus, who had been nurtured on his subtleties in

---

¹ So Gascoigne, 152. But cf. Little, 220 *n*.
² *Chart. Par.* ii. 117 ; Little, 220.
³ Wadding, vi. 116 f.; Tanner, 239, for his epitaph. His tomb was repeatedly opened, the last time in 1642 (Sbaralea, 414).
⁴ Wadding, *Vita Scoti*, 63. ⁵ *Ben. Incarn.* 51, 161.

Paris, to abhor him also.¹ Luther, in his reaction against the teaching of his nominalist university, arrayed against Duns the hatred of the Reformers. Tindale in 1530 wrote of the ' old barking curs, Dunce's disciples, the draff called Scotists, the children of darkness ', who ' raged in every pulpit against Greek, Latin, and Hebrew '.² In 1535 Layton wrote to Thomas Cromwell :

' We have set Dunce in Bocardo, and have utterly banished him Oxford for ever with all his blind glosses, he is now made a common servant to every man, fast nailed up upon posts in all houses of common easement id quod oculis meis vidi. And the second time we came to New College, after we had declared your injunctions, we found all the great Quadrant Court full of the leaves of Dunce, the wind blowing them into every corner. And there we found one Master Greenfield, a gentleman of Buckinghamshire gathering up part of the said bookleaves therewith to make him sewells or blaunshers to keep the deer within the wood and thereby to have better cry with his hounds.' ³

With such guides as these, little wonder that at Oxford in 1560 ' certain rude young men could carry great spoils of books about the city which being so done set them down in the market-place ' and there burnt them. ' This was by them styled the funeral of Scotus.' ⁴ But the new learning had neither sympathy nor understanding of the fallen schoolmen. With the cry of *Vae victis !* it overwhelmed them all with contempt, indifferent to their immense diligence and their high ideal of a science which should embrace all knowledge in one great whole within the fold of the Church.

Of the influence of Duns and of the acuteness of his intellect there can be no doubt. Though not himself a nominalist, no one did more to secure for nominalism the triumph which it won in the fifteenth century. In twelve volumes, this remarkable Scot, whose relation to Aquinas was similar to that of Kant to Leibniz, destroyed by his criticism of Thomas the rational grounds of faith and therefore the validity of the whole scholastic method.⁵ Reason, he held, relates solely to the

¹ Seebohm, *Oxford Reformers*, 102–12. Hobbes, *Behemoth* (in *Works*, 1840, vi. 214, quoted in *N. E. D.*), calls Peter Lombard and Duns ' two of the most egregious blockheads in the world '.
² Tindale, *Answer to More* (1573), 278.
³ Wood, *Univ.* ii. 62.   ⁴ *ib.* ii. 108.
⁵ Especially true if the *Theoremata* be by Duns. See Mallet, i. 207 *n*.

realm of the sensible. Philosophy and theology once more parted company. Belief is obedience to the unconditioned will of God, or rather is subjection to the authority of the Church, whereby that will is manifested. Thus he shook confidence in the Augustinian conceptions of grace. The Augustinian doctrine of sin was equally destroyed by his reduction of morals to arbitrary decree, as we see in his statement that murder, e. g. that of Holofernes by Judith, would be right if commanded by God, for Duns will not allow that the will of God can be determined even by His wisdom.[1] The ease with which such ethics could be changed into the doctrine that the end justifies the means, and that the Church's power of binding and loosing is equivalent to ' the good ', has probably led to the favour with which Duns has always been regarded by the Jesuits, who also look with approval upon his insistence on the primacy of the will over the intellect. Though himself an ardent champion of the Roman creed, even in its extremer forms—Duns defended as a Franciscan the dogma of the Immaculate Conception which Thomas the Dominican had refused to recognize—his criticism of the validity of the arguments put forward in defence of faith prepared the way for the coming rupture of the alliance between philosophy and theology. We see this rupture also in his emphasis of the independence of all secular sciences—a necessary step, we may remark, for their true development—and the independence of the world as over against God. He will not allow any place for demonstration by reason in such doctrines as immortality, the Trinity, or creation. His appeal to the sacred and inviolable authority of the Roman Church—he would not believe, he said, even the gospels save on the witness of the Church—was a mere personal conviction, full use of which, however, was made by his later disciples in the development of papal autocracy. His destructive criticism bore fruit after he had passed away. With Duns, in whom we note a lessened acceptance of the authority of Aristotle, we mark for scholasticism the beginning of the end. He criticized everything until he left everything in tatters. In some minds his philosophy led to scepticism; in others we see its results in " the emotional

[1] Pluzanski, 274 f.

prostration before authority, popularly called faith ".[1] It is this which gives him his prominence in the life and thought of Wyclif's world.

The influence of Duns on Wyclif was twofold. The Reformer inherited his dissolvent spirit without sharing his blind obedience. He accepted also the belief of Duns in the omnipotence of the arbitrary will of God as over against the Thomist conception of the possession by all rational beings of will dependent on understanding. Duns, it is true, preached the supremacy of the will of man, but only to throw the will of man over against the will of God, and thus virtually to deny the freewill he claimed. With Wyclif this last idea takes the place of Augustine's doctrine of original sin. Arbitrary as this last may appear to us to-day, it is certainly less arbitrary than the basing all things on the caprice of omnipotent will. Though both Wyclif and Duns profess to believe in the freedom of the will, both so fetter us with arbitrariness or confront us with the divine will that we cease to be free, in spite of the semi-Pelagianism of the Scotists. In the fact that Duns with all his orthodoxy, and Wyclif with all his evangelical zeal, both glide towards a philosophical pantheism we may detect also the common danger of all schools of realism.

In the Middle Ages the sons of St. Francis were the fruitful parents of new philosophies, heresies, orthodoxies, rebellions, and democracies—in all things a contrast to the conservatism and moderation of the Dominicans, with their belief in the infallibility of Aquinas. Now at Oxford the Dominicans were comparatively weak, the Franciscans all-powerful. The consequence was a ceaseless intellectual ferment in which we find the lead taken by the Franciscans. The reaction against realism, though begun by Duns's own pupil, Walter Burley, was led by another English Franciscan, a fellow student with Burley at Paris, William of Ockham, ' Doctor Invincibilis '.[2] Ockham, the ally of Marsiglio, was the second founder of nominalism. Hitherto nominalism had been branded by the

[1] Rashdall, ii. 534 ; cf. Harnack, vi. 164, 312. Popular versions of Duns took the form of Hoccleve's declaration (*Works*, iii. 14), that if faith could be proved the holding it would not be meritorious (cf. ' credo quia impossibile ').

[2] Wood, *City*, ii. 464, who says that he was so ' surnamed by the pope '. His usual title was ' Venerabilis Inceptor '.

Church as heretical. Its dangerous tendencies had become manifest first in Roscelin, who, starting with the assumption that the individual only is real, and the universal a mere *flatus vocis*—at any rate such conclusions were credited to him—had driven the theologians to choose between an absolute Unitarianism and the Tritheistic explanation of the Trinity. This early outcome, rather than any prescient discernment that if the individual is the only real nominalism must end in sensationalist scepticism, had alarmed the fathers of the Church. For long years realism and orthodoxy were looked upon as almost synonymous. But when Ockham refounded nominalism, its fortunes became curiously reversed. As it was no great leap from the realism of Duns, who ascribed a certain objective existence to general ideas, to the conceptualism of Ockham, who recognized the real existence of universals in the mind, the Scotists for the most part became nominalists.

In many respects the nominalism of Ockham is a philosophy of centuries later. Some of it might have come from the pen of Hobbes. Realism, Ockham argued, in whatever form it may be expressed, was bound to lead to absurdities ; the universal exists only in the thinking mind, and is thus essentially a relation.[1] Even in the mind of God universals do not exist, but are simply God's knowledge of singulars, which alone have reality. A common name is like an algebraic symbol ; it is a purely denotative term whose meaning is accepted on the basis of thought and experience. This doctrine of conceptualism, as we should now call it, was followed up, as it is often followed up to-day, by the relegation of all knowledge which transcends mere experience to the sphere of faith, for Ockham held that many dogmas are not only undemonstrable but irrational, though the soul has a faculty of its own for apprehending their truth. But the more Ockham realized this the more his religious nature clung to the plank of divine arbitrariness. In this point, especially, we see the essential oneness, though from different causes, of Duns and Ockham. Thus Ockham, as Duns before him, heralds the dissolution of scholasticism. The Thomist doctrine of the unity of reason

---

[1] *Summa Logicae*, i. cc. 15, 50. Cf. also Ockham's *Quodlibeta* (Paris, 1487), vi. 18–30, or his *Summulae in lib. Physicorum* (Venice, 1506), pt. 3, c. 5.

CH. IV   PLACE AMONG SCHOOLMEN   113

and faith gave place to a growing consciousness of their discrepancy.

The nominalism of Ockham, which seems, in the verdict of Rashdall, "to the modern non-metaphysical man of science the perfection of common sense", in spite of opposition swept all before it. Four times between 1339 and 1347 were his writings proscribed by the faculty of arts in the university of Paris, and his doctrines condemned.[1] At Avignon, as the catalogue of the papal library shows, nominalist writers were not admitted. But from the first the condemnation was vain, as its frequent renewal proves. In 1346 Clement VI complained that many masters of Paris, the renowned John Buridan included, were turning from Aristotle to Ockham.[2] By the time of the council of Constance, nominalism was in the ascendant in Germany, and, though to a lesser extent, in France also. At Paris the chancellor of the university, the celebrated John Gerson, was its open advocate. The effect of this revival of the age-long battle between realism and nominalism was felt most disastrously by the reformers of the day. Nominalism, especially after its adoption by the Scotists, became the ally of the extreme materialistic conceptions of transubstantiation against which Wyclif protested.

The examination of Wyclif's positions as to transubstantiation must be deferred. But it is well at this stage to point out the strength of the alliance at Oxford between nominalism and the Church. In defence of its central dogma of transubstantiation the Church was prepared with Duns to abandon reason and fall back upon the arbitrary fiat of God or of His vicar. Now the nominalists who held that the universal was a mere *flatus vocis*, and who grounded religion not in reason but in a mystical doctrine or the decrees of a supreme will, found it easy to believe in the annihilation of the substance of the elements, a dogma that for the realist was full of impossibilities. So a strong party in the Church, especially among the friars, abandoned its ancient antagonism and embraced nominalism. The consequences were remarkable. Hence arose the strong

---

[1] 29 Sept. 1339 ; Dec. 1340 ; adopted by the English nation 13 Jan. 1341 ; renewed 1347 (*Chart. Par.* ii. 485, 505, 507 *n.*, 680).
[2] *ib.* ii. 588, 590 *n.*

opposition which Wyclif, the realist, encountered at Oxford from nominalists and Scotists, chiefly, according to Wood,[1] of the 'Southern nation', who had set aside the cautious Thomist doctrine and substituted their arbitrary annihilations and recreations.

From Oxford, where as Wyclif tells us there was 'shameful strife' and a new logical system every twenty years,[2] the struggle surged elsewhere, with consequences writ large in history. The modern man, who looks upon philosophy as the harmless occupation of a few dreamers, can form little conception of the fury with which the rival schools attacked each other. In Prague the *odium philosophicum* descended into the streets. In the fight that raged there before the migration of five hundred Germans in May 1409 to found a new university at Leipzig, it would be difficult to say which hatred was uppermost, that of Czech against Teuton, of heretic against orthodox, or of realist against nominalist.[3] The Germans had embraced nominalism; of itself a sufficient reason for the Czechs, in their hatred of the Germans, to become uncompromising realists, and to welcome the works of so thoroughgoing a realist as Wyclif. As a matter of fact, Hus was condemned as much for being a realist in philosophy as for being a heretic in theology; his most bitter enemies were men who had at one time been realists, but who became what he calls 'Terminists', i. e. nominalists. At Constance the opponents of Hus were the two leading nominalists of Paris, both of them reformers in their way, Peter d'Ailli and John Gerson. Only slowly did the rival philosophical creeds learn tolerance, as slowly as the rival theologies at whose roots to some extent they lay.[4]

§ 2

From this general survey we pass to the more local philosophic influences. In one of his early Oxford sermons Wyclif

[1] Wood, *Univ.* i. 439, who adds ' the North held, 'tis said, with Scotus '.
[2] *Misc. Phil.* ii. 135 ; *Ver. Script.* i. 54.
[3] See my *Age of Hus*, c. 4, for details. From G. Erler, *Die Matrikel der Universität Leipzig* (in *Codex Dep. Sax. Reg.* xvi), we see the total entries at Leipzig in 1409 were 369, and not the thousands usually assigned.
[4] For illustrations see Rashdall, ii. 250, 263 *n.*, 269, 271.

gives a list of theologians through whom 'renown had come to England, all doctors of theology and great philosophers who had sown excellent doctrines throughout the world ': Bede, St. John of Beverley, 'the venerable' Robert Grosseteste, St. Edmund Rich, St. Thomas Cantelupe, and a mysterious name given as 'St. John Hollzdeyn'.[1] The presence of Cantelupe among the 'great philosophers' is as much a surprise as the absence of Duns and Ockham, unless indeed, as is probable, Wyclif was preaching before an assembly of seculars, to whom Cantelupe's recent canonization would appeal. But this will not explain his silence about two seculars to whom he was specially indebted, Bradwardine and Fitzralph. That Bacon [2] is not included is not strange. Except for a quickened interest in mathematics and science, Bacon was almost without influence in his own generation ; and at Oxford his memory was scarcely known save for the legend of his necromancy. " Not a doctor of the 13th or 14th century " writes Charles, " quotes Bacon ; not one combats or approves his opinions ".[3] Wyclif never mentions him. Bacon, to quote his own pathetic words, was 'unheard, forgotten, buried '.[4]

The value of the list lies in Wyclif's acknowledgement of his debt to Grosseteste.[5] There is, in fact, no writer save St. Augustine to whose authority he more frequently appeals. 'The great clerk, Grosseteste', commonly known as 'Lincolniensis' or as the uncanonized 'St. Robert', was the leading bishop of the thirteenth century, 'conspicuous by his good

[1] *Serm.* iv. 488. Dr. Poole suggests to me that this may be Howdeyn, i.e. John Hoveden, who was sometimes called a saint (*D. N. B.*). Can it be a Czech misinterpretation and conflation of Sacro Bosco and Holywood, where the ' sacro ' has been turned into Sanctus ?

[2] For Bacon see *D. N. B.* ; Brewer's pref. to *Op. Ined.* ; E. Charles, *Roger Bacon* (Paris, 1861) ; and Little, 195-211, who gives a list of his works and editions. Add *Un fragment inédit de l'Opus Tertium* (Quaracchi, 1909), a further fragment found by A. G. Little and printed in *Eng. Hist. Rev.* xxvii. 318-21. For the *Opus Majus* there is a poor ed. by J. H. Bridges (2 vols., 1897 : for criticism see *Eng. Hist. Rev.* xiii. 151-5), corrected in the 3rd vol. published in 1900. Add also R. Steele, *Communia Naturalium* (1911 f.) and H. Rashdall, *Compend. Stud. Theologiae* (1911).

[3] Charles, 42. But Woodford refers to Bacon's 'curious' *de Retardatione Senecututis* (Brown, *Fascic.* i. 197). For other references see Little, 195 *n*.

[4] *Op. Ined.* 7. The traditional date of Bacon's burial is 11 June 1292 (Rous, *Hist.* 82, followed by Wood, *Univ.* i. 332 ; *City*, ii. 384).

[5] For Grosseteste see F. S. Stevenson, *Grosseteste* (1899), and his *Epistolae*, ed. Luard in R. S.

faith, and his fidelity in addition to his other virtues and the endowment of his mind '.[1] From 1214 to 1232 he was the potent force at Oxford as lecturer, chancellor—really the first of the long line—and friend of the Franciscans. When in 1235 he became bishop of Lincoln he threw himself into the support of all that made for liberty in national life. His resistance in 1253 to the demands of Rome by his ' sharp epistle ' to ' master Innocent ', the representative of Innocent IV in England, secured him European reputation.[2] As a scholar there were few branches of study of which he had not some knowledge. Wyclif refers again and again to his eminence as an expositor of Aristotle.[3] Among his contemporaries he had repute as a French poet, lawyer, physician, preacher, theologian, and agriculturist who procured the translation into English of Walter de Henley's *Treatise on Husbandry*. Grosseteste's *Compendium Scientiarum* is a classification of all the departments of knowledge then accessible. He introduced the new translations of Aristotle to Oxford; the first translation of the *Ethics* from the Greek was made at his expense by ' master Nicholas, a Greek, a monk of St. Albans '.[4] ' Though he did not know Greek and Hebrew sufficiently to translate works himself '—this judgement of Bacon is too severe as regards Greek [5]—he did all that was possible to secure translations. His friend, John of Basing, translated a Greek grammar into Latin. At the same time he encouraged the study of the physical sciences. ' The lord Robert ', says Bacon, ' on account of the wonderful methods which he employed excelled all men in his knowledge of the sciences '. ' One man ', he says elsewhere ' alone had really known the sciences, namely Robert, bishop of Lincoln '.[6] Even more important in its influence on Wyclif was Grosseteste's constant appeal to the authority of Scripture.

[1] Girald. Camb., *Op*. i. 249.
[2] This epistle is reproduced by Wyclif with commentary in *Civ. Dom.* i. c. 43, *Pot. Pap.* 190 (from Higden, viii. 240), and thence passed to Hus, *Mon. Hus*, i. 236. For ' master Innocent ' see *Pap. Let.* i. 298, 395.
[3] *Ente Praed.* 25, 33, 35, &c. [4] *Chron. Maj.* iv. 233.
[5] See Stevenson, *op. cit.* 53, 223-8. For a *Psalterium Graecum* and a *Nov. Test. Graecum* which belonged to him see James, *MSS. Corpus*, ii. 422; *MSS. Caius*, ii. 469, and for his translation of the *Testament of the Twelve Patriarchs*, *ib.* ii. 462, see Lightfoot, *Apostolic Fathers*, ii. (1) 76 ff.
[6] *Op. Ined.* 33, 472.

In this list Wyclif is not only silent over Duns and Ockham but makes no reference to the lesser Oxford lights, whose renown in his day must have been considerable. Chief of these was the pride of Merton, Walter Burley—'doctor perspicuus', a title that assuredly few schoolmen deserved. Burley was a noted opponent of Duns, a commentator on Aristotle with tendencies towards Averrhoism.[1] The friend of Richard de Bury and the tutor of the Black Prince, Burley left Merton, probably in 1326, when he was sent to Avignon to procure the canonization of Thomas of Lancaster. In 1335 he was appointed by Benedict XII one of the committee to examine into pope John XXII's heresy of the Retardation of the Beatific Vision.[2] He died about 1346 at the age of seventy.[3] His numerous works were long in use as text-books, and Wyclif sometimes refers to them; in fact there were many points of agreement between the two thinkers.[4] So great was his repute that twenty editions[5] of his works were printed before the close of the fifteenth century, two being among the earliest books printed at Oxford.[6] One of his books must have interested Wyclif, his *de Vita et moribus Philosophorum*, printed at Cologne in 1467, and a few years later translated into Italian and German. This book of lives and anecdotes of 120 poets and philosophers was the first work of its kind.

Of the older Oxford Franciscans the fame would still linger of John Canon,[7] a pupil of Duns Scotus, whose *Commentary on the Physics of Aristotle* was noted, as the numerous manu-

[1] Renan, *Averroes*, 320.
[2] Lea, iii. 590–5; *Chart. Par.* ii. 414–42. For Wyclif's obscure allusion to this see *Op. Evang.* i. 53.
[3] For Burley see *D. N. B.* His death is often dated as in 1337, when he was 62 (Bale, i. 413). But he was alive in Jan. 1344 (*Pap. Pet.* i. 34; cf. *Chart. Par.* ii. 454 n.). Whether he was the Walter de Burley who in 1345 petitioned for the archdeaconry of Richmond is uncertain (Tanner, 142 n.). For a long list of his writings see Bale, i. 411–12; Leland, *Com.* 354. Many MSS. are at Oriel (Coxe, 4, 21).
[4] *Misc. Phil.* i. 49, 149; Wood, *Univ.* i. 514.
[5] Hain, i. 574–8; Reichling, i. 116; ii. 132; iv. 163; v. 91.
[6] Madan, *Oxford Books*, 5 in 1517–18. Madan, *ib.* 12, points out that the supposed Oxford print of 1512 of Burley's *super Libros Posteriorum* (Panzer, vii. 494) is a fiction.
[7] Tanner, 150; Bale, i. 387, who excels himself in vituperation; *D. N. B.* The first edition of Canon's work, Padua, 1475, was reprinted at St. Albans in 1481, and several times at Venice before 1500 (Tanner, l.c.; Little, 223). For the respect in which Canon was held at Oxford see Wood, *City*, ii. 402.

scripts and printed editions still testify. His work would be one of the text-books which Wyclif would study. Canon's rival in the schools was Adam Wodham or Godham, a follower of Ockham,[1] manuscripts of whose *Commentary on the Four Books of the Sentences* abound.[2] He appears to have lectured in Oxford about 1340. There he entered the lists in defence of the friars' right to hear confessions against Richard Wetherset, the chancellor of Cambridge,[3] and wrote commentaries on *Canticles* and *Ecclesiastes*.[4] Godham, according to Bale, died near Bury in 1358.[5] But no work on the *Sentences* was more in demand in England than the *Commentaries* of Robert Cowton whom Wyclif describes as ' an abbreviator of Duns '[6]—a job that sadly needed doing. Cowton came from a village in Yorkshire not far from Wyclif's home, and Wyclif would first hear of him through the rector of his own parish, John de Clervaux, who owned property in the place. More important, probably, as one of the factors accounting for Wyclif's earlier sympathies with the friars would be John Gwent, a native of Wales, who lectured at Oxford about 1340, and who from 1340–50 was the twentieth Provincial Minister of the order. Gwent was more noted for his holiness than his learning; he was credited with working miracles even in his lifetime.[7] Nor must we forget the Dominican, Robert Holcot, who died at Northampton through the Black Death. Holcot [8]—who hailed from a village of that name in Northamptonshire—took his doctorate in theology at Oxford, and in 1333 was one of the half dozen scholars whom

[1] ' Vir modestus sed non inferioris doctrinae aut ingenii quam Ockham ', J. Major *de Gest. Scot.* (1521), iv. 21.

[2] Little, 173. There were really two editions, not one as Little, of his *Sentences* printed at Paris in 1512, one by Jean Petit, the other by J. Granian (Brit. Mus. Cat.).

[3] Tanner, 329 *n.*, and for Wetherset, *ib.* 759; *D. N. B.*

[4] Leland, *Coll.* iv. 50; Little, l.c.

[5] Bale, i. 447.

[6] Wyclif, *Ben. Incarn.* 57, where Harris the editor wrongly identifies him with J. Colton, archb. of Armagh (1382–1404). Cowton (for whom see *D. N. B.*, Little, 222) entered the order when young and was with Duns (Wood, *City*, ii. 386, 388). A *Tabula super Cowton*, compiled by Partridge (*infra*, ii. 352 *n.*) is in Lincoln Cathedral (Tanner, 577).

[7] *Mon. Franc.* i. 538. He died and was buried at Hereford, March 1349 (*ib.* i. 560; Bale, i. 432; Tanner, 366). Leland, *Itin.*, pt. viii, f. 80, identifies him with a rector of Bredon, near Evesham.

[8] Poole in *D. N. B.*; Tanner, 407–8; Bale, i. 433; Quétif, i. 629–32. MSS. of his works abound.

Richard de Bury bishop of Durham[1] summoned to his house. There he would meet with Fitzralph, and with Bradwardine. At Oxford he made a great name for himself by his expositions of the Bible[2] and his commentary on the *Sentences*, all of which have been repeatedly printed.[3] In addition he edited an important collection of moralized stories.[4] Some writers, following an inscription found in several manuscripts,[5] would also assign to him the authorship of the *Philobiblon*, usually attributed to Richard de Bury to whom Holcot may have dedicated it. As a theologian he differed from Bradwardine, and from Wyclif, by the stress that he laid upon free will as an antecedent to merit. Nor must we forget the ' Resolute doctor ', the Carmelite John Baconthorpe († 1346), grandnephew of Roger Bacon. Between Baconthorpe and Wyclif there was the common link of opposition to ' the cloudy Scot '. Both doctors also insisted on the subordination of the priestly office to the kingly, a doctrine which Wyclif may have learned from Baconthorpe through his pupil, Fitzralph.[6]

But it was not in the Holcots, nor Burleys, nor even in Grossesteste, nor Aquinas, that Wyclif saluted his masterteacher. ' His disciples ', we are told, ' called him by the famous and distinguished name of John, son of Augustine ' and claimed for themselves the same proud title.[7] In this they did right ; for Wyclif owed the better part of his teaching to Augustine, whose exegesis and thoughts he repeatedly quotes and whom he praises because he founded his theology on reason and scripture. In Augustine Wyclif is versed beyond almost all his contemporaries, and this comes out on every page

---

[1] For Bury who died at Auckland 14 Apr. 1345 see *D. N. B.* A few dates not in *D. N. B.* may be added. In July 1328 Richard Aungerville—for this was his real name—(of Bury St. Edmunds) was provided to a prebend in Chichester (*Pap. Let.* ii. 275). He had been appointed by the king rector of Croydon on 30 Nov. 1327 and on 2 Dec. 1327 the king added a prebend in Crediton (*Reg. Grand.* i. 19). In Jan. 1330 Bury, now Edward's secretary, obtained a prebend in London (*Pap. Let.* ii. 339) and in Nov. 1330 a canonry in York and in St. Martin's le Grand (*ib.* 342). In March 1333 dean of Wells (*ib.* ii. 385), and in Aug. 1333 granted non-residence for three years (*ib.* 392).
[2] For printed editions see Poole l. c., and Tanner.
[3] See Hain, ii. 8763 for Lyons, 1497. Also at Lyons in 1510, 1518.
[4] Often printed ; Venice, 1505 ; Paris, 1507, 1510, 1513.
[5] Quétif, i. 631, gives details.
[6] *D. N. B.* Netter *Doct.* ii, art. 3, p. 379, draws attention to this.
[7] So Netter, *Doct.* i. c. 34, p. 186. Cf. *Ziz*, 167.

even of his philosophical treatises. He maintained that Augustine knew the truth better than Plato or Aristotle.[1] Now the general effect of scholasticism, until Aquinas began a return to Augustine, had been "to throw into the shade the more Pauline side of Augustine".[2] In revolt against this, Bradwardine began at Oxford, and Wyclif, influenced by Bradwardine, continued the emphasis of certain elements in Augustine, whose complete statement was reserved for a later age.

Bradwardine[3] has been neglected by all but Lechler.[4] But his influence in the development of Wyclif's ideas, his fame as a mathematician, must not be overlooked. Thomas Bradwardine was born towards the close of the thirteenth century at Hertfield or Heathfield in Sussex,[5] halfway between Tunbridge and Eastbourne, to which his family had removed from the village in Herefordshire to which they owed their name. At Chichester, where probably he would go to school, the lad may have learned to know Richard of Bury, who at that time held a prebend in its cathedral.[6] When in 1333 Bury became bishop of Durham and a noted patron of learning, he secured for Bradwardine his first preferments. At Oxford Bradwardine entered Merton.[7] There he studied theology and philosophy, wrote his *Speculative Arithmetic*, his *Principles of Geometry*, and other mathematical works which secured European reputation.[8] About this time an incident occurred, best described in Bradwardine's own words :

'I was at one time', he tell us, 'while still a student of philosophy, a vain fool, far from the true knowledge of God, and held captive in opposing error. From time to time I heard theologians treating

---

[1] *Ver. Script.* i. 35 f.   [2] Rashdall, ii. 540 ; Harnack, vi. 295 f.
[3] See *D. N. B.* and the preface by Savile to his *Causa Dei*.
[4] *Op. cit.* 64 f. Cf. however Harnack, vi. 307.
[5] *Ang. Sac.* i. 42. But Bradwardine, *Causa Dei* ii. 559, says that he was born in Chichester. The statement in *Ang. Sac.* i. 376 that he was born in Cowden, diocese Rochester, should be rejected.   [6] See note 1, p. 119.
[7] He first appears in the college books as an M.A. of some years' standing in 1323 (Brodrick 188).
[8] For MSS. and early printed editions see Tanner 121. The *Arithmetic* and the *Geometria Speculativa* were printed at Paris in 1495, 1512, 1530 (Tanner l. c.). For Bradwardine's mathematical importance see Cantor ii. 113 f. who rates him very highly. For his 'squaring of the circle' see *supra*, p. 100, n. 5. In the Paris edition of the *Geometria* in 1530 there is added a *tractatus de quadratura circuli noviter editus*. There are several copies of his mathematical works in the Brit. Mus.

of the questions of grace and freewill, and the party of Pelagius seemed to me to have the best of the argument. For I rarely heard anything said of grace in the lectures of the philosophers, except in an ambiguous sense. But every day I heard them teach that we are the masters of our own free acts, and that it stands in our power to do either good or evil, to be either virtuous or vicious, and such like. And when I heard now and then in church a passage read from the apostle, which exalted grace and humbled freewill—such, for instance, as that word in Romans, ix. 16, " Therefore it is not in him that willeth, nor in him that runneth, but in God that sheweth mercy ", I had no liking for such teaching, for towards grace I was still graceless. I believed also with the Manichaeans that the apostle, being a man, might possibly err from the path of truth in any point of doctrine. But afterwards, and before I had become a student of theology, the truth before mentioned struck upon me like a beam of grace. It seemed to me as if I beheld in the distance, under a transparent image of truth, the grace of God as it is prevenient both in time and nature to all good works—that is to say, the gracious will of God, which precedently wills that he who merits salvation shall be saved, and precedently works this merit in him,—God, in truth, being in all movements the primary Mover. Wherefore also I give thanks to Him who freely gave me this grace.' [1]

After his conversion, Bradwardine while as yet only a bachelor in theology [2] delivered at Merton a course of lectures in which he systematized his views on the all-determining power of grace. In September 1333 Bradwardine was provided with a prebend in Lincoln, in value but 20s. yearly.[3] In 1335 Bradwardine, with six other Merton men, was summoned to London by Bury, now chancellor of England, who made him one of his chaplains.[4] In 1339 he became the chaplain and confessor of Edward III, who appointed him (8 Feb. 1347) archdeacon of Norwich.[5] The memories of his piety lingered long both at Court and in the army, which he accompanied on the French campaigns.

Bradwardine, for whom on the 1st November 1348 Clement VI reserved the deanery of Lincoln,[6] was twice elected by the

---

[1] *Causa Dei* i. 308.   [2] *Chart. Par.* ii. 454 *n.*
[3] *Pap. Let.* ii. 395, 524. The date in *Chart. Par.* ii. 454 *n.* (25 Jan. 1336) seems inaccurate. He was admitted 23 Dec. 1333 (Tanner 120 *n.*). He still retained this prebend in Feb. 1349 (*Pap. Let.* iii. 284).
[4] Bury obtained for him several preferments, a benefice of 40 marks in Chichester, Jan. 1336 (*Pap. Let.* ii. 529); non-resident rector of Llanpadrn Vawr (*ib.* iii. 273); Chancellor of St. Paul's (19 Sept. 1337; Hennessy, *Nov. Rep.* 13).   [5] *Cal. Pat.* vii. 251.
[6] *Pap. Let.* iii. 273; *Pap. Pet.* i. 145. Bale in *Index Script.* wrongly calls it the bishopric.

monks of Canterbury to be their archbishop. On the first occasion (1348) their haste and informality angered the king, and Bradwardine was set aside. But on a second vacancy, a few months later, Edward himself nominated his friend.[1] So on the 19th July 1349 Bradwardine was consecrated at Avignon and the pallium conferred upon him the next day.[2] In the palace of Clement VI fires were kept burning night and day, and few were admitted. But fears of the plague did not prevent cardinal Hugh of Tudela, a kinsman of Clement, from indulging in a studied insult. In the banquet which followed the consecration, he led into the pope's presence an ass, on which rode a clown with a petition round his neck that he too might have a bishopric. Bradwardine had angered the papal officials by his unwillingness to pay the customary doles.[3]

Bradwardine returned to England to assume his duties. On the 19th of August he landed at Dover, having walked the whole way from Avignon to Calais at an average of twenty miles a day under an August sun. A week later (Aug. 26) he lay dead at Lambeth at a manor called La Place belonging to the bishop of Rochester,[4] the second archbishop within a few months to fall a victim to the Black Death. We can measure the loss by the love and esteem which people and King alike bore for him. His whole character is summed up in the prayer with which he begins the fifteenth chapter of his work :

'Good Master, my only Master, Thou who from my youth upwards hast taught me until this day all that I ever learned of the truth, and all that, as Thy pen, I have ever written of it, send down upon me also now of Thy great goodness, Thy light, so that Thou, who has led me into the profoundest depths, mayest also lead me up to the mountain heights of this inaccessible truth. Thou, who hast brought me into this great and wide sea, bring me also into Thy haven. Thou Who hast conducted me into this wide and pathless desert, Thou, my Guide, my way, my end, lead me also unto the end. Show to Thy little child, how to solve the knot of Thy Word.'

[1] On 19 June 1349 Clement affected to provide him (*Pap. Let.* iii. 339).
[2] *Ang. Sac.* i. 42 ; Reading, *Chron.* 108 ; *Pap. Let.* iii. 337.
[3] Reading, *Chron.* 112 ; *Ang. Sac.* i. 43.
[4] *Ang. Sac.* i. 119. He was buried in the chapel of St. Anselm. 'La Place' was a house built by Gilbert de Glanville bp. of Rochester (1215). After 1500 it was called Carlisle house (T. Allen, *Parish of Lambeth*, 1827, p. 333).

The influence of Bradwardine's determinism was far reaching. We see this in the confession which Chaucer puts into the mouth of his nun's priest as regards the distinction between predestination and free will:

> But I ne cannot bulte (bolt) it to the bren (bran)
> As can the holy doctour, Augustyn,
> Or Boëce, or the bishop Bradwardyn.[1]

In scholastic circles Bradwardine's opinions were much canvassed. We see his influence in the opinions of John de Mirecourt, condemned at Paris in 1347, as the Austin friar Hugh, who took the lead in the prosecution, pointed out at the time.[2] For the doctrine of Bradwardine put in a nutshell was this, that the divine will is the antecedent necessity of every effect. This Mirecourt pushed into the extreme 'that God causes that a man sins and is a sinner', and that 'no one sins by his own volition except as God wills that he should will'. Mirecourt thus made sin into a good, for the man who sins is but 'conforming his will to the will of God'. Applying these speculations to ethics, Mirecourt whittles away the heinousness of sin as due to 'custom'. Every act is predestined from eternity; if a man feels hatred let him remember that God is the 'antecedent cause'. Possibly also we may trace Bradwardine's influence in the views of the Paris master, Nicholas de Autrecourt,[3] several of whose letters written to a certain Bernard of Aretis still exist in the National Library at Paris. On the 21st November 1340 Benedict XII ordered the bishop of Paris to dispatch Autrecourt and five others—one of whom was an English Cistercian named Henry—to Avignon that the Curia might inquire into their heresies. Autrecourt duly appeared, with the result that in May 1346 he was condemned on some sixty counts. Nicholas was deprived of his mastership, his *Epistles to Bernard* were burnt in the Pré-aux-clercs, and he himself was compelled to recant, first before Clement and then before the university. For his submission he was rewarded by

---

[1] Chaucer, *Nonne Preestes*, 420–3.
[2] See *Chart. Par.* ii. 610–14. Wyclif mentions this condemnation in *Ente* 253, and states that though the council has no authority in England yet the articles would not be condemned without reason. Dziewicki, *Ente*, p. xxxv, thinks that it was Bradwardine that was condemned.
[3] For Autrecourt see *Chart. Par.* ii. 576-87, also *ib.* 505 *n*. The story that he fled to Lewis of Bavaria rests upon a confusion with Ockham (*ib.* ii. 720 *n.*).

obtaining a licence in theology and the deanery of Metz. Corrupt copies of the grounds of his accusation have been recently edited by Denifle. Many of his theses are mere quibbles of logic. But others are remarkably acute and remind us at times, by their denial of necessary connexion between phenomenal cause and effect, of the teaching of bishop Berkeley.[1] Influenced perhaps by Bradwardine, as Denifle suggests, Nicholas laid down that we are ' evidently ignorant of any cause which is an efficient cause, except God '. Logic, he asserted, cannot prove that anything is eternal, or that, in bread for instance, there is any substance at all. Nor is it possible to show that ' all things phenomenal are real '. In his ethical system the same idealism is also apparent, and led him to reduce action to desire. According to his enemies he followed this out to the conclusion that ' in some cases theft is lawful '.

In the sixteenth century Bradwardine's works were neglected, for his doctrines were expounded with more clearness by the greater master, John Calvin. But in 1618 archbishop Abbot shared with Sir Henry Savile the cost of publishing [2] Bradwardine's collected Latin lectures, previously known as the *Summa Doctoris Profundi*, under the title *On the Cause of God against Pelagius, and on the Nature of Causes*.[3] A copy of this work may have fallen into the hands of Milton. In a familiar passage he grimly speaks of the fallen angels as the first professors of " vain wisdom and false philosophy ".

> Others apart sat on a hill retired,
> In thoughts more elevate, and reasoned high
> Of providence, foreknowledge, will and fate,
> Fixed fate, free will, foreknowledge absolute,
> And found no end in wandering mazes lost.
> Of good and evil much they argued, then
> Of happiness and final misery.[4]

[1] Rashdall, ii. 538 ; *Eng. Hist. Rev.* viii. 134.

[2] See *D.N.B.* i. 20. For Savile see *D.N.B.* He was warden of Merton from 1585 to his death 19 Feb. 1622, not 1621 as Brodrick 167. He founded in 1619 the two Savilian chairs.

[3] *De Causa Dei contra Pelagium*, a work of 1,000 folio pages. The date of the *de Causa Dei* is uncertain. But Denifle, *Chart. Par.* ii. 590 *n.*, shows that it was before 1344, the date which Bale, *Index Script.* 433, assigns, possibly before 1340, if indeed Nicholas de Autrecourt was influenced by it. In 1348 the Corpus MS. was procured for the monastery at Worcester by the monk John Preston of Somerset (James, *MSS. Corpus* i. 47).

[4] *Par. Lost.* ii. 555 f.

Of Bradwardine's influence on Wyclif there can be no doubt, though the differences between the systems of the two men [1] prevent us from regarding Wyclif as a mere copyist. Even before he commenced his theological studies Wyclif had adopted Bradwardine as one of his masters—' Doctor Profundus ' as he called him [2]—though at times he contests some of his conclusions, especially as regards free will.[3] From Bradwardine he learned the doctrine that there is nothing evil *per se*, and that nothing positive has evil inseparably attached to it.[4] By Bradwardine the Reformer would be confirmed in that rigid predestinarianism which he had learned, together with an abhorrence of all Pelagianism,[5] from Augustine. In his earlier writings Wyclif appears to assert human freedom in something more than the equivocal sense in which it is admitted by Augustine. He defines it, with Anselm, as ' the faculty by which an intelligent nature willingly cleaves to rectitude or righteousness '.[6] Free will is thus not the power of choice between alternatives, for the power of choice is really only the sign of freedom.[7] Wyclif by differentiating between contingency and necessity [8] was evidently trying to steer a middle course between the indeterminism of Fitzralph, against which he protests,[9] and the predestinarianism of Bradwardine with whom the will of God is accepted as the cause of every action,[10] including sin.[11] Wyclif argued that a man may be in part the determining cause of God's will because that will presupposes that man will act in a particular way. But in later years, though he still did lip-service to the doctrine of free will, determinism grew upon him.[12]

[1] Pointed out by Wyclif, *Ente*, 165 f.
[2] *Dom. Div.* 115 ; *Ente Praed.* 83, 104, 124, *et passim*.
[3] e. g. *Ente Praed.* 214 ; *Ente* 152 f. ; *Dom. Div.* 167 f.
[4] *Ente Praed.* 159 ; cf. *Dom. Div.* 120.
[5] *Ente*, 193–6.
[6] *Ente*, 137 f., 160 ff.; *Pot. Pap.* 4, 17. Anselm's *Dialogus de libero Arbitrio* considerably influenced Wyclif. Cf. *Dom. Div.* 132.
[7] *Ente*, 142–52. But Wyclif is not consistent. In *Serm.* iv. 305 he maintains that God gives us free will since He will have none to be His unwillingly.
[8] *Log.* iii. 194–5 ; *Misc. Phil.* i. 71 f. ; *Dom. Div.* 166 f.
[9] *Ente*, 272 f. ; *Dom. Div.* 128.
[10] *Ente Praed.* 133, where there are over twenty references to the book, and cf. Poole, *Dom. Div.* p. xxix.
[11] See Wyclif's criticism, *Dom. Div.* i. 125 ; *Op. Evang.* i. 445–6.
[12] *Dom. Div.* 165. Cf. Dziewicki, *Misc. Phil.* i. p. xxi f. ; *Op. Min.* 375.

In the struggle of Oxford with the mendicants, a leading part was taken by one to whom Wyclif was profoundly indebted, Richard Fitzralph,[1] commonly known as 'Armachanus'. Fitzralph, though claimed by many as a native of Dundalk[2] in Ireland, was, possibly, of Devonshire origin,[3] a fact which will account for the friendship of Grandisson. At Oxford he entered Balliol, where he took his master's degree before 1325,[4] but by the rules of the college was forced to go elsewhere for further study. So he migrated to University.[5] Before 1329 he obtained his bachelor's degree in theology. From 1332–4 he served as chancellor of his university.[6] Owing to his favour with Avignon his promotion was rapid.[7] In April 1337 he was provided by Benedict XII to the deanery of Lichfield.[8] As dean he found himself harassed in his frequent absence at Avignon by the regulations which forced him

'to say mass in person on the greater double feasts, and if not present to entertain the ministers of the church in his house; and on the four principal feasts to treat the whole choir, inviting the canons separately for eight days beforehand.'

So in May 1344 he secured the revocation of these statutes, as well as the gift of prebends for his three nephews.[9] Through the favour of Clement VI he was provided with the archbishopric of Armagh (30 July 1346),[10] and was consecrated at

[1] For Fitzralph see Poole in *D. N. B.* to which I have added some references.
[2] *Chron. Ang.* 48. Cf. *Pap. Let.* ii. 355, where he is called 'of the diocese of Armagh'; and of course Ware, *Works*, 81.
[3] So Prince, 294, who assigns him to the Fitzralphs of Norral near Widecombe.
[4] Salter, *Ball. Deeds*, 285; *Reg. Grand.* i. 233; *Hist. MSS. Com.* iv. 443.
[5] Wood, *Coll.* 54 *n.*; borne out by a petition in 1379 in which 'Richard Armecan's' residence at University is expressly claimed (*Rot. Parl.* iii. 69 a). Poole in *D. N. B.* questions this, inasmuch as the appeal was part of the claim to antiquity of University. But while the major part is myth, it is hardly likely that so recent an Oxford man as Fitzralph could thus be treated.
[6] He was confirmed as chancellor by Burgersh on 30 May 1332, his successor, Hugh Willoughby being confirmed 14 May 1334 (Salter, *Snappe*, 75–6). In *Mun. Ac.* 127; Wood, *City*, iii. 104, and Wood, *Fasti*, 21, 'Ricardus Radi', i.e. Radulphi, is extended into Ricardus Radin and an unknown chancellor invented!
[7] Canonry at Crediton, value £8, in Sept. 1331, chancellor of Lincoln, 10 July 1334; archdeacon of Chester; prebend Lichfield (Dec. 1335 *Pap. Let.* i. 566, ii. 355, 524, iii. 78; *Reg. Grand.* iii. 1286).
[8] *Ang. Sac.* i. 443, 465.
[9] *Pap. Let.* iii. 117; *Pap. Pet.* i. 53.
[10] *Pap. Let.* iii. 217. In Jan. 1347 he received a faculty to select his conse-

Exeter by Grandisson on the 8th July 1347. After his consecration he rode through Exeter in his robes, and then acted for a time as a suffragan for Grandisson.[1] In the previous April he received instructions concerning certain wandering heretics, chief of whom was a Robert de Cowton, who were 'fostered' in the diocese of Dublin by Archbishop Alexander de Bicknor. If necessary he was to call in the secular arm.[2] This was the beginning of a struggle between Fitzralph and Bicknor over the primacy in Ireland in which Edward III took sides against him.[3]

In 1349 Fitzralph was once more at Avignon, commissioned by the English clergy to lay before Clement VI their complaints against the friars. But this action did not prevent friendly relations with the friars, for he was chosen by them to preach in the Franciscan church at Avignon on the festival of their order, 5th July 1350.[4] Perhaps this honour was conferred because he had already been deputed by Clement to make inquiry into the questions whose discussion had so long disturbed the order.[5] To this we owe the publication of his treatise *de Pauperie Salvatoris*. During this visit also Fitzralph took part in the negotiations with the Armenian church, and wrote by request an elaborate treatise in nineteen books refuting their heresies.[6] On the 18th February 1350 Edward III ordered Fitzralph to return to his see. In the following summer Fitzralph obeyed, and gave himself to the restoration of his

crating prelates (*ib.* 225). For a letter from Grandisson to him in 1328 see *Reg. Grand.* i. 173; in 1329 *ib.* i. 233. On 29 Aug. 1347 he received the pallium with an exhortation 'to serve humility and justice' (*Pap. Let.* iii. 262; Theiner, 288).

[1] *Reg. Grand.* ii. 1022-3.
[2] *Pap. Let.* iii. 227, 231; Theiner, 286. In *D. N. B.* v. 12 this is wrongly dated as in 1330. Bicknor (for whom see *D. N. B.*) died 14 July 1349 (Cotton, ii. 14). The hunt began in 1343; in 1346 the heretics despoiled the bishop of Ossory of his goods; we hear of the hunt again in 1351 (*Pap. Let.* iii. 136, 432; *Pap. Pet.* i. 115, 216; Theiner, 299).
[3] Rymer, iii. 190, 192.
[4] Sermon still exists in the Bodleian (Poole, *Dom. Div.* p. xxxv *n.*; Tanner, 285 *n.*).
[5] See Fitzralph's statement in the dedication of his *de Pauperie Salvatoris* (Wyclif, *Dom. Div.* 273), who dates as in 'anno octavo' of Clement, i. e. between 8 May 1349 and 8 May 1350.
[6] *Summa de Erroribus Armenorum* or *Summa in Questionibus Armenorum*, printed at Paris in 1512. For MSS. see Tanner, 248 *n.* In *Pol. Wks.* ii. 474 Wyclif calls Fitzralph 'dominum Armenium', a copyist's mistake for 'Armenorum'. For the negotiations see Leclercq-Hefele, vi. 846-8.

cathedral. Sermons also which he preached at Dundalk, Trim, and elsewhere in Ireland are still extant.[1] In April 1351 he obtained indulgences for all who within ten years should help the cathedral of Armagh, or visit it on St. Patrick's day. His object was to obtain funds for his bishopric, the rents of which amounted to but £400 a year. In consequence of this poverty he secured the appropriation to his *mensa* of four Irish churches, and a faculty to commute the vows of pilgrims to Rome, Santiago, or Palestine.[2]

In 1356 Fitzralph quitted Ireland and came to London. There he found a discussion in progress on the well-worn theme of the poverty of Christ, started, it would appear, by Richard Kilmington,[3] the dean of St. Paul's, with whom he had once lived in bishop Bury's house. Fitzralph, who may have just finished his own treatise on the subject, at once joined in the fray. In a series of ' seven or eight ' English sermons preached at St. Paul's Cross early in 1357, Fitzralph maintained that mendicancy had no warrant in scripture, and that the friars should be denied the right to hear confessions.[4] Fitzralph was opposed by the Oxford Franciscan, Dr. Roger Conway,[5] a native of the Welsh town, who had been brought up in the friary at Worcester, of which he became the guardian. In February 1355 Conway had obtained papal licence to remove from Worcester to the London friary ' for the spiritual recreation of himself and the nobles of England ', who were said to flock thither in great numbers.[6] To counter Fitzralph's attacks

---

[1] Tanner, 284 *n.* For Fitzralph as a preacher see Owst, c. 1, who exaggerates his character.

[2] *Pap. Let.* iii. 387, 398 ; *Pap. Pet.* i. 206, 207 ; Theiner, 295.

[3] So Wood, *Univ.* i. 475. For Kilmington (†1361) see *D. N. B.* which needs correction. He was the son of a priest and his first cure was Gateshead ; M.A. before 1331, doctorate before 1341. Provided deanery 9 Apr. 1354 (not 1353) and thereupon (not 1350 as *D. N. B.*) resigned his archdeaconry (see *Pap. Let.* ii. 364, 520, 554 ; iii. 394, 418, 516, 519, 530). According to Tanner 461 some of his sermons and a book on logic are extant at Peterhouse. But see James, *MSS. Pet.* 229.

[4] Brown, ii. 466. Of these, four were printed by Jean Petit in his ed. of Fitzralph's *de Erroribus Armenorum* (Paris, 1512 App.).

[5] At a later date he became 22nd English Provincial (*Mon. Franc.* ii. 538, 561). It is scarcely likely that he was provincial at this time, for he wrote his *Defensio* at the command of another. See Little, 240 *n.* For Conway see Little, 239–40 ; Poole in *D. N. B.* xii. 58, who, however, corrects some details in *D. N. B.* xix. 197.

[6] Wadding, viii. 106, 457. *Pap. Let.* iii. 563.

the friars procured his citation to Avignon. At first Edward forbade Fitzralph to leave the country,[1] but in the summer of 1357 Fitzralph arrived at the papal court.[2] Thither Conway followed him ' and strenuously defended his order in the curia ', for Fitzralph had already preached before Innocent against the friars and all their ways,[3] as well as published his main attack, his treatise *de pauperie Salvatoris*.[4] To this Conway replied in his *Defensio Mendicantium*[5]; Fitzralph's rejoinder is now lost.

As a result of the controversy a commission of four cardinals was appointed. Pending their report Clement ordered the English episcopate not to hinder the friars from hearing confessions or burying the dead.[6] The friars won their suit, in spite of the support given at first to Fitzralph by the English bishops,[7] who seem to have levied a tax for his expenses.[8] This victory was due ' to their lavish use of money in the curia ', and to the defection of the seculars; ' Pilate and Herod ', sneered Wyclif, ' who before were enemies were made friends '.[9] On the 3rd April 1359 Conway obtained from Innocent VI the confirmation of the decree *Vas Electionis* of John XXII.[10] Five months before formal judgement was given,[11]

---

[1] 1 Apr. 1357, Rymer, iii. 352.

[2] *Mon. Franc.* i. 358. In Reading *Chron.* 130 we have the unlikely statement that Fitzralph went to Avignon, concealing his destination from the friars.

[3] *Defensorium curatorum* (Nov. 8), in Brown, *Fascic.* ii. 466-86; Goldast, ii. 1392 f. A short summary in English by Trevisa is in *Mon. Franc.* ii. 276-7. Its popularity is shown by its many early editions. In the Brit. Mus. there are eds. printed at Louvain 1475, 1480, Lyons 1496, Paris 1500 (according to Coppinger c. 1485); Rouen 1485 (? not in Reichling). Reichling, vi. 233 adds Plannck, Rome 1485.

[4] For this see *supra*, p. 127. A MS. from St. Augustine's, Canterbury, is in Corpus, Camb., as also a copy which belonged to Adam Easton (*supra*, p. 101). On the frontispiece there is a portrait of the author, and also of four friars on whose shoulders demons sit beating them on their chins (James, ii. 229, 420; Tanner, 284 n.).

[5] Printed at Lyons in 1496 at the end of Fitzralph's *Defensorium*, then at Paris 1511, and in Goldast, ii. 1410 f. Conway's name is latinized into Chonnoe. For Conway's other works see Little, 240.

[6] *Pap. Let.* iii. 596; Wadding, viii. 127 f. Date 1 Oct. 1358.

[7] So Wyclif in *Trial*. 375. Cf. Walsingham, i. 285.

[8] Tanner, 284 n.; cf. *Ziz.* 284.

[9] Walsingham, i. 285; *Chron. Ang.* 38; *Ziz.* 284.

[10] Little, 239 n. One of Fitzralph's Sermons had been directed against this bull (Bale, i. 444; Tanner, 284 n.).

[11] *Chron. Ang.* 38; Mollat-Baluze, i. 324. We have no record of the formal decision.

Fitzralph passed away at Avignon (16 Nov. 1360),[1] an occasion for the friars ' for singing gaudeamus rather than a requiem '.[2] Conway outlived him some years,[3] and was buried in the choir of the Greyfriars, London.[4] But others were found to take up the struggle ; among whom on the side of Fitzralph were John Uhtred of Boldon [5] and Wyclif. As part of the fray, efforts were made to obtain Fitzralph's canonization, and a commission was appointed by Rome (Jan. 1399) to examine into the miracles wrought by him at Lichfield, as well as at his tomb at Dundalk.[6] Nothing came of the inquiry ' on account of the distance and expense ', though the lollards canonized him in their writings as 'St. Richard'.[7] Centuries later the common people of Ireland by ancient tradition were still wont to chant out this distich :

"Many a mile have I gone, and many did I walk,
But never saw a holier man than Richard of Dundalk." [8]

Fitzralph's *de Pauperie Salvatoris* attempts to solve the problems which had led to conflict among the Franciscans, by a careful examination of the disputed phrases.[9] He distinguishes ' lordship ' from ' property ', which it does not necessarily involve, and from ' possession ' which is the result of ' lordship '. ' Lordship ' or ' Dominion ', to use the word

[1] So rightly Cotton, iii. 15 ; Prince, 298 ; Ware, *Works* (1739), i. 83. The date of his death is variously given as 16 Nov. (Ware, *l. c.*) and 20 Nov. (*Chron. Ang.* 48 ; Bale, i. 444) ; Leland, *Comment.* 373, gives the year as 1359 ; so Poole in *D. N. B.* xii. 58, corrected in *D. N. B.* xix. 197. On 10 Sept. 1360 Fitzralph obtained at Avignon a prebend in Ferns for a kinsman there with him (*Pap. Pet.* i. 359).

[2] Mollat-Baluze, i. 324.

[3] Little, 240. In *D. N. B.* it is said that he died in 1360, following Bale, i. 460.

[4] Kingsford, *Grey Friars*, 72 ; Wood, *Coll.* 21.

[5] Wood, *Univ.* i. 475. For Uhtred see *infra*, p. 222. Wood adds archb. Thoresby, following Bale, i. 493. If true this would be an interesting link with Wyclif ; cf. *infra*, ii. 157 f. But Thoresby's *Processus contra fratres* merely dealt with the contention of the friars that mortuaries had not to be paid (Tanner, 711). Kingsford in *D. N. B.* considers the writer to have been the archbishop's nephew.

[6] *Pap. Let.* v. 245. Cf. Wyclif, *Lat. Serm.* iii. 311 ; *Chron. Ang.* App. 400 ; *Cont. Murimuth*, 225 ; Higden, viii. 392. For his removal to Dundalk see *Cont. Murimuth*, 193 or Higden, viii. 410. His tomb still existed in the time of Charles I (Ware, i. 83).

[7] *Eng. Works*, 128 ; *Sel. Eng. Works*, iii. 281 (both of doubtful authorship), 412, 416. Wyclif calls him ' Sanctus Ricardus ' in *Apos.* 36 ; *Blas.* 232 ; *Euch.* 292.

[8] Prince, 297.   [9] See the analysis in Poole, *Dom. Div.*, pp. xxxvii–xlvi.

which Wyclif has made more familiar, was the result of the Creation, and cannot be alienated from God by any user. Human lordship is therefore founded upon God's grant; it is merely an entrusted government and, as such, dependent upon 'grace'; 'without grace there is no lordship'. Originally 'lordship' was given by God to man in his state of innocency. By the Fall this lordship was lost, but can be recovered by repentance. Thus the original grant is still retained by the righteous man. 'Property' as distinct from 'lordship' is thus the result of the Fall—a doctrine which Wyclif pushed to its extreme conclusions. In the same way civil lordship is one of the results of sin; it is an accident that can be forfeited by mortal sin. 'Lordship' involves the 'right of use'. This right of use, which does not necessarily include 'lordship', is the gift of God and in nowise alienates God's lordship. Excess of use is abuse and therefore a sin against God's lordship, while to maintain that no one can have a thing except by way of 'property' is simply the cupidity of wicked men.

Wyclif's indebtedness to Fitzralph was twofold.[1] In his early years he did not agree with Fitzralph's denunciation of the friars,[2] though after his quarrel with the papacy he went farther than Fitzralph in his scorn of the mendicants. But before this quarrel Wyclif had adopted and enlarged a part of Fitzralph's *de Pauperie Salvatoris*.[3] A copy of the work, once the property of John Riseborough, a contemporary fellow of Merton,[4] still exists, and may have been the manuscript used by Wyclif. A comparison of the treatise of Fitzralph with the two works of Wyclif, *de Dominio Divino* and *de Civili Dominio*, shows

" that Wyclif has added no essential element to the doctrine which he read in the work of his predecessor. All he has done—this in the *de Civ. Dom.*—is to carry the inferences logically deducible from that doctrine very much farther than the purpose of Fitzralph's treatise required him to pursue them, and very much farther than it is likely Fitzralph would have pursued them." [5]

---

[1] For Wyclif's indebtedness to Fitzralph *in Questionibus Armenorum* see *Ente Praed*. 144, 152, 157; *Pot. Pap., passim*.

[2] *Infra*, ii. 98, and cf. *Civ. Dom*. iii. 62 f., 110.

[3] Of this work, books I-IV, which Wyclif followed, have been printed by R. L. Poole in *Dom. Div.*, pp. 257-476. The remaining three books deal with the bearing of his work on the controversies of the friars. Poole gives a table of their contents, *ib.* 264-72.

[4] Brodrick, 212; Poole, *Dom. Div.* 263.   [5] Poole in *Dom., Div.*, p. xlviii.

Wyclif's famous conclusion that 'no one in mortal sin is lord of anything' is directly taken, as Woodford pointed out,[1] from Fitzralph. When Wyclif's teaching on dominion was condemned by Gregory XI, and by the Council of Constance, both council and pope forgot that Wyclif and Hus were but reproducing the doctrine of an honoured archbishop, published in a work dedicated to Innocent VI.

Some mention should be made of the relation of Wyclif to the Italian thinker, Marsiglio of Padua. Marsiglio is one of the most interesting publicists of the Middle Ages, doubly interesting because of his association with Ockham and Lewis of Bavaria in the struggle against 'the great dragon and old serpent', John XXII. Marsiglio's *Defensor Pacis*[2] is undoubtedly the most original political treatise of the Middle Ages. No seer ever had a clearer vision of the new order towards which the world was slowly moving; no prophet ever glanced deeper into the future. In his works we find set out in clear outline ideals which now regulate all democratic governments, though not all of his concepts have as yet been put to the full test. The most characteristic political ideas of Wyclif, apart from Marsiglio's republicanism, are found expressed with greater clarity, though with the same intolerable prolixity, in the writings of the Italian; so much so that Wyclif's conclusions in the judgement of Gregory XI in 1377 'but represent with a few terms changed the perverted opinion and heretical doctrines of Marsiglio of Padua, of damned memory, and of

---

[1] See Brown, *Fascic.* i. 232, 237. Woodford quotes Fitzralph, *Paup. Salv.* ii. c. 11 (i. e. in *Dom. Div.*, pp. 352 ff.).

[2] For Marsiglio († 1343) see Poole's able analysis, *Med. Thought*, c. 9, and the valuable articles in *Eng. Hist. Rev.* xxxvii. 501 f., xxxviii. 1 f. Also S. Riezler, *Die literarischen Widersacher der Päpste zur zeit Ludwig des Baiers* (1874), 193–233. The *Defensor Pacis*, completed 24 June 1324 (see *Eng. Hist. Rev.* xx. 293-9, which also gives complete list of MSS.), is in Goldast, ii. 147–312, with useful summary, pp. 309–12. A new edition by C. W. Previté-Orton is in preparation. Its condemnation, 23 Oct. 1327, and formally in 1330, in the bull *Cum processum*, is in Rymer, ii. 719; *Chart. Par.* iii. 224. See also R. Scholz, *Unbekannte Kirchenpolitische Streitschriften aus der Zeit Ludwigs des Bayern* (Rome, 1911), 1–27, for three Curialist attacks. In 1374 the *Defensor Pacis* was translated into French, and in Sept. 1375 an inquisition was held among the masters of Paris to find out the guilty party (*Chart. Par.* iii. 223–7). The book was translated into English, with republicanism expurgated, in July 1535, by William Marshall, one of Cromwell's agents. Marsiglio should not be identified, as in Brit. Mus. Catalogue, with Marsiglio de Mainardino mistakenly called Menandrinus. See *Chart. Par.* ii. 158 *n.*, 717 *n.*

John of Jandun'.[1] Marsiglio, for instance, brushes aside all arguments for the pope's temporal jurisdiction. The State is supreme :

'What have priests to do with meddling of secular coactive judgements, for they ought not to be lords temporally, but to be servants and ministers after the example and precept of Christ? . . . Neither bishop nor pope have any coactive jurisdiction in this world, neither upon any priest, neither upon any other person being no priest, unless such jurisdiction be granted to them by the human power.'[2]

Excommunication in fact can only be decreed by the congregation. Other illustrations might be given which would abundantly justify Gregory's verdict. To the State belongs all patronage and ecclesiastical property. Church government is a question of expediency, the papacy of convenience. The Bible is the foundation of faith and of the authority of the Church. The power of the keys is limited, for the turnkey is not the judge. Errors of opinion, ' however so great they be,' must not be punished, unless dangerous to society. Of errors, Jesus alone is the judge in the world to come.

In reality Wyclif never seems to have heard of Marsiglio, and in all his voluminous writings there is no clear reference to him, though Wyclif, as is usual with medieval writers, is most careful to invoke the witness of others. The tenets of Marsiglio were worked out by Wyclif, without knowledge on his part that he was but following in another's footsteps, re-stating in a cloud of words theses that Marsiglio had enunciated fifty years previously. There does not in fact seem to have been any copy of Marsiglio's work at Oxford until one was presented to Lincoln College by Dr. Thomas Gascoigne,[3] probably because its defence of the conciliar theory would appeal to him as it did to Gerson. Such influence at Oxford as Marsiglio exerted, if any, must have been indirect through William of Ockham,[4] and this last merely the tradition of the struggle

---

[1] See *infra*, p. 297. For Jandun († 1328) see *Chart. Par.* ii. 186, 303 *n*., iii. 227, 244.

[2] ii. cc. 4, 5. In Marshall, 54 *a*, 60 *a*.

[3] Now in Brit. Mus. Royal MS. A 10. 15.

[4] For at least thirty years before his death at Munich on 10 Ap. 1350. Ockham was never in England (*Pap. Let.* ii. 490, 492, is due to confusion, cf. *ib*. 493, 496). Whether Ockham signed the recantation in *Pap. Let.* iii. 336 is uncertain.

between John XXII and Lewis of Bavaria, or rather between John and Lewis's allies, Marsiglio and Ockham.

§ 3

From these general considerations we pass to the study of Wyclif's early Oxford writings.[1] In his own age these works were held in the highest repute, as is evident from the many manuscripts which have survived. But now the problems they attempt to solve and the methods employed are dead, though "many of his arguments if stripped of their old-world form and dressed up in the terminology of the twentieth century would look strikingly new."[2] But by all except the enthusiast they will remain unread, for they repel not only by their subject-matter but also by their diffuseness, as well as by their heavy Latin, or rather English expressed in a Latin whose rules of syntax are those of Wyclif's native tongue.[3] These works divide themselves into philosophical and theological, corresponding to Wyclif's preparation for his master's degree in arts and for his doctorate in theology. From our study of the chronology of Wyclif's life we see that his philosophical works must have been completed before the spring of 1361 when he left Balliol. His early theological works may be dated between 1363 and his taking his doctorate in 1372. But the boundary line between theology and philosophy is not strictly delimited; the conclusions of one are always running into the basis of the other, as we see in Wyclif's references in his philosophical works to Bradwardine's *de Causa Dei*. Moreover, the philosophical works, written when Wyclif had no thought of revolt, were revised and published in their present form as part of a *Summa* at a later date. They are thus not always consistent, but bear marks of successive periods of thought.

As is usual with all schoolmen, Wyclif's works abound in quotations. In one of his writings there are no less than five hundred.[4] For the schoolman authority was supreme; he

---

[1] For a detailed account see Appendix D.
[2] Dziewicki, *Misc. Phil.* i. xxxiv.
[3] Poole, *Civ. Dom.* i. xviii f., gives some useful notes on its characteristics.
[4] *Ente Praed.*, p. xvi. In the *Comp. Hom.*, a scholastic exercise, quotations average four a page.

rarely ventured on an opinion that he could not support by a catena of writers. But even in his scholastic days Wyclif laid down the supremacy in all human thought of the Scriptures.[1] Next to the Bible he relied upon Augustine, whose power of psychological analysis appealed strongly to him. With these he tried to combine Aristotle and his commentators. Of Plato, except in so far as incorporated in Augustine, Wyclif shows no knowledge. That in his philosophic writings Wyclif rarely quotes from Peter Lombard's *Sentences* is due not to any revolt against that medieval text-book, but to the fact that he had not yet begun his theological reading. Wyclif's quotations are often vague and inaccurate even when taken from the more accessible writers, Augustine and Aristotle.[2] We must remember not only that Wyclif laboured under the usual disadvantages of the schoolman, that a good library with good transcripts[3] was not always at his hand, but that many of his writings are probably transcripts made by his disciples of his oral lectures. Wyclif evidently trusted largely to his memory, with consequent inexactness,[4] even in his references to the Vulgate. For Aristotle his only source would be Latin translations, often faulty themselves; in consequence there is scarcely a reference which is verbally accurate. In his quotations from Anselm, especially his *Dialogus de Veritate*, Gilbert of Porrée,[5] Aegidius Romanus, and the later schoolmen, he was more fortunately circumstanced. Wyclif sometimes quotes from sources almost unknown to modern scholars.[6] Such quotations were probably taken from commonplace books, though in our ignorance of the contents of Oxford libraries in Wyclif's day we cannot dogmatize.[7] In his theological writings we are conscious of a higher note; Wyclif was tired of mere sophistical discussion, and urged that 'we schoolmen' should seek for 'necessary truth' instead of making futile efforts 'to track impossible conclusions from impossible premises.'[8] Though

[1] *Comp. Hom.* 3. This was rare with the artists.
[2] Cf. *Ver. Script*, i. 7 *n.*, 33 *n.*
[3] For a bad manuscript of Augustine see *Civ. Dom.* i. 79.
[4] e. g. *Civ. Dom.* i. 56 from Boethius.
[5] For Gilbert see Poole, *Med. Thought*, c. 6.
[6] See Appendix E, and for Peraldus, Appendix K.
[7] Peterhouse, Camb. had 380 vols. in 1418 (James, *MSS. Pet.* 1–26).
[8] *Ben. Incarn.* 77, 116, 165.

quotation is as abundant as ever, the ' authorities ' are changed. Augustine is still predominant, but we hear little of Aristotle and less of Avicenna and Averroës. Wyclif has studied Jerome, Gregory the Great, John Damascenus, the theological works of Anselm, Aquinas; and Bonaventura, and freely uses his sources, while references abound to Duns Scotus on the *Sentences.* But chief of his authorities is the Bible, his lectures on which as a ' cursor ' had been no empty form. He leans upon the Bible absolutely, taking his stand upon the plain literal meaning. At the same time, in opposition to the current Scotism and following Aquinas, he maintains that all Christian truth may be established on grounds of reason ; even the miracles can be explained ' lumine naturali '.[1]

Wyclif's references to English history show that he had not neglected such sources as were available. He quotes freely from ' Cestrensis ',[2] i. e. Ralph Higden of St. Werburgh's Abbey, Chester, whose *Polychronicon*—from the Creation to 1352—was translated into English in 1387 by John Trevisa.[3] Was it Trevisa that first introduced Wyclif to this standard authority ? From ' Cestrensis ' he obtained and believed the fable of pope Joan, with which, more than once, he makes great play.[4] He uses also Ralph Diceto (†1222), dean of St. Paul's, from whom he obtained his knowledge of history outside England ;[5] as well as the *Flores Historiarum*[6]—from the Creation down to 1326—and Peter Comestor's popular *Historia Scholastica.*[7] He also refers to Josephus' *Antiquities*, a copy of which was in the library of Queen's.[8]

The work of Wyclif as a schoolman had its roots in a realism so uncompromising that he averred that whoever denied the reality of universals denied the reality of predestination, of eternal punishment, of the resurrection of the dead, of the law of confession and communion, and of the necessity of obedience to the dean of his faculty ! He compares individuals to private

---

[1] *Ben. Incarn.* 159.   [2] e. g. *Pot. Pap.* 130 ; *Off. Reg.* 128, 146, 159.
[3] *Infra*, p. 167. See also Gross, *Sources*, 371.
[4] *Pot. Pap.* 272, 309, 312 ; *Pol. Wks.* ii. 619.
[5] *Pot. Pap.* 181 f. Ed. Stubbs in Rolls Series.
[6] *Pot. Pap.* 223. Ed. Luard in Rolls. See also Gross, 362.
[7] ' The master of stories ' (*Eng. Works*, 2) ; *Ver. Script.* iii. 110 ; *Civ. Dom.* iii. 199, iv. 439 ; *Eccl.* 163 ; *Op. Evang.* ii. 14 ; *Pot. Pap.* 286.
[8] *Pot. Pap.* 283 ; *Op. Evang.* i. 124 ; see *supra*, p. 69 *n.*

CH. IV   PLACE AMONG SCHOOLMEN   137

persons, universals to commonwealths. Wyclif's realism was a protest against the conceptualism of Ockham. Wyclif refuses to allow that conceptualism, which he defines as the theory which makes universality to consist in abstractions, is permissible, in spite of the 'famous philosophers' who support it ; while to the earnest nature of Wyclif, nominalism was an impossible creed, a mere cult of 'signs'.[1] For in spite of all the objections that may be urged against the thirteen different schools of realism which Prantl has discriminated, this much may be said for the moderate realists, that their realism was a protest against any doctrine of illusion. They held that mental ideas are, in some sense of the word, strict realities, that in some way or other there is such a thing as 'heat', or even as 'panitas' and 'vinitas', that a houseful of virtues apart from acts or subjects would be worth nothing at all. Ideas alone, said Wyclif, have a being 'intelligible, possible, necessary and eternal'. These 'ideas' were the guarantee of the existence of the world around, imparting to it their own necessity and continuity.[2]

Wyclif's realism lay at the root of his views of the Church. It led him to warn his hearers against the nominalist heresy that there was no Church until after the death of Christ ; to contrast with the predestinate the foreknown who form one body, of which the devil is the head and 'the outward form is God's eternal foreknowledge'.[3] Above all, his realism brought him into collision with the prevailing nominalist heresies concerning the Eucharist, and the belief in the annihilation of the substance of the elements. To Wyclif this was more than an absurdity. If accidents can exist without substance, then why postulate substance at all? The annihilation of any one real meant the reduction of the universe to illusion, a world in which science could have no place. God could not annihilate any substance without annihilating the whole world of substances, for the annihilation of the universal in one is the annihilation of the universal in all ; the mere thought of annihilation is itself a contradiction in terms.[4] The real had for Wyclif a

[1] 'doctors of signs' (*Ben. Incarn.* 170 ; *Apos.* 155 ; *Ziz.* 105, 117, 125).
[2] *Ente Praed.* 41 ; *Misc. Phil.* ii. 39, 171 ; *Apos.* 136, 141-2.
[3] *de Eccl.* 77, 102, 437. See *infra*, ii. 10.
[4] *Ente*, 289, 292 ; *Logica*, iii, p. vii.

sacredness which sometimes leads him into irreverence, as when he protests that his opponents with their doctrine of phantasm degrade the Eucharist into something 'more imperfect than poison' or even than 'rat's food', both of which were realities.[1] So in the interpretation of his ideas, we must remember that when Wyclif speaks of the Host as a 'sign' he does not use the word in any Zwinglian sense. With him every figure has its own real though ideal existence, and every real is of necessity universal, since the universal is the intrinsic formal cause of any particular being.[2] He goes so far as to maintain that the paschal lamb being the figure of Christ is Christ, though less perfectly so than the Host.[3] With Wyclif, universal ideas have no existence apart from God; the Divine Essence is, as it were, a mirror in which all possible things are reflected, and this reflection is the ideal world.[4] All that exists has its origin in God's eternal thought.[5] He assented to Grosseteste's doctrine that 'God is the form of things'.[6] In his discussion of the relation between God's 'intellections' or acts of cognition, whereby He knows His creature, and his 'volitions', Wyclif supposes a world of divine acts which are not God, yet belong to God somewhat as the sun's rays are not the sun.[7]

Wyclif's realism is seen at its best in his 'sententiary' treatise, the *de Benedicta Incarnacione*, a long exposition of the Person of Christ. Here he opposes the current medieval obscuration of the humanity that we find in Abailard, in the *Sentences*, in Aquinas—"the Christ of Aquinas is after all not our brother, not a man but only a ghostly simulacrum"[8]—in Duns and others whom Wyclif calls 'the moderns', whose errors he attributed to the prevalent nominalism.[9] For Wyclif,

---

[1] *Apos.* 172. In *ib.* 205 he compares it with 'stercus ratonis'; in *ib.* 235 with a tortoise; in *Euch.* 347 with 'horse-bread'; *Blas.* 27 with a 'spider's web'. Cf. *Ziz.* 106, 108.
[2] *Misc. Phil.* ii. 29. In *Trial.* 66 he warns us against pushing this too far.
[3] *Apos.* 98.
[4] See especially *Misc. Phil.* ii. 1–30. Wyclif appealed to Augustine's punctuation of John i. 4 'quod factum est in ipso vita erat'.
[5] *Ver. Script.* ii. 119; *Ente Praed.* 274; *Euch.* 69, 70, 78 (important).
[6] *Misc. Phil.* i. 171; *Ente Praed.* 147 from Grosseteste, *Epist.* 1.
[7] *Ente*, Book II, cf. *ib.* pp. xviii f.
[8] Dorner, *Person of Christ*, ii. (i) 333 quoted by Harris, *Ben. Incarn.* 240.
[9] *Ben. Incarn.* 71, 144–5, 223.

the humanity of Christ is a ' most precious jewel ' which he will not surrender, in spite of the charges made against him of Arianism.¹ At His incarnation, a greater miracle by far than the Creation, Christ took upon Himself the nature not of a man, nor of many men, but the ' communis humanitas ' of all men, manhood as it is in the ' forma exemplaris ' of the Divine Idea. This likeness He can never lose ; it is the same yesterday, to-day, and for ever, not the likeness of men but the primal humanity itself which He retained even during His three days in the tomb, and which makes Christ to be of the same species as other men.² Nothing human is alien to Him,³ for the manhood of Christ is the basis of the manhood of every individual. Christ is thus not only the ' homo communis ' ; He is also by His incarnation ' unicus homo ', Who is one with every individual, Who lives, suffers, and dies like all His brethren, liable to all the ills that flesh is heir to. One effect of this exaltation of the humanity of Jesus is seen both in Wyclif and his disciples in their exaltation of humanity at large. The ' Universal man ' is the bond between man and man.⁴

We note also in this work another development. In spite of Wyclif's oaths as a ' sententiary ' that he taught nothing that was not orthodox, we see in the work, at any rate in its published form, the beginnings of theological strife. Though little notice was taken at the time, as Netter himself tells us, five positions were branded at a later date as heretical,⁵ and in consequence the book was burnt at Prague in 1410 by archbishop Zbinek.⁶ The book is also noteworthy insomuch as Wyclif now begins to be troubled about the remanence of the bread in the Eucharist. Hitherto he had held the Scotist theory of annihilation, or had not protested against it, in spite of its contradicting his philosophic realism.⁷ But now, though he did not openly

---

¹ *Ben. Incarn.* 23, 25, 54, 78 f. Cf. Netter, *Doct.* i. 207–36.
² *Sel. Eng. Works*, i. 319 ; *Ben. Incarn.* cc. 2–5, 123 f., 169, c. 4 as against Duns and Cowton.
³ So, but not in exact words, *ib.* 135.
⁴ *ib.* c. 13 and pp. 89, 101, 149 ; *Misc. Phil.* ii. 149–50.
⁵ *Ziz.* 1–2, namely positions 3, 4, 5, 6 and 7.
⁶ Palacký, *Doc.* 380, where it is called, as by Wyclif himself (*Dom. Div.* 55), the *de Incarn. Verbi*.
⁷ I do not think Wyclif was ever a nominalist. See Appendix D, p. 333. But he did not at once realize all the implications of his realism.

break away from the current views, he maintains that there must be a subject underlying the accidents, though what that subject is he cannot tell, nor is the definition necessary ' for the faith of pilgrims '.[1] But so little notice was taken of this that Woodford assures us that Wyclif still held to the current theory of annihilation. Wyclif's position was the beginning of a controversy that did not come to a head until some years later.

Wyclif's realism led him into many difficulties. As he deems that all names denote realities and every true thing is also a real thing, he is driven into affirming that death, sin, and falsehood are ' entitive ' beings, and that time, space, extension, and other ' successives ' are realities incapable of increase or diminution.[2] Now the primary cause of sin is a deficiency, and deficiencies are not entities in themselves, but only possess an occasional or secondary existence so far as there is a good for which God allows them to exist. Thus Wyclif claims that sin, i.e. sin taken with its punishment which is just and holy, is willed by God as a good thing, inasmuch as it shows God's providence in bringing good out of evil.[3] The sanctity with which he hedged the real led also to the paradox that the annihilation of any one atom of the universe, of which atom the universal is an essential part, is virtually an annihilation of God, as it is the diminution of the universe itself which can neither be increased nor decreased. Whatever is exists in eternity and for eternity, extending to all time past and future, for it has continuous existence in a real present which has neither non-existent past nor not-yet-existing future.[4] Wyclif is thus forced to deny that annihilation of a single atom is possible even for Almighty Power. When asked what becomes of the atoms in a chemical compound he answered, as against the Thomists, that they still exist. That which differentiates the compound is the relation of one atom to another, a position much in accord with modern science. But by the same realism he is driven to conclude that the flash of cats' eyes in the

---

[1] See the very important passage *Ben. Incarn.* 190-1, and *infra*, ii. 34.
[2] *Ente*, c. 3 ; *Ente Praed.* 199 ; *Apos.* 136 ; *Logica*, iii. 170.
[3] *Ente*, 10-23, 221 f., 283-6 ; *Ente Praed.* cc. 17 f. ; *Serm.* ii. 226 ; *Logica*, iii. 195.
[4] *Logica*, iii. 1, 39, 173-7 ; *Ente*, pp. xxvi, lvii n., 287 f.; *Apos.* 144-5 ; *Comp. Hom.* 41.

dark is due to real fire, and that heat apart from fire is a thing in itself.[1]

The crux for all realists, from Plato downwards, has been the relation of the individual to the universal idea. Nor is the difficulty lessened if we emphasize with Wyclif that 'all our life is but a momentary interlude' between two eternities.[2] This had been the difficulty of Aquinas, who taught that the principle of individuation lay in matter, in so far as it is the substratum of forms.[3] Wyclif felt the same difficulty; it was urged against him that as the universal has existence separate from any of its singulars, universal and individual are really two singulars. He tried to escape by teaching that the universal is indeed its singular, but not formally, i. e. not *qua* singular; and likewise the singular is indeed its universal, but not *qua* universal,[4] an answer which may have satisfied his opponents, but which seems to mean little or nothing. It is as wrapped in darkness as his discussion whether a universal taken with one of its singulars is one being or two.[5] This he answers by stating that they form two realities, a position which comes perilously near the heresy that the Divine Essence and the Trinity make four Persons. From this Wyclif saved himself by the juggle that the two realities, since one *is* the other, do not form a number. But Wyclif's theory of real universals, absolutely increate yet caused by God and dependent on Him, is often obscure.[6] It was also exposed to theological danger. For it is impossible to maintain that reality belongs only to the idea or universal, without falling into Pantheism, more especially if we hold with Wyclif that the world is 'animated being', or a reflection in the mirror of Divine Essence, or, as he phrases it elsewhere, 'the world is an accident of God'.[7] If then the only real thing in Wyclif himself was the 'form' of humanity, if, moreover, as Wyclif claimed, this had its existence from the dawn of creation, soul and body united eternally, the individuality of Wyclif

---

[1] *Logica,* iii. 74 f.; cf. *ib.* iii. pp. vii, xix; *Apos.* 141.
[2] *Serm.* iv. 349.
[3] This was called 'quantitas determinata' (Ueberweg, i. 446).
[4] Dziewicki in *de Ente,* p. xv; *Misc. Phil.* i. p. xii, 143–5.
[5] *Log.* ii. 48–54; *Ente,* book I, c. 5.
[6] *Ente,* 5 *n.* Wyclif's main teaching 'de universalibus' is in *Misc. Phil.* ii.
[7] *Misc. Phil.* i. 168, ii. 6; *Logica,* iii. 203.

becomes unreal and phenomenal. What then, the nominalist asked, becomes of the immortality of the soul if the individual himself disappears ? What becomes of the soul itself if it is only ' the form by which the body is animate ' ? If so, can the soul ever be separated from the body ? [1] Nay more, what becomes of the personality of God ? Are we not driven to conclude that all things are forms or modes of being of the one only substance or real ? Is not every man, as Wyclif puts it, *materia prima* and ' in consequence created in the beginning of the world ' ? [2] Is not matter itself eternal as Averrhoës claimed ? [3] Can the world, or for that matter the individual, ever have beginning or end ? Is it not identical with the Divine Life ?—a method of statement, as Wyclif owns, that may be offensive to the weak minds of many ' modern theologians '.[4] All realists, we own, were not logical, and generally succeeded in stopping short of the conclusions of their syllogisms. Wyclif, for instance, claims that while all things are eternal in God's knowledge they are not eternal in themselves ; the archetype alone is eternal.[5]

At this stage it may be well to point out what is involved in calling Wyclif the last of the schoolmen. With Wyclif scholasticism became played out. Wyclif as a schoolman added little or nothing " to the stores already accumulated, pressed down, shaken together and running over, in the daily debates of the schools ".[6] " The Aristotelian form refused to fit a matter for which it was never intended ; the matter of Christian theology refused to be forced into an alien form ".[7] In its earlier years, especially under Abailard, this great movement had brought a measure of deliverance to the human mind. Scholasticism had proclaimed in words that Wyclif

---

[1] In *Comp. Hom.* 57, 67 Wyclif confesses that he had erred—' deliramenta juvenilia '—in thinking this possible.

[2] Wyclif, *Comp. Hom.* 19 f., 33, 53, 55.

[3] So owned by Wyclif, *Logica*, iii. 121.

[4] *Log.* iii. 225 ; *Misc. Phil.* i. 235–42, ii. 12, 14 ; Quaest. xiii. no. 8 in *Ente Praed.*

[5] *Log.* iii. 192 ; *Misc. Phil.* i. 237, 240–1, ii. 10–11. Wyclif's pantheistic tendencies, apparent in his *Logica*, are more fully developed in his *de Materia et Forma* (in *Misc. Phil.* i. 163 f.).

[6] Poole in *Dom. Div.*, p. xxxi. Dziewicki in his ed. of Wyclif's *Logica* and *Misc. Phil.* pleads for a much higher estimate.

[7] Prof. Seth on ' Scholasticism ' (*Encyc. Brit.* 9th ed. xxi. 418).

borrowed from Plato that the ' human intellect was created on the confines of eternity '.[1] Her energies were now exhausted, her vital force spent. If in common repute scholasticism unjustly stands damned for ever, the cause must be found in the worse than uselessness of her latter days. Her services in the reconciliation of faith and reason have been forgotten in the memory of her follies and repetitions in which all but professed students of the history of philosophy have long ceased to take any interest. As an intellectual movement its work finished with Ockham. Wyclif, judged as a schoolman, does little more than gyrate on a well-beaten path, often concealing with a cloud of dust and digressions that he is but moving in a circle. His philosophical works contain little that can claim to be strictly original, with the partial exception of his political doctrine of ' dominion '. That he was serving up once more the old ideas, or rather groping vainly to adapt the old wineskins to hold the heady must of his new thoughts, may account for his being " perhaps the most intricate and obscure of all the scholastic host ".[2] Theology, too, in the latter part of the fourteenth century became sterile. No manuscript of the fathers dates from that century, with the exception of a few brief tracts.[3] What the age knew of the past it was content to obtain from commonplace books alphabetically arranged, without insight into its meaning or realization that much of it was dead. Its outlook into the future was cribbed, cabined, and confined by a mental architectonic that looked no higher than an endless output of barren syllogisms.

Scholasticism, in fact, in the days of Wyclif had become unreal. We see the unreality in the favourite idea of the later schoolman that there is a double truth, that what is true in philosophy might be false in theology. Ockham, for instance, revels in demonstrating as a philosopher the absurdity of doctrines which as a theologian he was prepared to swallow.[4] There was, in fact, nothing, however sacred, which the later schoolmen were not prepared to fling into their logical machine, as they mistook an endless output of syllogism and wind for reality and truth. They held that it was open to debate whether

[1] *Comp. Hom.* 8 ; *Trial.* 227 ; *Ente Praed.* 144 f.
[2] Rashdall, ii. 541.
[3] See Denifle's remarks, *Chart. Par.* iii, p. ix.
[4] Rashdall, ii. 538.

continence was a virtue, or voluntary fornication a sin. At Oxford in Wyclif's day

'a doctor publicly taught in the school of the father of lies that in many cases it is allowable and even meritorious to lie'.[1]

Wyclif himself was real; his bitterest foes could not label him otherwise. Unfortunately he was no prophet. He argued strenuously in favour of free inquiry, so long as it was conducted in a spirit of reverence and confined to the learned.[2] But the older methods of inquiry had become profitless; the need of the world was the discovery of a new approach to its problems. The soil of scholasticism was exhausted, and Wyclif's labours could not produce from it any further harvest of life. To the misfortune of the cause he advocated, Wyclif did not see that the methods of the later schoolman were mere mental gymnastics without bearing on life; researches which resulted in no discovery, elaboration of distinctions without difference; endless conflicts in which the foes lost sight of each other in more than Egyptian darkness and in labyrinths without issue. Whether the schoolmen debated, as is popularly supposed, how many angels could dance on the point of a needle, we know not. But other questions of equal absurdity—for instance, whether the blessed in heaven are able to talk—were common subjects of dispute.[3]

The reader may be glad of an illustration which will simplify and explain the interest which these logical puzzles evolved. If the universal can only become individual by becoming incarnate in matter, what then becomes of the angels? They must either possess matter, or else there must be no difference of the individual between them. To obviate this difficulty Thomas was obliged to assume that each angel is a different species, a doctrine against which Duns protested.[4] It is interesting to note that, as Wood tells us, the question of the composition of angels was still keenly discussed at Queen's in his days.[5] One of the questions debated by Aquinas was

---

[1] *Apos.* 67.   [2] *Dom. Div.* 76 f.
[3] Aegidius Romanus, *Quodlibeta* (Venice, 1502, i.e. 1503), iii. 88.
[4] The matter is also discussed by Aegidius Romanus, *Quodlibeta*, ii. 7. Aegidius decides with Thomas that each angel is a separate species. Wyclif discusses the matter in *Misc. Phil.* ii. 128–9.
[5] Wood, *Univ.* i. 309.

whether an angel can pass from one extreme to the other without passing through the middle, while Ockham canvassed whether an angel can move through a vacuum.[1] In 1614 Christopher Binder published at Tübingen his *Scholastica Theologia*. Its controversy with the Jesuits we may pass by. But his collection in his second chapter of the absurdities which formed the diet of the schools is still of value, provided that the student remember that such absurdities were not the whole work nor the abiding work of scholasticism. We find among other matters of debate the following: whether the body of Mary was exposed to the influence of the stars; whether if man had not fallen all would have been males; whether a dumb priest is able to consecrate; or whether a baptism would be valid ' if you inverted the syllables and read Trispa, Liifi and Ctisan Tusspiri ' or said ' Buff, Baff '.[2]

We could pardon the failure of scholasticism to discover a primary law governing the realm of mind and matter, for in the nature of things success was impossible. We could pardon the self-assurance of her sons, for as yet there was no consciousness of the infinite range of science to impress humility on all but the ignorant, nor in this matter were Luther and Calvin more praiseworthy than Wyclif and Ockham. But the unreality of the later schoolmen are sins unto death which brought their inevitable penalty. We need not wonder at the enthusiasm with which Europe turned away from these barren puerilities to the New Learning, with its revelation of the forgotten treasures of Hellas. With the incoming of a new intellectual method and outlook there came also a complete revolution in theological conceptions. But these were developments of which Wyclif, necessarily, had no prevision. In his efforts at reform he was forced, so far as he attempted to accomplish his aim by thought, to use the tools at his disposal. Unfortunately these had lost their cutting power.

The reader should beware of another prevalent error. It is customary to look upon the revolt of Wyclif as almost an isolated event, and to consider scholasticism a period of stagnant because uniform thought. Such a theory ignores the

---

[1] Taylor, ii. 465 ; Ockham, *Quodlibeta* (Paris, 1487), i. 5.
[2] Cf. an old Oxford Catechism in Coulton, *Med. Garner*, 588–90.

history of medieval speculation. The sin of scholasticism did not lie in any rigid, mechanical uniformity. We might even assert that scholasticism by the very logomachies on which it set such store made it its chief business to prevent uniformity. There was never a time when some angel or demon was not stepping down into the pool and troubling its waters. In consequence the record of scholasticism is the record of all sorts of minor heretics, for differences of thought soon became differences in belief. But as a rule these minor heretics were unreal; their beliefs were mere matters of argument vitiated by the tradition of a double truth, or adopted to advertise their Determinations or Quodlibeta. When the sun of official disapproval arose they straightway withered away, for they had no depth of soil. Marsiglio, Ockham, and Wyclif differed from these men, not so much by daring to think for themselves, as by the groundwork of reality which underlay their belief, and by their willingness to push their independence into defiance. This last, in fact, is always the acid test.

The student of Wyclif should take some notice of these minor heretics. As these pages will show, Oxford was in a ferment, and Wyclif's strength lay in his voicing the current intellectual unrest. Passing by the men who may be called his followers, there were others in that century who drew down upon themselves official disapproval. Unfortunately the details of their heresies are often obscure, so that it is difficult to know to what extent they were lone venturers. One of these heretics in the generation before Wyclif, the Dominican Nicholas Trivet, the son of one of the king's justices, was a writer of repute as an historian and as an expositor. In February 1315 [1] Trivet was condemned by the chancellor and the doctors of divinity. His offence lay in his utterances on the relation between the Father and the Word. Trivet retracted, resumed his lectures, and died in 1328 at the ripe age of seventy.[2]

One of the most interesting of these heretics was a Cornishman, Ralph de Tremur,[3] a member of an ancient family that

---

[1] *Mun. Ac.* 100–1 (wrongly 1314); Wood, *Univ.* i. 386.

[2] For Trivet see *D.N.B.*, which omits this incident but gives a list of his writings and their manuscripts. See also Tanner, 722–3; Bale, *Index Script.* 308–9; Leland, *Comment.* 326–8; Gross, *Sources*, 391.

[3] For this man see *Reg. Grand.* iii. *passim*.

had long resided at a manor on the edge of Bodmin moors. In July 1331 Ralph, who was at that time studying in Oxford, was instituted to the small benefice of Warleggan, near his home. On his seeking the usual licence for non-residence, bishop Grandisson ordered him to take minor orders and granted him letters-dimissory for the purpose. He continued his Oxford studies—he had already, it would appear, obtained his Master's degree—and in September 1334 resigned Warleggan. After this we hear nothing of him for twenty years. During this period he took deacon's orders and obtained the repute of being a fluent speaker in Latin, French, English, and Cornish. He returned to Warleggan, robbed his successor of his goods, and then set fire to his rectory—a fair commentary on the general lawlessness of the age. He now spent his time in wandering through Devon and Cornwall preaching to the people both openly and secretly ' that the bread and wine are not changed consubstantially into the Flesh and Blood of our Lord Jesus '. His knowledge of Cornish and his repute as a scholar gave his words more weight. ' O detestable tongue,' wrote Grandisson in his letter of excommunication (17 March 1345) :

' more poisonous than that of any mad dog, which ought to be cut out by the chirurgeons of the Church and of the Crown, to be torn into little bits and cast to the swine '.

A year later Grandisson found the case to be hopeless. Tremur had asserted :

' Ye adore like idiots the work of your own hands, for what doth a priest do but gape over a piece of bread and breathe upon it.'

He had further declaimed against the worship of the saints ; St. Peter he called ' a mere empty-pated rustic ', and St. John he deemed a braggart. But his chief offence was his stealing from a church the pyx. This

' he conveyed to a house, took out the Sacrament and threw it into the fire, carrying the pyx away with him.'

For this and his other offences Tremur had been excommunicated by Simon Islip, when dean of Arches, i. e. before October 1349 when he became archbishop. But Grandisson, who seems to have doubted Islip's zeal in the matter, pleaded for Tremur's degradation, and threatened, 'unless justice be done, I will deliver my own soul by appealing to the Apostolic See'. Of the result, unfortunately, we know nothing, nor is anything further heard of this unbalanced heretic whom, but for the date, we might mistake for one of the later lollards.

At Cambridge there was a contemporary of Wyclif, a heretic of whom we would gladly know more, Nicholas Drayton. Drayton had been appointed warden of the scholars at the king's hall [1] on the 1st December 1363 with a salary of 4d. a day and 8 marks per annum for robes. In 1369 he was suspected of heresy, and on the 20th March 1370 Sudbury was authorized to commit him to prison. What became of him there or how he purged his offence we know not, but his heresy, such as it was, withered away. He became one of the king's clerks, obtained a provision to a prebend in Hereford (20 Feb. 1377), and on the 14th November 1376 was appointed a baron of the exchequer. Two days previously Nicholas, a licentiate in laws, had been put on to a commission to correct the abuses 'in the free chapel of St. Stephen, Westminster'.[2] Assuming these identifications, the career of Nicholas Drayton presents interesting points of affinity with that of Wyclif's Oxford disciples.

At Paris [3]—for in those days of internationalism in thought the doings of one university profoundly impressed another—confining ourselves to the period from 1350 to 1372, we find in 1351 a certain 'Simon', of whom nothing else is known, enlarging in his vespers on the proposition 'Jesus non est Deus', and proving the same from His assumption of humanity. In 1354 an Austin friar, Guido by name, launched out in his responsions into the propositions that 'a love which once backslides never was true love'; in his collocation, that 'a man merits eternal life *de condigno*'; in his quodlibeta, that 'if there had been no free will there would have been no sin', as well as several semi-pantheistic ideas. In 1362 another Franciscan, Ludovic of Padua, was condemned to retract or modify fourteen propositions which he had advanced in his vespers. One of

---

[1] Now part of Trinity; see Rashdall, ii. 561.
[2] Rymer, iii. 716, 889, 1064; *Cal. Pat. Ed.* xii. 459, xvi. 410, 432.
[3] For the following heretics see *Chart. Par.* iii. 11, 21-3, 95-7, 108

them is interesting : God, he said, cannot love himself more than he loves the devil, which is not far removed from a similar well-known paradox of Wyclif. The others may be disregarded ; they flutter round the subtleties of the relation of Divine Foreknowledge to sin and do not indicate special indebtedness to Bradwardine. In 1363 another master, John de Calore, was in trouble over his vespers. But his flippant triflings, e. g. that if there were perfections which God did not possess He would be worthy (dignus) of possessing them, may be dismissed. We mention the incident but to show how the scholastic exercises, vespers, responsions, and the like, created an atmosphere of freedom of which Wyclif took full advantage.

A more important heretic was Denis Foullechat, another Paris Franciscan.[1] On the 21st November 1366 he was summoned before the Theological Faculty. So he stood ' holding in his hands two sheets written on paper ', the one a recantation written by the Faculty, the other an appeal written by himself to the pope. This he had concealed in his vest. ' Read the schedule written out for you by the doctors of the faculty ', said the chancellor. But Denis began to read ' in a high voice ' the schedule of his appeal. He had come to grief, it seems, in the " principium " of his *Sentences*. According to the recantation drafted for him, his opinions partly resemble Wyclif's, or rather Fitzralph's, partly are akin to those of the Spiritual Franciscans. The law of love, he said, takes away all ' lordship ' as well as gets rid of the two possessive pronouns *meum* and *tuum*. Perfect love makes all things common ; so also does extreme need. The following out of these laws was the principal duty that Christ enjoined upon His disciples, while in the relinquishment of ' dominion ' and temporal power lay the perfect state. So he concluded with a protest against the decision of John XXII. We may remark that Foullechat did not distinguish, as Fitzralph had done, between *dominium* and *proprietas*. In spite of his brave defiance, the next day (22 Nov.) Foullechat yielded. He was sent to Avignon and there forced to read his recantation (31 Jan. 1365). But his revocation was not very sincere. In November 1368 we find him once more in trouble, Urban V writing from Rome to

[1] For his trial see *Chart. Par.* iii. 114–24.

Cardinal John Dormans, the chancellor of France, to inquire into and punish his errors. These were, chiefly, subtle variations on his previous ideas. Christ, he maintained, in His death had abdicated all things, for when His body lay in the tomb love took from Him all *dominium*. The usual revocation followed (12 April 1369) without more serious consequence than his being refused his doctorate. In 1385 we find him still a bachelor, one of the witnesses in the suit against the chancellor, John Blanchart. In the interval, probably in 1372, he translated into French the *Policraticus* of John of Salisbury.[1]

[1] *Chart. Par.* iii. 102 *n.*, 185, 397.

V

FROM MASTER OF BALLIOL TO DOCTOR OF THEOLOGY

§ 1

IN a previous chapter we left Wyclif in his country living at Fillingham, his master's degree completed, the connexion with Balliol severed. In the present chapter we shall resume the story of the outer life of Wyclif from his leaving Balliol to the completion of his doctorate in theology.

Wyclif had been instituted to the living of Fillingham on the 14th May 1361, presumably travelling down for the purpose to Holbeach near Spalding, one of the manors of Bishop Gynwell. Before institution he must have taken orders, but where and when cannot now be stated. By a constitution of archbishop Rich a priest could only be ordained by the bishop of the diocese in which he was born, unless he secured a dimissory letter.[1] As Wyclif is called in official documents a priest of York it is probable that he was ordained by the archbishop of York, at any rate no dimissory letter has yet come to light. We may, therefore, take it for granted that he was ordained by archbishop John Thoresby. This may explain how Thoresby's *Lay Folks' Catechism*, translated or paraphrased by John de Gaytrik, fell into the hands of Wyclif with consequences that present another of the many puzzles of Wyclif's life. But to this we shall return later. We may also note that archbishop Thoresby would be in many respects a man after Wyclif's own heart. How long Wyclif resided at Fillingham we cannot say ; possibly he may have stayed at his benefice for a year or more, for it was not until the summer of 1363 that he made up his mind to secure a dispensation of absence in order to study for a degree in theology. Possibly, therefore, Wyclif was in his Lincolnshire

[1] See Lyndwood, *Prov.* 27. For specimen dimissory letters see Isaacson, *Reg. David*, 95.

parish when there happened the great tempest of 1363. 'On the fifteenth day of January, upon the day of St. Maurice,[1] there blew so exceeding a wind that the like of it was not seen many years passed. This began about evensong time in the south' and lasted six days 'suffocating men', blowing down the spire of Norwich cathedral, and working immense havoc.[2] At Oxford it cost eighteen shillings to repair the damage done to the roof of Queen's.[3]

If, as we may assume, Wyclif left Oxford in the summer of 1361, he would therefore be away from the university during the worst months of a new visitation of the plague. The plague of 1361,[4] though not so widespread or disastrous as that of 1349, carried off a great number of clerics including Michael Northburgh, bishop of London (9 Sept.), and Reginald Bryan, bishop of Worcester (10 Dec.). The abbots of Chertsey, Shrewsbury, Cirencester, Reading, and Abingdon, as well as the priors of Merton and Coventry, all fell victims to its ravages,[5] as also, among the many nobles,[6] Henry, duke of Lancaster, the father-in-law of John of Gaunt, who died at Leicester on the 23rd March 1361.[7] Its effects in Oxford were especially disastrous.

The next incident in Wyclif's life is one of the minor ironies of history. On the 24th November 1362 the university of Oxford in presenting its annual 'roll of masters' petitioned the newly elected pope, Urban V, to exercise the power of provision by granting Wyclif, whose name is misspelt by the

[1] So Fabyan, *Chron.* 475, extensively copied, e. g. Kingsford in *Chron. Lond.* 290. In reality it was 'St. Maur' as *Chron. Anon. Cant.* in Reading, *Chron.* 213, not 'St. Maurice', i. e. 21 Sept. Walsingham dates as 10 Jan. 1363. For verses on this wind, dated as in 1361, see James, *MSS. Caius*, i. 302.
[2] References in nearly all the chronicles; it is alluded to in *P. Plow.*, A. Pass. 12–20, and in *Rot. Parl.* ii. 269.
[3] *Hist. MSS. Com.* ii. 128. For the damages on the estate of Westminster Abbey see Flete, 135.
[4] Usually dated as from 15 Aug. 1361 to 3 May 1362 (cf. Reading, *Chron.* 212, where it is dated in July). According to Malvern in Higden, viii. 360, it broke out on 28 Mar., but the death of Lancaster shows that this date is too late (M. Bateson, *Records of Leicester*, ii. 124–5). By 10 May it had worked such ravages in London that the courts were prorogued (Rymer, iii. 616).
[5] See Tait's note in Reading, *Chron.* 292.
[6] Higden, viii. 411–12; Reading, *Chron.* 150, note that the mortality was chiefly among men.
[7] For his will dated 15 Mar. 1361 (not 1360) see Nicolas, *Test. Vet.* i. 64–6. He was buried in St. Mary's collegiate church, Leicester.

Avignon scribe as ' Wychif ', ' a canonry and prebend of York, notwithstanding that he holds the church of Fillingham value thirty marks '.¹ The pope granted instead a prebend in the collegiate church of Westbury-on-Trym, near Bristol, where the church was at this time ' destitute of counsel and ministers ', owing, probably, to the pestilence of 1361.² The prebend, though not specifically named, was the prebend of Aust, worth £6 13s. 4d.³ The previous holder had been an alien, Raymond de Sancto Claro,⁴ a priest of Cahors, who had been appointed by Clement VI on the request of one of his men-at-arms. Historians have waxed wroth with Wyclif over this incident. But it would be difficult to find a single graduate of any standing who did not conform to what was then the custom. Jean Gerson and Nicholas de Clémangis stand out for their scholarship and piety. Yet in the Paris roll of 1387 ⁵ we find their names side by side. The forwarding of these annual ' rolls of masters ' was the medieval equivalent of the modern fellowship, and, though greatly abused, was not without its good points.

On the 29th August of the following year, 1363, Wyclif, who was now the lord of the manor of Wycliffe, obtained from his bishop, John Buckingham, a licence for non-residence at Fillingham that he might ' devote himself to the study of letters in the university '.⁶ Dispensations of this sort were common,⁷ and were the right of all students at Oxford studying

---

¹ *Pap. Pet.* i. 390 ; *Eng. Hist. Rev.* xv. 529, where it is given in full. Along with Wyclif there were sent up the names of the chancellor, Dr. John de Renham, and the two proctors of the year. Among the non-regent masters on the roll we note William Rede.

² See the statement of Roger Ottery, who was elected about the same time as Wyclif (Wilkins, *Westbury*, 107).

³ Wilkins, *Westbury*, 41 ; *Taxatio*, 220.

⁴ Raymond was appointed by Clement VI to a prebend in Lincoln on 1 Feb. 1350 (*Pap. Pet.* i. 192 ; *Pap. Let.* iii. 316). In August of the same year he was provided to a prebend in Lichfield. This last he resigned in Feb. 1358 (*ib.* iii. 361, 592).

⁵ *Chart. Par.* iii. 452.

⁶ Buckingham, Mem., f. 7. See Cronin, *Trans. Hist. Soc.* (1914), 74 *n.* This first licence has been ignored by historians, e. g. Lechler, 101 *n.*, with consequent misunderstanding of the second.

⁷ e. g. *Chart. Par.* ii. 142, 225 ; *Reg. Stafford*, 8, 15, 22, 37, 56, 98, 101, 120 (for seven years at once), 231, 266. Other episcopal registers would show similar results, e. g. *Reg. Giffard*, i. p. cvii, fifty-five licences for study, twenty of which are for study abroad.

in theology.¹ Of this Wyclif in his later years expressed approval,² though he objected strongly to any extension of the privilege for the study of law. In his judgement this last was the cause of much of the secularization of the Church. Wyclif also protested against the fees that were exacted from theological students for this licence, possibly a reminiscence of personal loss.³ Non-residence ' of clerics at Oxford and Cambridge for their learning ' was so completely recognized that they were specially exempted in 1425 in a petition of the Commons that the clergy should reside in their benefices, provided they were not at the university ' for avarice or other vices, so they pass not the age of 40 winter '.⁴ As a rule the students in theology were beneficed seculars with a dispensation for absence, oftentimes for a period of five years. By reason of their immunities they often formed the most disorderly element in university life, in spite of statutes which ordained that during lectures they should sit ' as quiet as girls '.⁵ As no candidate for a doctorate in theology could absent himself from the university for a longer space than two months, Wyclif during the next few years was an absentee cleric, except during the vacations, not only from Fillingham but also from Aust.

The bishop of Lincoln who granted Wyclif this licence,

¹ By a constitution of Honorius III, 16 Nov. 1219, entitled *Super speculum* (*Chart. Par.* i. 91 ; Leach, *Charters*, 144 ; quoted by Wyclif, *Off. Reg.* 179), beneficed clerks studying theology at Paris or Oxford were allowed absence for five years and to hold the income during the period. In Dec. 1226 Honorius explained that this did not include ' daily commons which resident clerks receive ' (*Pap. Let.* i. 114). The privilege was renewed by Clement VI (3 May 1343 ; *Chart. Par.* ii. 537). As abuses arose, attempts at reform were made in Paris in Apr. 1361 and in 1366. Beneficed clerks were to appear before the faculty ' to give information concerning their scholarship ' (*ib.* iii. 73) that the faculty might see whether the case came under their privilege (*ib.* iii. 146, in 1366). The candidate had to swear that he would not stretch the privilege beyond five years. But as Clement VI on 4 Mar. 1346 had extended the privilege to all masters and students in any faculty, valid for seven years (*ib.* ii. 574 ; cf. Wyclif, *Off. Reg.* 179), by adding the two together it was possible to get a twelve years' leave of absence. On 11 Oct. 1382 Clement VII renewed this for Paris, the period to count ' from the time in which they began to be scholars in any faculty ' (*Chart. Par.* iii. 311). At Paris in May 1371 the king granted that the wine and corn of such students sent to them from their benefices ' whether for consumption or sale ' should pay no imposts (*ib.* iii. 198 ; cf. 202, 318).
² *Ver. Script.* iii. 39.
³ *Off. Reg.* 177–80 ; *Eng. Works*, 250.
⁴ *Rot. Parl.* iv. 306 a. ⁵ Rashdall, ii. 605.

John de Buckingham, demands some notice, if only because Wyclif for the rest of his life was under his supervision. Buckingham[1] was one of Edward's civil servants,[2] since 1359 keeper of his privy seal. This 'Caesarean' priest had been paid with several canonries and the archdeaconry of Northampton, and then in the autumn of 1362 with the bishopric of Lincoln.[3] Some difficulty, however, arose with Urban V who doubted 'whether John was of sufficient learning to rule so populous and noble a diocese', and asked that 'he should come to the Roman court, and it may be that his presence will sufficiently answer the objections made against him'.[4] Accordingly Buckingham was examined by two abbots at St. Omer with satisfactory results. By the help of money[5] difficulties were smoothed away and provision was granted on the 5th April 1363. On the 25th June 1363 Buckingham was consecrated at Wargrave by William Edendon, bishop of Winchester, Robert Wyvill, bishop of Salisbury, and an Irish bishop,[6] a few weeks before the granting of Wyclif's licence. For nearly thirty-five years—he died on the 10th March 1398—Buckingham ruled his enormous diocese, seeing the rise and

[1] Not in *D. N. B.* The note in Nicolas, *Test. Vet.* i. 80, is wildly erroneous. By some writers Buckingham is credited with the works of the schoolman Thomas Buckingham, a fellow of Merton in Edward III's reign, on whom see Tanner, 137.

[2] In 1348 he was 'chamberlain of the exchequer' (*Pap. Let.* iii. 291; *Pap. Pet.* i. 143). From 4 Feb. 1350 to 5 Jan. 1353 he was keeper of the Great Wardrobe. He then served, 5 Jan. 1353 to 23 Feb. 1353, as Controller of the Wardrobe (*Eng. Hist. Rev.* xxiv. 503, 505. For the importance of these offices see *ib.* 496–7). Buckingham's preferments had been many; a prebend in Exeter, Jan. 1332 (*Pap. Let.* ii. 358), the church of Sutton Coldfield and a prebend in Warwick before Feb. 1348, then in addition a prebend at Lichfield (*ib.* iii. 258; *Pap. Pet.* i. 143); in Jan. 1349 a canonry in York and the reservation of the archdeaconry of Nottingham (*Pap. Let.* iii. 291), and in Nov. 1349 the reservation of the deanery of Lichfield (*ib.* iii. 341; *Pap. Pet.* i. 184). As such in Apr. 1351 he obtained an indult for a portable altar (*Pap. Let.* iii. 385) and in the same month the archdeaconry of Northampton with permission to hold his canonries in Warwick, Lincoln, and York (*ib.* iii. 398, 415). He also retained his deanery of Lichfield, for which in Sept. 1359 he obtained an indult for non-residence for a year while engaged in the king's business (*ib.* iii. 608; *Pap. Pet.* i. 348), extended in the following year into a dispensation of absence for three years (*ib.* i. 356) and further extended for two years in July 1361 (*ib.* i. 371).

[3] He had been chosen bishop of Ely earlier in the year but had been passed over by Innocent VI in favour of Langham (*Ang. Sac.* i. 662).

[4] *Pap. Let.* iv. 1; 8 Dec. 1362.

[5] 'prece et pretio', Higden, viii. 365.

[6] *Ang. Sac.* i. 45; Eubel, i. 319; Stubbs, *Reg. Sac. Ang.* 79.

downfall of lollardy in his see. He looked well after the interests of his cathedral by securing the confirmation of all its charters.[1]

Shortly after obtaining his licence, on the 8th October 1363, Wyclif took possession for two years of rooms at Queen's on whose repairs 'two workmen had been engaged for four days at a cost of three shillings'.[2] He began the long course of at least nine years [3] for a doctorate in theology. Wyclif would thus be at Oxford in the severe winter of 1363 when a great frost lasted from the 30th November until the 19th March 1364.[4] The sufferings involved in the comfortless, fireless rooms of medieval Oxford can be imagined when we remember that during that winter the Rhone froze at Avignon and the Meuse at Liège.

§ 2

The relation of Wyclif to the prebend of Aust in the collegiate church of Westbury [5] is of considerable importance. But before entering on this difficult question, the church itself deserves some mention as of more than usual interest. The village of Westbury-on-Trym, now absorbed in Bristol, was in Wyclif's day three miles from the city across the famous Downs. "As early as the ninth century, when the outlying hollow which afterwards became Bristol was for the most part an uninhabitable swamp Westbury was an important ecclesiastical district." There a church, standing on a slight hill, with the village and the little river Trym at its feet, had been founded, probably loosely monastic in character,[6] about the year 715. After various vicissitudes Westbury was established in the thirteenth century as a collegiate church, with a dean

---

[1] See *Charter Rolls*, v. 251-4 (2 July 1378).
[2] Foxe, ii. 941. See *supra*, p. 65 *n*.
[3] See *supra*, p. 94. Nine years and a term will bring the doctorate to Dec. 1372 or Mar. 1373. See *infra*, p. 203.
[4] Reading, *Chron*. 160, with Tait's note; Higden, viii. 414; *Chron. Ang.* 54; Walsingham, i. 299.
[5] For Westbury see Dr. H. J. Wilkins, *Westbury College* (Bristol, 1917), and also his *Westbury and Bristol Records*, vols. 1-5; also A. H. Thompson, *Bristol and Glos. Arch. Soc.* xxxviii. 100 f.; the brief study by Miss Rose Graham in *Vict. Co. Glos.* ii. 106-8, whose list of deans is, however, incomplete. The older accounts are all taken from Tanner, *Notitia*, or from Rudder's *Gloucestershire*, 799.
[6] *Vict. Co. Glos.* ii. 106.

and five prebends, three for priests, one for a deacon and a fifth for a subdeacon.[1]

After the college had been in existence 100 years[2] bishop Godfrey Giffard of Worcester[3] made an attempt to enlarge it into one of the greater collegiate churches. He sought in 1385 to obtain from Honorius IV the annexation of the churches of Weston-on-Avon near Bath and Bredon near Evesham as prebends of Westbury and also ' to make all the churches in his patronage prebendal to Westbury '.[4] If Giffard could have matured his plans the college would have consisted of a dean, sub-dean, fourteen canons and prebendaries, a chaplain, and a schoolmaster [5]—the reader will notice this usual feature of a collegiate church—together with provision for six poor men and six poor widows. What bishop Giffard's motives were it is impossible to say. Some have considered that Giffard—and Carpenter after him—sought to provide for the needs of the growing city of Bristol.[6] But there was already in Bristol itself the monastery of Austin canons, now the cathedral, the conversion of which might have better served his purpose and whose disordered state in 1278 gave him an opportunity for making changes.[7] Others, again, have considered that he was anxious to have an episcopal throne in a church of secular canons as well as in a Benedictine monastery, after the analogy of the similar combination of Benedictines and seculars in Lichfield and Coventry, and Bath and Wells.[8] Probably he had no special object, except to annoy the monks of his

[1] This is expressly stated by bishop Wittlesey in 1366. See Wilkins, *Westbury*, 43.

[2] Writers have erred in attributing the foundation of the college to Giffard, following Tanner, *Notitia*. Its previous collegiate character is proved by *Reg. Giffard*, i. 20, 49 ; ii. 54, 71, 243, &c. Cf. Wilkins, *op. cit.* 12–16, 35–8. It is sufficient to note that between 1237–66 bishop Walter de Cantilupe issued statutes for Westbury, quoted by Wittlesey in 1366. See *infra*, p. 159. The prebends are in the *Taxatio*, p. 220.

[3] For Giffard see *Reg. Giffard*, i. pp. xxiii f. or *D. N. B.* For his will in full, dated 13 Sept. 1301, see *Reg. Ginsborough* (ed. Bund, 1907), 48–60.

[4] *Reg. Giffard*. ii. 301–3, 336, 340. For churches which Giffard tried to make prebendal see *ib.* ii. 362.

[5] In the Dissolution balance sheet (Wilkins, *Westbury*, c. 4) I can find no trace of this schoolmaster.

[6] See Wilkins, *op. cit.* 132.

[7] See *Reg. Giffard*, ii. 100. The ' abbot was not sufficiently instructed to propound the word of God '.

[8] *Vict. Co. Glos.* ii. 107. So Wilkins, *op. cit.* 152.

cathedral at Worcester. For Giffard, though in 1282 for purposes of policy he had become a Franciscan, had none of the Franciscan spirit. He was a typical medieval bishop of unyielding will and of a haughty, quarrelsome spirit that brought him into incessant litigation,[1] who visited his diocese with an escort of 100 horsemen, exacting full procurations, and spending his vast income in building. To him we owe the choir of Worcester with its slender, graceful columns. He fortified Hartlebury castle and erected magnificent episcopal mansions at Kemsey and Wick. Like Browning's bishop Giffard ordered a costly tomb to be erected in his lifetime, close to that of St. Oswald. A bishop's throne at Westbury might well have formed one of his dreams.[2]

But whatever Giffard's plans, they were unfulfilled in spite of a 'quickener' of £200 bestowed on the pope's secretary.[3] The monks of Worcester, frightened of losing fees and dignity, entered an appeal in the curia, and though at last Giffard won his lawsuits[4] death prevented him from carrying out his purposes. So Westbury remained a college with a dean and five prebends. Giffard, it is true, rebuilt the church, though only the south aisle remains as he left it and as it was in Wyclif's day.[5] Not until almost a century after Wyclif's death were Giffard's plans carried out by bishop John Carpenter of Worcester (1444-76), who actually styled himself bishop of 'Worcester and Westbury'.[6] Carpenter,[7] as Fuller tells us, was 'so indulgent to Westbury, the place of his birth, that of a mean he made it a magnificent convent, more like a castle than a college, walling it about with turrets, and making a stately gatehouse thereunto'.[8] At the same time he enlarged

---

[1] For a more favourable estimate of Giffard's character see Bund in *Reg. Giffard*, i. p. xxii. On p. clii he speaks of him as "possibly the greatest of the Worcester bishops".

[2] Wilkins, *op. cit.* 31.

[3] For these bribes in full see *Reg. Giffard*, ii. 301-3.

[4] *ib.* i. p. li f. Cf. *Ang. Sac.* i. 511.

[5] The dimensions are given by William of Worcester, who, as a native of Bristol (*Itin.* 190, 206), would be fully familiar with it: the college was 141 ft. long, 75 ft. broad; the church 126 ft. long, 72 ft. broad (Rudder, *Glos.* 799; Worcester, *Itin.* 133, 202).

[6] Godwin, 467.

[7] For Carpenter see Wilkins, *Westbury*, c. 6; *D.N.B.* For his new statutes for Westbury, confirmed by Calixtus III on 25 Sept. 1455, Wilkins, *ib.* 146 f. [8] Fuller, *Worthies*, i. 380.

the church, in which he desired to be buried. Carpenter had been enabled to do this through one of Bristol's merchant princes, William Canynges,[1] five times mayor and twice member of Parliament for Bristol. Canynges, after a most successful career as a trader to Iceland, Prussia, and Denmark—he owned 10 ships [2] and employed 800 seamen—retired from the world in 1467, and on the 3rd June 1469 became dean of Westbury, of which church he had already been collated a canon on the same day as he was consecrated priest (16 Apr. 1468).[3] Canynges it was who rebuilt St. Mary Redcliffe, which still remains one of the glories of English architecture. Very different was the fate of his stately college. At the Dissolution, the college, whose clear annual income was £232,[4] was sold with other church property to Sir Ralph Sadleir, though the fine church was spared. Of the college, a turret and gatehouse and part of the boundary walls are all that now remain. After serving as smithy and tenements these were vested in 1902 in the National Trust, under the impression, probably, that the college was at one time the home of Wyclif.

Wyclif's relation to Westbury presents problems of exceptional difficulty. The doubts that have been cast upon Wyclif's acceptance of the prebend may be dismissed;[5] for in the spring of 1366 William Wittlesey,[6] bishop of Worcester, made a visitation of Westbury.[7] He found it neglected, as Giffard

[1] For Canynges see *D.N.B.*; Wilkins, *Westbury*, c. 8; or J. Dallaway, *Antiquities of Bristol* (1834), 167 f. For his will, made 12 Nov. 1474—he died 17 Nov.—and proved at Lambeth, 29 Nov. 1474, see T. P. Wadley, *The Great Orphan Book and Book of Wills at Bristol* (1886), 151–3.

[2] The size given in *D.N.B.* from the description on his tomb is probably an exaggeration, especially the one alleged to be of 900 tons. The inscription was composed much later. See Dallaway, *op. cit.* 183–4.

[3] Wadley, *op. cit.* 154; Robert Ricart, *The Maire of Bristowe is Kalendar* (1872), p. 44.

[4] In full in *Valor*, ii. 432–5, or Wilkins, *Westbury*, c. 4.

[5] e.g. Rashdall in *D.N.B.* lxiii. 205.

[6] For Wittlesey, see *D.N.B.* He was archdeacon of Huntingdon when in 1348 he secured permission to study civil law in a university for three years (*Pap. Pet.* i. 133); warden of Peterhouse, Cambridge, from 10 Sept. 1349–51, obtaining on its behalf many preferments (*ib.* i. 211). On 23 Oct. 1360, Islip secured his election to Rochester (Thorpe, *Reg. Roff.* 181). To this he was provided 4 Aug. 1361, and translated to Worcester 6 Mar. 1364 (Eubel, i. 444, 561). For his donations of books, see James, *MSS. Pet.* 35, 111; *MSS. John*, 72.

[7] We are indebted for this discovery and for all the documents to Wilkins, *Was John Wyclif a Negligent Pluralist?* (Bristol, 1915).

had similarly found it in 1293,[1] and Thomas Cobham, bishop of Worcester, in November 1319.[2] So on the 16th April he wrote from his palace at Henbury—a village close to Westbury—ordering the dean, Richard de Cornwall, to hold an inquiry immediately after Ascension Day. Cornwall reported on the 27th June that all the five canons had been non-resident from the time they had obtained their prebends. Only one of the five, viz. Hyndele, had complied with the statutes and provided his vicar; the other four were in default. Bryan had provided no deacon for four years, Michel had provided no chaplain for a year, Ottery no subdeacon for five years, while as for John Wyclif the dean reported:

'Master John Wynkele (sic)[3] canon and prebendary, whom I inducted into corporal possession of the same prebend, who also took corporal oath to observe the statutes of the said collegiate church: and he ought to have provided a chaplain in the same according to the manner set forth and has provided none at all, but has entirely withdrawn him for the whole year last past, neither has he kept any residence from the time of his obtaining (the prebend).'[4]

Immediately on receipt of the report Wittlesey wrote from Alvechurch (28 June) that the dean was to cite Wyclif and the other defaulting canons to appear before the bishop, ' on the twentieth day after your citation, canonically made ', to show cause why they should not be ' suspended from office and benefice '. In the meantime he must ' sequestrate all fruits, rents, and produce whatsoever belonging to the said prebends '.[5] Of further action by Wittlesey there is no record, but this colourless prelate who owed his position to his uncle, Simon Islip, was not inclined to strong measures of any sort. Probably the matter soon dropped, more especially as on the 11th October 1368 Wittlesey was translated to Canterbury.

---

[1] See Wilkins, *op. cit.* 10–14, 19–21.
[2] Reg. Cobham, f. 41 d., in Wilkins, *Westbury*, 43. Cf. Reg. Wittlesey, f. 1.
[3] There is no doubt that this is Wyclif. The scribe was most careless. He has misdated Giffard by one hundred years, his Latin is often unintelligible. Several documents are undated, and several not in order. "It is clear that there was an accumulation of entries waiting to be made in the register" (Wilkins, 26, 27, 46–7). For ' Wynkle ' as a name, see *Cal. Pat. Ric.* iii. 461; *Pap. Let.* iii. 93; *Pap. Pet.* i. 2, 4 (1342), Dr. Richard Wynkele, the king's confessor, and his kinsman John Wynkele, prebendary of Salisbury.
[4] Wilkins, *op. cit.* 16, 24, from Reg. Wittlesey, 1 and 1d.
[5] Wilkins, *op. cit.* 43–6 from Reg. Wittlesey, ff. 11 and 11d.

At this point we should inquire what were the duties which Wyclif and his colleagues had neglected. According to Giffard's statutes, which Wittlesey cites, residence by the canons 'must be kept for one month, either discontinuously or continuously'. Canons who were non-resident must 'provide their vicars within a year'[1] who should be 'subject to the correction and obedience of the dean of Westbury'. Moreover, 'if a canon shall not have thus provided a vicar after the lapse of a moiety of a year, reckoned from Michelmas, he shall incur suspension from office and benefice, and after the lapse of a whole year the greater excommunication in addition to a fine of four marks to the common funds of the canons in residence.'

Oath that they would obey these statutes was to be taken by the canons annually.[2] Furthermore, and on this Wittlesey lays stress, the canons, who individually and severally received the emoluments of their prebends,[3] were responsible for the repairs of the 'chancels of the church appropriated to them'. This they had neglected to do 'to the grave peril of their own souls and the open scandal of the people'.

Wyclif's neglect must be admitted. But before examining any excuse that may be offered we may dismiss the further charge that part of Wyclif's duties lay in ministering to the flock at Aust. Aust is a village, about ten miles from Westbury, charmingly situated on the Severn. It owes its importance to the fact that in ancient times the chief ferry over the Severn was at this point. Hence, possibly, its Latin name of *Augusti* (*trajectus*), of which it is a corruption. It was at Aust also, according to incorrect local tradition, that St. Augustine met the Welsh bishops. Another legend is that Wyclif was vicar of the church—a plain confusion of the prebend of Aust with Aust itself and a generous ignoring of the charges that were made in 1366. In support of this legend a key is shown which is called Wyclif's key. Unfortunately for the story, Aust at this date was a chapelry attached to the parish of Henbury, and Wyclif, therefore, had neither rights nor duties there.[4]

---

[1] For the more lenient rules at Exeter, see *Reg. Brant*, i. 171.
[2] Wilkins, *op. cit.*, 11 f., 20.
[3] This was the rule until Carpenter in 1452 instituted a common fund. See H. J. Wilkins, *Appendix to John Wycliffe* (1916), p. 12.
[4] See Wilkins, *An Appendix to John Wyclif*, 6, 9–11, who thus corrects his

What excuse can be made for Wyclif?[1] If Wyclif were other than himself it would be easy to reply that he was only doing what ninety-nine out of every hundred of the higher ecclesiastics in his age had done. The prebends of Westbury were habitually treated as *sine cura*. Moreover Wittlesey does not complain so much of non-residence, as of a neglect to appoint vicars to do the duty of the absent canons. But a reformer cannot plead in defence the customs which he denounces. It is better to fall back upon the general difficulty in 1365–6 of obtaining vicars. We must remember that by the joint legislation of Church and State in 1362 vicars were limited to the receipt of six marks, and that any one who offered more was condemned to pay the excess to the Crown.[2] Such legislation was heroic in its defiance of the laws of supply and demand. Two epidemics of the plague had left the Church stripped of curates and priests.[3] Those who remained, even if they were prevented from commanding their price, were at least able to fix their location. A few years later, as Wyclif tells us himself, the average price for a vicar rose to ten marks a year.[4] In London it would not have been difficult for Wyclif to obtain a vicar; it was more difficult in a country village. Only one of the canons, Hyndele the prebendary of Henbury, had in fact succeeded. But Wyclif was at Oxford in the thick of his fight, as we shall see later, over Canterbury college —a college founded, be it remembered, because of this very dearth of curates—and may not have had the same opportunities. Vicars of sorts he might have secured, but Wyclif at Oxford would probably look higher than a hedge-priest.

The student will note that Wyclif, writing in the late winter

---

Negligent Pluralist, pp. 48 f. Cf. A. H. Thompson in *Bristol and Glos. Arch. Soc.* xxxviii. 132. The vicar of Henbury was well paid. In the *Taxatio*, 220, his reserved 'portion' is £18. In Rudder, *Glos.* 494, Aust is given as a tithing of Henbury. It is of interest to note (*ib.* 495) that the manor belonged to the lollard, Sir Thomas Broke.

[1] Wyclif had obtained a licence for non-residence from the bishop of Lincoln (see *supra*, p. 153). But this would not hold for the diocese of Worcester.

[2] *Statutes*, i. 373; *Rot. Parl.* ii. 271; Wilkins, iii. 50.

[3] For Bristol, see especially Wilkins, *Negligent Pluralist*, 55–60. For monasteries forced by the pestilence to apply for licences to ordain certain of their inmates at the ages of 20, 22, &c., see *Pap. Let.* iv. 37 (Apr. 1364).

[4] *Sel. Eng. Works*, i. 291.

of 1381, made excuses for absenteeism which may be an answer to some taunt on his absence from Aust or neglect of Lutterworth. Pastors who 'for the greater advantage of mother church' find it necessary to leave their flocks must take care that the sheep do not suffer; otherwise they must surrender the income. But such non-residence, even though 'the curate absent in body is present in efficiency', is not justified 'by serving in secular business, taking one's ease in the schools, or travelling abroad to visit the Roman pontiff'.[1] That Wyclif 'took his ease in the schools' is a charge that his bitterest enemy could not bring. In view of his delegacy to Bruges it is more difficult to claim that he was never an absentee because of 'secular business', though probably he took a high view of the nature of this mission.

These excuses may be accepted or not. A modern writer has claimed, basing his judgement on this absence from Aust, " that the estimate of Wyclif's character in the past has been too high ".[2] But after the experiences of the Great War the excuses seem to us to have some weight. During the War there were hundreds of positions, clerical and educational, which were not filled or filled most inadequately. In the age of Wyclif the "Great War" was the succession of plagues, to whose effects upon the supply of clergy we shall more than once draw attention. In this plea for extenuating circumstances we may point out that in 1377 all the five prebendaries of Westbury, though it must be confessed they were still absentees, had duly elected vicars, whose names are given.[3] As regards dilapidations at Aust the charge is too sweeping. It is not possible that in four years the chancel should have become so ruined. Dilapidations are always difficult to adjudicate, and the previous holders of the prebend of Aust cannot be exonerated from their share of the blame.

One other matter must be mentioned. Wyclif, it would seem, was the only one of the prebendaries of Westbury who

[1] *Blas.* 178–9. In *Pot. Pap.* 359, written in 1379, Wyclif protests against appropriated prebends where duty was not done; in 1378 in *Ver. Script.* iii. 37, that the appointment by a prebendary of a vicar does not absolve the priest from his duties.
[2] H. S. Cronin in *Trans. Hist. Soc.* (1914), p. 57.
[3] Wilkins, *Westbury*, 90.

neglected to make a return of his pluralities, in accordance with Urban V's constitution *Horribilis* [1]—to many pluralists this must have appeared an inspired designation. Such returns ought to have been made to the bishop of the diocese in which the pluralist was accustomed to reside, i. e. for Wyclif to the bishop of Lincoln. Two of his colleagues made their return to the bishop of London, another to the bishop of Hereford, and a fourth to the bishop of Lincoln. Wyclif's return does not exist. Either the return is lost, or Wyclif was overlooked, or else, possibly because the expenses of his vicar swallowed up the revenues, Wyclif neglected to make it.[2] Thereby he ran considerable danger of incurring excommunication and the sequestration of his revenues.[3] That he did not suffer either may be credited to the friendliness of the authorities, or to the remissness of bishop Buckingham.

As every fact connected with Wyclif is of interest, we may linger for a moment over the Reformer's fellow delinquents at Westbury. For the most part they illustrate the worst features of the medieval church. In later life Wyclif would not look back with any pleasure on his association with them—if indeed he ever met any of them at all, except the dean. The dean of Westbury, who states that he had personally inducted John ' Wynkele ' into ' corporal possession ' and taken his ' corporal oath ',[4] was Richard de Cornwall. This ' king's clerk ' had been appointed on the 12th June 1362,[5] six months before Wyclif, and had been instituted by proxy on the 20th July.[6] In 1386 he exchanged with Robert Wattes of Abingdon.[7] Cornwall was therefore dean the whole time that Wyclif was a canon. One of the canons was John de Bryan, who had been appointed by Edward in 1349 [8] in succession to his brother Richard, then bishop of St. Davids. He seems

[1] Cf. Reading, *Chron.* 156
[2] See A. H. Thompson's note in Wilkins, *Westbury*, 86.
[3] See the case for which queen Philippa intercedes, May 1368, *Pap. Let.* iv. 68.
[4] This would seem to show that Wyclif must have visited Westbury for his institution either in 1363 or early in 1364.
[5] *Cal. Pat. Ed.* xii. 220.
[6] Reg. Barnet, f. 2, cited in Wilkins, *Westbury*, 50.
[7] Reg. Wakefield, f. 45, in Wilkins, *op. cit.* 50.
[8] *Cal. Pat.* viii. 403 (28 Sept.). Instituted 29 Oct. 1349 (*Sed. Vac. Worc.* 238).

to have held the prebend until 1387. This noted pluralist was the brother [1] of Sir Guy de Bryan, whom we shall meet again in our story. In addition to the church of Bishop Hatfield [2]—where as a rule he resided [3]—Bryan held prebends in Lincoln, Wolverhampton, Wells, Lichfield, Exeter, St. Davids, and Dublin,[4] as well as the deanery of St. Patrick's, Dublin,[5] and the church of Bishop's Cleeve.[6] For some reason or other he resigned his prebend at Westbury in 1353, but was immediately readmitted.[7] In July 1351 he obtained an indult to receive for five years the fruits of his deanery while studying at a university in Civil Law, and was therefore at Oxford with Wyclif. He died on the 4th February 1389, and hungry wolves, even before his decease, secured the reversion of his sinecures.[8]

Another prebendary, Richard Michael, had been provided when but 14 years of age with a prebend in St. Paul's.[9] In February 1358 he was further provided with the rectory of Pulham in Norfolk.[10] In November 1362 he exchanged his benefice in St. Paul's for Westbury,[11] and shortly afterwards received in addition the rectory of Harlow in Essex.[12] These he held until his death in 1374.[13] The third prebendary was William de Hyndele, the only one who had provided his vicar according to statutes, ' though he kept no residence ' and had taken his oath by proxy.[14] He seems only to have held Westbury from the autumn of 1365 to the 3rd November 1367, when he exchanged his prebend and his church of Belbroughton for

---

[1] *Pap. Pet.* i. 141.   [2] *Pap. Let.* iii. 334.
[3] Thompson in *Bristol and Glos. Arch. Soc.* xxxviii. 133.
[4] Wilkins, *Westbury*, 68–9; *Pap. Pet.* i. 268; *Pap. Let.* iii. 258, 268, 277, 334, 426, 429, 445, 477, 568; *Cal. Pat. Ed.* xv. 92; *Cal. Pat. Ric.* i. 371, ii. 416.
[5] Provided Aug. 1350 (*Pap. Let.* iii. 1361; *Pap. Pet.* i. 202).
[6] Instituted by proxy on 25 June 1374 on presentation of Edward III on 18 June release by deed from cure of souls (*Sed. Vac. Worc.* 308).
[7] *Cal. Pat. Ed.* ix. 405 (20 Feb. 1353). Readmitted 4 Apr. 1353 (*Sed. Vac. Worc.* 200).
[8] See *Cal. Pat. Ric.* iii. 361 (28 Sept. 1387). As it was discovered that he was not dead, new grants were made in Feb. 1389 (*ib.* iv. 10, 18, 19, &c.). He was succeeded in his Irish prebend of Lusk by Robert de Farrington (*infra*, p. 169; *ib.* iv. 98).
[9] Aug. 1349 (*Pap. Let.* iii. 314, 459; *Pap. Pet.* i. 188).
[10] *Pap. Let.* iii. 593, 596; *Pap. Pet.* i. 326.
[11] Wilkins, *Westbury*, 98–9.   [12] Newcourt, *Rep.* ii. 312.
[13] *Sed. Vac. Worc.* 317. He died in debt to the Crown for 6s. 8d. for his tenths (*ib.* 329).   [14] Wilkins, *Neg. Pluralist*, 16, 24.

the church of Essenden.[1] On the 22nd September 1366 he also received the prebend of Islington in St. Paul's.[2] He was subsequently rector of Oxted, and by a series of exchanges received the churches of St. Alphege, London Wall, in 1384,[3] of Little Bardfield in Essex (1386),[4] and by exchange Borley in Essex in 1397,[5] resigning Borley in September 1399 on an exchange for Hinderclay in Suffolk.[6] There, we may presume, this 'chop-church' died in peace.

The fourth delinquent was Roger Ottery, LL.B., who had been collated on the 10th November 1360. In 1361 he was appointed sequestrator-general for Worcester,[7] an office which, presumably, he held in 1366 when dean Cornwall made the sequestration order against the canons, among whom Ottery had not kept any residence for five years.[8] He was in the service of bishop Charlton of Hereford, whose chancellor he became in 1364.[9] When in May 1366 Urban V ordered a return of pluralists Ottery gave a full statement with a defence of his position.[10] He held pluralities worth £55 1s. 4d., but on the pope's inquiry seems to have resigned all except his church at Bledlow worth £22 which he held from 1344, and his prebend at Westbury. These he enjoyed until his death in the late summer of 1387.[11]

Wyclif did not live in an historical age, and probably knew little of his predecessors. Nevertheless Westbury could boast some distinguished men among its canons, all of them sad pluralists. Several bishops and even archbishops had started their career with a prebend at Westbury. We may mention John de Stratford, archbishop of Canterbury (1333–48), William of Edington of Winchester (1346–66), John Trillek of Hereford (1344–60), Reginald de Bryan of St. Davids (1349),

[1] *Cal. Pat. Ed.* xiv. 19.
[2] Hennessy, *Nov. Rep.* 33.
[3] *ib.* 86, where the date 1385 seems a mistake for 1384; estate ratified 27 May 1384 (*Cal. Pat. Ric.* ii. 565).
[4] Newcourt, *Rep.* ii. 31, 5 June 1386.
[5] *ib.* ii. 76, 4 Dec.; *Cal. Pat. Ric.* vi. 263.
[6] *Cal. Pat. Ric.* vi. 595; *Cal. Pat. Hen.* i. 7.
[7] Wilkins, *Westbury*, 106; *Neg. Pluralist*, 29 n.
[8] Wilkins, *Neg. Pluralist*, 17.
[9] *Reg. Charlton*, 6, 7, 17. Not in Le Neve, i. 498.
[10] Discovered by A. H. Thompson in *Reg. Langham*, f. 26; see Wilkins, *Westbury*, 106–7, or *Bristol and Glos. Arch. Soc.* (1916), xxxviii. 126–8.
[11] *Cal. Pat. Ric.* iii. 361.

then of Worcester (1352-61), and the renowned Richard de Bury of Durham. Another canon of Westbury, Adam de Murimuth, won repute as a chronicler and diplomatist.

One canon of Westbury, contemporary with Wyclif, deserves a longer notice, John de Trevisa, the eminent translator. Trevisa, a native of the parish of St. Mellion near Saltash, was a fellow of Exeter college from 1362-5,[1] but in May 1369 migrated to Queen's,[2] where he was joined by three associates of Wyclif—Nicholas Hereford, William Middleworth, and William Selby. The appointment of so many fellows from the south of England, contrary to the statutes, led to trouble. On the 6th April 1378, and again on the 20th October 1379, the Crown appointed a commission, on the complaint of the provost of Queen's, Thomas de Carlisle, to inquire into the conduct of certain fellows of Queen's who had been expelled ' for refusal to account for money which came to their hands '. They had also taken away ' charters, books, jewels, and muniments belonging to the college ', as well as the common seal of the college. As a result of the inquiry the provost was removed and certain fellows expelled.[3] One of these delinquents was Trevisa, who had ceased drawing his fellowship after 1374.[4] Another was William Middleworth, who, in fact, seems to have begun the strife, as, possibly, in earlier years he had been a source of discord at Merton. But there is no reason for the supposition of Wood that the trouble was due to the infection of Wyclif's heresies.[5] It is more likely that the seceders, who seem all to have hailed from Exeter, were an anti-northern faction who objected to the reservation of half the places in Queen's for natives of Cumberland and Westmorland.[6] Whatever the cause of his expulsion, Trevisa in

---

[1] *Hist. MSS. Com.* ii. 128. For Trevisa there is a brief sketch in *D. N. B.* to which I have added several references. Cf. Babington in Higden, i. p. liv f.

[2] Boase, 11-12. See Foxe, ii. 941 or Wilkins, *Westbury*, 88, for Trevisa's accounts at Queen's from 5 May to 29 Sept. 1369.

[3] *Cal. Pat. Ric.* i. 204, 420 ; also on 7 Feb. 1380, *ib.* i. 470. Cf. *Close Rolls Ric.* i. 42 (10 Jan. 1378) ; Wood, *Univ.* i. 496 ; *Rot. Parl.* iii. 69, from which we see that the archbishop of York intervened as visitor and removed the provost ; Rymer, iv. 65 (Orders on 26 June 1379 to the chancellor to find who have these jewels). [4] Magrath, i. 108.

[5] Wood, *Univ.* i. 496, doubtfully ; Boase, p. xiv ; Magrath, i. 106 f.

[6] Wilkins, *Neg. Pluralist*, 78 n. According to Wilkins, *Westbury*, 113, the riot was caused by the election of a provost.

the autumn of 1382 was once more back at Queen's, though no longer as a fellow. He hired a set of rooms, for which, however, for four years he neglected to pay rent. Only by means of two writs could the college in November 1386 recover £3 6s. 8d. for rent and " costs ".[1] After this, presumably, he left the college and retired to his parish at Berkeley. Thence in 1387 he joined in a disgraceful raid upon the dean of Westbury, Robert Wattes. The party

' took the dean lying in his bed and dragged him out of the house into the streets, tearing his clothes, and there assaulted, beat, wounded, and maltreated him '.

In the end the dean promised ' to give them all his goods to suffer him to have his life '.[2] It is a curious commentary on the age that two years after this raid, possibly earlier, Trevisa was appointed to a prebend in Westbury.[3] Trevisa was always a great traveller—he tells us himself in the *Polychronicon* that he had bathed at ' Aken in Almayne and Egges in Savoye '[4]— and his prebend of Westbury, if he ever obtained actual possession,[5] simply found more money for a new expedition for which he had received licence on the 5th November 1390. In 1394-5 he was once more at Queen's, and in 1398 paid off an old debt due to the bursar. He died and was buried at Berkeley, where he made many of his translations, in the early months of 1402.[6] Through the usual English indifference his grave is unknown, and an ancient writing upon the walls of the chapel of ' the apocalypse, both in Latin and French ', was destroyed in 1805, though, possibly, written by Trevisa himself.[7] Trevisa's translations from Latin into English earned for him the just title of the Father of English prose. But of these translations more anon.

[1] Wilkins, *Westbury*, 89; Foxe, ii. 942.
[2] Ancient Pet. 7355 in Record Office, trans. in full in Wilkins, *Neg. Pluralist*, 80-1.
[3] Wilkins, *Neg. Pluralist*, 84-5, often erroneously assigned (e. g. *D. N. B.*) to Westbury-on-Severn (Tanner, 720) or Westbury, Wilts. (Wilkins, *op. cit.* 82-3).
[4] Higden, ii. 61; i. e. Aachen and Aix.   [5] Wilkins, *Westbury*, 113.
[6] Usually dated in 1412, e. g. *D. N. B.*; Tanner, 721 (who, however, gives the alternative of 1399); Boase, 11; Babington in Higden, i. p. liv; Magrath, i. 123; Fuller, *Worthies*, i. 217, dated ' about 1400 '; cf. Bale, i. 518, who gives ' 1397 claruit'. From Reg. Clifford, f. 14 d, it appears he died before 21 May 1402 (Wilkins, *op. cit.* 86).   [7] *D. N. B.*

From these records we see that the prebends at Westbury, generally bestowed upon men who are designated as 'king's clerks',[1] were generally regarded as involving no residential duty. Wyclif was no exception to the rule. Writers have drawn eloquent pictures of Wyclif preaching not only at Westbury, but also in the neighbouring churches of Bristol.[2] To this has been attributed the early prevalence of lollardy in Bristol, its general strength in the West of England, as well as the publication in Bristol by Wyclif's secretary, Purvey, of his revised translation of the Bible. Of all this there is no evidence, though it may be that after the visitation of 1366 Wyclif was more careful to provide a vicar, or even himself to spend at Westbury the required one month a year. He had also visited Westbury in 1363 for his institution. That we hear no further complaints with reference to Westbury[3] may be deemed by some to be proof of their contention. If Wyclif thus annually visited his prebend—very doubtful as it seems to the present writer—he would certainly preach at Westbury, and possibly, though improbably, in adjoining Bristol churches —secular clergy were not accustomed to hold missions of this sort. But in all this we are reduced to mere conjecture.

Biographers of Wyclif have hastily concluded that Wyclif resigned the prebend of Aust in November 1375. The mistake has arisen in this wise. On the 6th November 1375, for reasons that are not clear, Wyclif was confirmed in the prebend of Aust by the Crown.[4] A fortnight later, 18th November, the same prebend was conferred by the king upon Robert de Farrington,[5] a clerk in the king's service whose greed had already received a number of livings.[6] The inference that

---

[1] For Wyclif as such, see *infra*, p. 237 f.
[2] So even Maunde Thompson in Usk, *Chron.* 140, *n.* 3. Cf. Seyer, *Bristol*, ii. 164.   [3] Wilkins, *Neg. Pluralist*, 64.
[4] Edward's order, dated 6 Nov., to make out the ratification is printed in Wilkins, *op. cit.* 33. For the ratification itself, made out the same day, see *Cal. Pat. Ed.* xvi. 121, printed in Wilkins, *op. cit.* 34. Writers have treated this as the first presentation of Wyclif to Aust, and regarded it, naturally enough, as a reward for his services at Bruges. So Vaughan, *Mon.* 180; Lechler, 156; Lyte, 252; Sergeant, 132, who states that he refused it.
[5] *Cal. Pat. Ed.* xvi. 121, 195. Given in full in Wilkins, *Neg. Pluralist*, 35, who points out that there is no mention of any institution of Farrington in the Worcester registers.
[6] e. g. Blackawton (Devon) and Ludlow, both in 1371; Spettisbury (Dorset) in 1372; Bishopstrow (Wilts.) in 1373; St. Clether (Cornwall),

Wyclif resigned because he " objected to pluralities, while the prebend by itself was insufficient for his support "[1] is not borne out by a later entry (22 Dec. 1376) that the grant to Robert de Farrington was revoked ' for causes laid before the king and council ' on the ' information ' of John of Gaunt. Whether the prebend was restored to Wyclif is not notified. It is, however, plainly stated that the king's grant to Farrington had been made owing to his ' belief that the prebend of Aust was vacant, as it seemed to us from the inspection of the rolls of our chancery '.[2] From this we infer that John of Gaunt, Wyclif's patron, with whom at that time he was in close alliance, had pointed out to the officials that Wyclif was still the rightful owner of the prebend. On the same day (22 Dec. 1376) Farrington was offered the *solatium* of the living of Ivinghoe in Bucks.[3] But this, evidently, he declined, for five days later (27 Dec.) it was conferred by the king on John Searle, who in time became chancellor of England. In the previous October Farrington had been collated to the prebend of Carton Paynel in Lincoln, and obtained the king's ratification of his possession (29 Nov. 1376).[4] With this he seems for the time to have been satisfied.[5]

Our contention that Wyclif continued to hold the prebend of Aust until his death is strengthened when we find that from the time of this trouble with Farrington there are but two recorded changes in the college of Westbury, and both these in connexion with the prebend of Henbury.[6] Eight months before Wyclif's death the nomination to the first vacant prebend in Westbury was given by Richard II to one of his clerks, Richard de la Felde,[7] who in fact seems to have been

29 Oct. 1374; Harlow (Essex), 30 Nov. 1376; St. Dunstan-in-the-East (24 Dec. 1374–9); Hennessy, *Nov. Rep.* 135. See *Cal. Pat. Ed.* xv. 154, 156, 191, 261; *ib.* xvi. 22, 32, 44, 392.

[1] Rashdall in *D. N. B.* lxiii. 205.

[2] *Cal. Pat. Ed.* xvi. 393, printed in Wilkins, *op. cit.* 36. Mistakes as to Aust vacancies were not uncommon.

[3] *Cal. Pat. Ed.* xvi. 394; worth in the *Taxatio*, 33, £33 13s. 4d.

[4] *Cal. Pat. Ed.* xvi. 392.

[5] In 1388 Farrington was prebendary of York (*Cal. Pat. Ric.* iii. 622). In June 1398 he was vicar of Dodington in Ely (*Pap. Let.* v. 97). He became also rector of Crofton. His will was proved 23 Mar. 1405 (*North Country Wills*, Surtees Soc. 1908, pp. 1–2; cf. *Cal. Pat. Hen.* iii. 20).

[6] Wilkins, *op. cit.* 37, for details.

[7] *Cal. Pat. Ric.* ii. 408, on 31 May 1384; in full in Wilkins, *op. cit.* 38.

appointed shortly afterwards to the prebend of Aust.¹ The proof is not absolute, but the presumption is strong that after the rectification of the king's error Wyclif continued to hold the prebend for the rest of his life, even in days when he waxed fierce in his wrath against absentees and pluralists. Richard's nomination of Richard de la Felde was made, probably, in anticipation of Wyclif's death; nor would it add to the comfort of the paralysed reformer, if he heard of the arrangement, to know that it was part of a deal between Richard II and Urban VI whereby Richard obtained the nomination of two persons to all vacant dignities in cathedral and collegiate churches in England, Ireland, and Wales.

§ 3

Wyclif's tenure of Westbury was thus a sinecure. From February 1363 to the close of 1365 he resided at Queen's at work on the initial stages of his doctorate, going home, we presume, to his living at Fillingham during the long vacation.² On his first journey up from Fillingham to Oxford he seems to have brought with him, possibly for protection, a servant, who travelled back with one of the fellows called Henry Hopton, or Upton, receiving from the college one penny for his services.³ Though his rent at Queen's was paid up to the 26th September 1366 ⁴ it is possible that during the spring of 1366 he did not reside in his rooms. In a deed dated at Mayfield (9 Dec. 1365) a certain John Wyclif was nominated by archbishop Islip ⁵ to

---

¹ Ratification delayed until 28 Sept. 1387 (*Cal. Pat. Ric.* iii. 361, printed in Wilkins, *op. cit.* 39). But the delay seems accidental, for it would be hard to account otherwise for four out of the five being ratified at the same time.

² The Long was limited by Gregory IX to one month (Apr. 1231; *Chart. Par.* i. 138). But in Wyclif's day it lasted from 5 July to 9 Oct. (*Mun. Ac.* cxlv, cxlviii; Boase, *Exeter*, 339, gives wrongly 7 July to 18 Oct.; and cf. for Paris, *Chart. Par.* ii. 709–10). At Paris, and possibly, therefore, at Oxford, there were 'legible' days in the Long; so Wyclif may have stayed up part of it.

³ Magrath, i. 113. Thus I interpret the record 'pro famulo Wiclif quando rediit cum Hopton i d'. Hopton had been bursar of Queen's in 1361–2.

⁴ *Supra*, p. 65 n. Wyclif's rent was high. See Trevisa's, *supra*, p. 168.

⁵ For Islip, see *D. N. B.* For an account of the village in Oxfordshire from which he took his name, see *Journal of Brit. Arch. Soc.* (O.S.) v. 39–51. For his pension of six marks a year granted by Grandisson on 28 May 1331 as 'advocate of the curia of Canterbury', *Reg. Grand.* ii. 616. For Islip's work, *de Speculo regis Edwardi III*, written 'de mala regni administratione', on

be the warden of Canterbury hall.¹ The identity of this Wyclif is another of the controversies in the biography of the Reformer.²

The story of this hall is of more than usual interest. In earlier days the monks of Canterbury had studied at home, where, indeed, they possessed an excellent library.³ When scholarship in the monasteries declined they did not avail themselves of the arrangement for a joint Benedictine college at Oxford, but so far overcame their jealousy of the mendicants as to allow a friar to read to them lectures in theology.⁴ So successful was this that in 1321 the prior constructed 'eighteen new studies' in the cloisters, thus relieving the infirmary where the lector's readings had much distressed the sick.⁵ But the 'new studies' did not solve the problem, nor the two scholarships that by personal influence were secured at Merton.⁶ So in September 1331 the monks hired a hall at Oxford, at a rent of six marks a year, in the parish of St. Peter's-in-the-East, near the later St. Edmund's hall, for those of their number, at first but three soon reduced by death to two, who should receive permission to study in the university.⁷ For their benefit in March 1332 the bishop of Lincoln granted a licence for an oratory.⁸ There was no endowment, but food, money, and all that was necessary for Inception and other feasts were provided by the bailiff of the monastery's manor of Newington near Henley.⁹ This hall, it would appear, was abandoned—

procurations, &c., see the ed. by J. Moissant, Paris, 1891. There are many manuscripts (*ib.* 10 f.). Moissant dates in 1337 (*ib.* 19–23), Stubbs (ii. 535) in 1349.

¹ Wood, *City*, ii. 284 ; *Univ.* i. 484, and better, from Reg. Islip, f. 306, in Foxe, ii. 926.

² The authorities for Canterbury hall are in *Hist. MSS. Com.* v. 450 ff. ; Sheppard, *Lit. Cant.* ii. pp. xxv ff. ; Wood, *City*, ii. 275–90. For the dispute the main documents are printed in Foxe, App. ii. 922 ff., and less fully in Lewis, 235–52 ; Vaughan, *Mon.* 549–59. In the view I have taken I have been influenced by an able article of H. S. Cronin in *Trans. Hist. Soc.* (1914), 55–76. I had, however, come to the main conclusions independently before reading his article. See also Lyte, 176–80.

³ Details in M. R. James, *The Ancient Libraries of Canterbury and Dover* (1903). James, p. xlvii, points out that of the books sent to Canterbury hall not one has survived. For Greek books in the fourteenth century in the library, see *ib.*, p. lxxxv.

⁴ Little, *Grey Friars*, 66, about 1310. In 1314 one of his pupils was able to take his place.   ⁵ *Lit. Cant.* i. 46.

⁶ *ib.* i. 258, 267.   ⁷ *ib.* i. 392–3, 414, 417.   ⁸ *ib.* i. 358.

⁹ *Lit. Cant.* i. 415, 468. The expenses of the three students going from Canterbury to Oxford in 1331 came to £1 17s. (*op. cit.* i. 415).

possibly because of its heavy expense in proportion to numbers —and in its place a set of rooms was hired in Gloucester college. These they retained until they had secured complete possession for themselves of the new Canterbury hall. Thereupon they sold their rooms at Gloucester college to the monks of Westminster, reserving, however, a power of re-entry should any misfortune through process of law happen to their abode.[1] Of the life of these Canterbury monks in Oxford before Islip enlarged the foundation an amusing story has come down to us. One of their number, a certain John Bodi, in 1357, complained that he had been publicly ridiculed by a bachelor of theology. He obtained as redress that the said bachelor should go to the house of every doctor of theology, and make an humble apology.[2]

With the fatality which dogs all Wyclif's story, we are met in our study of the history of Canterbury hall with a " double " not of persons but of statutes. Two sets of these have come down to us, and much turns upon the question which of the two was the original. The one set, which for convenience we will call Islip's statutes, was published by Wilkins in his *Concilia*,[3] and assigned by him to February or March 1363. Another set, hereinafter called the Courtenay statutes, was promulgated by Courtenay in 1383,[4] but assigned by the archbishop, so far at least as its fundamental clauses are concerned, to his predecessor Islip. The two sets of statutes are distinct, and in some respects contradictory. Unfortunately, Islip's statutes are undated—the date given by Wilkins is a guess— while their position in Islip's *Register* would suggest a date " not earlier than the middle of March 1366 ".[5] On the other hand, it is difficult to suppose that Courtenay was without justification in assigning to Islip the statutes he quotes in 1383. Courtenay was a trained man of affairs, who had been chancellor of Oxford in 1367, and in residence in the university in the years immediately preceding. He was not dealing with

[1] So Sheppard in *Lit. Cant.* ii. p. xxvii, and *Ch. Ch. Let.*, p. xv, in which he dates as 1371.
[2] *Mun. Ac.* 203.　　　　[3] iii. 52 f.
[4] Partially printed in *Lit. Cant.* ii. pp. xxx ff. In full in Ch. Ch. Cant. Reg. B. f. 381 f. (Cronin, *loc. cit.* 58 n.).
[5] See Cronin's arguments, *loc. cit.* 60–2.

a matter of which he knew nothing; nor was he biassed in favour of the regulars, especially the regulars of his cathedral church, with whom he was not at that time on very good terms.[1] It is not likely that he either deceived himself [2] or was imposed upon by the monks.[3]

We believe that what happened was as follows. Early in 1361 Islip, impressed by the ravages among the secular clergy of the Black Death of 1349,[4] to which in fact he had owed his own elevation to the see of Canterbury,[5] as well as by the recurrence of the plague that very year, anxious also to place the provision for the monks of Canterbury at Oxford upon a sure foundation,[6] determined to found a joint college at Oxford in which seculars and regulars should be instructed in theology together. Joint education of monks and priests was a favourite dream of the times, as we see from the attempt of Hugh Balsham, bishop of Ely in 1280, to introduce seculars among the canons regular of the Hospital of St. John at Cambridge,[7] and from the ordinance of bishop Hatfield of Durham in 1381 for Durham college at Oxford. Islip's first business was to obtain funds. He himself gave certain property at Oxford, and his nephew, William de Islip, granted the manor of Woodford in Northamptonshire.[8] As these were insufficient and the delay

---

[1] Cronin, *loc. cit.* 60.

[2] As Sheppard in *Lit. Cant.* ii. p. xxx, who thinks he mistook Simon Langham for Simon Islip.

[3] As Rashdall, ii. 499 *n*. Monks were quite capable of forging, but generally took refuge in forgeries dated in a distant past. For illustrations see Jaffe's *Regesta, passim.*

[4] Wilkins, iii. 52. In time this appeal to the Black Death became a formula, and is reproduced both in the statutes of New College in 1400 (Leach, *Winchester*, 70) and in the preamble of King's at Cambridge; J. Heywood and T. Wright, *Ancient Laws of 15th Cent. for King's* (1850), 18. For the lack of clergy in 1367, see Wilkins, iii. 69, 'raritate capellanorum', and cf. *supra*, p. 163.

[5] Provided 7 Oct. 1349, appointed 15 Oct. (*Pap. Let.* iii. 41, 312).

[6] Cronin, *loc. cit.* 56 *n.*, thinks negotiations began about Nov. 1359 with Islip's letter to Christ Church. See *Lit. Cant.* ii. 386. In 1355 Islip had written a strong letter to the prior urging him to send more monks to Oxford (*Lit. Cant.* ii. 332).

[7] *Cal. Pat. Ed. I.* i. 420 (24 Dec. 1280); *Doc. Rel. Univ. Camb.* (1852), ii. 1. The failure of the attempt led to the foundation of Peterhouse (T. Baker, *Hist. Coll. S. John*, ed. J. E. B. Mayor, 1869, i. 22 f.). Willis and Clark, i, p. l, quote a bull of Sixtus IV in 1481, no longer extant, which sanctioned the monks of Norwich residing with the seculars of either Trinity Hall or Gonville.

[8] Documents dated 13 Apr. and 4 June 1363 in Foxe, ii. 922, 925; *Lit. Cant.* ii. 443, 447. There is evidence in J. Bridges, *Northamptonshire* (1791),

in obtaining possession was considerable, Islip fell back upon the unfailing source of all medieval founders, the appropriation of livings. He had in his gift one of the wealthiest livings in the country, Pagham in Sussex, valued in 1291 at £110 per annum.[1] There the archbishops possessed a palace, for manor and advowson had belonged to the see of Canterbury from days before Domesday.[2] So on the 20th October 1361 he obtained the royal licence for the alienation to his new foundation of the advowson of Pagham.[3] But the archbishop's difficulties were not at an end. The monks of Canterbury cathedral had certain rights in Pagham, nor could the endowment be alienated without the chapter's consent.[4] The chapter naturally made the best terms for itself that it could; it secured that the government of the new hall at Oxford 'both in spirituals and in temporals' should be retained by the monks, and that the warden should be selected from their number.[5] The seculars associated with the monks were to be distinctly inferior in status, though with rights of their own.

In the spring of 1363 a beginning was made. On the 13th March 1363,[6] in accordance with the scheme agreed upon,[7] three monks were nominated to Islip for the post of warden, Henry Wodehull, John de Radyngate, and William Richmond.[8] Islip selected Wodehull, a doctor of divinity, a monk of Abingdon who three years previously had obtained licence to migrate to Christ Church, Canterbury,[9] in consequence of a dispute with his abbot. Wodehull's desire for economy in his inception feast in 1361 had led to a riot in the university.[10] But

i. 130, ii. 265, that neither the manor of Woodford in Warden hundred nor Woodford in Huxlow hundred passed to Canterbury.

[1] *Taxatio*, 1386.
[2] Horsfield, *Sussex*, ii. 66. Ceded by Cranmer to Henry VIII.
[3] *Lit. Cant.* ii. 409; Foxe, ii. 922; *Cal. Pat. Ed.* xii. 139. In 1370 this was contested by the monks of Christchurch as illegal, *Hist. MSS. Com.* viii. 341.
[4] See Lyndwood, *Prov.* iii. 8; Decretum II, c. xii, 9. 2, C. 71, part of which is quoted by Wyclif in *de Eccles.* 371.
[5] Expressly stated by Langham (Foxe, ii. 929).
[6] Foxe, ii. 88, 923. Not 1362 as in *Vict. Co. Ox.* ii. 68; *D. N. B.* xxix. 77; *Hist. MSS. Com.* ix. 89.
[7] That this existed in 1363, see Cronin, *loc. cit.* 58; for later appointments by this agreed form, *ib.* 60 n.
[8] Possibly a neighbour of Wyclif. Richmond was appointed warden of Canterbury in Sept. 1371 (Reg. Wittlesey, f. 86 in Foxe, ii. 927 n.).
[9] *Lit. Cant.* ii. 497; *Hist. MSS. Com.* viii. 342.
[10] Wood, *Univ.* i. 477; *Mun. Ac.* i. 220–2.

this parsimony, as the statutes show,[1] would commend him to Islip who had a reputation for frugality, especially as the cause of the dispute, Wodehull's desire to incept under the archdeacon of Huntingdon,[2] would argue a willingness to work with seculars. Following upon the election of the warden there came the acquisition of Woodford, and the archepiscopal licence for the alienation of Pagham.[3] Difficulties with the monks had evidently been overcome, at least temporarily. The next step was to secure premises. Islip—or more probably the new warden, for in January 1363 Islip had a stroke of paralysis which deprived him of the power of speech[4]— selected a site adjoining St. Frideswyde's on which stood eleven tenements, one of which belonged to Balliol.[5] These were adapted to form the new college, and were so used until the freehold was acquired and the ground cleared for the new buildings erected at the close of the fourteenth century, the bills for which are still in existence.[6] That the monks of Christ Church did not look on the new foundation as taking the place of their previous provision, is clear; not until nearly thirty years later did they deem it wise to sell their accommodation in Gloucester college.[7]

Thus, in the summer of 1363 Canterbury hall was set going, with four monks and eight seculars, together with a chaplain, who had to wait on the first table and dine with the servants at the second.[8] For two years matters went on, not without

[1] Cf. Wilkins, iii. 56. At Inception feasts not more to be invited than the hall will hold, &c.
[2] i.e. Wittlesey (*supra*, 90 n., 159 n.).
[3] 11 May 1363. The living was resigned on 24 May (Foxe, ii. 922, 924; *Lit. Cant.* ii. 445; Reg. Islip, f. 301). The endowments of the chapelries of Bergstead and Bognor were reserved. But the sanction by Urban V to the appropriation was received 21 Sept. 1363 (*Pap. Pet.* i. 460).
[4] Due to a fall from a horse, and sleeping at Mayfield in a stone bedroom (*Ang. Sac.* i. 46).
[5] The royal licence was granted 1 June 1363, but the property was not fully acquired until 20 July 1364. See Foxe, ii. 924; Rymer, iii. 703; *Cart. Frid.* i. 136. Other Balliol property was acquired on 6 May 1380 (*Cal. Pat.* i. 487; Savage, *Ball.* 66).
[6] *Lit. Cant.* ii, p. xxvii. Cf. *ib.* 509-10, which shows that in Feb. 1373 the freehold of the St. Frideswyde's tenements was bought.
[7] On 15 June 1392 (*Lit. Cant.* iii. 14).
[8] Wood, *City*, ii. 282; Wilkins, iii. 56. Islip wisely adds that if no chaplain 'sic subtilis' can be found, the fellows must make the best of a bad job and let him dine at the first table. For the licence for the chapel, granted 21 Sept. 1363, see *Pap. Pet.* i. 460.

friction if we read human nature aright, especially the human nature of seculars studying at a university where seculars were supreme and yet placed in a hall where they were in an inferior position. But on the 9th December 1365 Islip—probably because he had discovered that a monk from Christ Church was not the man to further his plans even if he did not do all that he could to subvert them, possibly because financial deficiencies had led to trouble [1]—dispensed with Wodehull, and put in his place ' John de Wyclyfe ' [2] who

' had obtained the Master's degree, and on whom we have fixed our eye, both because of our confidence in thy fidelity, circumspection, and industry as also by reason of the laudable conversation and honesty of thy life, and also thy knowledge of letters '.

The acquaintance of Islip with Wyclif may have arisen from his interest in Balliol. Twenty-five years previously Islip had been one of the witnesses to Sir William de Felton's gift of three livings to that college. A change of warden was within Islip's competence as visitor, though whether he could make the new warden a secular would depend upon the bargain he had struck with the chapter of Christ Church. But with complete illegality, inasmuch as this altered the terms upon which he had obtained his licence,[3] Islip drove out the regulars, and put in their place three seculars : William Selby,[4] William Middleworth, and Benger or Beneger, all three hailing from Merton.[5] While accepting this position Wyclif did not sur-

---

[1] From the first the hall was not on a sound financial basis. The revenues at Islip's death amounted to £68 8s. 6d. (Wood, *City*, ii. 289). This would not pay for the £10 a year plus his robes which Islip intended each fellow to receive (*ib.* ii. 286), unless the fellows were reduced below the twelve. The monks had thus financial reasons for refusing to call the seculars ' fellows '.

[2] Foxe, ii. 926. Langham claimed that Islip's measures were due to his ' grave illness ' and that Wyclif took possession when Wodehull and the monks were absent (*ib.* ii. 929).

[3] This the royal courts later pointed out (Foxe, ii. 936).

[4] In *Lit. Cant.* ii. 504 called ' Soleby '.

[5] Benger was from the diocese of Exeter (reading ' Exoniensis ' for ' Oxoniensis ' in Foxe, ii. 930). Benger, Christian name not given, probably Richard, had been seneschal of the week at Merton in 1360-1 (Foxe, ii. 940). For later career, see *infra*, p. 242. Selby and Middleworth were from the Salisbury diocese (Foxe, ii. 930). ' Middleworthy ' was a Sarum foundationer at Exeter from 1361–5 (Boase, *Exeter*, 10) who then migrated to Merton (Brodrick, 211). I have identified Middleworthy of Exeter with the ' Middleworth ' who figures in the ' Compota ' of Queen's (Foxe, ii. 941), and with the struggle of some of its fellows with the provost (*supra*, p. 167), and not

render his rooms at Queen's, for which he paid a rent of forty shillings from the 21st March 1365 to the 26th September 1366.[1] Either the improvised accommodation at Canterbury was not to his mind, or his rent had been paid in advance.

Not content with driving out the regulars, Islip changed the statutes. This was within his competence as visitor [2] provided he did not violate the conditions on which endowments and royal licences had been received. This proviso Islip either overlooked, or trusted to obtaining later the royal consent. Possibly he may have been influenced by the fact that his existing foundation was contrary to the constitution of Benedict XII in 1335 that 'seculars shall on no account be admitted to be taught with monks in the same churches, monasteries, priories, or other places'.[3] Whatever the cause, he now promulgated statutes without any consent from his Chapter; possibly he thought that such was not necessary.[4] These altered the character of the college, for they suited " a purely secular society and such a society alone ", though nominally regulars from Christ Church were still to be received. In the new statutes [5] we see the influence of Islip's old college, Merton. The 'studentes seculares' of the original foundation now became fellows (socii), 'masters of arts, or at least bachelors in arts' anxious to study theology, who were to lose their place 'if any one of them shall enter any religion'.[6] Henceforth the warden must have made considerable progress towards the degree in arts, a matter that monks neglected. His nomination rested with 'all the fellows' who were to select three names 'de toto collegio'.[7] Islip's beneficent provision that a sick fellow without friends should receive five

assume, as *Ziz.* 519, another double. I also identify our Middleworth with the 'William Middleworth, lawyer', who in May 1374 was appointed to visit Exeter college (Boase, *Exeter*, p. lix; *Reg. Brant.* i. 147).

[1] See *supra*, p. 65; Foxe, ii. 941; Wilkins, *Westbury*, 88-9.
[2] Wilkins, iii. 58. [3] Leach, *Charters*, 291.
[4] According to Wyclif, *Eccles.* 371, the lack of this consent formed the basis of the later papal judgement.
[5] Wilkins, iii. 53-4.
[6] Wilkins, iii. 54. I need scarcely explain that 'religio' is the technical term for membership in a regular order (Workman, *Evolution of Monastic Ideal*, 4 n.).
[7] This is the fundamental difference between the two sets of statutes. In Courtenay's statutes the warden is restricted, 'monachus ecclesiae nostrae'.

marks a year from the community shows the secular character of the new scheme; such provision was needless for monks from Canterbury. Other clauses that point to seculars was his regulation that vacancies arising in the Long Vacation must be deferred ' because there will then be in the town but scanty material for choice ', as also his permission for a fellow who obtains a benefice to stay on in the hall for one year longer, that thus he may be able to pay back to the hall his expenses out of the revenues of his new living.

Islip's proceedings formed part of the constant struggle at Oxford between the regulars and the seculars. The battle had been renewed on several fronts. Strong action had been taken in 1364 or early in 1365 against mendicants enticing youths under eighteen into their orders, and the friars had appealed to Rome. On the 1st June 1365 Urban V ordered the offending statute to be cancelled. He followed this up on the 15th July by a mandate to Islip and the bishops of Llandaff and Bangor, Roger Cradock [1] and Thomas Ringstead—the latter a Dominican doctor of theology of Cambridge of some repute [2]—to cite the chancellors and masters of both Oxford and Cambridge to show cause why certain statutes, which the pope suspended for a year, should not be perpetually revoked.[3] The statutes in question—that no one shall obtain his doctorate in theology unless he has first obtained his master's degree in arts, that ' there shall not be two regents in any one cloister of mendicants ', and the restriction of the reading of the *Sentences* to those who had studied one year—were precisely the statutes to which the regulars most objected. In our judgement it is probable that the turning out of the monks from Canterbury hall was a return-stroke of the seculars. What knowledge of the move a busy, sick archbishop would have is doubtful. Plausible reasons would be given him by the university

[1] Cradock (not in *D. N. B.*) was a Franciscan whom Clement VI had provided to the see of Waterford (3 March 1350); on 15 Dec. 1361 translated to Llandaff. He died 16 Aug. 1382 (Eubel, i. 304, 548).

[2] For Ringstead, see *D. N. B.*; Tanner, 633. Many manuscripts still exist of his *Parabolae Solomonis*, e. g. James, *MSS. Pet.* 144, unless indeed it be the work of Thomas Ringstead, junior, in 1461 (*D. N. B.*). He died at Shrewsbury, 8 Jan. 1366 (Tanner, *loc. cit.*). His brother Ralph was a great pluralist (*Reg. Grand.* iii. 1251-2).

[3] *Pap. Let.* iv. 52.

authorities, who at the same time would secure the nomination as warden of so zealous a secular as Wyclif.

Wyclif's tenure of the wardenship was but brief. On the death of Islip (26 Apr. 1366),[1] five months after Wyclif's appointment, the monks of Canterbury lodged an appeal with his successor, Simon Langham. By refusing assent to the new statutes they had preserved their *locus standi*. Langham was a stern man, who had been prior then abbot[2] of Westminster. As bishop of Ely[3] he was more respected than beloved either by his monks or his clergy. On his translation from Ely to Canterbury (24 July 1366)[4] an epigram was circulated :

> Exultent caeli, quia Simon transit ab Ely;
> Cujus in adventum flent in Kent millia centum.

Secure in the sympathies of a Benedictine archbishop, who was also chancellor of the realm, the monks claimed that Islip had acted contrary to his own statutes. Langham, ' considering that the government of the college by a secular was a great prejudice to the monks of Canterbury ', deprived Wyclif of his wardenship and appointed in his place John de Radingate, the second of the three monks originally nominated (30 Mar. 1367), and then a month later (22 Apr.) reinstated Henry de Wodehull.[5] Three monks from the monastery at Canterbury were also dispatched to Canterbury hall. Whether they were

---

[1] *Ang. Sac.* i. 46, 60 ; Reading, *Chron.* 176, dates on 27 Apr. As he died about midnight both are correct.

[2] From May 1349 to 20 Mar. 1362. His election, in which John de Reading took part, was confirmed by Clement VI on 20 July 1349, *Pap. Let.* iii. 339 ; temporalities restored 16 Sept. 1349 (*Cal. Pat. Ed.* viii. 404).

[3] On the death of Northburgh of London of the plague (9 Sept. 1361) Langham was nominated for London (Reading, *Chron.* 149 ; Higden, viii. 411). But Innocent VI provided Sudbury, 22 Oct. 1361 (Eubel, i. 324 ; cf. Rymer, iii. 628), and Langham was elected to Ely, 10 Jan. 1362 (Eubel, i. 247 ; *Ang. Sac.* i. 663) ; temporalities restored, 19 Mar. 1362 (*Cal. Pat. Ed.* xii. 184 ; Rymer, iii. 642).

[4] *Ang. Sac.* i. 47. As Langham was not enthroned until 25 Mar. 1367 proceedings against Wyclif were among his first official acts.

[5] Foxe, ii. 926–9. The terms of Radingate's appointment read as if it were a stop-gap arrangement. Possibly Langham hoped to come to some arrangement with Wyclif. The name is erroneously given as Radington or Radinghall (Wood, *City*, ii. 287). According to *Hist. MSS. Com.* ix. 89, before Radingate there was the short appointment of Richard de Hatfield. The wardens of Canterbury seem to have been changed at short notice (cf. Foxe, ii. 927 *n.*).

received or not we cannot say; all that is certain is that they were at Oxford.¹ Wyclif, to whom the letter of reinstatement was addressed, and the other seculars proved obdurate, for probably they were supported by the sympathies of a secular university. So Langham sequestrated the revenues of Pagham and confiscated certain books which Islip in his will left to Wyclif for the use of the college. As these measures proved unavailing, Langham ordered the expulsion of Wyclif and the three associate seculars.² Wyclif thereupon appealed to Urban V, and nominated as his proctor one of the three, Richard Benger, a step that shows either indifference to the result, consciousness that his plea would not hold, or else but little of the wisdom of this world in dealing with the curia. For Benger, after forwarding a petition that summarized the case, seems to have been withdrawn by Wyclif himself, at any rate he failed to put in an appearance in spite of summonses duly posted on the doors of the cathedral at Viterbo.³ Possibly, in addition to the expense of the journey, the reason was an anxiety on Benger's part lest he should be called to book for holding the living of Donington in Berkshire ' value 50 marks ' for a year or more without having obtained ordination as a priest.⁴

The result of a struggle against such powerful opponents was a foregone conclusion, for the university did not come to his support. Wyclif in his petition failed to present any justification for Islip's action other than the archbishop's mandate; no appeal whatever was made to any statutes that would have regularized the position.⁵ On the other hand, the curia was not unwilling, if only by delay, to punish Langham for the part he had played in the uncompromising answer in 1366 to Urban's demand for tribute. Urban, after hearing the outlines of the case ' in consistory ', referred the matter to cardinal Androin,⁶ with power to act. The decision

¹ *Hist. MSS. Com.* viii. 89.
² For Wyclif's continued residence at Canterbury, see *infra*, p. 198.
³ Foxe, ii. 930–1. For procedure in contested suits, see Mollat, 329 f.
⁴ *Cal. Pap. Let.* iv. 421.
⁵ Cronin, *loc. cit.* 66, points out the bearing of this on the late date of the alleged Islip Statutes.
⁶ Androin de la Roche, abbot first of Seine near Langres (*Pap. Let.* iii. 47), then appointed by Clement VI in 1351 to Cluny (Mollat-Baluze, i. 257).

was given at Monte Fiascone, about twelve miles north of Viterbo, on the 23rd July 1369.[1] Owing, however, to Androin's death (29 Oct. 1369) it was not attested by cardinal Bernard [2] until the 15th May 1370. Langham was upheld and the appeal dismissed. Simon Sudbury (bishop of London), Thomas de la Mare (the abbot of St. Albans), and Thomas Southam (archdeacon of Oxford) [3] were appointed by the pope to see that his decision was carried out. The costs were thrown upon the estate of the college, impoverished already by the years of struggle.

The proctor for the monks, Roger de Freton, dean of Chichester,[4] lost no time in setting the ecclesiastical machine to

On 17 Sept. 1361 he was nominated a cardinal by Innocent VI, but had not received his title on Innocent's death. As he voted, however, at the election of Urban this established a precedent (Mollat-Baluze, i. 327, 350). In Apr. 1362 he was sent to England to deal with certain details of the peace of Bretigny (Reading *Chron.* 296). He was specially qualified for this as on 24 Oct. 1360 he had administered in St. Nicholas, Calais, the oath to the two kings, along with the dauphin and Black Prince, to keep this peace (Delachenal, ii. 252). On the death of Albornoz he was appointed 'pastor' of the States of the Church (Mollat-Baluze, i. 353), a most unfortunate appointment (see *infra*, ii. 49), and his difficulties with 'English companies of adventurers in the pay of the Visconti' were great (*Pap. Let.* iv. 23, 24).

[1] Foxe, ii. 927 f. Urban V was at that time at Viterbo.

[2] Bernard de Bosqueto, archbishop of Naples, created cardinal 22 Sept. 1368, died at Avignon 19 Apr. 1371 (Eubel, i. 20).

[3] Thomas Southam in 1366 claimed that he had studied at Oxford for fifteen years, and held a bachelor's degree in Canon Law, and a canonry at Wells. In Apr. 1366 he was granted the archdeaconry of Llandaff but refused it (*Pap. Pet.* i. 521, 522), and was appointed archdeacon of Oxford before Christmas 1367 (*Pap. Let.* iv. 73). He also held canonries in Lincoln (*Cal. Pat. Ed.* xv. 230, in 1372) and Salisbury (*Pap. Pet.* i. 544), for which in Sept. 1391 he obtained permission to have coadjutors ' on account of age and weakness' (*Pap. Let.* iv. 354). In the previous April he obtained permission to visit his archdeaconry by deputy (*Pap. Let.* iv. 408). This was renewed in July 1398 for some years (*Pap. Let.* v. 98). Before the expiration he had died, his executors lending Henry IV £100 on 1 Apr. 1403 (*Privy Council*, i. 202). Le Neve, ii. 65, therefore, is in error in stating that Southam exchanged the archdeaconry of Oxon. for that of Berks. on 30 Jan. 1404. On 13 Sept. 1389 he was appointed by the Privy Council one of the court to try the Montague dispute (*ib.* i. 129).

[4] Roger Freton, D.C.L., was dean of Chichester from 1362–81, in which year he is said to have died (Le Neve, i. 256). But as on 22 Feb. 1383 pardon was granted to certain people who had taken out of the stocks a man who had stolen thirty-nine of Freton's sheep, he was probably still alive (*Cal. Pat. Ric.* ii. 229). In Hennessy, *Clergy List*, 2, he is given as dean from 1369–83. But in Jan. 1367 he was already dean (*Pap. Let.* iv. 71). In addition he held prebends in Wilton, York, from 19 Aug. 1370 (Le Neve, iii. 169), and Salisbury (*Pap. Let.* iv. 174, in 1372 ; *Cal. Pat. Ed.* xv. 195). On 18 Mar. 1384 he is mentioned as deceased, his successor being Richard Lescrope from 1383–90

work. While still at Viterbo the judgement was promulgated by Thomas Southam (27 May 1370). Wyclif and his allies were given six days in which to leave Canterbury, and to cease from troubling Wodehull and the monks. As ' through the stress of other business in the Roman curia ' Southam was not able personally to attend to the execution of the decree, he appointed ' the prior of Lewes,[1] the prior of the Black monks in the university of Oxford,[2] the chancellor of Salisbury,[3] Master Roger de Freton, and Master Walter Backton, doctor of decrees, canon of Chichester ', to act in his place, with full powers of excommunication. Southam possessed ' for the present no authentic seal of his own ' ; so he sealed the document with the seals of Langham, one of the witnesses being the famous Adam Easton.[4] That nothing should be lacking, the monks of Christ Church appointed two of their number to eject all seculars and to obtain the sequestrated revenues of Pagham.[5] In 1375, as if to show their final victory, they secured from Gregory XI a licence to dispense with the university statute requiring ' every master in theology to become a regent in arts '.[6] In 1383 Islip's statutes were remodelled by archbishop Courtenay,[7] who determined that there should be no room for any future Wyclifs. The seculars were reduced to ' five poor scholars ', as at Durham—whose statutes might almost have been the guide—for whose discipline elaborate regulations are set forth.[8] For their maintenance they were to receive ten pence a week apiece.[9] As the college was now

(*Cal. Pat. Ric.* ii. 388 ; Hennessy, *op. cit.* 2). Freton had been provided with Ratlisden in Suffolk in Mar. 1351 (*Pap. Let.* iii. 362), to which was added in Jan. 1355 a prebend in Bromyard (*ib.* iii. 545 ; *Pap. Pet.* i. 277). At this time he was one of the household of bishop Bateman of Norwich, who had been sent to Avignon to treat for peace. The death of the bishop (6 Jan. 1355) left them stranded, and they all began to sue for preferments as ' destitute '. In Mar. 1372 Freton was attached to the retinue of cardinal Langham (*Close Rolls Ed.* xiii. 423).
[1] John de Cherlew ; *Vict. Co. Sus.* ii. 70.
[2] Probably the prior of Durham and therefore, probably, Uhtred Boldon.
[3] According to Le Neve, ii. 650, John Norton.
[4] Foxe, ii. 932–5. For Easton, see Addenda.
[5] *Lit. Cant.* ii. 504 ; 3 June 1371.
[6] Foxe, ii. 937. See *supra*, p. 91.
[7] Courtenay's statutes from his Register at Canterbury (B. f. 388) are printed in part only in *Lit. Cant.* ii, pp. xxix–xxxiv.
[8] For forms of appointment for these scholars, see *Lit. Cant.* iii. 184–5.
[9] Wood, *City*, ii. 285.

too large, rooms were let to monks from other Benedictine houses.¹ These were all put under the control of the head of Gloucester college, who in 1426 complained that they failed to observe the regulations as regards eating meat.² Courtenay's amended statutes remained in force until the college was swallowed up in Wolsey's great foundation, leaving a faint memorial of itself in the Canterbury quadrangle and Canterbury gate of the present Christ Church.³

On a review of the whole case it is clear that, legally, Wyclif had little to be said in his favour ; nor for that matter had Islip or Langham, both of whom had violated the provisions of the Trust with its endowments for a joint college of seculars and regulars. It was a moot point, therefore, whether the hall and its revenues could not be forfeited to the Crown. To prevent this the prior and convent of the cathedral, in asking for the confirmation of the pope's judgement, solicited the royal pardon for their trespass and also the renewal of their endowments. On the 8th April 1372 this was granted,⁴ on payment of the enormous fine of 200 marks,⁵ the raising of which sadly crippled the monks as we see from a piteous letter that they wrote to cardinal Langham.⁶ In explicit words the royal pardon states that Langham's removal of the seculars was altogether illegal and adds that Islip had equally sinned against the original licence in mortmain in driving out Wodehull and the regulars. With this decision, from which there was no appeal, the legal questions may now be left. The student will note with interest the evidence it gives of the intention of the State to be supreme in all matters of property and endowments.

---

¹ *Hist. MSS. Com.* v. 451. Lyte, 180, is wrong in stating that the monks never exceeded five. This was the number in 1376 (Wilkins, iii. 110), but in 1373 we find seven (*Lit. Cant.* ii. 511).

² Reyner, App. iii. 188.

³ *Lit. Cant.* ii. p. xxxiv ; Wood, *City*, ii. 289. At archbishop Warham's visitation of Christchurch, Canterbury, in 1511, out of seventy-nine monks in the abbey six were at Oxford and two at Paris (*Eng. Hist. Rev.* vi. 20 *n.*).

⁴ Foxe, ii. 935 f.

⁵ ' Nearly £1,000 of our money ', writes Lewis in 1720 (*op. cit.* 15 *n.*) ; at least £4,000 to-day. Lewis was the first to point out the bearing of this fine.

⁶ *Lit. Cant.* ii. 510.

§ 4

As yet we have left undecided the identification of this Wyclif, warden of Canterbury. We believe that the older opinion that the Wyclif of Canterbury was the Reformer is correct, as against the claim that he was Whitclif of Mayfield.[1] We shall first present the arguments advanced on both sides.

Two contemporary writers, William Woodford or Wadford[2] and the author of the *Chronicon Angliae*, without hesitation indicate the Reformer. Of Woodford's life little is known save his opposition to Wyclif. The struggle between the two began at Oxford, which Woodford entered between 1360 and 1368[3] as a Franciscan.[4] He was thus probably a few years younger than Wyclif, against whom he took up the cudgels as a doctor ' in the year before ' Wyclif wrote his *Determination*.[5] After a distinguished career at the university Woodford in 1390 became the vicar of the provincial minister. In 1393 he took part by his pen in the trial of the lollard Walter Brut.[6] He usually resided at the Greyfriars, London, where in 1396 he obtained from Boniface IX the confirmation of certain privileges, including the right to a private room.[7] This ' doctor

---

[1] The identification with the Reformer is accepted by N. Harpsfield in his *Historia Wicliffiana* (printed in his *Hist. Anglic.*, ed. 1622), 668 ; by Wood, *City*, ii. 284 ; *Univ.* i 482–5 ; *Coll.* 82 *n.* ; Lewis, Milman, Lechler, Poole, *Med. Thought*, 287 *n.* ; Matthew, *Eng. Works*, p. iv ; Brodrick, 36–7 ; and preb. Wilkinson in *Ch. Quart. Rev.*, Oct. 1877. The identification was first rejected by Courthope, *Gent. Mag.* Aug. 1841, v. xvi, N.S., p. 146 ; Vaughan, *Mon.* 547 ; Shirley, *Ziz.*, 513–28 ; Rashdall, ii. 498 *n.* ; *D. N. B.*, s.v. ; *Vict. Co. Ox.* ii. 68. Courthope also unearthed some doubts from *The Life and Reign of Richard II* (1681), 37, a work by Sir R. Howard, quoted in *Ziz.* 518 *n.*, where it is argued that if Wyclif had ' affected any such small business as Canterbury college the duke of Lancaster who was his great patron could have helped him to it '. But the alliance with Lancaster was later.

[2] So Wyclif in *Civ. Dom.* iii. 351 ; possibly an error of the copyist.

[3] ' Postquam ego fui primo Oxoniae habuit episcopus Lincoln jus confirmandi cancellarium electum etc.', *Defensorium*, viii. c. 19 ; Wood, *Univ.* i. 482. This fixes the date, see *supra*, p. 87. This also disposes of the idea in Twyne MS. xxii, f. 103 (Little, *Grey Friars*, 80 *n.*) that Woodford defended the friars against stealing children (*supra*, p. 93). The author of this tract was William Folvyle (Wood, *Univ.* i. 475 ; Tanner, 292).

[4] The idea of Loserth, *Civ. Dom.* iv. p. xi, that Woodford was both a friar and a Benedictine monk must be rejected.

[5] *Op. Min.* 415 ; for date see *infra*, p. 239.

[6] See his work, no longer extant, *Epistola bp. Hereford de decimis contra Gualt. Britte* (Brown, *Fascic.* i. 220, 222).

[7] Little, *Grey Friars*, 247 and more fully 313. For Woodford, see *D. N. B.*

egregius' died in London in the reign of Henry IV [1] and 'lies buried under a stone cross in the Greyfriars, London, on the right-hand side of friar William Goddard '.[2] His writings won for him the title, engraved on his tomb, of 'hereticorum extirpator acerrimus'. In addition to the inevitable *Determinationes Quatuor*, delivered at Oxford against the lollards in 1389–90 in the schools of the Franciscans,[3] he wrote several commentaries on books of the Bible, and a number of polemical works against Wyclif and his followers, as well as against Fitzralph [4] and his attacks on mendicancy. Their popularity is seen in the number of manuscripts still existing.[5] Among his pupils was one greater than himself, Thomas Netter of Walden.

In his polemical work, *Septuaginta duo quaestiones de Sacramento Altaris*, Woodford writes as follows: [6]

'And this rage against the religious owed its origin to corruption. For before he had been expelled by the monks and the prelates from the hall of the monks of Canterbury he (Wyclif) attempted nothing of any moment against them; and before he had been publicly reproved by the mendicants for heresy with reference to the sacrament of the altar he attempted nothing against them, but after his reproof defamed them hugely. Thus his evil and baleful teaching against the religious, monks and mendicants, was the offspring of corruption and disappointment.'

That Woodford believed that the Reformer had been the warden cannot be gainsaid. There is a similar statement in the more recently discovered *Chronicon Angliae*, known, how-

[1] See the reference to Henry IV in his *de Causis Condemnationis articulorum* (*infra*, ii. 344 n.). His death is after 1411, in which year he seems to have been deputed to attend a council in London (Sbaralea, 333). The statement in Bale, *Script. Cat.* i. 512, that he died in 1397 and was buried at Colchester is therefore an error.

[2] Kingsford, *Grey Friars Lond.* 72.

[3] Little, *op. cit.* 246 n. In Bale, *Index Script.* 153; *Script. Cat.* i. 511, called *contra Wyclif de Religione* by a confusion with a work *de Religione* of William of Waterford, see *infra*, p. 188.

[4] viz. (i) *Defensorium mendicitatis contra Armachanum*; (ii) *de Erroribus Armachani*.

[5] For Woodford's works, see Little, *op. cit.* 247–8; Tanner, 784; Sbaralea, 332. His chief works against Wyclif were: (i) *Septuaginta duo Quaestiones de sacramento Altaris*; (ii) *de Causis Condemnationis articulorum xviii damnatorum Johannis Wyclif* (see *infra*, p. 298); (iii) *Responsiones contra Wiclevum et Lollardos* otherwise called *ad LXV quaestiones Wiclevi contra fratres*; (iv) *contra Wiclevum de Civili Dominio*. See Bale, *Index Script.* 152, 154.

[6] Quoted in *Ziz.* 517.

ever, in an old English translation long before the publication of the Latin original.¹ We are told that Wyclif ' was justly deprived by the archbishop of Canterbury from a certain benefice that he unjustly was incumbent upon within the city of Oxford '.² Nor can it be reasonably argued that the evidence of these statements is neutralized by their *theologicum odium*. Some additional proof, also, might be claimed from the further statement of the *Chronicon Angliae* :

' that (Wyclif) might the more delude the people's minds he adjoined himself unto the begging friars, approving their poverty and extolling their perfection, that he might the better deceive the vulgar sort '.³

This would fit in with Leland's statement that Wyclif when ' at Canterbury went about in a long russet gown, with naked feet ', as also with Wyclif's early sympathy with the Spiritual Franciscans.⁴

These two contemporary records are of great importance. The *Chronicon Angliae* is a valuable source of information for the period from 1376 to 1387.⁵ More striking still is the testimony of Woodford. The work in which it occurs, according to Shirley, was " a course of theological lectures, delivered perhaps at the Grey Friars in London, of which he was a monk (friar),

¹ This translation, well known to John Stow, was printed by T. Amyot in 1829 in *Archaeol.* xxii. 212–84; the section with reference to Wyclif is on p. 253. Lowth, *Wykeham*, pref. xxii, made use of it (MS. Harleian 6217), and noted that it was part of a large historical work which he wrongly identified (*ib.* 130 *n.*) with Malvern's *Continuation of the Polychronicon*. Foxe (ii. 797–806) used the Latin original, as Lowth noticed, and in a note gives (p. 801) the source of his translation. The original was found in the Parker collection (Harl. MS. 3634) and published by E. M. Thompson as *Chronicon Angliae* in 1874, thus refuting Shirley's scepticism as to its existence (*Ziz.* 520–1).
² *Chron. Ang.* 115.   ³ *ib.* 116.
⁴ Leland, *Collect.* iii. 409. Cf. Wyclif's statement (*Blas*, 237) that gowns of russet hue were very costly. The going about barefoot was one of the marks of the Spiritual Franciscans. The 7th conclusion of the *Introduction to the Eternal Gospel* (*infra*, ii. 99) was this: ' quod nullus simpliciter idoneus est ad instruendum homines de spiritualibus, nisi illi qui nudis pedibus incedant ' (*Chart. Par.* i. 272).
⁵ The *Chronicon Angliae* was afterwards expurgated by Walsingham (who wrote at St. Albans at an earlier date than used to be assigned) by cutting out passages hostile to John of Gaunt. Among those thus cut out from Walsingham's *Hist.* were the pages in the middle of which this charge against Wyclif takes up two or three lines. Hence, it is not mentioned by Walsingham or Capgrave, while Knighton is largely local in his interests. (See Thompson, *op. cit.*, for details.)

in preparation for the feast of Corpus Christi (1381) ". Its date would appear to be fixed from its constant references to Wyclif's *Confession* "which appears to have been newly issued and certainly not yet condemned at the time of the delivery of the lectures ". The *Confession*, as we shall see, was published on the 10th May 1381 and the feast of Corpus Christi fell that year on the 13th June. " In the following year Wyclif's conclusions were condemned eighteen days before Corpus Christi day. As the Synod met at the neighbouring house of the Black Friars, the condemnation of the conclusions must have been immediately known to Woodford." Against this positive statement of Woodford all that Shirley can adduce is that Woodford wrote his lectures in " extreme haste, at a moment of great controversial excitement, when any story to Wyclif's discredit would have been told and listened to without examination ", and that he can only have heard of the matter second-hand, as he would be " a mere boy " when the event took place.[1] The " controversial excitement " may be granted, nor must we forget, as Dr. Rashdall reminds us, " how easily even at the present day ridiculous stories about theological opponents are circulated and believed ".[2] But the argument that Woodford was " a mere boy " at the time is a mistake founded upon the erroneous identification, through the patriotic zeal of Wadding, of William Woodford with a certain William of Waterford who about the year 1435 wrote a tractate, *de Religione,* dedicated to cardinal Giuliano Caesarini.[3] Woodford, in fact, and Wyclif were not far apart in age. In the schools he came into close, friendly contact with Wyclif. He himself tells us :

' When I was lecturing at the same time as he was on the *Sentences* [4] Wyclif used to write his answers to the arguments which I advanced in a note-book which I sent him with my arguments, and to send me back the note-book.' [5]

---

[1] *Ziz.* 517, 523-4.   [2] *D. N. B.* lxiii. 204.
[3] Tanner, 364 ; Sbaralea, 333. J. Ware, *Writers of Ireland* (1704), 22, rejects the identification and should have kept Shirley right.
[4] ' Quando concurrebam cum eo in lectura sententiarum '. Little (*op. cit.* 81 *n.*) confesses that he does not understand the phrase, but quotes *Mun. Ac.* 393, ' Statutum est quod duo magistri in theologia, si velint, possunt concurrere disputando '.
[5] Little, 81, from Woodford, *Quaestiones de sacramento altaris,* qu. 63. Little, *op. cit.* 246, states that he was not a D.D. until after 1381. But this seems incompatible with the early date of his entrance into Oxford, see *supra,* p. 185.

Though after 1381 Woodford attacked Wyclif, his evidence cannot be discounted as the gossip of a stranger or the malice of a partisan. Wyclif, Selby, and Middleworth were still alive, and nothing could have been easier than for Wyclif to have shown up the mistake that Woodford was making. The argument from the silence of Wyclif's opponent Netter (who attributes the outbreak of Wyclif as due to his not obtaining the bishopric of Worcester [1]) can scarcely prove, as Shirley would have us believe, that Netter, a disciple of Woodford, disbelieved the story of one whom he calls ' my father and master '.[2] It may show that he regarded the charge, as Wyclif seems to have done, as not of great moment, and, at any rate, did not see anything discreditable in it.[3]

There are other arguments in favour of the Reformer, some of which are of slight value, though taken together they are of considerable strength. Much, for instance, has been made of the flattering language in which the warden was nominated.[4] But he would be a bold man who would take medieval compliments as more than token coins. Nor should much stress be laid upon the fact that the name of the warden is consistently written some thirty times as ' de Wyclyve ' or ' Wiclif ', and never as ' Whitclif ' or the like.[5] Though medieval spelling, even in official documents, was subject to few laws, this uniform spelling should have some weight. Of more importance is it that the warden is described as having already obtained his master's degree, and as a bachelor in theology, whereas the vicar of Mayfield in four episcopal registers and in the probate of his will is only styled ' dominus ', a proof that he had not taken the higher degree.[6] This fits in with the academic status of the Reformer at this time, as also with the require-

---

[1] See *infra*, p. 252.   [2] Netter, *Doct.* ii. 310 ; Bale, i. 511.
[3] Netter, *Doct.* i. 560, 934. I suspect a reference in *ib.* iii. 485, where Netter speaks of Wyclif's disobedience ' numquam ulli praeposito aut honesto collegio alius quam rebellis hospes discors, contumax et inobediens '.
[4] *Supra*, p. 177 ; Foxe, ii. 926.
[5] The name of the vicar of Mayfield is spelt in four different registers with a ' t ' (Foxe, ii. 944). But in *Close Rolls Ric.* i. 91–2 it is spelt ' Wycclyve '. Cf. *Gent's Mag.* (N.S.), xxii. 136.
[6] Foxe, ii. 945. See the documents in *ib.* ii. 943. Shirley, *Ziz.* 519 pleads that ' dominus ' is the usual " style of a priest whenever there was no question of his degree ". That is true, but episcopal registers and wills are formal documents in which the question of degree would enter.

ments in Islip's statutes.¹ We may further point to the association of Wyclif, Middleworth, and Selby when they hired rooms at Queen's, as some corroboration of their previous alliance.² Important also is it to note that the warden is officially stated to be ' of the diocese of York ', the designation which is given to the Reformer as master of Balliol.³ We may add that the archbishop could not have found any one more likely than the Reformer to carry out his purposes with enthusiasm. Throughout life Wyclif was intensely anxious to improve the outlook of the secular clergy.

Wyclif's appeal to Rome may also be explained when we remember the relations at that time between Edward III and Simon Langham. On the 22nd September 1368 Urban V created Langham cardinal-priest to the title of St. Sixtus.⁴ Langham accepted the honour without waiting for Edward's consent; whereupon the offended king argued that the see of Canterbury was vacant, took possession of the revenues, and appointed Wittlesey (11 Oct. 1368).⁵ On the 27th November 1368 Langham, who had been driven by lack of money to sell his cross,⁶ formally resigned his archbishopric, and with some difficulty obtained permission to leave the country for the papal court (28 Feb. 1369). A survey of dates will show that Wyclif's appeal was lodged probably during the period of Langham's disgrace.⁷ Wyclif's carelessness over the prosecu-

---

¹ A student of Canterbury must be ' Magister artium studens in theologia, vel saltem regens in artibus et theologias in proximo auditurus, alioquin baccalarius in artibus ad proficiendum aptior' (Wilkins, iii. 53). Wodehull did not fulfil the statutory requirements, nor the vicar of Mayfield, except under the last clause.

² See *supra*, p. 167. Poole, *Med. Thought*, 288 *n.*, considers this " one of the strongest arguments in favour ". But of the six colleges in existence practically only Queen's, with its rooms to let, was open.

³ Foxe, ii. 945.

⁴ For date see Mollat-Baluze, i. 368, where he is called ' Symonem de Langari'; Eubel, i. 20. In *Ang. Sac.* i. 47, given as 23 Sept.

⁵ *Ang. Sac.* i. 48; Eubel, i. 169. Temporalities restored 15 Jan. 1369 (Rymer, iii. 857).

⁶ *Ang. Sac.* i. 47.

⁷ Langham as cardinal was appointed by Gregory XI in Jan. 1371 to go to England to treat for peace between England and France. Gregory sent letters on his behalf, but in July 1371 complained that he had as yet failed to secure a safe conduct from Edward, ' some prelates having presumed to hinder the same' (*Pap. Let.* iv. 92–4). Not until the end of Oct. 1371 would Edward receive him (*Pap. Let.* iv. 97; Rymer, iii. 929) or even allow him tithes from his archdeaconry of Wells (see *Close Rolls Ed.* xiv. 105–6). There were the

tion will thus be explained. For the winning of his suit he trusted to the royal displeasure with Langham rather than to direct influence with the Curia. That the appellant had grounds for such confidence is seen in the heavy fine which Edward levied upon the monks of Canterbury.

On behalf of Whitclif of Mayfield the following arguments have been adduced. Islip himself was a Merton man and founded Canterbury hall on Merton lines. He chose, for instance, the warden out of a list of three in strict Merton fashion. Stress also is laid upon the provision that the books of the library were not to be loaned except to Merton men.[1] Now the clannishness of Merton men was well known. William Rede, bishop of Chichester, who probably gave this Whitclif his prebend, was a fellow of Merton.[2] We may therefore infer, so it is argued, that Islip of Merton would probably select the Whitclif of Merton, already identified with Whitclif of Mayfield. Mayfield was a favourite residence of the archbishops,[3] and according to Matthew Parker the living had been appropriated by Islip for the support of Canterbury college.[4] If this were true, nothing could be more natural than that Islip should compensate Whitclif[5] for the loss of revenues, or that after four years' favourable experience of him at Mayfield he should entrust him with the higher duties of the wardenship of Canterbury. The argument is strengthened when we find that two of the warden's associates, Benger and Middleworth, were also from Merton.[6] But the objection taken against the Reformer that " the warden of Canterbury seems to be spoken of as a scholar of that house at the time of his appointment,

usual difficulties over his procurations (*Pap. Let.* iv. 102, Apr. 1372; *Reg. Brant.* i. 248–53; *Reg. Wykeham*, ii. 145–8). Langham died 22 July 1376 (Flete, 132; *Ang. Sac.* i. 60) and was buried first at Avignon, then afterwards at Westminster (Stanley, *West.* 358). One of his executors was Thomas Southam (*supra*, p. 182), who was detained at Avignon in settling the will after Gregory XI's departure for Rome (*Ch. Quart. Rev.*, 1908, p. 358).

[1] Brodrick, 199; Wilkins, iii. 51.   [2] Brodrick, 211, 218; *Ziz.* 516.

[3] For the archbishop's manors in Sussex, including Mayfield and Pagham, see *Jour. Brit. Arch. Soc.* (N.S.), xx. 107–14.

[4] M. Parker, *Antiq. Brit. Eccles.* (1605), 248.

[5] Whitclif had been appointed to Mayfield 21 July 1361 (Foxe, ii. 943) on the death of Ralph Baker of Sevenoaks. But as Mayfield was already a vicarage and not a rectory it is difficult to see where there would be ground for compensation. In the *Taxatio* Mayfield was worth £60.

[6] Brodrick, 202, 211; Foxe, ii. 930.

an impossible position for the vicar of Fillingham ",[1] let alone for an ex-master of Balliol, is founded upon a double mistake. In the first place the idea that he was a scholar of the house is due to a false reading;[2] in the second there was nothing whatever to prevent a vicar of Fillingham or of any other place studying at Canterbury for his degree in theology, as, in fact, the statutes provided, if he could obtain a licence for absence.

The argument from Merton clannishness is hardly sufficient to counterbalance the positive statements for the identity of the warden and the Reformer. Nor can the clannishness of Merton be maintained, considering the constant hospitality the college gave to fellows of Exeter.[3] Moreover, the vicarage of Mayfield was one that carried with it the duty of residence, as is clearly laid down in the record of Whitclif's original appointment.[4] We may own with Shirley[5] that as Islip was patron both of the living and of the hall, with ample powers of giving such dispensations as he might choose, this last argument cannot be pressed. On the other hand, no trace has been found of the granting of such dispensation,[6] nor is there any proof that archbishop Parker was correct in his statement that Mayfield had been appropriated to Canterbury. Whatever may have been Islip's intentions, this scheme does not seem to have been carried out, and, according to Stephen of Birchington, who in 1382 became a monk of Christ Church, Canterbury, and finally its treasurer, and who therefore should have been in a position to know, the living that Islip intended to bestow, had not death intervened, was ' Ivechirche ' not Mayfield.[7]

Assuming as we may that the Reformer was the warden of Canterbury, there is no ground for imputing to him dishonourable action. Any illegality lay at the door of Islip himself. The idea that Wyclif so felt his expulsion that he was thereby stirred up to revenge seems to have originated with Woodford,

---

[1] So Rashdall in *D. N. B.* lxiii. 204, from Lewis, 13.
[2] ' quendam secularem Custodem ' was misread by Lewis, 13, as ' scholarem '. See Foxe, ii. 929, 936.
[3] Boase, p. lxvii.
[4] Reg. Islip, f. 287 b, quoted in Foxe, ii. 943.
[5] *Ziz.* 579.   [6] Foxe, ii. 944.
[7] *Ang. Sac.* i. 46. Ivychurch is a parish in Kent near New Romney.

and to have been copied by Reyner.[1] But imputation of motives has always been prevalent in theological disputes.

In most biographies we should look with confidence to the assistance of the subject in solving a problem such as we have presented. Wyclif, it is true, alludes to the affair in his *de Ecclesia*,[2] a work written in 1378. Unfortunately Wyclif's usual strange impersonalness colours this reference. It is impossible to say whether he is treating it as an event in his own life or not. Some critics have detected in it personal interest; others have remarked that it reads like a detached illustration. The reader shall judge for himself. Wyclif is dealing with the objection that if his reasoning were true it would follow that all university endowments are evil, and that this would issue in detriment to the poor. Wyclif owns that he would gladly see all endowments ended, but urges that sin may creep in by inadvertence in a thing good in itself or in its motives. This he illustrates by a 'rather familiar example', the founding of a college in Oxford by Islip for '*pure clerici scholares*'. No name is mentioned, but that Canterbury is intended is beyond doubt. Islip's motives, Wyclif pleads, were perfectly good, and yet Islip 'sinned', for the appropriation of a parish church—he is alluding to Pagham—'or the alienation of an estate in mortmain, can never be without sin', both in giver and receiver, as bishop Wykeham should remember. But 'Antisimon', Islip's successor Langham—the gibe is characteristic of Wyclif—sinned even more in upsetting the arrangement. The reader will notice that save for one doubtful phrase[3] there is not a word which would lead us, if we had no other knowledge, to imagine that Wyclif had any part in the matter. The whole narrative is characteristically colourless. Equally so is a possible reference in his last work, the *Opus Evangelicum*. His treatment there of lawsuits about benefices shows that if once concerned in an appeal to Rome he had now changed his mind as to the desirability of such

---

[1] Reyner, i. 219.   [2] *Eccles.* 571.
[3] Lechler, 108 f., urged that the Latin 'in familiariori exemplo' (*Eccl.* 371) should be translated 'by an example touching myself more closely'. Dr. Poole truly remarks (*Med. Thought*, 288 *n.*) that "those who are best acquainted with Wyclif's grammar will be the least disposed to attach weight to a point of this kind".

methods.[1] In his earlier *de Ente*, written as we hold shortly after the time of his Canterbury controversy, Wyclif makes vague reference to the trial of his patience by delay in securing a promised benefice, but gives no further particulars.[2] In all probability he is alluding to a prebend in Lincoln, a matter to which we shall return.

We wish that our proof that Wyclif was thus the warden of Canterbury could carry with it the pleasant legend of Wood that while Wyclif was warden ' he had to his pupil the famous poet called Jeffrey Chaucer who following the steps of his Master reflected much upon the corruptions of the clergy '. The famous picture of the ' poor parson of the town '[3] with which Chaucer had enriched his portrait-gallery of fourteenth-century England could in that case be assigned without hesitation to the Reformer. But the legend is without any possible foundation.

§ 5

While the conflict over Canterbury hall was still raging, Wyclif's licence for absence for five years from his living expired. There was especial reason why he should be careful to renew it. So long as he was acting for Islip non-residence at Fillingham would be condoned. But when he defied Langham non-residence without licence became dangerous. Wyclif was not inclined to repeat the troubles he had experienced at Westbury. Possibly the Paris requirement of 1366 that the applicant for leave of absence must appear before the faculty to justify the privilege, had been extended to Oxford—the two universities largely borrowed from each other. Possibly Wyclif may have dreaded unfriendliness on the part of the chancellor. For on Whit-Saturday, 1367, grace had been given ' that the reverend doctor and lord, Master William Courtenay, son of an earl and of the royal blood, should be called to the chancellorship ',[4] and it is difficult to imagine that the future archbishop would have much sympathy, even at this date, with the future reformer. Whatever the cause,

---

[1] *Op. Evang.* i. 200, 211, 213, 294.
[2] *Ente*, 126. This should be read along with his remarks in *ib.* 32.
[3] Chaucer, *Prol.* 480 f.; Wood, *Univ.* i. 485.   [4] *Mun. Ac.* 226.

Wyclif took steps betimes to regularize his position. So on the 13th April 1368 licence was granted at Stow Park by Buckingham to 'Master John de Wyclif that he may absent himself from his church for the space of two years to devote himself to the study of letters in the university of Oxford '.[1] The summer of that year, memorable for the renewal of the plague,[2] would probably be spent by Wyclif at Fillingham. A few months later Wyclif exchanged his Lincolnshire rectory for Ludgershall in Buckinghamshire.[3] The nearness to Oxford—but sixteen miles—compensated Wyclif for the loss of income, ten marks a year instead of thirty marks. In making this exchange we see a desire on Wyclif's part to keep more oversight over his flock than had been possible at Fillingham. So on the 12th November 1368 he was instituted in his new living, on the presentation of John Paveley, the prior of St. John's, Clerkenwell.

The old church of Ludgershall,[4] with its embattled tower, stands at the top of a sloping green. The church is dedicated to the Assumption of the Virgin. The patronage of the living had been given in or before the reign of Henry III to the Knights Hospitallers of St. John of Jerusalem, who also possessed in the parish the manor of Tetchwick.[5] In 1291 the living was valued at ten marks after deducting two portions of tithes settled in 1190 upon the priory of Bermondsey.[6] Wyclif was thus brought into direct contact with the system of monastic appropriations. The parish, about 2,000 acres, had been granted at the Conquest to Geoffrey, bishop of Coutances. In process of time it formed part of the estates of Hugh le

[1] Buckingham, Mem., f. 56 d; not f. 7 as *D. N. B.* lxiii. 204.
[2] Wilkins, iii. 74.
[3] Reg. Buckingham Inst. x, f. 419; cf. f. 130 d.
[4] For details concerning Ludgershall, see Lipscomb, *Bucks.* i. 305–22. The parson with whom Wyclif changed was a certain John de Wythernwick appointed the previous year, 27 Feb. 1367 (Lipscomb, i. 318). This parson was alive in Sept. 1391 when a cup was bequeathed to him (Gibbons, 69). Four parsons in succession exchanged the living. The taxation of Ludgershall, including pannage of hogs in the forest of Bernwood, amounted to $11\frac{1}{2}$ marks (Lipscomb, i. 312). There were neither merchants nor cattle-dealers in the village. For the value of the living, Lipscomb, i. 316 should be corrected by Bacon, *Thes.* 503. The name of the village is not derived from a hall of king Lud as Lipscomb suggests, but contains the Celtic Lug, a water-god, found in Ludgate, Ludlow, Lugdunum, &c.
[5] Lipscomb, *Bucks.* i. 313.
[6] *Taxatio*, 41; Dugdale, v. 97.

Despenser, and passed to the Crown on his forfeiture. On the 21st October 1335 it was granted to John de Moleyns,[1] who in 1346 received permission to impark the woods and 100 adjacent acres ' for the better support of his dignity as a bannaret '.[2] Standing near the church the sky-line to the south is broken by the heights of Brill and Ashendon which divide the plain of North Bucks. from the Vale of Aylesbury. Over the southern porch of the church there was formerly a parvise or priest's chamber which Wyclif occasionally may have used—a worthless local tradition asserts that in it he wrote his *de Civili Dominio*. This chamber was unfortunately destroyed in a ' restoration ', though the spiral stair leading up to it from the aisle may still be traced. At Ludgershall, even more than at Fillingham, Wyclif would be brought into contact with the peasants. At Fillingham, as throughout Lincolnshire, serfs were few : at Ludgershall the majority were serfs and villains. Fillingham and Ludgershall saved Wyclif from becoming academic ; they taught him a great pity for the poor. At Ludgershall Wyclif would come across difficulties of winter floods, troublesome even now, which made intercourse dangerous. Wyclif would be at Ludgershall also in 1369 when there was ' a great pestilence of men and of great beasts ', a ' falling of waters ' that destroyed the crops, insomuch that ' a bushel of wheat was sold for 40 pence '.[3] At Ludgershall, moreover, Wyclif may have come into contact with the coarse side of English village life. In one of his tracts he gives us a vivid picture of the bedridden peasant ' couching in muck or dust ', of men getting drunk on borrowed money, and of the prevalence of ' dalliance with women '.[4] In another he refers to the frequent sale and loan of wives.[5]

The student of economics, translated to a medieval village such as Fillingham or Ludgershall, while finding many things unchanged, would be struck with one great difference from present-day conditions upon which Wyclif is silent. To-day woman and her work looms large ; the question did not then

[1] *Chart. Rolls*, iv. 351. [2] Lipscomb, i. 307.
[3] *Brut*, ii. 321 ; Walsingham, i. 309. [4] *Eng. Works*, 210, 217, 218.
[5] *Op. Evang.* i. 172. In *Sel. Eng. Works*, iii. 167, Nicholas Hereford speaks of this as frequent at fairs.

INTERIOR

By permission of H.M. Stationery Office

CHURCH OF ST. MARY, LUDGERSHALL

arise, for as a matter of fact the unmarried girl over fourteen scarcely existed. Marriages at ages that seem to us immoral were then the rule, especially in the villages. We hear of a widow of ten whose husband at death was but eleven.[1] For men this was exceptional, but the records of the poll-tax show that there were few spinsters or widows.

The first long vacation that Wyclif would spend at Ludgershall was a time of stir and tumult. On the 3rd June 1369 Edward had once more assumed the crown of France.[2] A week later new seals 'engraved in two pieces, on the one *Rex Angliae et Franciae*, on the other *Rex Franciae et Angliae*' were delivered to the officers of state in the chancery at Westminster.[3] Orders were issued for the muster of ' all fencible men between the ages of 16 and 60 '. Freedom of egress from towns was taken away, while the sheriffs were instructed to set about the provision of arrows—Bedford and Bucks. for instance to provide 1,200 sheaves, afterwards increased by 1,000 sheaves each, cause of no small stir in the villages, including Ludgershall. Nor were the clergy to be exempt from doing their duty. ' Abbots, friars, men of religion and other ecclesiastics ' were to be ' armed and arrayed '.[4] Fears were expressed lest the Welsh, assisted by the French, should rise and destroy the principality,[5] and in February 1370 ' the fencible men ' throughout the country were arrayed to prevent invasion.[6] Alien priors who were suspected of intercourse with the enemies were seized.[7] All this and more Wyclif may have heard from his friend William de Askeby, chancellor of the exchequer,[8] even if he took no part in the stirring events himself.

Rector of Fillingham or vicar of Ludgershall, where did Wyclif live when in Oxford ? Did Wyclif leave Canterbury hall or did he continue in possession during the appeal ? Some

---

[1] Deiser, 154.
[2] *Close Rolls Ed.* xiii. 93–4 ; Rymer, iii. 874 ; *Rot. Parl.* ii, App. 460. Parliament had been summoned on 6 Apr. (*Close Rolls Ed.* xiii. 83 ; *Dig. Peer.* iv. 644–5). It went down on 11 June (*Close Rolls Ed.* xiii. 100 ; Prynne, *Writs*, iv. 278, 281).   [3] *Close Rolls Ed.* xiii. 94.
[4] *ib.* 18, 20, 23, 38, 41, 57–8 ; Rymer, iii. 876, 6 July 1369.
[5] *Close Rolls Ed.*, xiii. 61 ; Rymer, iii. 883, 24 Dec. 1369 ; also 10 Nov. 1370 (Rymer, iii. 901 ; *Close Rolls Ed.* xiii. 158).
[6] *Close Rolls Ed.* xiii. 124 ; Rymer, iii. 887.
[7] *Close Rolls Ed.* xiii. 63, prior of Hayling on 12 Nov.
[8] See *infra*, p. 201.

historians have argued as if Wyclif's expulsion by Langham in the spring of 1367 had been immediate,[1] and have dismissed as mere spite the statement of his enemies that while the appeal to Rome was in progress Wyclif lived on at Canterbury with his three allies, spending freely, it was affirmed, the college goods.[2] We should do well to refresh our memory of the dates. In April 1367 Wyclif was still in possession at Canterbury hall, as we see from Langham's order to him to receive Henry Wodehull.[3] This Wyclif refused to do. He was still, as it would appear, in possession on the 23rd July 1369 when cardinal Androin made his decision. Judging from the terms of cardinal Bernard's decree on the 15th May 1370 Wyclif still prevented Wodehull's entrance, and with his companions was enjoying such revenues as the college possessed after the sequestration of Pagham.[4] But Bernard's decree should not be pressed into other than the legal phraseology of a judgement that would leave no loophole for further complications; for it is certain, from the fine afterwards paid to the Crown, that the regulars succeeded in driving out the seculars. Probably this was done as soon after the 23rd July 1369 as the news of the decision, though not formally promulgated, reached England.[5] We are confirmed in our view when we find that during this period Wyclif ceased paying rent for rooms at Queen's. That Wyclif left Canterbury before he was forced seems to us improbable. He was too ardent a fighter tamely to surrender a battle, especially one so dear to the university as seculars versus regulars. That Wyclif quitted Canterbury in the autumn of 1369 may be inferred from the fact that one of the company, Middleworth, obtained a fellowship at Queen's on the 5th May 1369; his old college, Merton, was probably closed to him.[6] This he held for the next four years, being

[1] So *D. N. B.* lxiii. 204.   [2] *Lit. Cant.* ii. 491.
[3] Foxe, ii. 927.   [4] *ib.* 930.
[5] Cf. *Lit. Cant.* ii. 492, ' saeculares, quorum tamen nullus . . . superstes sit '. This was in Oct. 1370, not 1369. But it shows that by 1370 the hall was cleared of the seculars.

[6] Shirley (*Ziz.* 520 *n.*) exaggerates this when he claims that the archbishop, as visitor of Merton, would prevent his return. The archbishop had merely " power to enforce the statutes " (Rashdall, *Univ.* ii. 485), though it is impossible to read the visitations of Kilwardby in 1276 and of Peckham in 1284 without seeing that archbishops interpreted this power very amply (Brodrick, 24–5).

joined there by Nicholas Hereford¹ and John Trevisa. In September 1374 Middleworth became the bursar, and had the pleasure that year of letting a room to his former chief, Dr. John Wyclif, for twenty shillings, as well as of spending sevenpence on his door fastener and keys.² Middleworth's departure from Canterbury hall may be interpreted as a leaving of the sinking ship ; on the other hand it would enable Wyclif, if he so disposed, to continue residence for a little longer, by lessening the financial strain caused by the sequestration of Pagham.

The later career of Middleworth and the other associates of Wyclif at Canterbury hall is of some interest. In Middleworth, whatever his theological views, Wyclif certainly found a kindred fighter. In 1378 he was one of the leading spirits in the disturbance at Queen's to which we have already referred. With him were associated Richard de Thorp and William Frank. Frank was an old hand at disorder. In October 1371, when senior fellow at Exeter,³ he prevented the others from electing a rector. In consequence he had been expelled by bishop Brantingham, excommunicated, and, after the usual forty days' grace, handed over to the secular arm⁴ (27 Jan. 1372).⁵ So he migrated to Queen's, where in Middleworth he found a congenial spirit. He seems even to have secured election as provost by the southern party, though soon expelled to make place for Thomas Carlisle, the leader of the northerners.⁶ For their brawls at Queen's Middleworth and his two friends were brought up before a special commission and ordered to make restoration.⁷ Middleworth took no notice, but a year or so later ⁸ handed over the stolen goods to Trevisa and others, who had been 'expelled for their unworthiness'.⁹ Sterner

¹ See the 'compoti' of Queen's quoted in Foxe, ii. 941–2 ; Wilkins, *Westbury*, 89 ; Magrath, i. 116.
² See *supra*, p. 65, n. 8.
³ He must therefore have entered Exeter on a Sarum foundation before 1362 (Boase, 14). Possibly he is the William Franke who became rector of Broughton, Wilts., in 1400, resigned 1407 (Hutchins, *Dorset*, i. 585–6).
⁴ *Reg. Brant.* 143, 246.
⁵ Boase, pp. lv, lvi. Latin originals in *ib.* (first ed.), pp. xliv, 233, 270. See also *Rot. Parl.* iii. 69 a, or abstract in *Collect.* iii. 146.
⁶ Magrath, i. 106 *n.*, 117. ⁷ *Cal. Pat.* i. 204.
⁸ Trevisa was not brought up until 20 Oct. 1379 (*Cal. Pat.* i. 420).
⁹ Magrath, i. 108 *n.*, 115 *n*.

measures were taken, and Middleworth was outlawed. In consequence the books and goods were restored, and on the 1st May 1380 Middleworth was pardoned.[1] So on the 9th October 1381 [2] Middleworth was back at Queen's as a fellow, though from 1382 to 1386 and again in 1396 he paid rent for his rooms. While he was absent in disgrace, in 1380, his companion, William Selby, another of Wyclif's comrades at Canterbury, hired a chamber at Queen's at the same time as Wyclif. For this he paid twenty shillings rent. This chamber Selby rented again and again until his death in 1393, in which year a man was sent to Lincoln by the provost of Queen's ' pro testamento Willelmi Selby '. Middleworth survived his friends. In the Christmas of 1385 Queen's spent £3 19s. 6d. upon the expenses of a journey of the provost and Middleworth to London, so completely were the old feuds forgotten. In 1395 he bought from Queen's, for £3 13s. 4d., a ' great concordance ',[3] probably the *Concordantiae Magnae* of Hugh de S. Caro. In the same year he made a donation for a curtain, possibly the money he had received for his books. Medieval halls were draughty, and Middleworth was growing old. In 1406 Middleworth died, leaving to his old college Exeter £17, of which £5 was paid in the following Lent ; to Queen's he left nothing. On the day of his death 14d. was distributed among the fellows of Exeter—one penny a head.[4] As for Richard Benger he took himself off to the rectory of Donington in Berkshire, and when in trouble, in the summer of 1374, obtained the help of his old chief, John Wyclif.

In one of his writings Dean Stanley drew a picture of Wyclif at Oxford as " a poor boy in a threadbare coat ".[5] Poor in this sense he never was, and before 1362 he had become lord of the manor of Wycliffe, though as his mother was still alive the income he would thence receive would suffer reductions. In fact about this time, probably, Wyclif was hard pressed financially. In 1366-7 he had been compelled to provide a

[1] *Cal. Pat.* i. 432. The indenture of restitution, dated 13 May 1378, is in *Stonor Letters*, ed. C. L. Kingsford (1919), i. 12, from *Anc. Deeds, C.* 1782. It is of interest *inter alia* as showing us what books would be available for Wyclif in Queen's library.
[2] Foxe, ii. 942, ' a festo S. Dionysi '.
[3] In 1373 2s. 8d. was spent on binding it (Magrath, i. 79 n.).
[4] Boase, 10.   [5] Stanley, *Cant.* 134.

vicar at Westbury; this would cost him 8 to 10 marks a year, the whole value of the prebend. In 1368-9 he lost his position at Canterbury hall, worth 15 marks a year. In addition there were expenses for the lawsuit. Moreover, in the autumn of 1368 he exchanged a living worth 30 marks a year for one only worth 10 marks, less the expense of a curate for a good part of the year. In December 1368 or March 1369 there would be the expenses of his baccalaureate in theology.[1] In 1372 he must find the heavy cost of his inception feast as a doctor.[2] We are not surprised that shortly after this degree was obtained Wyclif took service under the Crown. Moreover a little time before his doctorate he had accepted, probably from Gregory XI, though possibly from Urban V, the reservation of a prebend at Lincoln. But this forms another story. Meanwhile we shall not be far wrong if we connect the offer with the results of the Canterbury lawsuit, and look upon it as in some way an effort on the pope's part to compensate Wyclif for the award.

In 1371 we come across another record, which, unfortunately, like almost every other event in Wyclif's life, is not without its ambiguities. In the will of William de Askeby made on the 11th November 1371 and proved a month later, there is a legacy of '100s. or one best robe' to 'John de Wyclif, rector of Leckhamstead'. The executor of the will was 'John de Wyclif, rector of Ludgershall'.[3] Some have thought that here there is evidence of another John Wyclif to add to our existing doubles. Others have hinted that the executor and the legatee were one and the same, and that this was a cunning device to hide that the Reformer was a pluralist. But at Leckhamstead

[1] Wyclif is not styled B.D. in any document until the *Expositio causae* (Foxe, ii. 927). This may be dated 23 July 1369 or 15 May 1370. As he was not a B.D. at the time he obtained his extended licence from Buckingham (Apr. 1368, see *supra*) we have the limits. Cronin, *loc. cit.* 73, takes the later date for the *Expositio* and dates the baccalaureate a year later. As I incline to 1372 for the doctorate I incline to March 1369 for the B.D. See *Mun. Ac.* 388-93 and *supra*, pp. 96-7.

[2] In *Civ. Dom.* i. 387 Wyclif speaks of his 'sumptus non modicos et labores'. I take this to refer to his inceptions, &c. Cronin, *Eng. Hist. Rev.* xxxv. 566, strains it to mean expenses connected with his reservations. See *infra*, p. 206.

[3] Gibbons, 25-6, and for London in *Gent.'s Mag.* xxii. 136. It was proved in London on 20 Dec. 1371 (Foxe, ii. 946), and at Stow, Lincolnshire, on 5 Jan. 1372 (Reg. Buckingham, f. 101). The senior executor was one John Swynstead.

from 1361 to 1375 a certain John de Barton was the rector, and he was succeeded on the 2nd July 1375 by a John D'Autre or Dantre.[1] So there is no room at Leckhamstead for a Wyclif as rector, and we must imagine that failing memory led the dying archdeacon into a blunder (unless indeed it were a slip of the notary), and that John de Wyclif of Ludgershall was intended in both cases and would obtain the hundred shillings.[2] It is of interest to note that as one of the executors of Askeby Wyclif would have the pleasure of forwarding to bishop Wykeham—at whose enthronement on the 9th July 1368 Askeby had acted as agent [3]—' two silver cups and a *Liber Decretalium* '. Probably Wyclif would be more interested in the twenty marks left by the archdeacon to the poor of Askeby and the ten marks left to the poor of Waynflete.

The connexion of Askeby [4] with Wyclif gives to the former a momentary interest. But the record of Askeby's career does not reveal the bond between the two men. Probably they were together at Oxford, where Askeby seems to have obtained his master's degree about the year 1350. He was then a canon of Lincoln and held the church of Elton and the ' poor hospital of Newark '. His real name—for he was the illegitimate son of a priest—was William de Scoter. In 1351 he petitioned for additional benefices, and in February 1352 obtained by exchange the chancellorship of St. Paul's. As he was ' neither a bachelor nor master of theology ' a special dispensation was necessary to enable him to hold this office. In the April of the same year he obtained a dispensation for the private celebration of mass even in places under an interdict. He was also created a papal chaplain, and on the 1st June 1352 the archdeaconry of Lincoln was reserved for him by Clement VI. In July of the same year he secured the right of conferring the office of notary on four clerks chosen and examined by himself. In 1359 Askeby was commissioned to appoint guardians for the two children of Sir Philip Despenser. Entering the service of the Crown he became archdeacon of Northampton

---

[1] Lipscomb, *Bucks*. iii. 27.   [2] Summers, 32 ; Pratt in Foxe, ii. 946.
[3] *Reg. Wykeham*, ii. 1–3.
[4] Not in *D. N. B.* For what follows see *Pap. Let.* iii. 357, 363, 387, 423, 433, 435, 462, 464 ; *Pap. Pet.* i. 196 ; Gibbons, 23.

and chancellor of the exchequer. A worthy priest, no doubt, but of the 'Caesarean' order, as in later years Wyclif bitterly called these civil servants.

In the spring of 1373, or probably in the autumn of 1372, Wyclif completed the long course of eight or nine years necessary for obtaining his doctorate in theology. As a consequence on the 26th December 1373 Gregory XI, dealing, probably, with the usual requests of the university on behalf of successful doctors, renewed the grant to Wyclif of 'a provision lately made to him by the pope of a canonry of Lincoln with reservation of a prebend, possession of which he has not yet obtained'. He added to this permission to retain

'the canonry and prebend in the collegiate church of Westbury, notwithstanding that by the terms of the said provision he was bound to resign the same on obtaining the said canonry and prebend of Lincoln'.[1]

As is usual we are at once up against certain difficulties. When was this provision first made? Was the provision ever carried out? and if so in what way? According to Gregory

'John (Wyclif), who is also Master of Arts, became licentiate of theology soon (*cito*) after the date of the said (former) letters of provision, and afterwards (*demum*) became master (of theology)',

this last the usual title at Oxford for a doctor of divinity. The provision therefore was first made shortly after his obtaining his licence in theology, and some time (*demum*) before his doctorate. Now the *terminus ad quem* of the doctorate is, as we see, December 1373. How many months earlier we should place it is uncertain. Probably the spring of 1373 is the latest date, and very possibly it was the late autumn of 1372. According to Gregory some time (*demum*) elapsed between the doctorate and the previous licence. As a rule the time was very short,[2] but there may have been special reasons for

---

[1] For this important document, see *Eng. Hist. Rev.* xv. 530, in full, or *Pap. Let.* iv. 193. This first gave an approximate date for the doctorate. Shirley had dated (*Ziz.* 527) 'at the very latest in 1366', with a preference for 1363 (*ib.*, pp. xvi–vii), and others, e.g. Lechler, 116, had followed Shirley with disastrous results for Wyclif's chronology. Wood's guess (*Univ.* i. 498), 'the year not certain, unless 1376', erred at the other extreme, while Bale's date of 1372 (margin, *Ziz.* 2) may be quite accurate. Cronin, *Trans. Hist. Soc.* (1914), 67 n., dates 'late 1371 or early 1372'. This seems somewhat early. [2] *Supra*, p. 98.

extension. In no case, however, is it likely that we must date back the licence beyond the early months of 1372 or the last months of 1371, especially when we bear in mind the necessary time that must elapse from October 1363 when Wyclif began to read for the degree. We are therefore inclined to look upon the provision as first made, not by Urban V but by Gregory XI, at some date in 1371, not many months after his own election.

That Gregory had not carried out the provision in December 1373 is clear from his own statement. Did the pope ever complete his grant? In January 1376, in an official letter sent from the chancellor of Oxford, John Wilton, to the curia at Avignon, the witnesses to the chancellor's signature are given as ' mag. John Wyclif, sancte theologie doctore, canonico Lincolniensi, Willelmo Thursfordo, archdiacono Gloucestrie, mag. Rob. Aylesham sancte theologie baccalario, mag. John Balcon procuratore universitatis '.[1] This letter is proof that Wyclif was at Oxford in January 1376, and that in that year he officially signed himself as ' canon of Lincoln '. From this it has been argued that between December 1373 and January 1376 Wyclif received his promised canonry and prebend, for it was very unusual in English documents for any one to be called a canon unless at the same time he had a prebend. The argument is not conclusive, for in the documents of the papal court such a custom was by no means unusual, and the document in question was intended for the papal court.[2] Gregory, therefore, may have given Wyclif, possibly in the first provision, the terms of which are not directly known, a canonry without a prebend but ' with reservation of a prebend ' —the words, in fact, of Gregory's statement in December 1373. Wyclif himself, writing in 1377, gives us some information on this prebend. ' The pope ', he says,

' gave to me a prebend in the church of Lincoln, but afterwards, care being taken to collect the first fruits of £45,[3] bestowed the same prebend on a young man from across the seas by way of

[1] For this, see *Eng. Hist. Rev.* xxxv. 98.
[2] See H. S. Cronin in *Eng. Hist. Rev.* xxxv. 564-9, whom I have followed closely.
[3] ' facta sollicitudine ad colligendum sibi primos fructus ', a very ambiguous sentence.

general reservation, making no enquiry whether I was the right man for it (*de habilitate persone mee*) nor taking note of any possible dispensation on my part '.[1]

Unfortunately Wyclif's language is far from clear. Wyclif's reference to the papal grant (*dedit*) by no means implies that he received it. Provision of a prebend and the obtaining thereof even after a considerable lapse of time were not always the same, owing to the ' multitude of expectants ' whom the pope provided, oftentimes to the same cathedral, though in Wyclif's day things were not quite so bad as they afterwards became under Boniface IX. Nor is it clear that Wyclif refused or hesitated to pay the first fruits, for the language may be a sneer at his successful rival, and Wyclif himself may never have had the chance of paying or refusing. We must therefore not assume that Wyclif had been dispossessed of his prebend because he declined to pay.[2] It would not be Wyclif's way to speak so moderately had he been treated like this,[3] and when Wyclif obtained the reservation he must have known what was expected.

The truth seems to be that very shortly after his first grant of a reservation, doubts began to be entertained at Oxford as to his orthodoxy, and in July 1373, or whenever the *de Ente* was published, Wyclif's enemies at Oxford began to threaten him with deprivation of his reservation.[4] In December 1373, however, the reservation, as we have seen, was renewed, but Wyclif's opponents took care that Gregory should display no anxiety to fulfil his promise. Wyclif's mission to Bruges in

---

[1] *Civ. Dom.* iii. 334. Cf. also the undoubted reference in *Civ. Dom.* i. 387. I detect also a reference in *Pot. Pap.* 348, where he speaks of the pope and ' his examiners ' appointing persons, ' unexpert in the art of the cure of souls '. Cf. *Sel. Eng. Works*, i. 304, 305, where the language is stronger but similar. In *ib.* iii. 278-80 there are three references to the pope's advancing ' lewd men ' that ' kunnen not good ' but ' came to benefices by flattering and prayer of mighty men ' and ' much gold for lead ', and to the pope's heresy in ' taking the first fruits '. In his *de Mandatis*, 118, cf. 381, Wyclif declares that a bishop ought to ignore the pope's orders to promote one who is ' ineptus ' or ' minus ydoneus '.

[2] As Loserth, *Civ. Dom.* ii. p. xxx ; Rashdall, *D. N. B.* lxiii. 205.

[3] Cronin, *l.c.* 568.

[4] *de Ente*, ii. c. 6, end. See Cronin, *l.c.* 568. Cf. *Op. Min.* 425, where Wyclif in his *Determinatio* (on which see *infra*, p. 231) says that Binham had attacked him in order that the curia might deprive him ' of his ecclesiastical benefices '.

1374, his later publication of his *Determinatio*, would not lead to any expression of papal gratitude. Wyclif almost alone among the delegates came away empty-handed. In 1375 two vacancies in Lincoln arose. The first was the prebend of St. Cross, worth eleven marks. This was bestowed in April on Thomas Stowe, the pope pointing out that he did not reserve it for his own use,[1] though he might very well have taken this opportunity of discharging his promise to Wyclif; nor would Gregory have troubled that the benefice was so small. In the spring or summer of 1375 there was a vacancy in the prebend of Caistor, a lucrative benefice worth sixty-eight marks.[2] Judging from his complaints it is clear that Wyclif thought himself entitled to this and seems to have put himself to some expense to obtain it.[3] But so far from receiving it, or being dispossessed of it later because he refused to pay the first fruits, it was granted to Philip de Thornbury,[4] an illegitimate son of Sir John Thornbury, an English leader of mercenaries in the pope's service in Italy. Thornbury was a young priest in the diocese of Modena; and though Wyclif in wrath calls him ' ydiota ' he was really a man of some ability and standing. Owing to Gregory's indebtedness to his father he had received a general reservation which took precedence of Wyclif's special reservation. Thornbury received also a licence for non-residence,[5] a fact which Wyclif did not fail to note.[6] Shortly after 1375 Wyclif's quarrel with the Church commenced, and Gregory, in place of fulfilling his grant, condemned Wyclif's *Conclusions* in a series of bulls. Friends of Wyclif may be glad that he neither received any gift from Gregory, nor was given the chance of paying him first fruits. But the matter rankled, and, human nature being what it is, due note must be taken of the incident in our study of Wyclif's development.

[1] *Pap. Let.* iv. 208.
[2] *Pap. Pet.* i. 535.
[3] *Civ. Dom.* i. 387, ' ad sumptus non modicos '.
[4] Cronin, *l.c.* 565. See *infra*, p. 226.
[5] Non-resident canons of Lincoln were mulcted of one-seventh of their income. This was granted to resident canons (*Pap. Let.* v. 169, Sept. 1398).
[6] *Civ. Dom.* iii. 334.

ABOOK II

THE POLITICIAN

"BRING ME MY ARROWS OF DESIRE"

O quam sanctum et fertile foret regnum Anglie, si ut olim quelibet parrochialis ecclesia haberet unum sanctum rectorem cum sua familia residentem, quodlibet regni dominium haberet unum iustum dominum cum uxore et liberis cum proporcionali familia residentem; tunc enim non sterilescerent in Anglia tot terre arabiles nec rarescerent ex defectu yconomie tante caristie artificialium peccorum terre nascencium, sed regnum habundaret omni genere huiusmodi bonorum, adessentque servi atque artifices labori debito, per civiles dominos mancipati. . . .

Si enim [cleri] verbo et opere docerent efficaciter legem Christi sicut ab olim, cessarent abusus . . . Si autem civiles yconomi haberent temporalia in propriis, multiplicantes coniugia, liberos atque familias, ex quibus secundum Aristotelem elementis crescit respublica, tunc nimirum resultaret regnum in omnibus bonis suis uberius.

WYCLIF, *De Civili Dominio*, ii. p. 14.

1

THE MISSION TO BRUGES

§ 1

SHORTLY before obtaining his doctor's degree [1] Wyclif entered the service of the Crown. The transition was natural, and would pass unnoticed by his contemporaries. For the fact itself we have not only indirect evidence, but Wyclif's own statement, though this last it must be owned is ambiguous.[2] In accordance with custom, against which at a later time no one protested more strongly than Wyclif, Wyclif was paid for his services by being appointed by the Crown to the rectory of Lutterworth. The patronage belonged to the family of Ferrers of Groby. But as Henry de Ferrers [3] was still a minor [4] the right of collation to the vacancy devolved on the Crown, and the king presented Wyclif on the 7th April 1374.[5] Wyclif took steps to resign his living at Ludgershall, and on the 29th May 1376 a certain William Newbold is named as the parish priest of the village in a licence giving him leave of absence for two years.[6] We must own that for some time after his appointment to Lutterworth Wyclif was an absentee. But the silence

---

[1] Cunningham in *Ziz.* 14, in a tract written before Wyclif's doctorate, taunts him with having become of the house of Herod (Lancaster).

[2] ' Peculiaris regis clericus ', see *infra*, p. 239, and cf. Devon, 200.

[3] Not " lord " as Lechler, 157 ; he was never more than a knight (*Cal. Pat. Ric.* iv. 326). He died before 20 March 1388, and though a minor, was married when Wyclif was appointed (*Close Rolls Ed.* xiv. 36 ; *Close Ric.* iii. 385).

[4] For the will of his father, proved 19 Aug. 1372, see Nicolas, *Test. Vet.* i. 76. The vacancy arose through an exchange between the then rector and John Belvoir, rector of Charlton-on-Otmoor, Oxon. On 9 May 1372, bishop Buckingham appointed a commission to institute Belvoir to Lutterworth (Reg. Buckingham Mem., f. 59). " But there is no certificate of institution, and I think it likely that Belvoir was judged *inhabilis* as he certainly held a benefice incompatible with cure of souls (Crick, Northants) at this time, and no papal dispensation is recorded." A. H. Thompson, in Wilkins, *Westbury*, 87.

[5] So in Buckingham's register (Vaughan, *Mon.* 180 n.). Lewis, 40, states Wyclif was presented after return from Bruges, a mistake extensively copied.

[6] Reg. Buckingham, f. 143 d, or new pag. 141 d. A. H. Thompson in *l.c.* or in *Bristol and Gloucester Arch. Soc.* xxxviii. 135.

of his enemies is proof that he made sufficient provision for the cure of souls.

We believe that Wyclif entered the service of the Crown before obtaining his doctorate, i. e. a little earlier than 1372. We are strengthened in this conviction when we find that Wyclif gives us a report of a speech made in the parliament of 1371,[1] which Wyclif states that he himself 'heard'. The necessities of the Crown, especially the risks of invasion, forced it on the 8th January to summon parliament. On its assembly on the 24th February Wykeham, the chancellor, and Brantingham of Exeter, the treasurer, laid before it the critical condition of England, and asked for help. So great were the king's necessities that he had been driven into borrowing £4,621 from Fraunceys, Phillipot, and other leading citizens of London. The discussions between the lords and commons lasted a month. In the course of the debate the representatives of the monasteries, probably the mitred abbots, claimed exemption from the payment of tenths and fifteenths. Such a demand would interest Wyclif, who had already distinguished himself by his attack upon the 'possessioners'. So it is with much satisfaction that he gives us the reply of 'a certain peer, more skilled than the others', possibly the new treasurer, Richard le Scrope:

'Once upon a time there was a meeting of many birds; among them was an owl. But the owl had lost her feathers, and made as though she suffered much from the frost. So she begged the other birds, with a trembling voice, to give her some of their feathers. They sympathized with her, and every bird gave the owl a feather till she was overladen with strange feathers in unlovely fashion. Scarcely was this done when a hawk came in sight in quest of prey. Then the birds, to escape from the attacks of the hawk, demanded their feathers back again from the owl, and on her refusal each of them took back his own feather by force, and so escaped the danger, while the owl remained more miserably unfledged than before. Even so, when war breaks out we must take from the endowed clergy a portion of their temporal possessions, as property which belongs to

---

[1] For this parliament (24 Feb.–28 March) see *Rot. Parl.* ii. 303 f.; *Close Rolls*, xiii. 288–90; Stubbs, ii. 440–4. For the English history of this chapter and the next I have not added references to sources. The reader should consult the standard histories, adding Armitage-Smith, *John of Gaunt* (1904). Much new information will be found in the *Close Rolls*, *Patent Rolls*, and Sharpe, *Letter-Books*.

CH. I   THE MISSION TO BRUGES   211

us and the kingdom in common, and so wisely defend the country with property which exists among us in superfluity.'[1]

The claim of the monasteries brought out in opposition two Austin friars, with whom in later years Wyclif quarrelled, but who at that time were working with him as allies. The two, John Bankyn and probably Thomas Ashbourne, laid before parliament certain articles 'maliciously drawn up against prelates and possessioners' of which no official notice was taken. That they caused some stir is evident from their preservation in a Bury cartulary.[2] The abbot of Bury, John de Brinkley, had been present in this parliament. Possibly he brought back a copy of these hostile propositions with the intention of writing a reply in his official capacity as president of the provincial chapter of English Benedictines. The protest of Bankyn is chiefly legal in character, though it ends with quotations from St. Augustine and St. Bernard. But its claim that 'all possessions both of the clergy and of others should be in common in all cases of necessity', though founded on the *Decretum* of Gratian, shows a link of connexion with the ideas then fermenting in Wyclif's brain.[3]

Another incident in the same parliament would strengthen Wyclif's belief that he could best help the cause he had at heart by attaching himself to the service of the Crown. Under the leadership of John Hastings, earl of Pembroke, the son-in-law of the king, and of lord Richard le Scrope, first baron of Bolton in Wensleydale,[4] an address was presented to Edward, in which it was urged that the government had been carried on too long by prelates whom it was impossible to bring to account, and

[1] *Civ. Dom.* ii. 7. This tale was a favourite with the Spiritual Franciscans, and seems to have been a prophecy of their missionary, Juan de la Rochetaillade (de Rupescissa), who in 1349 wrote in prison at Avignon his wild *Vade mecum in Tribulatione*, on the vices of the clergy and the need for disendowing the Church. For his career and works see Mollat-Baluze, i. 318; Wadding, viii. 132 f.; Sbaralea, 460 f.; Brown, *Fascic.* ii. 496–507; Lea, iii. 86–8. One of his books was a proposal to find the philosopher's stone to relieve the poverty of the pope. The tale was common talk. Froissart, who gives it under its original circumstances, says: 'I heard it when I was but young and Innocent reigned in Avignon' (ii. c. 42).
[2] For the articles in full see V. H. Galbraith in *Eng. Hist. Rev.* xxxiv. 579–82.
[3] Gratian, *Decretum*, i. d. viii. 1, where it is argued that private property exists merely 'jure constitutionis et jure consuetudinis', which are both subordinate to 'jus naturale'.
[4] For whom and their genealogy see *D. N. B.*; Wylie, *Hen. IV.* ii. 192 f.

that in consequence great evil had befallen the State. In future, laymen only should be chosen for the offices of chancellor, treasurer, privy seal, and exchequer. As a result Wykeham surrendered the great seal on Monday, the 24th March, ' in a privy chamber of the king, upon the Queen's bridge by the River Thames, called the Red Chamber ',[1] and Brantingham the treasurership on the 27th March. In their places Pembroke secured the elevation as chancellor of the chief justice of Common Pleas, Sir Robert de Thorpe, the second master of Pembroke hall, Cambridge,[2] while Scrope became treasurer. John of Gaunt was away in Gascony, but there can be little doubt of his indirect support of Pembroke. To Wyclif the substitution of a lay ministry for a clerical was so fully in harmony with his views that he would easily be persuaded to accept office under them. With the new chancellor, Thorpe, he would feel more at home than with Wykeham, though Thorpe's sudden death would be a blow to his hopes. To his enthusiastic idealism it would appear that a new era was already dawning, more especially when he heard that the temporalities of sixteen bishops had been seized in July 1372 for alleged detention of part of the subsidy granted of £50,000.[3] Nor would he be undeceived by the crude schemes of taxation to which, under the lead of its new governors, parliament consented.[4]

We know little of the circumstances or reasoning which led ' the flower of Oxford scholarship ' to throw himself into the struggle of politics. But Wyclif probably could not act otherwise. We know that he was already committed to a doctrine of disestablishment ;[5] if he desired that this should not remain mere theory it was necessary that he should become more than a schoolman. Church and State were too intertwined in

---

[1] *Close Rolls*, xiii. 287. I imagine in the Tower Royal at the Queen's Wardrobe (Stow, *Survey*, i. 71).

[2] 1347–64. Cooper, i. 111. His will, dated 27 June 1372 (Sharpe, *Wills*, ii. 149), was made in the ' lodging of Robert (Wyville), bishop of Salisbury in Fleet street '. On the same day he handed over the chancellorship and died ' about one hour before midnight ' (*Close Rolls*, xiii. 445 ; Rymer, iii. 951). For Thorpe see *D. N. B.* and *Close Rolls*, xiii. 70, 94.

[3] Cf. *Reg. Wykeham*, ii. 577–9. Restored 4 Aug. 1372 with apologies (Rymer, iii. 958).

[4] See *infra*, ii. 222.   [5] Compare *Op. Min.* 402 with *Ziz.* 4.

medieval life for the innovator in the one not to find himself involved in the other. On all sides there was a strange confusion of religious and political interests. For the questions of the day were chiefly ecclesiastical—at any rate before the Peasants' Revolt—and the parties in the State ranged themselves for the attack or defence of the Church. Even the war with France, in which the whole nation persisted with an infatuation blind to all disaster, had an ecclesiastical side. The people believed, rightly or wrongly, that the head of the Church was a 'French pope', that aliens 'worse than Jews or Saracens, who neither see nor care to see their parishioners, convey away the treasure of the realm'. Parliament discovered in 1376 that the gold annually paid to the pope amounted to five times the sum paid to the king [1]—a gross exaggeration characteristic of the loose financial knowledge of the times—while the insufficiency of the revenue led all to insist that the Church, which in common repute held a third part of the land of England, should bear a third part of the taxation.

We do well to bear in mind the main political movements which formed the background to Wyclif's public life. When Wyclif left Oxford three issues stood out conspicuously: the first the humiliation of England; the second the rise of the power of John of Gaunt; the third the continued friction with the papacy. When Wyclif entered the king's service the pride and glory of England had been for some years in decline. In 1363 three suppliant kings had gathered at the court of Edward III and the Black Prince, the captive John of France, David of Scotland recently released from durance, and the king of Cyprus bent on obtaining aid against the Turks. Already the fiction was arising that Henry Picard, vintner and ex-mayor of London, had entertained five kings at a banquet on the same day.[2] The nation still remembered Crecy; Poitiers was but of yesterday; the archers of England were still deemed invincible; the Black Prince was recognized as the first of Christian

---

[1] *Rot. Parl.* ii. 337. The Crown revenue was a minimum of about £65,000 (Stubbs, ii. 581). But see Addenda.
[2] Stow, *Survey*, i. 106. To this day the Vintners drink their special toast with five cheers in memory of this banquet. For its lack of historical basis see Reading, *Chron.* 312.

knights. The great sea-fights off Sluys (June 1340) and Winchelsea (Aug. 1350) in which Edward had destroyed the fleets of France and Castile were still the talk of our seaports. Within ten years all that was changed. For the Merry England of Chaucer's Pilgrims the student of the latter years of Wyclif will search in vain. He will discover instead on all hands signs of weakness and decay. Nor will he be deceived by Edward's proclamation resuming the title of king of France (June 1369). The Black Prince, to whom the proclamation was addressed, was slowly dying and the hope of England dying with him. His last days were days of shame and disaster. In 1370 Aquitaine, stirred into revolt by the rapacity of his tax-gatherers, had joined France in her renewal of the struggle. For Charles V, the successor of John, had only waited his opportunity to break the Peace of Bretigny. The Prince quelled the revolt by the brutal massacre of Limoges, which provoked even the censures of the chroniclers. But death was already upon him, and in January 1371 he was compelled to return to England. The present of plate worth £1,000 which the citizens of London were forced to give him [1] could not hide the fact that he was a broken man. Edward, too, was sinking into a dishonourable old age, the captive of the rapacious Alice Perrers. The condition of the royal chapel at Windsor, where the gravest scandals were disclosed,[2] was typical of the whole court. Nor was corruption at home redeemed by success abroad. Of all the conquests in the north Calais alone remained; in Aquitaine, Bayonne and Bordeaux alone were left. Our navy was gone, our shores were exposed and insulted, for the victory of the Spaniards in 1372 over the English convoy off Rochelle had wrested from us the mastery of the seas. In April 1370 there were fears of a raid on the Sussex coast. In the following August a French fleet off the North Foreland was expected to make an attack on the City. In February 1372 there was dread of an invasion from Scotland, and in the following July castles in South Wales were hurriedly put in order 'to repel the malice' of the French. Without allies, with resources impoverished by plague, famine,

---

[1] Riley, *Mem. Lond.* 350-2; Sharpe, *Letter-Book G.*, 275, 283.
[2] Wilkins, iii. 132-4.

and extravagance—in 1366 Edward paid £350 for an embroidered vest![1]—as well as by the loss of her commerce, with amateur bunglers at the head of her finance, England still stubbornly continued a war that could only end in defeat. She attempted tasks beyond her strength. Fortunately she escaped the later fate of Spain and Holland in similar circumstances by her early disasters. A series of triumphs such as Crecy and Poitiers would have proved her undoing.

One ray of hope was soon extinguished. In the autumn of 1372, roused from his lethargy by Pembroke's defeat at Rochelle, Edward announced that he would succour Aquitaine in person. The Black Prince, in spite of his illness, decided that he would accompany him. John of Gaunt also promised that he would serve for a year with 500 men and 500 archers. Peace was made with Flanders, and the assistance of Brittany purchased by the restoration to its dukes of the earldom of Richmond—an event, no doubt, that would arouse some interest in Wyclif. On the 11th August prayers were ordered throughout the realm for the success of the expedition, and on the 1st September Edward sailed from Sandwich. But after five weeks' buffeting in the Channel the king returned, his money wasted and Aquitaine unsuccoured, while the English party in Brittany was shattered by du Guesclin.

Peril abroad was accompanied by disaster at home. The closing years of the reign of Edward III were years of plague, famine, and violence. The insecurity for life and property was extraordinary. Pardons for murder and other serious crimes are numbered in the existing rolls by the hundreds, while the estates of landowners, lay and clerical, were invaded by armed bands, often led by priest or knight, who cut down trees, destroyed crops, fished the ponds, carried off the cattle, and ravished the women. At Shoreham in Sussex in August 1371 the men of Sussex boarded a ship of Dordrecht, killed the crew and passengers including the women, carried off the plunder, then sank the ship. Nor could excuse be made that it was an enemy ship.[2] Such an event was typical. Pestilence also did its work, and depopulation proceeded apace. In March 1371

---

[1] Devon, 186. In May 1375 Edward owed one citizen £220 for wine (Sharpe, *Wills*, ii. 187).   [2] *Pat. Ed.* xv. 177.

Wykeham found it necessary to prohibit the citizens of Winchester from carrying away the materials of disused churches, whose sites the corporation endeavoured to appropriate. In 1378 Truro was said to be ' almost uninhabited and wholly waste '; traders had fled from the plague-stricken Appleby to surrounding villages where they sold their goods in the churchyards on Sundays, while in 1380 Newcastle-on-Tyne is said to have lost in the pestilence 6,054 men. No doubt these figures were exaggerated to secure the desired assistance toward the repair of ' towers, wall and bridge '. But Edward's exchequer was empty; in his last years he borrowed from all and sundry, £1,000, for instance, from Sir Walter de Manny ' by bills of his wardrobe ', which that good knight in his last will evidently despaired of ever seeing again. The king resigned himself to his pleasures ' and for a year and more before his death was not worth more in discretion than a boy of eight '.[1] So John of Gaunt seized his chance and grasped the reins.

John of Gaunt, if conscious still of things mundane, must feel gratified as he realizes that not only our English kings, but all the houses of Europe reigning at the outbreak of the Great War, and some also even then no longer reigning, are descended from him. For the ambitions of the duke were not confined to England. On the death of duchess Blanche, a victim like her father and sister to the plague (Sept. 1369), he began to dream of securing by a second marriage a place among the princes of Europe. At one time he had thoughts of claiming the county of Provence, as the descendant of Eleanor, the wife of Henry III. But the papacy was averse and nothing came of the negotiations, while his marriage in September 1371 to Constance, the heiress of Pedro of Castile, pointed to a bigger prize. Henceforth he claimed to be called the king of Castile and Leon.

Disastrous as were his ambitions abroad, his policy at home was not less dangerous. His intentions, no doubt, were to secure what he deemed to be the best for the nation, provided that his own interests were not affected. But these last out-

---

[1] *Reg. Wykeham*, ii. 125, 166; Nicolas, *Test. Vet.* i. 86; *Pat. Ric.* i. 208, 510; *Chron. Ang.* 401.

JOHN OF GAUNT
From the window in the Chapel of All Souls College, Oxford

weighed all else. He became not only the enemy of constitutional progress, but the leader of the court-party, the 'cat of a court' who played with the 'rats' of parliament, laughing at them and pushing them about. Sundry propositions were made to the 'rats and mice' for restraining him. At last a bell was brought. But alas !

> There ne'er was rat in all the rout for all the realm of France
> That durst have bounden the bell about the cat's neck.

All that men could do was to comfort themselves that an old cat was better than a young kitten, such as Richard might prove. Moreover, cats had a use when the 'rout of rats' took to destroying 'men's malt', peasant insurrections and the like.[1] As the leader of the court-party the duke found himself at the head of a small, well-organized band of nobles and knaves whose one object was their own aggrandisement. For statesmanship except as an instrument of selfishness and extortion they cared little. They allowed the national defences to rot while they bought the leases for four years of the subsidy in cloth, made their " corners " in wool and victuals, or levied illegal customs. They encouraged Edward III in the intrigue of his old age with Alice Perrers. By their lawless insolence they prepared the way for the deluge of the next century, when the Wars of the Roses laid liberty at the feet of a triumphant crown.

§ 2

Wyclif's period of service under the Crown, and the alliance that followed with John of Gaunt, involved him in conflict with two prominent principles of his teaching : that clerics should not discharge secular duties, and that absenteeism should be done away. Wyclif's personal sin was small, especially when compared with the abuses against which he protested. Nevertheless the historian must confess to a measure of inconsistency between Wyclif's ideals and his conduct. But his first appearance in politics was rather as a representative of the nation in its resistance to papal exaction than as an associate of a selfish faction. For some years the relations between

---

[1] *Piers Plow. Prol.* 146–207. Dr. Cust in *Mod. Lang. Rev.*, July 1925, points out that this is taken from Brunton's *Sermons* (*infra*, ii. 256).

England and the papacy had been strained, or, as Innocent VI put it, Rome had learned 'how suspicious the English are'.[1] Time after time the attention of Parliament and Crown had been directed to ecclesiastical abuses, papal provisions, the pope's claim to exercise jurisdiction over English subjects and to excommunicate English judges, the receipt of papal bulls, and the drain of gold to the papal curia. More than once steps were taken to strengthen the statutes of *Provisors* and *Præmunire*, nominally, according to the parliament which met in January 1365, in the interests of the Holy Father himself, to protect him from the evil suggestions of selfish advisers. Time after time orders were issued for a strict search at Calais to discover persons conveying gold, silver, or papal bulls, and a limitation put upon the number allowed to leave the realm.[2] But when the parliament of 1365 further decided to withhold the grant of Peter's Pence, Urban V retorted on June 6[3] by a demand for John's annual tribute of 1,000 marks together with the arrears since the last payment on the 7th July 1333.[4] Urban further threatened to take proceedings, in case of default, in his own courts. The cess, he urged, was needed 'for the defence of the territories of the Roman church against the incursions of impious companies of perverse men'—English adventurers of 'the company of St. George' in the pay of the Visconti. He added that

'the Curia hitherto had not made its demands from regard to the necessity of England, which has been involved in grievous wars. But now that peace is restored, England is rich and can satisfy her obligations.'

Edward laid the matter before both houses on their meeting at Westminster in May 1366. The prelates begged for deliberation, but on the morrow agreed with the lords that 'neither John nor any other person could place the realm under such subjection without their consent'. So parliament declared that the compact was a violation of John's coronation oath,

---

[1] *Pap. Let.* iii. 613.
[2] e. g. Reading, *Chron.* 164; Rymer, iii. 775.
[3] *Pap. Let.* iv. 16; Theiner, 329. In Raynaldi, xxvi. 116, dated June 13, and hence extensively copied.
[4] On Peter's Pence and the tribute see Appendixes F and G. For the parliament of 1365 see *Rot. Parl.* ii. 283 f.

CH. I   THE MISSION TO BRUGES   219

and assured Edward that should the pope attempt to enforce his claims ' dukes, earls, barons, grandees and commons ' would join in resisting him to the utmost. Two knights were dispatched to Avignon with this defiant answer, and were instructed, as a counter move, to revive the claim for certain cities in Provence by right of Henry III's queen, Eleanor of Provence.[1]

Until recently—to the utter confusion of the chronology of Wyclif's life [2]—it was believed that " this solemn declaration set the question at rest for ever ", and that " since that day not one word more has ever been said on the part of Rome of her feudal superiority over England ".[3] Rome is not accustomed lightly to relinquish her claims; in 1374 this was once more revived by Gregory XI. During the intervening eight years the struggle with Rome continued, though intermittently. On the 12th December 1370 the ports were closed and orders given for the arrest of all attempting to bring bulls or papal provisions into the realm.[4] At times, according to the whim of the king, licence was given for some one to pass to Avignon, ' taking 40s. for his expenses and £10 by exchange ', rarely as much as £40, bail being given in £100 or other large sum that the applicant ' shall prosecute nought to the king's disadvantage '.[5] At other times ecclesiastics who attempted the journey to Avignon without permission were thrown into prison [6] or

---

[1] *Rot. Parl.* ii. 289 f.; Reading, *Chron.* 171; Rymer, iii. 798.

[2] By dating Wyclif's intervention in this year. So Lechler, 122, and all previous writers, e. g. Arnold in *Sel. Eng. Works*, ii. 61 n., as well as Poole, *Med. Thought* (1st ed.), 290, who thus misdates *Dom. Div.* The idea still persists, cf. *Lay Folks' Cat.* 118, Nolloth's note. The mistake was first corrected by Loserth, *Eng. Hist. Rev.* xi. 320.

[3] Lingard, *Hist.* iii. 253; Lechler, 123. To the same effect Ramsay, *Gen. Lanc.* i. 465; Barnes, 667, 670 " quashed for ever ". In 1500 the ambassador of Venice wrote : ' This subsidy seems to be forgotten by the Roman Church, which certainly is a wonderful thing.' But the claim to suzerainty was brought forward by the nuncio, Vergerio, on 7 Nov. 1535 in a conversation with Luther who repudiated the idea (*Eng. Hist. Rev.* xxv. 668). On 18 Aug. 1409 there looks something like the revival of the tribute in the payment by Henry IV ' of the yearly cesses in the realm pertaining to the *camera* of the pope to the sum of 1,000 marks ' (*Cal. Pat.* iv. 101).

[4] *Close Rolls Ed.* xiii. 200–1; Rymer, iii. 907.

[5] e. g. June 1371 (*Close Rolls*, xiii. 312); Oct. 1371 (*ib.* 330, 331, 337); in Feb. 1372 (*ib.* xiii. 422–3); Jan. 1373 (*ib.* 481).

[6] e. g. March 1372, *ib.* xiii. 428; May 1372, *ib.* 434, 435; June 1372, *ib.* 442; Dec. 1372 (*ib.* 479); July 1373 (*ib.* 583) and Nov. 1373 (*ib.* 599; *Cal. Pat.* xv. 398). For an instance of the subterfuges to which resort was had see *ib.* xv. 19.

ordered to be brought before the Council.¹ In the summer of 1373 a writ was issued for the removal from the realm of all alien friars, an order which on the 18th October 1373 was extended to Oxford.² Nor would the friction be lessened by an incident which occurred early in 1372. On the 29th October 1371 ' Arnold Garnier, papal nuncio and collector in England ', crossed the seas to Dover with a train of servants and a dozen horses. He had secret instructions to recover, ' if necessary with the aid of the secular arm, all property bequeathed for the deliverance of the Holy Land '.³ Six months later (13 Feb. 1372) he was forced by the Crown to swear at Westminster in the presence of the chancellor Thorpe and others an oath ' divided into ten articles ', that he would not in anything act contrary to the rights and interests of the realm, nor introduce papal mandates or letters, ' nor forward treasure out of the realm in money or bar gold or silver for pope or cardinals '.⁴ Wyclif, who had just entered the service of the Crown, may have been present at the ceremony ; at any rate the incident made a considerable impression upon him.

In November 1373 parliament once more raised complaints that the rights of patrons were made illusory by papal provisions. Alien clerics, especially the religious, by their removal of treasure and their betrayal of national secrets were a danger to the realm. To this petition the king gave answer that he had already commanded his ambassadors then engaged in negotiations with France, to discuss the position with the Roman curia.⁵ For this purpose he had also given a commission to John Gilbert, bishop of Bangor, Uhtred Boldon, John of Sheppey, D.C.L., and Sir William Burton.⁶ Their leader, John

---

¹ 20 June 1373, *Cal. Pat.* xv. 315 ; Rymer, iii. 986.
² *Close Rolls*, xiii. 517 ; Rymer, iii. 991. I detect a slight reference to this in Wyclif, *Op. Min.* 419.
³ *Pap. Let.* iv. 100 ; Rymer, iii. 924, where wrongly dated Oct. 18. News of the appointment was sent to Garnier on Oct. 8 (*Cal. Pap. Let.* iv. 149). He returned to Avignon in July 1374.
⁴ For the text of this oath see Rymer, iii. 933 ; Lechler, *Wiclif* (ed. German), ii. 575–6, and cf. *Close Rolls*, xiii. 424. It is preserved in two Vienna MSS. (Buddensieg, *Pol. Works*, i. p. xxx, xlii).
⁵ *Rot. Parl.* ii. 320 ; Walsingham, i. 316 ; Higden, viii. 379.
⁶ In Lechler 141 *n.* misnamed " Bolton of Dunholm " and " William of Barton ". For their names see *Pap. Let.* iv. 127, where the pope states on 21 Dec. 1373 that he has received them at Avignon.

CH. I   THE MISSION TO BRUGES   221

Gilbert,[1] whom we shall meet with again and again, was a strong adherent of John of Gaunt. Gilbert's history is not without interest. A simple friar, without the prestige of family,[2] we first hear of him on the 11th October 1366, when a certain John Gilbert, a Dominican ' baccalarius formatus ' in theology at Oxford,[3] appealed to Urban V that he might be allowed to finish reading the *Sentences* at Paris, and ' in the following year incept in theology '. He alleged that in consequence of the dispute between the university and the friars he had been persecuted, nor was there any chance of his being allowed to proceed to his degree. The petition was granted,[4] but Gilbert does not seem to have taken any doctor's degree. When on the 17th March 1372 he was provided by Gregory XI with the see of Bangor, he was still only a bachelor, as indeed he so remained at the Blackfriars Council ten years later.[5] Following up this deputation to Avignon, Gilbert was despatched in 1374 to Bruges, with Wyclif as his companion. As a result he was translated by papal writ to Hereford (12 Sept. 1375). Immersed in high politics—e. g. in 1380 the chancellorship of Ireland,[6] in May 1381 accompanying Lancaster on a commission to the Scots—Gilbert committed his diocese to vicars-general and suffragans.[7] In 1382 he sat in condemnation of Wyclif at the Blackfriars. He took a prominent part in the preaching of Lancaster's disgraceful crusade against Castile in 1386. In the same year, on the 24th October, Gilbert was made both treasurer and chancellor, owing to his sympathies with the opposition to Richard's absolutism. Accordingly he was dismissed (3 May 1388) when Richard threw over the tutelage of the "Appellants". We are told that Gilbert always ' excelled more in speech than in fidelity ',[8] a fact which may perhaps account for his recall to the treasury three months later, when a decision was made by the Privy Council that his business

[1] Not in *D. N. B.* For his promotions see Le Neve, i. 100, 295, 463.
[2] His only known relative was his sister Margaret (*Reg. Gilbert*, 19).
[3] *Supra*, p. 97.   [4] *Chart. Par.* iii. 157–8 ; *Pap. Pet.* i. 536.
[5] *Ziz.* 286–8 ; *Chart. Par.* iii. 158 *n.* But in spite of this Gilbert became chancellor of Oxford. See *infra*, p. 307 *n.*
[6] *Cal. Pat.* i. 459, 463 ; Rymer, iv. 110.
[7] *Reg. Gilbert*, 1, 57, 101–2 (where ' Archil ' cannot be identified, Eubel, i. 103. Correct also date 1386 to 1387).
[8] *Chron. Ang.* 374 ; Walsingham, ii. 152.

should have precedence of all other. He was once more dismissed or resigned after but a few months' service (4 May 1389), but was shortly afterwards again reappointed.

Of Gilbert's diplomatic ability we have a proof in his selection as the head of a mission to secure peace with France in March 1385. As a preacher he had some repute; at any rate some of his sermons were published.[1] On the 7th May 1389 he was translated by Urban VI to St. David's. Probably the transfer had been arranged before he had been dismissed from the treasury. Other embassies fell to his lot, and he was employed by the pope to settle tangled disputes. In April 1391 he was sent by Boniface IX as nuncio to Brittany, his expenses being fixed at twenty gold florins a day.[2] His attendance at the Council, even after he had resigned the treasurership, still continued,[3] and in 1393 he acted as the chief executor of the will of Edmund Mortimer, an inheritance, probably, from his old Herefordshire days. Gilbert lived to a ripe old age, his death taking place in London on the 28th July 1397, his will being proved in the following month.[4] After his death his goods were seized by Richard to meet claims against him by the Exchequer, but on the 5th January 1398 the dead bishop, at the instance of his successor, Guy Mone, was pardoned his 'ill behaviour toward the king and his regality'.[5] Owing to his immersion in political business Gilbert saw little of his dioceses, which became a refuge for lollards from all parts of the country.

Another member of the deputation was the noted controversialist, John Uhtred or Owtred,[6] who, according to

---

[1] Found by Leland at Ford, *Coll.* iv. 150.

[2] *Pap. Let.* iv. 279. Comparing this with *ib.* 280-2 we see that the exchange for gold florins in Wyclif's day varied between 37 and 38 pence.

[3] See the journal of John Prophet in Baldwin, 503.

[4] Le Neve, i. 295; cf. *Cal. Pat.* vi. 186. Walsingham, ii. 476, refers therefore to Trefnant.

[5] *Cal. Pat.* 286, 327. For other references see *ib.* iv. 89, v. 50, 315; *Pap. Let.* iv. 326, 458, 479; Rymer, vii. 466, 617.

[6] See the sketch in *D. N. B.*; and also Leland, *Comment.* 392, to which Bale, i. 482 and Tanner, 743 add little. There is an account also by J. Loserth in his 'Die ältesten Streitschriften Wiclifs' in *Sitzungsberichte der Phil.-Hist. Klasse* (Vienna, 1909), pp. 7-23. The chief source of his life is the brief but circumstantial *Vita Compendiosa Uhtredi*, by John Wessington or Washington, bursar of Durham college, Oxford, 1398-1403, and prior of Durham, 1416-46, now in the British Museum. In the MSS. of Wyclif's *Determinatio* (see

Leland, hailed from the Western side of the Severn, but more probably was born at Boldon in Durham, about the year 1315. In 1333 Uhtred became an inmate of the cell of Durham at Boldon, and in 1340 he was sent to Oxford to complete his studies. There he would enter Durham college, of which in 1381 he was appointed one of the trustees for the carrying out of bishop Hatfield's bequest. In 1344 he was sent for three years to the Benedictine cell at Stamford, but in 1347 returned to Oxford and took his master's degree in arts. In 1352 Uhtred obtained his licence as bachelor in divinity, completing his doctorate in 1357. He stayed on at Oxford, possibly as warden of Durham college, receiving from Wearmouth in 1361 and 1362 two sums of 6s. 8d. as contributions to his expenses, and in 1363 a grant from Finchale.[1] His success, according to Leland, was remarkable: 'never was there a monk at Durham college more learned than he'; while the esteem in which he was held by his brethren is shown by his election as prior of Finchale abbey, a cell of Durham (25 Aug. 1367), and in 1368 as sub-prior of Durham, offices to which he was afterwards several times reappointed.[2] As prior he would frown upon the use by the brethren of the pack of hounds which the monks recently had kept for their sports. During this period he would come into contact with Wyclif, first in his election as Master of Balliol, and again when Wyclif left Balliol and went to Canterbury. In 1373 he served on the deputation to Avignon[3], and in 1374 Uhtred took part in the council which determined the question of papal tribute, making on that occasion a memorable speech. In 1381 he brought to Finchale William du Stiphel of Brittany, and employed him in transcribing the *Ecclesiastical Histories* of Eusebius (as translated into Latin by Rufinus), of Rufinus and of Bede, as well as of Nennius and Gildas. All these manuscripts are now in the British

Op. Min. 405) he is called 'Magistrum Owtredum de Omesina', possibly a Czech misreading for some contraction of Oxoniensis.

[1] *Collect.* ii. 23; *Jarrow and Wearmouth Rolls* (Surtees Soc., 1837), 42, 155, 157, 235-6; *Finchale*, p. lxiv.

[2] Prior, 1367-9, 1376-80, 1388-96 (*Finchale*, pp. lxxviii-lxxxiv, xcviii-cxvii). For Finchale see *Vict. Co. Hist. Dur.* ii. 103 f., or *Finchale* preface with plan and views. There were usually eight monks there. Its revenues in 1535 were £122 15s. 3d. (*Valor.* v. 303-4).

[3] Pollard in *D. N. B.* gives the double error that he was sent " with Wyclif to Rome ".

Museum.¹ In 1383 Uhtred was once more in Oxford, but from 1388 to 1396 was back at Finchale. He died on the 24th January 1396 and was buried in the priory before the entrance to the choir.² Uhtred was a resolute man of affairs who knew his own mind. He was also a voluminous writer. But of his twenty works, of which Bale gives the incipits of nine, not more than four can now be traced.³ For years Uhtred was a stout opponent of Wyclif,⁴ but was equally opposed to some of Wyclif's adversaries. In consequence he won from Bale the title of 'athleta magnanimus'.⁵ His special opponent was the Dominican, William Jordan, with whom, while reading for his theological degree, Uhtred entered into violent controversy on the old theme of poverty. According to Bale Jordan went so far as to seek Uhtred's excommunication,⁶ while the Franciscan, Richard Tryvytlam, attacked him in a poetical squib 'as a beast armed with two horns, who with all his powers insults the friars'.⁷ In addition to these controversial themes two spiritual works, *Devout Meditations* and *On Loving Enemies*, are attributed to Uhtred.

The other cleric of the deputation, John of Sheppey—a village in Leicestershire—was a secular doctor of civil laws, often employed about this time by the Crown.⁸ This John must be distinguished from another John of Sheppey, a monk

---

¹ Burney MS. 310. Several of the fragments have been printed. See Brit. Mus. Catalogue. From Finchale Stiphel moved to Durham, writing there the splendid *de Lyra* still existing (*Finchale*, p. xxiii n.). Pollard, *D. N. B.*, writes as if the translation of Eusebius was made by Uhtred.

² *Jarrow Rolls*, 181.

³ Pollard, *l.c.*, gives five, by including the *Eusebius*. MSS. are found in Corpus, Camb., and Durham cathedral (James, *MSS. Corp.* i. 200 ; Raine, *Durham*, 360 ; Bernard, iii. 12), also Brit. Mus. Royal MSS. Of his *Meditationes*, copies exist in Camb. Univ. library, Bodleian, and Brasenose.

⁴ Wyclif, *Op. Min.* 405 f., and cf. *Ziz.* 241.

⁵ Bale, i. 482–3 ; *Index Script.* 463 ; Wood, *Univ.* i. 491 ; all write as if Uhtred and Hilton (†1376), another Franciscan opponent of Uhtred, were followers of Wyclif.

⁶ Bale, i. 482, on the authority of Adam of Rewley. See also Wood, *City*, ii. 320 ; *Univ.* i. 491.

⁷ See Tryvytlam's '*de laude Oxoniae*' in Hearne, *Vita Ricardi II*, App., or *Collect.* iii. 188–209. See also Wood, *Univ.* i. 492, for part quotation. Tryvytlam's name—possibly, as Hearne, the Cornish Trevytham—was not John (as Pollard *l.c.*) but Richard (Little, 254). Hearne identified him with the Franciscan, Robert Finingham (*c.* 1460). But the author was certainly a contemporary of Owtred. As there is no allusion in the poem to Wyclif it is possible that it was written before 1377.

⁸ See Appendix H for his career.

of Kent, who became bishop of Rochester.[1] The only layman of the deputation was Sir William Burton [2] who was more than once employed on similar errands. Burton, who had thrice served as a member for his county, was a man of strong religious feelings ' who purposed to fast on all days on which he did not hear mass ', and had obtained a portable altar, as well as plenary absolution for himself and his wife Eleanor at the hour of death (May 1359). In the following June he founded a short-lived college for five chaplains in his wife's manor of Tolethorpe in Rutland, for which nine months later he obtained indulgences. Possibly this foundation overtaxed his resources, for in October 1371 he was £160 in debt.[3] As a result —no doubt Wyclif would hear of it from him—his college had come to an end. Shortly after his return from Bruges he died in mysterious circumstances in Cumberland. Four years later there was a sad fracas. His widow Eleanor, assisted by the parson of Casterton, broke into the manor of Thomas Stapellio, in the neighbouring village of Conington, ' mowed his grass, fished his fishery, burned his houses, depastured his corn and grass at Stilton ', and ' abducted ' three of his bondmen.[4]

On their way to Avignon the commissioners fell among thieves. Near Chambéry they were robbed of their horses and goods, and only released after urgent letters from the pope (Aug. 1373). On arrival at Avignon at the commencement of October, the commissioners treated with Gregory XI for the

[1] For this John Sheppey (†19 Oct. 1360), see Kingsford in *D. N. B.* Kingsford rightly suggests that the two legal treatises attributed to the bishop in Tanner, 666, *de Ordine Cognitionum* and *de Judiciis*, are probably by this John. The bishop, however, was the author of some *Fables*, printed by L. Hervieux, *Les Fabulistes Latins*, iv. 417–50. These, abridged from Odo of Cheriton (*infra*, ii. 226), are part of his *Sermones*, of which three vols., dated as preached in Rochester, exist at New College (Tanner). See *infra*, ii. 216.

[2] For his pedigree, property, &c., see T. Blore, *Rutland* (1811), 91–2, 215 f. Commission (13 Nov. 1375) to inquire into his death (*Cal. Pat.* xvi. 222). For his will, 20 July 1373, see Gibbons, 37 ; he was worth about 200 marks a year. His first ' dear wife Mabel, whom God pardon ' (not in Blore), was buried on his right side ; Eleanor, ' if she will consent to it ', on his left. He was M.P. in 1353, 1354, 1357 (*Members*, 154, 156, 162). For his hospital at Tolethorpe, name corrupted in surnames to Trollope, see *Vict. Co. Rut.* 161. For his many requests to the pope see *Pap. Pet.* i. 340, 353, 360 ; *Pap. Let.* iii. 607, 630. He probably went to Avignon to further his projects for a collegiate church at Little Casterton (*ib.* iv. 192 ; granted Dec. 1373, but never matured, Blore, 11–12). His tomb there has perished.

[3] *Close Rolls*, xiii. 334.   [4] *Cal. Pat.* i. 419 (Sept. 1379).

removal of the various causes of complaint. They received a conciliatory but indefinite answer. In one thing Gregory was peremptory. As to the subsidy that he had demanded from the clergy he would only grant a delay until a month after the next Easter; he desired Edward III not to encourage the clergy in their rebellion.[1] The commissioners thereupon returned.

They found the relations between England and the pope severely strained, especially over this subsidy. In his war with the spirit of Italian nationality [2] Gregory XI had attacked the Visconti of Milan [3] with the help of mercenaries led by that 'champion (*pugil*) of Christ and athlete of the Lord, John Aguti'—for so the Italians pronounced Hawkwood [4]—and another Englishman, John 'Tournebarri' (Thornbury) whom Gregory calls 'the marshal of the forces in Italy for the pope', whose illegitimate son he had rewarded with the prebend in Lincoln that Wyclif deemed his due. To carry on this war Gregory demanded on the 2nd February 1373 from the clergy of England 100,000 florins, the sum that he claimed had been paid to Innocent VI in a like case. Failing the payment of this lump sum, Gregory XI was prepared to impose 'upon the clergy of England, who abound in revenues',[5] a tenth, to be paid to his Florentine agents at Bruges, one half at Easter, the other at Michaelmas. 'So that there could be no pretence of ignorance'—for his previous mandates had not been allowed to reach England—Gregory 'ordered the letters to be posted on the doors of the churches at Avignon, and in the parts near England'.[6] The demand was impossible, for the clergy were already confronted with a precept from Edward III for a tenth for his French war, and the king's taxes must come first. So king and prelates turned a deaf ear to all Gregory's appeals.

[1] *Pap. Let.* iv. 125 f., and cf. *ib.* iv. 201, and Walsingham, i. 316.
[2] See the severe strictures in Pastor, i. 100 f.
[3] Not Florence as Ramsay, *Gen. Lanc.* ii. 37, 39. This war did not break out until July 1375. See *Pap. Let.* iv. 116, 121, 124.
[4] *Pap. Let.* iv. 118, 132. As a commentary see Gregory's mandate to Sudbury to provide Hawkwood's illegitimate son 'if he be not an imitator of his father's incontinency' (*ib.* iv. 191, June 1373).
[5] A favourite theme with Gregory. Cf. *Reg. Wykeham*, ii. 245.
[6] *Pap. Let.* iv. 106. For tentative demands by Gregory in March and Dec. 1372, see *ib.* iv. 115-18. For the exemption of Cistercians, *ib.* iv. 153.

To the pope's disgust, the police arrested a Carmelite friar who had ventured to introduce into the country 'papal letters touching the subsidy'.[1] A straw may show the direction of the wind. On the 18th November 1373 the chamberlain of the pope complained that Wykeham's proctor on his recent visit to Avignon had 'paid no oblation and rendered no homage'.[2]

At Edward's request (Oct. 4) Wittlesey summoned on the 20th October a meeting of convocation for the 1st December. Dragging himself from his sick-bed he preached on the text 'the truth hath set us free'. Exhausted with the effort he fell back into the arms of his chaplain and retired to Lambeth, leaving convocation to be managed by Sudbury. As regards the tax the clergy showed a disposition to resist; they stated that they could only meet the demand by 'the removal from their necks of the intolerable yoke' of the papal exactions.[3] After some delay the tax was voted, though not before Courtenay

'had arisen in the midst of the assembly, and proclaimed with a loud voice that neither he nor his diocese would pay any more taxes until the king should remedy the evils from which the clergy had suffered so long.'[4]

Chief among these evils was the demand of Gregory, to which no reply had yet been made. On the return of the Avignon deputation Edward, on the 11th March, wrote to the pope offering to appoint further commissioners who would come to Bruges or Calais and deal with all outstanding matters of dispute. Meanwhile no 'censures' should be made against the king's subjects. Gregory replied that he had appointed three nuncios who would arrive in Bruges on the 24th June.[5]

The anxiety of the pope to treat with the king had been stimulated by recent events. On the 6th March 1374, Edward had sent orders to the archbishops and bishops, as well as to

---

[1] May, 1373, *ib.* iv. 123-4.   [2] *Reg. Wykeham*, ii. 197.

[3] *Close Rolls*, xiii. 588; *Dig. Peer*, iv. 662; *Wilkins*, iii. 95 f.; Parker, *Antiq.* 380; *Reg. Brant.* i. 317-18; *Reg. Wykeham*, ii. 196.

[4] Wilkins, iii. 97 from Parker, *Antiq.* 380. The demand for the collection of the tenth was forwarded by Edward III on 20 March 1374 (*Sede Vac. Worc.* 305). From *Close Rolls*, xiv. 37 it would appear that in many parts of the diocese of Lincoln the previous subsidy of £50,000 was not yet collected, many refusing to pay. In Leicestershire the secular arm was threatened. We assume that Wyclif as a servant of the king paid promptly.

[5] On May 1. Rymer, iii. 1000; *Pap. Let.* iv. 132, 202, 203; *Close Rolls*, xiv. 69.

all the sheriffs, to make an exact return before the 16th April of the benefices held by aliens, of 'the true value thereof', and whether the said aliens were resident or not.[1] As these aliens were for the most part provided papal nominees Gregory felt cause for some alarm. The return, which is said to have filled 'several sheets of paper', has not come down to us, except in fragments.[2] One thing it would have revealed—the number of benefices held in England by cardinals. The anxiety of the pope to avoid the return showed the Crown that it possessed a new weapon which in later years it was not slow to use again.[3] As an offset to this, the renewed demand of Gregory for the payment of John's tribute [4] was ineffective.

Some answer to the pope's demand must be carried to Bruges. So a council of prelates and barons—the division of function between council and parliament was yet fluid, nor was the matter regarded as coming within the purview of the Commons—was held at Westminster on the 21st May, 1374, presided over by the Black Prince and Wittlesey.[5] On the right of the archbishop sat the prelates; to the left of the prince the barons. 'On a form' in front of the archbishop and prince sat four doctors, the provincial of the Dominicans,[6] and three others who had specially asked to be present, John Uhtred of Durham, recently returned from Avignon, John

---

[1] *Close Rolls*, xiv. 65; Rymer, iii. 999; *Reg. Brant.* 193; *Sede Vac. Worc.* 293.

[2] Barnes, 865. For the return for Exeter see *Reg. Brant.* i. 193-5. The prior of Totton was a non-resident alien drawing £92 a year. Of the prior of Montacute, who drew £55, Brantingham did not even know the name; William de la Haye drew about £130. The list, however, includes some who are 'indigena'. For the return for Worcester see *Sede Vac. Worc.* 307-8. There is in it nothing very serious.

[3] e. g. 16 Jan. 1385 (*Reg. Gilbert*, 68).

[4] For this demand our sole authority is *Eulog. Cont.* iii. 337. But the whole chronology of Wyclif's later life, though in one sense resting upon it, in reality supports the statement.

[5] The report of this assembly is only in *Eulog. Cont.* iii. 337-9. In *D. N. B.* lxi. 159 this narrative is treated as a fiction. I have given credence to it in the main, in spite of its manifest exaggerations. It seems to me to have been edited, or written later. A proof lies in the fact that in his opening statement the chancellor represents the subsidy as wanted for the 'rebel Florentines and others'. For this mistake see *supra*, p. 226. It may have arisen from the author misplacing his account of this quarrel, for *Eulog. Cont.* iii. 335 should chronologically come after iii. 337-9.

[6] He was either William Andrew, who was provincial from 1370-4, or more probably Thomas Rushoek, 1374-8. See *Eng. Hist. Rev.* xxxviii. 243-51, and cf. viii. 523.

Mardisley, a Franciscan,[1] who had preached before the king on the previous Whitsunday, and Thomas Ashbourne, an Austin friar. The doctors of law sat on a carpet in the centre. Knyvet the chancellor opened the proceedings by stating the pope's claim. A subsidy was demanded on the ground that the pope ' as vicar of Christ and thus lord spiritual was general lord of all temporals ', especially in this realm of England, owing to the ' gift of King John '. The prelates, said Knyvet, must decide now the spiritual claim ; the barons the temporal, on the morrow. ' My lord archbishop,' he concluded, ' what do you say ? ' There was only one answer possible for the medieval prelate when the question was put in this way. ' We cannot deny ', said the archbishop, ' that the pope is lord of all.' To this judgement the other prelates assented. The provincial of the Dominicans was not so easily ensnared. He complained that neither mass nor the hymn *Veni Creator Spiritus* had yet been sung, and that until this had been done by the custom of his order no answer could be given ' on so difficult a question '. Uhtred, however, when asked, boldly asserted the papal supremacy in both spheres, falling back on the favourite text of Hildebrand, ' Lo here are two swords.' Mardisley, in words that must have delighted Wyclif, if he were present, replied with the counter-text, ' Put up thy sword again.' He argued that Christ neither possessed temporal dominion, nor bequeathed it to his apostles, and justified his arguments by citations from the gospels and scriptures, from the doctors of the church, from the example of the religious, and from the confessions of the popes themselves. He pointed to the deplorable end of Boniface VIII and maintained that in aspiring to ' earthly dominion the pope was the successor not of Peter but of Constantine, according to the

[1] Wrongly named ' Marcheley ' in Bale, i. 486, ' Mardelegy ' in Leland, *Comment*. 397 (corrected in Tanner, 509 *n*.), and in *Mon. Franc.* i. 561 as ' Mardiston ' (see Little, 242 *n*.). He was probably a Yorkshireman and took his D.D. at Oxford before 1355, in which year, on April 10, he disputed in the chapter-house of York with William Jordan (see *supra*, p. 224), upholding the Immaculate Conception. As his manner of disputing gave offence, the York Chapter testified that he had ' behaved modestly and courteously, without introducing personalities or improprieties ' (Tanner, 509). Between 1374–80 he was 25th Provincial Minister (*Mon. Franc.* i. 538, 561). The date of his death is not known—Bale, *l.c.*, ' 1376 ' is incorrect—but he was buried at York (Kingsford, *Grey Friars Lond.* 194 ; Bale, *l.c.*).

blessed St. Thomas'. Ashbourne followed on the same side. The pope carried the keys, as did Peter; the Black Prince, like St. Paul, the sword; 'Wield your sword, and Peter shall recognize Paul'. Ashbourne's words were brave; nevertheless a few years later we find him sitting in judgement on Wyclif for holding similar conclusions.[1]

The arguments of the friars sorely displeased the archbishop. When the council met the next day he sneered that the assembly would have been better without the friars, as also the country itself. The Black Prince retorted angrily: 'If we had listened to your counsel the kingdom would have been lost.' The archbishop, who was really a dying man—he passed away a fortnight later on the 5th or 6th June—now refused to give any answer to the question at all. 'Answer, you ass', said the Prince, who was equally irritable and worn with disease; 'it is your business to inform us.' The archbishop feebly replied that he was quite willing that the pope should not be lord in England, and to this the other prelates assented. Uhtred also, on second thoughts, agreed with the argument. 'What becomes then of the two swords?' mocked the Black Prince. 'My lord', replied the monk, 'I am now better instructed.' Nothing remained but to ask the barons for their verdict on the 'gift of John'. They replied [2] that the gift was invalid 'without the consent of the realm and the barons'. The envoys were instructed to report to the pope to this effect.

---

[1] For Ashbourne see *supra*, p. 211, also *infra*, ii. 262. The Austin Ashbourne must be distinguished from Thomas Ashbourne the Carmelite poet, a scholar at St. Benedict or Corpus Christi, Cambridge (James, *MSS. Pet.* 58, for an inscription of expenses of his patron. See also *D. N. B.* lvi. 175; Tanner, 52, speaks doubtfully). Bale, *Script. Cat.* i. 494, as also Pitts, 539, assign him six works, including his polemic against Wyclif entitled *Contra Trialogum*. As Thomas became prior of the Austin friars in London before Feb. 1380 (*Cal. Pat.* i. 429), and was still prior in the Patteshull riots in 1386 (Walsingham, ii. 158), we must reject the statement of Wood, *City*, ii. 467, that he became a monk of Stafford, or was born at Stafford (Bale, i. 494), a mistake arising from his birthplace probably being in Dovedale in Staffordshire. On 18 July 1387 he was succeeded as prior by Bankyn (*Cal. Pat.* iii. 386), and was alive on 4 March 1392 when Richard of Arundel in his will wrote: 'My body to be buried in the priory of Lewes in a place behind the high altar which I have shown to . . . friar Thomas Ashbourne my confessor' (Nicolas, *Test. Vet.* i. 129, 133).

[2] There is no report in *Eulog. Cont.* But see *infra*, p. 235.

§ 3

The interest that Wyclif took in this question of the tribute [1] is seen by the references he made to it in a short treatise usually entitled his *Determinatio*. Though this work was not written, in our judgement, until after Wyclif's return from Bruges in the autumn of 1374, it is advisable to consider it in connexion with the debate of May 1374. The *Determinatio* [2] consists of two tracts, in reality forming one work—the first a reply to the arguments of Uhtred of Boldon, the second to an attack by William Binham.[3] Binham [4] was a native of the village of that name in Norfolk, where there was a cell of St. Albans. Embracing the monastic life, Binham naturally became a monk of St. Albans and in due time the prior of a cell of St. Albans at Wallingford. Entering Oxford about the same date as Wyclif, the two at first had been friendly rivals. But when Wyclif ' began to tear to pieces the authority of the old theologians ', Binham, who had taken his doctorate before 1374,[5] was the first, if we may trust Leland, to oppose him by publishing a book *Contra Positiones Wiclivi*.[6] To this Wyclif replied in a tract still extant, *Contra Willelmum Vynham monachum S. Albani*, afterwards published as the second chapter of the *Determinatio*. As Leland confesses with regret, Binham was no match for Wyclif

' by reason of his inferior knowledge, his unequal skill in controversy, and his lack of a similar rush of words '.

[1] Wyclif refers to this tribute in his later *de Apost.* 66, 204 ; *Serm.* ii. 424 ; *de Euch.* 315 ; and loosely speaks of it as ' 900 marks annually for England and Ireland ' (cf. *Sel. Eng. Works*, ii. 61).

[2] Until recently historians, in addition to dating in 1366, were dependent on the fragment published by Lewis, 363–71, from the defective Bodleian MS. Lewis's reprint was amended by Matthew, *Eng. Works*, p. v, n. 2, from Lambeth MS. no. 537. The complete text was published by Loserth in 1909 (from a Paris MS. in possession at one time of the confessor of Louis XII) in the article already referred to (see p. 222, n. 6), pp. 1–74, and in Wyclif's *Op. Min.* (1913), pp. 404–30.

[3] So expressly stated in the Paris MS. Loserth, *Eng. Hist. Rev.* xi. 322–4, argued that the opponent was Woodford, who as a friar could not have been ' unum monachum '.

[4] For Binham, in *Op. Min.* 415 wrongly called ' Wiham ' or ' Vyringham ', see Poole, *D. N. B.* ; Leland, *Comment.* 381 ; Bale, i. 458, copies Leland ; Tanner adds a few notes. See also Walsingham, *Gesta*, iii. 426.

[5] *Op. Min.* 415, ' secundus doctor '.

[6] Not known to be extant.

Retiring to Wallingford, Binham was still alive on the 9th October 1396, though too ill to journey to St. Albans to take part in the election of a new abbot on the death of Thomas de la Mare.

The general argument of the *Determinatio* we may dismiss briefly ; Wyclif asserts nothing that is not more fully dealt with in his later work, *de Civili Dominio*. Uhtred, whom Wyclif calls ' my reverend doctor *et magister specialis* '—a reference possibly to old Balliol associations—had laid down in certain lectures at Oxford, where Wyclif in the autumn of 1374 was residing, that the rule of the priest is preferable to that of layman, that in no circumstances has the secular power a right to judge the priesthood, and that any one who taught or induced the secular power to spoil the Church of its endowments was acting for the ruin of king and kingdom. To all these Wyclif, who had already entered into controversy on the subject ' in the previous year ' with friar William Woodford, replied with courtesy and moderation. He grants that the patron is only to act against the scandalous priest by depriving him of his endowments if the bishop should fail to do his duty. His conclusion that it would be better if selected laymen administered Church property while the clergy attended solely to their spiritual duties is one that appeals to-day to men of all schools of thought.[1]

The second part of the *Determinatio*, the reply to Binham, is of extraordinary interest because of the problems it presents, for it is Wyclif's fate whenever he strikes a personal note to raise a cloud of difficulties. At the heat displayed in Binham's attack Wyclif expresses surprise, and in consequence treats Binham with scant courtesy, accusing him of misrepresentation. Three reasons, he states, have been named accounting for this vehemence :

' (1) that Wyclif might be personally compromised with the Roman Curia and thus, after severe censures, might be deprived of his benefices ; (2) that his opponent might conciliate for himself and his friends the favour of the Curia ; and (3) that, as the effect of

[1] *Op. Min.* 405, 410, 414. For correspondence with *Civ. Dom.* see Loserth's notes in *Op. Min.* and *Eng. Hist. Rev.* xi. 320. That *Civ. Dom.* is the later work (as against *ib.* xi. 321) is proved by *Civ. Dom.* iii. 100. For the controversy with Woodford see *Op. Min.* 415–16 ; *Civ. Dom.* iii. 351.

a more unlimited dominion of the pope over England, the clergy [1] might grasp in greater numbers the secular lordships of the kingdom, without being checked any longer by brotherly control.'

To all this Wyclif replies that he is 'a humble and obedient son of the Roman Church', who 'desires to assert nothing which would reasonably offend pious ears', the usual formula of all medieval apologists who ventured into the region of innovation.[2] Both Uhtred and Binham were monks; but only in his controversy with Binham does Wyclif strike the note of antagonism to the 'possessioners':

'If any monk does not keep the poverty of his first profession I dare to say that he is not a follower of St. Benedict but a dangerous apostate, a disciple of Antichrist.'

But the chief interest of the tract does not lie in its abstract arguments but in its references to the papal tribute. Binham had maintained that by the non-payment of this tribute 'the king of England had forfeited his right to dominion in England'. In reply Wyclif, instead of giving his own views, refers 'my reverend doctor to the answer to arguments of this sort which I heard was given by secular lords in a certain council'.[3] Seven lords, all of them anonymous, are brought forward and their speeches reported.

The first lord, a valiant soldier, is reported to have expressed himself thus:

'The kingdom of England was of old conquered by the sword of its nobles, and with the same sword has it ever been defended against the enemy. The tribute exacted by Julius Caesar has been withdrawn, for, as Aristotle teaches, nothing violent is eternal. Even so does the matter stand in regard to the proposed tribute to the Roman curia. My counsel is, let this demand of the pope be refused, unless he is able to compel payment by force. Should he attempt that, it will be our business to withstand him in defence of our right.'

The second lord had made use of the following argument:

'A tax or a tribute may only be paid to a person authorized to receive it; now the pope has no authority to be the receiver of this

---

[1] Lewis, 365–6; Lechler, 123, introduced the word 'abbatis'. In the text of *Op. Min.* 425 there is no such reference.
[2] *Op. Min.* 425; cf. *Pot. Pap.* 396.
[3] *Op. Min.* 417, 425. The Latin 'quam audivi in quodam concilio esse datam' is ambiguous as to whether Wyclif claims to have heard the speeches himself. See *infra*, p. 237 n.

payment, and therefore any such claim on his part must be repudiated. For it is the duty of the pope to be the chief follower of Christ; but Christ disdained all civil dominion. As, therefore, we should hold the pope to the observance of his holy duty, it follows that we are bound to withstand him in his present exaction.'

The third lord argued thus:

'It seems to me that the ground upon which this demand is rested admits of being turned against the pope; for as the pope is the servant of the servants of God, it follows that he should take no tribute from England except for services rendered. But he builds up our land neither spiritually nor temporally; his whole aim is to turn its possessions to his own personal use and that of his courtiers, while assisting the enemies of the country with money, favour and counsel. We must, therefore, apart from all else, refuse his demand. That pope and cardinals leave us without any help either for body or soul is a fact which we know by experience well enough.'

The fourth lord, whose speech could be put together out of passages in Wyclif's *de Ecclesia*, continued the debate:

'I am of opinion that it is a duty which we owe to the laws of our country to resist the pope in this matter. For, according to his principles, he is owner-in-chief of all the property which has been granted to the Church or alienated to her in mortmain. Now, as one-third of the kingdom at least is so held in mortmain, the pope is lord over the whole of that third. As a proof of this on a vacancy arising in any particular church by death as lord he exacts the first fruits. Now in civil lordship, there cannot be two lords of equal right, but there must be one lord superior, and the other must be vassal; from which it follows that during the vacancy of a church either the pope must be the vassal of the king of England, or vice versa. But we have no mind to make our king the inferior of any other man in this respect. We desire to reserve to the king the right of feudal superiority. It follows therefore that the pope ought to be for the time of vacancy the inferior or vassal of the kingdom or king. But since for a long time the pope has neglected to do his homage and service the pope has forfeited his rights.'

The fifth lord addressed himself to the grounds upon which King John had entered into the supposed agreement:

'Was that annual payment the condition on which he obtained the benefit of absolution or the relaxation of the interdict or his reinstatement in his hereditary right to our realm? For I am sure that he never granted such a gift to the curia as pure alms for all time. Now on the first or second suppositions the condition is invalid because of the dishonest simony it involves. For no spiritual gift can be bestowed on the promise of temporal returns. As St. Matthew tells us: Freely ye have received; freely give.'

This argument the fifth lord proceeded to develop. If the tax was imposed as a penitential penalty,

'it should have been granted to the poor Church of England which the king had wronged. But it did not savour of the religion of Christ to say : I absolve thee on condition that you give me so much money every year. It is perfectly right thus to break faith with one who has broken faith with Christ. Moreover it is rational that a punishment should fall upon the sinner and not upon the innocent. But as this annual tribute falls not upon the sinning king but upon the poor innocent people it seems to savour more of avarice than of salutary penalty.'

The fifth lord then addressed himself to the third supposition, that by virtue of his pact with John the pope had become the feudal lord of the realm. He pointed out that in consequence the pope could dethrone whom he pleased, and choose whom he liked as his successor. 'Are we not bound', he asked, 'to resist such a doctrine ? '

The sixth lord continued the argument and claimed that

' the pope's act could be turned against himself. The pope claimed that he had given the kingdom back to John as a feudal fief, of which he was the overlord. Now as it is not right to alienate the goods of the church without reasonable recompense, it seems to me that it was not right for the pope to alienate so wealthy a realm for so poor an annual tribute. By the same reasoning he might at his pleasure demand our country back again, under the pretence that the Church had been defrauded of more than the fifth part of the value. It is necessary, therefore, to oppose the first beginnings of this mischief. Christ Himself is the Lord-Paramount, and the pope is a fallible man, who, in the opinion of theologians, must lose his lordship should he fall into mortal sin, and therefore cannot make good any claim to the possession of England. It is enough, therefore, that we hold our kingdom as of old, immediately from Christ in fief, because He is the Lord-Paramount, who, alone and by Himself, authorizes every right of dominion allowed to created beings.'

In the latter part of this argument we recognize Wyclif's tenet of dominion founded upon grace.

The seventh lord represented Wyclif's views of constitutional history and practice. He argued as follows :

'I cannot but wonder that you have not touched upon the imprudence of the king, and upon the rights of the kingdom. It stands to reason that an ill-considered treaty, brought on by the king's fault, without the country's consent, can never be sustained if it cause permanent mischief. According to the custom of the realm, it is necessary, before a tax of this kind is imposed, that every individual in the country, either directly or by his lord-superior, should give his consent.¹ Although the treaty was ratified with the king's golden seal and a few seals of misguided lords, they had no warrant to give the lawful consent of the realm in the absence of so many dissenting lords.

With the speech of the seventh lord Wyclif concludes his tract. He claims that their arguments have demolished the pope's demand.

The problem raised by these speeches is of interest. Lechler and Shirley have maintained that we have here " the earliest instance of a report of a parliamentary debate " ² and that Wyclif may be justly called the father of the press-gallery. To such a claim it might be sufficient to retort that to imagine that the House of Lords—the very title is an anachronism— in the fourteenth century, numbering not more than forty in all, was a society of schoolmen who arose one by one, arranging their arguments with perfect precision and in ascending order, is only a degree less ridiculous than to attribute to it the democratic sentiments and heretical doctrines—for several of the arguments were condemned by Gregory XI in 1377 as the teaching of Marsiglio and Wyclif—to which these seven speeches gave expression. " Practice in political business ", to which Lechler appeals as one ground of his belief that we have here the actual speeches of seven barons, does not as a rule lead men into the academic method of approaching deep issues from *a priori* principles. One thing also must be noticed that seems conclusive. The speeches give no idea of any opposition. But what were the spiritual peers doing ? Did the bishops and mitred abbots sit in silence while one by one these shadows of Wyclif rose to continue the debate ? The idea betrays a complete misunderstanding of the nature of fourteenth-century parliaments. In our judgement Wyclif has thrown his reply to Binham into dramatic form. Though he

¹ Wyclif did not know that Peter des Roches in Henry III's reign successfully claimed immunity from a tax because as an individual he had not assented to the levy (Pollard, *Evol. Parl.* 143).

² Shirley, *Ziz.* xix ; Lechler, 129 ; Vaughan, *Mon.* 110, who talks of it as " a field day in the house of lords " ; Milman, viii. 163. As there was no meeting of either parliament or convocation in 1374 (Wake, 303 ; *Members*, 191–3), the meeting must have been one of the Great Council, probably the Whitsuntide meeting (*supra*, p. 228).

may have availed himself to some extent of utterances actually made at the recent Whitsuntide assembly [1] as reported to him, yet in the main the seven anonymous speakers are but mouthpieces through whom he utters his own thoughts, cast in the dialectic that his treatises on *Dominion* have made familiar to us. They are speeches after the manner of the ancients and not of the modern press. In this guise Wyclif's arguments would probably less ' offend pious ears ' than if they had been developed as his own. In this form the *Determinatio* was a dialectic exercise of the recognized kind ; in the latter it would have been a personal challenge which could hardly have been ignored by the curia.

There is another question raised by this tract that is also of interest. In taking up Binham's challenge, Wyclif speaks of himself as ' peculiaris regis clericus '.[2] This phrase has been variously interpreted. Pauli and others considered it to mean " royal chaplain ".[3] But for this " no trace of a proof is to be found ".[4] Nor can it mean that Wyclif considered that the recent gift by the Crown of the living of Lutterworth gave him the right to this title. Such gifts were far too common. Lechler argued at length that it meant that Wyclif was a member of parliament, and that this membership had given him the chance of hearing the debate he had reported.[5] Such an interpretation is the result of a confusion of thought, the falsity of which has been shown by recent studies of the evolution of parliament. That Wyclif may have had a place in Convocation as one of the representatives of the inferior clergy, or as the proctor for some official, is possible, but that he could ever have been summoned, except indeed purely formally under the *praemunientes* clause, as such a representative to the Commons is almost inconceivable, and certainly without historical justification. This interpretation may therefore be dismissed, as may also the

---

[1] Wyclif in *Civ. Dom.* iii. 100 again refers to the ' replies of the seven lords ' which ' audivi respondisse ', quoting the second lord.

[2] *Op. Min.* 422.

[3] So Vaughan, *Mon.* 106 ; Poole, *Med. Thought*, 289 ; Shirley, *Ziz.* xix. It is hardly worth while to mention the suggestion that it means " a cleric of the national church, in opposition to a cleric of the papal church ". This reads into Wyclif's thoughts the extreme ideas of his later years.

[4] Loserth, *Eng. Hist. Rev.* xi. 325. So Lechler, 132.

[5] Lechler, 130 f. See Appendix I, *infra*, p. 340.

idea of Lechler that " the king required his presence in that parliament as a clerical expert, or, in modern phrase, as a Government commissioner ". What precise interpretation Lechler would give to this we do not know, unless indeed all that is meant is that Wyclif was one of the special clerks in attendance. But such clerks were certainly never members, but usually notaries or lawyers, not theologians ; as, for instance, Dr. Adam Usk who, speaking of the parliament held in 1397, tells us that he, ' the writer of this chronicle, was present every day '.[1]

Lechler's whole conception rests upon the modern idea of a sharp distinction between " the high court of parliament " and the Council of the King. The King's Council [2] until the very close of the Middle Ages is almost protean in the forms it may assume ; it can appear as a Great Council or a Privy Council, as a Council in Parliament or a Council out of Parliament, as a Council in Chancery or a Council in the Star Chamber. The barons try to make it a council of magnates, and Edward III and Richard II tried other lines of demarcation. But throughout the period of our story all was ill-defined and formative. The House of Lords, in the modern sense of the word, did not exist ; it was merely ' the King's Great Council in Parliament ', to which, as in the trial of Oldcastle, others were summoned than peers of the realm. Of this indefinite overlapping of function between parliament and council we shall meet more than one illustration in our pages. In one sense parliament was but a more formal session of the Great Council, the difference being that parliaments were summoned under the great seal and councils under the privy seal. Knights and burgesses also were summoned to Great Councils as well as to parliaments. From the neglect of this evolution we fall into many difficulties when we enquire whether an act of the council, e. g. the anti-lollard legislation of 1382 or the burning of Sawtre, was an act of parliament, or assert, with Lechler, that Wyclif was a member of parliament. As one of the king's clerks he may well have been present in the council.

[1] Usk, *Chron.* 152.
[2] For the King's Council and its functions see J. F. Baldwin, *The King's Council in England during the Middle Ages* (1914). See also Pollard, *Evol. Parl.* (1920).

A better interpretation would be to take the phrase 'peculiaris clericus regis' as referring to Wyclif's special services to the Crown, including his appointment to the commission at Bruges. We date therefore the work as written shortly after his return from Bruges, when, as we know, he retired to Oxford. If so it was published in the spring of 1375. We are confirmed in this belief when we find that Wyclif states that Binham dragged in this matter of the tribute in order to set the curia against him and so deprive him of ecclesiastical benefices.[1] Lewis and the older writers, giving to the *Determinatio* a date impossibly early, interpreted this to refer to his wardenship of Canterbury;[2] but that had long since been settled by Wyclif's eviction. Nor can it refer to the Crown's gift of Lutterworth. It may refer, possibly, to some intrigue to deprive him of his prebend at Aust. If so we may have an explanation of his temporary deprivation of this living in November 1375. More probably, however, it refers to the slight which at this time Wyclif received in being twice passed by for a prebend in Lincoln. The *Determinatio* can scarcely have been published before Wyclif's appointment to Bruges, for that would have stamped him as a partisan rather than a commissioner. But the fall of 1374 or the early months of 1375 gives a satisfactory explanation of difficult yet vital phrases.[3] Moreover this date is not too removed from the 'certain council' and its events for interest therein to have been lost, and yet is sufficiently removed for Wyclif to be able to edit its speeches after his own heart. If our interpretation be correct, Wyclif, as late as 1375, was still proud to proclaim to his opponents that he was in the civil service of the Crown. His change round to violent attacks upon this root of offence was as complete as it was rapid.

[1] *Op. Min.* 425.
[2] Lewis, 18. So also Matthew in *Eng. Works*, p. vi.
[3] Loserth, *Op. Min.*, pp. liv ff., and in *Eng. Hist. Rev.* xi. 319–28, dates as 'about 1377'. This date seems altogether too late. His main argument is that the *Determinatio* was preceded by polemics with Woodford. But as the *Determinatio* was written at Oxford (see *infra*, p. 257) this is easily explained.

§ 4

On the 26th July 1374 the envoys to the pope were finally appointed.[1] At their head was Gilbert, and associated with him his former colleague, Sir William Burton. By his recent speeches Uhtred Boldon had made himself impossible, and was passed by, as also was John Sheppey. Five new members were added, of whom the first, next in order to Gilbert himself, was 'Master John de Wicliff, professor of theology'. Some writers urge that the appointment shows the value attached to his recent *Determinatio*. The author could be trusted not to betray the realm, while the form in which the tract was cast would make it difficult to challenge his personal opinions. In his appointment, it is argued, we may recognize the victory of the national party. But this assumes a date for the *Determinatio* that seems to us too early, though no doubt the ideas it expresses were already widely known as held by Wyclif. One thing is clear, John Wyclif was the only theologian in the mission.

One of Wyclif's colleagues was a trusted agent of John of Gaunt, the Spaniard Juan Guttierez,[2] dean of Segovia, in Old Castile. As his name shows, he was probably a native of Guetaria, with which port England had considerable trade.[3] We meet his name as early as 1366, several years before the duke made his claim to the crown of Leon and Castile. He was then a witness to treaties made with Navarre and Castile. Guttierez, who was a 'notary by papal and imperial authority', described himself at Bruges in 1375 as 'clericus Couchen.', i. e. from the diocese of Cuenca. As his deanery probably brought him no money, John of Gaunt procured him on the 26th September 1376 a grant of £40, and paid him a salary of about £20 a year for his services. In 1380 he was made bishop of Dax in Gascony. As such, in 1886, he was one of the three bishops instructed to preach the crusade on

---

[1] Rymer, iii. 1007 ; Foxe, ii. 790 ; Wilkins, *Neg. Pluralist*, 31 ; *Cal. Pat.* xv. 462.

[2] Lewis, Lechler, &c., misled by Rymer and Wilkins call him Guter and assume he was English. For references to him see Rymer, iii. 800-7 ; Wilkins, iii. 102 ; *Close Rolls*, xiv. 416 ; *Reg. Gaunt.*, i. 53, 138 ; ii. 44, 228, 300.

[3] See *Cal. Pat.* xvi. 507 for 1345.

behalf of Lancaster's Castilian expedition. He died in the autumn of 1393.[1]

Another colleague was Simon de Multon, D.C.L.—from Multon or Moulton, the name of two villages, one in Suffolk, the other in Lincolnshire. From him Wyclif would learn firsthand the workings of the system whereby king's clerks were foisted upon wealthy monasteries. Multon had obtained his B.C.L. before October 1367, when he received the enlargement from thirty to forty marks of the benefice 'reserved to him in the gift of the abbot and convent of Ramsey'. He obtained his doctorate before July 1372, about the same time as Wyclif, and then received a grant of £50 a year for life. On the 12th August 1372 Multon had been admitted 'a clerk of the Chancery of the first form'. As such he obtained some pickings of his own, for instance on the 20th May 1373 the grant of the marriage of a minor. In the parliament of 1373 Multon served as one of the receivers of petitions from Gascony and the Channel Isles. On the 6th May 1374 he was granted the prebend of Bole in York. He did not long survive the mission to Bruges, to which he was sent a second time in the spring of 1375, for he died before May 1376.[2]

The other new names were Robert Bealknap[3] and John Henington.[4] Of these Bealknap had been for some years in the civil service. Of good Kentish family, his varied experiences with poachers and others would make him an interesting companion. In 1366 Bealknap was appointed one of the justices of assize. On his return from Bruges Bealknap was made chief justice of the court of common pleas, and received a knighthood.[5] As chief justice he had a narrow escape in the Peasants' Revolt. On the 25th August 1387 when the judges were summoned by Richard II to Nottingham and forced to draw up answers favourable to his absolutism, Bealknap protested, but eventually yielded to the threats of de Vere

---

[1] His successor was appointed 5 Dec. 1393 (Eubel, i. 97).

[2] For Multon see *Rot. Parl.* ii. 317; *Pap. Let.* iv. 64, 216, 226; *Cal. Pat. Ed.* xv. 187, 193, 287, 431.

[3] For Bealknap see *D. N. B.*, to which add numerous references in *Cal. Pat.* and *Close Rolls*.

[4] Not "Kennington" as Lechler, 142. I can find nothing about him.

[5] Rigg in *D. N. B.* says not until 1385. It was before 28 Dec. 1374 (*Cal. Pat.* xvi. 16; cf. *Close Rolls*, xiv. 207 with 201).

and Michael Pole. When next year de Vere was overthrown, Bealknap and the other judges were arrested and condemned to death; but on the intercession of the queen he was banished to Drogheda. His estates were forfeited, but £40 a year was granted for his maintenance. In 1397 Bealknap was allowed to return to England, but on the accession of Henry IV was again banished and probably died shortly afterwards.

Very shortly after his appointment Wyclif and, presumably, the others set off. There was in fact no time to be lost; the pope's nuncios were already at Bruges. Wyclif would find to his relief that orders had been given to provide 'hackneys at reasonable charge' for all the king's messengers and envoys.[1] The payments to the commissioners are still preserved. Wyclif received for his travelling fare there and back 42s. 3d., and for his expenses 20s. a day. This was the usual liberal allowance for a cleric; it certainly paid better to be in the civil service of the king at 20s. a day than to confine oneself to the spiritual duties of a parish. As Wyclif was away from the 27th July to the 14th September—on which day he returned—his total expenses amounted to £60. Gilbert of Bangor's expenses, of course, were on a higher scale.[2] He received £133 6s. 8d.; but, probably, a good deal of official hospitality would fall upon him as the head of the embassy.[3] To obtain foreign money Wyclif would need to pay a visit to Bucklersbury, where by law all exchanges of gold and silver were located.

A few days before his departure Wyclif took some legal steps of interest. Along with Ralph Strode, whom we shall meet again, 'John Wyclif of Leicestershire' obtained on the 26th July an order to the sheriff of Wiltshire 'by mainprise',

'to stay the execution of the king's late writ ordering him to take Richard Beneger, parson of Donynton and imprison him until he should find [security] not to depart over sea nor send thither in order to do aught to the prejudice of the king or crown or of the realm, and if the said Richard be taken order to set him free; as the said

---

[1] 28 May 1373, *Close Rolls*, xiii. 505.

[2] In 1328 a bishop was paid £3 6s. 8d. daily, and a bishop's clerk 18d. (Devon, 140). Knights were paid 40s. a day. Sometimes bishops were rated at double, a knight as one and a third a doctor's fee (*Privy Counc.* iv. 119, 120).

[3] Devon, 197. As payment is entered under date July 31, some part was evidently made in advance.

John and Ralph have mainperned in chancery that he shall not prosecute or attempt aught, or cause aught to be prosecuted or attempted over sea which may tend to the prejudice of the king or crown or of the laws of England.'

This, being interpreted, signifies that Wyclif and Strode had gone bail, or, as it was technically called, become 'mainpernors' for Richard 'Beneger', whom we identify with Wyclif's old associate at Canterbury Hall, Richard Benger, once his somewhat negligent proctor at the court of Rome. Benger had obtained Donnington, a parish in Berkshire, by papal letters on the resignation of the previous rector, who had entered the Charterhouse at Hinton, near Bath. Benger had held the living for over a year without being ordained a priest. Now he was anxious to see what further he could obtain for himself by a journey to Avignon. Wyclif, though we may respect his loyalty to old associates, was not always fortunate in his friends.[1]

To meet the envoys of Edward, Gregory sent as his nuncios Bernard de Folcaut, bishop of Pampeluna,[2] Dr. Ralph de Castello, bishop of Sinigaglia,[3] and Giles Sancho, D.C.L., provost of St. Minion's, Valence.[4] They were appointed on the 1st May with instructions to arrive at Bruges on the 24th June.[5] Procurations, twelve gold florins a day for Bernard and Sancho, six gold florins a day for Ralph, were levied, under the usual threats of citation, upon the English clergy, secular or regular,[6] at the rate of one halfpenny in every mark. Ralph and his suite possessed fifteen horses; the other two would have more. As a result of the effort to make the levy there followed a vast correspondence which reveals how hated these impositions were. Disputes arose as to the length of time for which the procurations were due.[7] As the embassy

---

[1] *Close Rolls*, xiv. 94; *Pap. Let.* iv. 421–2, and *supra*, p. 181.

[2] He was bishop of Huesca from March 1362, translated to Pampeluna, Jan. 1364, died 7 June 1377 (Eubel, i. 396, 406).

[3] 19 Aug. 1370 to c. June 1375 when he died (Eubel, i. 470).

[4] In Wilkins, iii. 106 called 'Mimionis'. The see in question is Valence-Die near Vienne in France.

[5] *Pap. Let.* iv. 132. Cf. Raynaldi, xxvi. 258.

[6] *Pap. Let.* iv. 202, 203; cf. *ib.* 133. On 17 Aug. 1374 nothing had yet been paid and the pope was impatient (*ib.* iv. 109).

[7] On 16 Nov. 1374 Sudbury protested that these envoys were asking for 100 days whereas they were only entitled to 25 days (Sheppard, *Christ Church Letters*, 3–5).

was continued from month to month the sum demanded grew, until finally it was necessary to impose a levy of $1\frac{1}{2}d.$ in the mark to meet the 4,380 florins required from the province of Canterbury, a sum increased by January 1375 to 6,564 florins. The levy was long in arrears, and in the diocese of Hereford was still unpaid on the 3rd May 1376. Even Wykeham needed a threat of excommunication to make his first levy on the 28th December 1374.[1] We wonder if Wyclif on his return paid his share of the levy for the diocese of Lincoln ?

At the time of Wyclif's visit Bruges was one of the leading cities of Europe, the centre of its commerce and banking, in population probably twice the size of London,[2] distinguished alike for its wealth and its civic spirit. Wyclif's life is so impersonal that it is vain to ask what he thought of this first experience of foreign travel. In Bruges he would find himself in the town which more than any other save Venice drew to itself the merchants of Europe. So many English resorted to the city that in 1391 they obtained leave to have a chapel and priest of their own.[3] But there were also in the city permanent settlements of foreigners of every nation giving their names to whole streets and districts. Its merchants dominated the Hansa of London ; its market was the centre of the English and Spanish wool-trade. Wyclif would marvel at the busy life, at the quays stacked with goods, for the Zwijn which connected the city with the sea had not yet silted up. But we wonder if his keen eye detected the deepest characteristic of this Flemish town ? For the most important monument of the past in Bruges, or in Ypres—these words were written before the fury of the Germans—is neither the castle, nor the cathedral, but the Cloth Hall and the Belfry, whose carillon

---

[1] *Reg. Wykeham*, ii. 225–7 ; cf. *ib*. ii. 219 ; *ib*. 252, 295 ; *Reg. Sede Vac. Worc.* 323, 325 ; Wilkins, iii. 98–100, 106.

[2] For Bruges see Rudolf Häpke, *Brugges Entwickelung zum mittelalterlichen Weltmarkt* (Berlin, 1908) with a map indicating the then approaches from the sea. It contained in 1302, 9,300 burghers of whom over 8,000 were craftsmen, and was governed by a clique of fifty families. In Bruges, in the library of the monastery of St. Bartholomew of Eeckhout, demolished in 1798, Wyclif may have seen a *Passio mirabilis*, a blasphemous chronicle concerning Peter de Coninck. Of this Adam Usk has left us a copy. It was evidently to his taste (*Chron.* 107–10).

[3] *Pap. Let.* iv. 374. From *ib*. v. 72 we learn that the inhabitants in their suspicion would not let the English celebrate mass with closed doors.

called the artisans to work in time of peace, to arms at any attempt to invade their rights. Nowhere in Europe, save in Ghent, did the new civic spirit reveal itself more clearly; nowhere did the burghers assume such control of public affairs. But how much of this would come under Wyclif's observation and what were his opinions thereon it is useless to inquire. One comment is very pertinent. We may frankly confess that it was a misfortune for Wyclif that he was an Englishman. How different would have been the fate of his teaching if sown in the more congenial soil of Flanders we can see from the success that his doctrines met when linked on in Bohemia to a fierce national resentment against the Germans. Wyclif's theory of dominion, with which at this time his mind was full, in a Flemish town would speedily have become the intellectual basis for the civic independence which the burghers prized even more than wealth.

The first conference at Bruges did not last long. By the middle of September Wyclif was back in England[1] and Giles Sancho had returned to Avignon for further instructions.[2] Conference by committee, at any rate by this committee with its irreconcilable elements, was found undesirable by both king and pope. Neither was anxious to push measures to an extreme, and the views of Wyclif, if brought down from theory into practice, were as little to the liking of Edward as of Gregory. Wyclif retired to Oxford, once more hiring rooms at Queen's, for which from September 1374 to September 1375 he paid a rent of twenty shillings. As usual the rooms needed some repair, and the account is still preserved of the penny paid 'pro nouschyn', i. e. for a new door-fastener. On the 23rd November 1374 he preached before the university a sermon which still exists.[3] By this retirement Wyclif showed that he realized that his services at Bruges were not wanted. He had discovered that the Crown, whatever parliament might say, was scarcely in earnest over the whole business. The civil service must be carried on, and the easiest way of payment

---

[1] Wyclif only makes one indirect reference to his travels. In *Serm.* i. 374 he tells us that foreign wheat is less spiky than English but not so good for bread.

[2] For this paragraph see *Pap. Let.* iv. 109, 134-5, 184, 202.

[3] *Serm.* iv. 468 f. and for date *ib.* 474 and *infra*, ii. 206, n. 7.

for an impecunious Crown was by the plunder of the English Church and its wealthier benefices. But this could be more easily managed by arrangement with the papacy than by obtaining the reluctant consent of English chapters and patrons. Possibly this may account for the absence of all documents on the English side. Such a compromise was difficult to draw up in language that would have satisfied even the most subservient parliament. From Avignon, however, we learn more of the actual results. The conference broke up, or rather was carried on by other less formal methods. Wyclif had retired, but Gilbert of Bangor still continued the negotiations with the three papal envoys, who were given powers to postpone the publication of certain articles until a concordat could be secured. In the spring of 1375 the negotiations fell into the hands of John of Gaunt and Sudbury, who had himself been appointed to his bishopric by papal provision. Edward III on his part supplied a gentle stimulus to the pope's anxiety to secure a concordat by levying in April 1375 a tenth on the benefices of cardinals held in England, and by a prohibition in the previous November of any attempt to procure provisions ' to the prejudice of the king '.[1]

As a result of these negotiations, in August 1375 another deputation was appointed by Edward to go to Bruges to confer with Giles Sancho.[2] For us the chief interest of the new deputation lies in the fact that Wyclif was left out, in all probability, as we may surmise from his actions in the ensuing parliament, because he was not sufficiently accommodating to be a party to the pre-arranged deal between king and pope. Wyclif's omission, overlooked by most historians, is of vital moment, the more to be noted when we remember that his former associates, Moulton, Guttierez, and Burton, were retained as subordinate members. Bealknap had become chief justice of common pleas. In his place and Wyclif's the famous Sir John Cobham and Sir Hugh Bryan were appointed. Bryan was probably a son of Sir Guy de Bryan, Edward's steward and secretary, and nephew of bishop Reginald Bryan. Hugh's

---

[1] *Pap. Let.* iv. 143; *Close Rolls*, xiv. 103. For Sudbury's ' provision ', Oct. 1361, see Rymer, iii. 628.
[2] *Pap. Let.* iv. 144 dated 1 Sept. In this Burton is miscalled ' Borton '.

brother John had been granted in 1349 the prebend at Westbury, vacated by his uncle's elevation to the see of St. David's. This he held along with many other preferments until his death in 1389.[1] Sir Hugh, it is clear, belonged to a family whose interests lay in preserving existing methods.

But the real authority was left with Adam Houghton, bishop of St. David's, and Ralph Erghum, the chancellor of John of Gaunt. The career of these two men will illustrate the difficulty of obtaining reform, and show why Wyclif was left out. Houghton[2] was born at Caerforiog in Pembrokeshire, not far from the city of which he became canon, precentor, and finally bishop. As an Oxford student he was in trouble in 1337 for wounding a clerk and his wife.[3] After obtaining his doctorate in civil laws he was taken into the king's service and rewarded by a prebend (Marthire) at St. David's (1347), a second at Hereford (1 Feb. 1347), the archdeaconry of Chichester (1352), a prebend at Abergwyli (Sept. 1360) and the living of Croydon. On the 20th September 1361 Houghton was papally provided to the see of St. David's, but obtained for himself from the pope a continuance for two years of his benefice of Bedington, on account of the expense he had been put to in restoring the 'hospitia' or lodgings. Compelled to relinquish his prebend of Marthire, he secured it for his brother Philip, his prebend of Abergwyli for his clerk Philip Martin, his prebend in Hereford for his illegitimate clerk, John de Carew, who already held a licence for two sinecure benefices, for his chaplain Peter de Hakeness, a benefice value forty marks, for another of his clerks, Adam Bobelyn, who already held the prebend of Howden, further papal provision. Nor did he forget his kinsman William Russell, for whom he secured a prebend at Penkridge. On the 11th January 1377 Houghton was appointed chancellor of England and held the office for fifteen months. He secured from the Crown for himself and

[1] *Cal. Pat.* xvi. 303 ; *Pap. Pet.* i. 202 ; *supra*, p. 165.
[2] For Houghton see Kingston in *D. N. B.*, Rymer ; *Rot. Parl.*, to which add numerous references in *Pap. Pet.* (in itself significant) ; also *Pap. Let.* iii. 238, 336, v. 285 ; *Cal. Pat. Ed.* xvi. 404 ; *Close Rolls*, xiv. 409 ; *Chart. Rolls*, v. 290. For his church &c. see *Monast.* vi. 1376 ; Browne-Willis, *Cathedral Church of St. David's* (1717), 24, 108-9, 143 and plan of his tomb.
[3] Wood, *Univ.* i. 434. This became a test case of the powers of the chancellor, *Close Rolls* (1338), 318-19.

his successors all the liberties of lords marchers. To-day he is remembered for his foundation in 1365, in conjunction with John of Gaunt, of his stately college of St. Mary's at St. David's for a master and seven chaplains. Houghton believed in a money reserve for emergencies and ordained that

' forty pounds of silver be kept for the protection of the rights of the college in a chest in the treasury under three locks and keys '.

He died on the 13th February 1389 and was buried in his college under a tomb long since destroyed.

With Erghum, whose name is variously spelt in the records [1] —often in the form ' Argam ' which still survives locally— we shall meet more than once. If we may judge from certain presents of game made from the duke's park, at Erghum's request, the home of his parents, William and Agnes, was not far from Pickering in Yorkshire, probably at the house still known as Little Argam, on the Argam dyke, not far from Rudstone and Bridlington.[2] But the family itself, whose name possibly may indicate original emigration from Arkholme [3] near Lancaster, belonged to Preston in Lancashire. In 1397 William de Erghum became guild mayor ; and representatives of the family, under the name of Arrom, appear in Preston documents down to the seventeenth century, " Arom " house finally becoming the town residence in Preston of the earls of Derby. Other members of the family were found in Beverley, where one of them had sufficient influence with John of Gaunt to secure his exemption in November 1382 from the fine levied on the people of that turbulent town. Another Erghum, a certain William of Rudstone, in all probability his brother, openly threatened Ralph in March 1383 that he would destroy his manors and his rolls ; the bishop was driven in consequence to secure his arrest.[4] Erghum's first preferment was to the rectory of Winestead, near Patrington in Yorkshire.

[1] ' Argam ' (Knighton, ii. 298), ' Argirii ' (*Pap. Let.* iv. 144), ' Argins ' (Wals. i. 319), ' Erghum ' in his will. No record in *D. N. B.* This Erghum must be distinguished from his nephew, Ralph Erghum, who held many preferments in Bath and Wells and died in 1409, and to whom the bishop in his will left the cancellation of his ' letters of obligation '.

[2] *Reg. Gaunt.*, ii. 80, 324, which show that his father died between 1372 and 1375. On 20 Jan. 1399 he founded a chantry for them at Wells (*Ang. Sac.* i. 570). [3] In *Lanc. Inquis.* iii. 40 written as ' Erghum '.

[4] *Vict. Co. Lanc.* vii, 85, 100 *n.* ; *Cal. Pat. Ric.* ii. 213, 261.

This he held before his ordination as sub-deacon and deacon in April 1362. He had already by that time taken his master's degree at Oxford. To this before 1374 he added a doctor's degree in civil law, and before September 1375 a doctorate in canon law.[1] As an inceptor in civil law he had been appointed by Sudbury to obtain the two sets of statutes for Balliol college, and so may have had fleeting association with Wyclif.[2] Erghum's services to John of Gaunt brought him many preferments. In addition to Winestead he held in 1371 a canonry in York, and the chapel of St. Mary Magdalene (York), to which John of Gaunt added the wealthy living of Preston (September 1374) in addition to an annuity of twenty marks (March 1372). As chancellor Erghum kept the duke's seal, as also his 'plat seal' with the arms thereon of Spain.[3] In October 1375 he was rewarded by duke and pope with the see of Salisbury,[4] but, not content, on the 7th June 1385 he was collated archdeacon of Dorset. His duties at Salisbury he handed over to a vicar-general.[5] In 1376 he was appointed one of the commission to settle the disputes between the Artists and Lawyers at Oxford, and through the influence of Lancaster was nominated on Richard's council of regency.[6] In 1388 he was translated to Bath; for this paying 1,000 gold florins to Urban VI's Florentine agents in London. In September 1395 he obtained permission from Boniface IX for six of his chaplains or clerks to farm out their benefices 'while engaged in his service' or studying at the university.[7] Age was creeping on, and in November 1395 Erghum requested exemption for life from attending parliament or council 'as too old and too weak to render further service'. Erghum died on the 10th April 1400 and was buried at Wells.[8] In his will he left one third of

[1] *Pap. Let.* i. 144; iv. 136; *Ziz.* 286; *Reg. Charlton*, 80, 83. For two short legal notes by Erghum see Tanner, 263.
[2] Salter, *Deeds*, 301 (5 Feb. 1365). See *supra*, p. 81.
[3] *Pap. Let.* iv. 167; *Reg. Gaunt.*, i. 89, 165; ii. 343.
[4] One of his duties was to crenellate Salisbury (*Cal. Pat. Ric.* i. 10).
[5] Wilkins, iii. 102.
[6] *Chron. Ang.* 164; *Cal. Pat.* xvi. 325; Rymer, iii. 1055; Wood, *Univ.* i. 488.   [7] *Pap. Let.* iv. 268, 527; *Cal. Pat.* v. 635.
[8] Godwin, 431; *Ang. Sac.* i. 570 *n.* says 20 March. For his will proved 19 April 1400 see Weaver, ii. 294–7. For his sister with the curious name of Agnas Rabbas still living in 1406 see *Cal. Pat. Hen.* iii. 136; *Ang. Sac.* i. 570 ('Robas').

his goods to poor scholars at Oxford, especially boys of his chapel and clerks of his household.

With Houghton and Erghum at the head of a deputation the pope had nothing to fear, especially as he had already come to terms with John of Gaunt. Neither Houghton nor Erghum would be hard upon a system which had given them so much of this world's goods. Wyclif was well out of the whole business. On the 1st September 1375 Gregory XI addressed to Edward six bulls relating to the proposed concordat. They amounted briefly to this—to recognize accomplished facts, and to leave the *status quo* untouched. Whoever was in possession of a living in England that had been "reserved" for some papal nominee—a long list is given—should not have his incumbency challenged by the curia; whoever had had his right to a church office disputed by Urban V should at once be confirmed in the office; benefices which the same pope had "reserved", in the event of a vacancy, should be filled up by the patrons themselves; and all firstfruits not yet paid should be remitted. In addition, the Church revenues of cardinals who held prebends in England should be subject to impost, to cover the costs of the restoration of churches or other buildings which the holders had allowed to fall into ruin.[1]

At first sight these appear to be important concessions. When examined they resolve themselves into very little, for they all relate to the past. For the future the pope remitted nothing of his claims. These concessions regulated only matters of detail, and left the principle untouched. The concordat, it is true, if Walsingham may be trusted, effected one important change—the pope abandoned for the future his claim to the reservation of English church livings; but the king was also bound, on his side, to abstain in future from conferring church dignities by brief of *Quare impedit*.[2] But even if Walsingham's

---

[1] *Pap. Let.* iv. 111, 144; Rymer, iii. 1037–9.

[2] Walsingham, i. 317. Lechler 147 wrongly supposes that this is in the bulls. Nor is it mentioned in the pope's verbal promises as published by the king on 15 Feb. 1377 (Rymer, iii. 1072). It is in *Brut.* ii. 327. "By the writ *Quare impedit* the king was accustomed, on the ground of wardship or of his rights to the patronage of vacant churches, to treat as vacant livings which had been filled up by the pope" (Stubbs, ii. 447 *n.*).

statement be credited, the result will be discounted when we remember that the pope surrendered his claim only in consideration of a corresponding concession on the side of the Crown; and that the concession contained no security that henceforth there should be no tampering with the rights of cathedral chapters. And yet this had been one of the chief points of reform aimed at by parliament. That this had not been dealt with is noted with censure by Walsingham. He attributes it to the slackness 'of some who knew that they were more likely to be promoted to the bishoprics they desired by the curia than by the election' of the chapters.

Of the results of this second conference this proposed concordat is our chief document. That the settlement proved much on the lines suggested is fairly certain, if only from its preservation without note or comment in our archives. They agree also with the brief statements of Walsingham and Adam of Murimuth,[1] and the verbal promises of the pope as published by Edward III in February 1377. That the concordat was not reached at once is also certain, for on the 6th September 1375 we find Gregory still offering 'to prorogue the articles of concord, provided the king of England do the same', until Christmas 1375, or even until Easter 1376, pending an agreement. On the 1st October Gregory further wrote to the archbishop of York and John Gilbert urging them to give credence to Giles Sancho, who was being dispatched from Bruges to Edward personally 'so that the business [of the Concordat] may attain its conclusion and effect'.[2] But the actual arrival of Sancho seems to have been delayed until the following year, when there were associated with him two archbishops,[3] Pileus of Ravenna[4] and Guillaume Lestrange[5] of Rouen. At length, after 'almost two years of negotiation', as Walsingham informs us, a concordat was reached, which proved for all reformers a sore disappointment. On the occasion of his jubilee, Edward III, in giving up on the 15th

---

[1] Walsingham, i. 317; Murimuth, *Cont.* 214.
[2] *Pap. Let.* iv. 111, 147, 218.
[3] Rymer, iii. 1055–6, and cf. Wilkins, iii. 106.
[4] Pileus de Prata (†*c.* 1400) archbishop of Ravenna (23 Jan. 1370), appointed cardinal 28 Sept. 1378 (Eubel, i. 22).
[5] 22 Dec. 1375, d. March 1389 (*ib.* i. 174, 447).

February 1377 the right of presentation to certain preferments which had fallen into his hands during vacancies, published six articles. In these he stated that the pope had verbally promised to abstain from reservations, to allow free election to bishoprics, to be moderate in bestowing preferments on foreigners, to relieve the clergy from giving firstfruits, and to be moderate in granting provisions and expectations.[1] Thus the mountain delivered itself of a mouse. With these tardy and small results, which were not even carried out, the nation was forced to be content. They strengthened rather than weakened the papal claims, but added to the anti-papal feeling to which, soon after their promulgation, Wyclif appealed.

To show the unreality of the conference, several of the chief actors were rewarded with preferments by means of the papal provisions against which they had been sent to protest. Gilbert was translated from Bangor to Hereford,[2] and Erghum appointed to Salisbury.[3] Wyclif, whose part had been insignificant, received no reward, for Lutterworth had been given him before the first conference met. In after years his enemies invented the story that he expected to obtain the bishopric of Worcester, vacant through the death of that stormy prelate William de Lynn,[4] and that his disappointment in being passed over led to his turning reformer. The gossip is worthless, in spite of the fact that Netter heard it repeated 'in a great synod of the Canterbury clergy' by the eminent Robert Hallum, bishop of Salisbury.[5] All that it shows, in our judgement, is that his enemies assigned to Wyclif in their reminiscences greater authority at Bruges than the records warrant. The vacancy of the see for eighteen months would lead to many rumours among those unacquainted with the facts. On the 7th December 1373, half a year before Wyclif sailed to

[1] Rymer, iii. 1072 ; Wilkins, iii. 114.
[2] 12 Sept. 1375, Eubel, i. 285 ; Rymer, iii. 1044 and *Cal. Pat.* xvi. 199.
[3] Oct. 12 ; *Pap. Let.* iv. 215 ; *Cal. Pat.* xvi. 208 ; consecrated at Bruges on Dec. 9 (Stubbs, *Reg. Sac.* 80).
[4] Died 18 Nov. 1373 (*Sede Vac. Worc.* 289 ; *Ang. Sac.* i. 535). Shirley, *Ziz,* p. xvii, misled by his chronology, refers to the vacancy at Worcester in 1363 filled by the translation of Wittlesey from Rochester. The vacancy in 1368 when Wittlesey was made archbishop is also out of the question.
[5] Netter, *Doct.* i. 934 (bk. iv, c. 33) ; i. 560 (bk. ii, c. 60). The story was repeated at Basel in 1433. See Zatacensis, *Lib. Diurnus,* 317. For Hallum see *D. N. B.* and my *Age of Hus, passim.*

Bruges, Walter Leigh, the prior of Worcester, had been nominated by the chapter, with Edward's consent.[1] But this choice was set aside, and on the 12th September 1375 Henry Wakefield, the keeper of the king's wardrobe,[2] was provided by Gregory XI and accepted by Edward[3]—another illustration of the unreality of the Crown's action.

The victory of the papacy seems more complete when we remember that in return for his concessions Gregory had obtained his subsidy—not his full demand of 100,000 florins, paid immediately, but 60,000 payable in two sums, half on the 1st November 1375, the other half on the 24th June 1376. A clause was also added that if peace should be made between England and France the clergy should also pay 40,000 florins more. Accordingly on the 15th July 1375 the pope issued his mandates to the archbishops reciting the terms to which 'the representatives of the clergy' at Bruges had 'recently' agreed. Study of the dates shows that Wyclif was no party to this disgraceful surrender to the papal claim.[4] The only representatives of the clergy who were present at Bruges in the spring of 1375 were Sudbury and the two subordinate members, Sheppey and Multon. But to their negotiations John of Gaunt must have been a consenting party, for a right of veto had been specifically lodged with the duke and the bishop.[5] We do not think we shall do either of them an injustice in

---

[1] *Sede Vac. Worc.* 283, 290–1, whence we see that on 24 Dec. 1373 Edward wrote to the archbishop to do what pertained to him over the matter.

[2] From 27 June 1369–13 Oct. 1375 (*Eng. Hist. Rev.* xxiv. 501, and numerous references in Devon, *Roll Brant.*). Wakefield, not in *D. N. B.*, had received many preferments for his Crown services, e. g. prebend in Salisbury, 17 March 1371 (*Cal. Pat.* xv. 58); archdeaconry of Northampton, Dec. 1371 (*ib.* 165); archdeaconry of Canterbury, June 1374 (*ib.* 443). On 1 July 1373 Edward gave his assent to his election to the see of Ely (*ib.* xv. 319), which, however, ultimately went to Arundel. He was appointed treasurer of the exchequer, 26 June 1377 (*Cal. Pat. Ric.* i. 3), but resigned before 19 July (*ib.* 7). He died 3 March 1395 (*Ang. Sac.* i. 536; in Stubbs, *Reg. Sac. Ang.* 80 the date is given as 11 March from Godwin).

[3] Eubel, i. 561; *Ang. Sac.* i. 535. Intimation of the provision was forwarded from Lambeth on 3 Oct. 1375, received at Worcester 8 Oct. (*Sede Vac. Worc.* 353). Wakefield was consecrated at Hatfield on 28 Oct. (*Ang. Sac.* i. 535).

[4] On 30 Dec. 1374 Gregory wrote to Sudbury to exact this subsidy. But his letter shows that this refers to the old demand to which no attention had been paid (*Pap. Let.* iv. 136). In *ib.* iv. 111, 218 (dated 15 July 1375) the tone is altogether new, and the references are to the 'late' agreement at Bruges. So expressly *Reg. Wykeham*, ii. 241.

[5] See Rymer, iii. 1025.

supposing that in granting these terms the duke was thinking of possible assistance from the papacy in his campaign in Castile. Ten years earlier, on his seeking to arrange a marriage between his younger brother Edmund, earl of Cambridge, and Margaret of Burgundy, he had learned the power of Avignon to thwart his projects.[1] He was already dreaming of a new endeavour, with the forces of the papacy enlisted on his side. Nor shall we do Sudbury a wrong if we attribute to him some thought of the see of Canterbury, now vacant for over a year through the death of Wittlesey. If so, he had his reward in his translation by papal bull on the 12th May 1375 to the stool of St. Augustine, with an exhortation from Gregory ' to multiply the talent entrusted to him '.[2] Our suspicions are increased when we find that Sudbury, immediately after he had secured the prize, displays a lively interest in the raising of Gregory's subsidy.[3]

Before we pass away from this Bruges concordat there are two matters which demand correction. Historians,[4] almost without exception, have exaggerated the part that Wyclif played at Bruges. We have shown that he was soon pushed aside, and others more yielding took his place. We confess that we are glad that we can thus clear his name from complicity in a great sham. It is ill to conceive of Wyclif as rowing in the same boat with Houghton, Erghum, or Gilbert. Another mistake that has also arisen from not distinguishing between the two missions has been the assigning to Bruges the opportunity for Wyclif to meet in person with John of Gaunt. Lechler has gone so far as to draw a picture of the two men "having constant exchange of ideas with each other, both on matters of business and in social intercourse, during the time that they were occupied with the congress in Flanders ".[5]

[1] On this see Armitage-Smith, 28–32.
[2] Wilkins, iii. 97 ; *Pap. Let.* iv. 147 ; Rymer, iii. 1029.
[3] Wilkins, iii. 101, letter to Wykeham, dated Lambeth, 29 Sept. 1375, but as the postcript shows written at Bruges. The subsidy was not easily raised. Wykeham paid his first instalment on 18 Dec. 1375 (*Reg. Wykeham*, ii. 250), but he was almost alone. See Gregory's stern letters on 30 Dec. (*Pap. Let.* iv. 112), and to the ungrateful Gilbert on 3 May 1376 (Wilkins, iii. 106). Nothing paid in the province of York (*Pap. Let.* iv. 154).
[4] Lechler, 145 ; Ramsay, *Gen. Lanc.* ii. 46 ; Rashdall in *D. N. B.* ; Stubbs, ii. 447.
[5] Lechler, 144, accepted by Wells, *Manual*, 465.

The picture is attractive, and has been pushed to many conclusions. Unfortunately, it is wholly incorrect. John of Gaunt, it is true, was at Bruges in the autumn of 1375 at the head of the English legation. But in 1374 the duke was never at Bruges,[1] and in 1375, when John of Gaunt was there, Wyclif, dismissed from the deputation, was back in Oxford.

During the greater part of 1374, in fact, John of Gaunt had been sulking in his tents. He was at that time the most unpopular man in England, for he had been guilty of a great failure, the greater in reality because of its daring pretentiousness. On the 4th August 1373, after two months of preparation, the duke had set out from Calais with 15,000 men, and had marched through Picardy, Champagne, and Burgundy, burning and destroying as he advanced,[2] in spite of all the efforts of Gregory XI to stop hostilities. Charles of France forbade any fighting. ' If a storm rages over the land ', he said, ' it disperses of itself. So will it be with the English '. His prescience was justified by events. Leaving the wealthy lands behind them, Gaunt's freebooters had plunged into Auvergne. In that volcanic region his baggage was swept away by the winter torrents, his men killed by cold and hunger at the very time that Edward's chancellor, Sir John Knyvet, was assuring parliament of the success they had accomplished. Lancaster reached Bordeaux in December, to find the remnant of his army reduced to begging in the streets and deserting by scores. Through the efforts of Gregory, who went so far as to threaten to excommunicate both Lewis of Anjou and John of Gaunt, a truce was at last patched up,[3] and the duke, with borrowed money, returned to England (Apr. 1374). There he was openly reprimanded by Edward for his mismanagement of the campaign. For the rest of the year the duke retired from public affairs, spending the time at Hertford or on his northern estates. His disasters had led him to the conviction that the

[1] *Reg. Gaunt.* i. 79, 80 ; ii. 329, 331, 341, 342. In Aug. 1374 when Wyclif was at Bruges the duke was at Ravensdale, and in Sept. 1374 at Cowick and Lincoln (*ib.* i. 63–4). He seems only to have been at Bruges in May and June 1375, and from the end of Sept. to Jan. 1376 (*ib.* ii. 332, 335, 341–2).
[2] For this march of John of Gaunt see Armitage-Smith, 100–15, with excellent map. Prayers for success were ordered 16 June 1373 (*Close Rolls*, xiii. 563 ; Rymer, iii. 983).
[3] *Pap. Let.* iv. 108–9, 125, 131, 135.

continuance of the struggle with France was hopeless; moreover he saw clearly that if that war was stopped there would be greater chance of receiving English support for a second invasion of Castile. He therefore flung himself into the cause of peace, and persuaded Edward to listen to the overtures of the papacy [1] to arrange a truce. In the spring of 1375, as the head of an English embassy, the duke met the envoys of France at Bruges, and after three months parleying concluded a truce (27 June 1375). In November 1375 he returned to Bruges together with his duchess to continue the negotiations. After six months of extravagant outlay in feasts and tournaments, the unseemliness of which amid so much distress provoked the rebuke of the chroniclers,[2] John returned to England, having secured the prolongation of the truce until the 1st April 1377. To the English at home, with their dreams of the ratification of the peace of Bretigny, the results seemed pitiable. Walsingham in his vexation draws a sharp contrast between the cunning of the French and the absence 'of all foresight and prudence' among the English, who fight rather 'after the manner of brutes'. It was during this second embassy to Bruges, of which Wyclif was not a member, that the concordat with the pope was concluded.

[1] For this section see *Pap. Let.* iv. 142 f.; Rymer, iii. 1021 f., 1031 f., 1039-40, 1048, 1054.
[2] *Eulog. Cont.* iii. 336; cf. Walsingham, i. 318.

II

THE GOOD PARLIAMENT

§ 1

WYCLIF returned from Bruges a disillusioned man. The wars in France were abhorrent to him. In a work that he was then writing he breaks through his usual reserve to protest that 'the Great Company devastating France is hateful to God'.[1] The hollowness of the long negotiations would be borne in upon him. So Wyclif seems to have contemplated abandoning politics, preferring to fall back upon his academic position for the advancement of his ideas, to which henceforth, as he tells us, he would devote his life.[2] He retired to Oxford, taking rooms at Queen's in September for a year. Probably, for we hear nothing to the contrary from his enemies, he kept in touch with his new parish of Lutterworth, which, fortunately, was at no great distance from Oxford. But his main work during the year was literary. He formed the intention of publishing a vast *summa* of philosophy, ethics, and theology, partly by the recast of previous lectures, partly by new work. His recent experiences had shown him the need of making clear the foundations of thought upon which action must rest. He devoted himself at once to the publication of his *Determinatio*. But this was only the skeleton of a larger work, his vast treatises on *Divine and Civil Dominion*. No doubt publication was preceded by many arguments in the schools which brought out the antagonism of those who now began to see more clearly whither his views were leading. The first to break a lance with Wyclif, before either Boldon or Binham or the publication of the *Determinatio*, was William Woodford, on the limit and nature of civil dominion and the right of the clergy to possess property.[3] Of direct work for the Crown during the next two years we hear nothing, though it is evident from later events that Wyclif was not forgotten. On the other

---

[1] *Civ. Dom.* iv. 412. [2] See his striking preface to *Dom. Div.*
[3] *Op. Min.* 415 ; *Civ. Dom.* ii. 1 ; iii. 351, 358.

hand the student who would understand the inwardness of Wyclif's writings at this time must not overlook that they are the academic side of the political movement reflected in the Good Parliament. "In them are precipitated those ideas by which the Good Parliament was governed." [1]

The student should remember that the subject of Dominion was neither so original nor so academic as at first blush he might assume. It was only one form of the age-long controversy on the jurisdiction and limits of Church and State; direct descendant, as we may put it, of the treatises on the Translation of the Empire and the like which had attended the growth of the Hildebrandine doctrine. In an age when the jurisdictions of Church and State were ill-defined and yet interwoven, the subject, on one side or other, whether in the works of Pierre Dubois,[2] Augustin Trionfo, Marsiglio of Padua, Manegold of Lutterbach, or John of Salisbury, formed a constant staple of discussion. In Oxford, especially, the whole subject was familiar. The writings of William of Ockham, with their intimate reference to the struggles of Lewis the Bavarian, might be regarded as rather of continental than English interest, but in Fitzralph Wyclif had a direct predecessor at Oxford itself, whose conclusions, as we have seen, he adopted and amplified. In an age when authority was paramount it was a great advantage that at every turn of the discussion Wyclif could fall back upon the opinions of one popularly regarded as 'St. Richard' of Armagh.

The discovery of printing has somewhat reversed the order of controversy. To-day the publication of a work is the beginning, as a rule, of discussion; in the Middle Ages publication marked the culmination of a long tournament in the lecture rooms and schools. We shall do well, therefore, at this stage to examine more fully the nature of Wyclif's work on *Dominion*, both 'divine' and 'human' or 'civil',[3] which at this period occupied his thoughts. Moreover in this work we find the key to the political actions of Wyclif. For Wyclif's theory of Dominion led him to the enunciation of a policy

[1] Loserth in *Civ. Dom.* iv. p. vi.
[2] For these see *Owens College Historical Essays* (1902), c. 6.
[3] *de Dominio Divino*, ed. R. L. Poole, 1890; *de Civili Dominio*, vol. i, ed. R. L. Poole, 1885; vols. ii–iv, ed. J. Loserth, 1900–4.

which brought him into alliance with John of Gaunt. The importance of the subject is also seen in the place which Wyclif assigned to it when making his *Summa*. As the *de Ente* stood at the head of his philosophical writings, so the *de Dominio Divino* stood at the head of his theological.[1]

At the outset the student should remember one essential caution. Wyclif's political writings must not be construed as if they were programmes of actual reconstruction. They should be read in the same way as Plato's *Republic* or More's *Utopia*.[2] Wyclif thought out a society such as he desired England to become, and with which he contrasted the England of his age; there is no evidence that he thought that such a society could be inaugurated when Richard was king. In fact so merely idealistic is the reconstruction that neither Fitzralph nor Wyclif seriously attempted the first step of all, to adjust the two titles to possession: that given by lordship in grace, and the claim of the civil law. But Fitzralph and Wyclif would have answered that without ideals no progress can be made; to attain the goal we must salute it from afar. With Fitzralph, it must be confessed, this distant homage was about all; his life in every other respect was on the ordinary level. Moreover Wyclif's reconstruction, unlike that of Marsiglio, is thought out in the terms of an out-worn philosophical and political system; it looked to the future but was too rooted in a dead past to have in it the promise of life. Unfortunately it was the metaphysical groundwork rather than the working out in life of the doctrine of lordship itself which seems to have attracted Wyclif, and to whose explication he devotes his strength.

Wyclif, following the order of Fitzralph, commences his *de Dominio Divino* with a distinction between 'lordship' or 'dominion' and 'use'. The discussion was not without its interest for the land-owning class. For years they had been engaged, with the assistance of such lawyers as Robert Wyclif, in trying to turn feudal 'use', with duties to the lord in chief,

---

[1] See the early catalogues of Wyclif's works in *Pol. Wks.* i. pp. lxvi, lxxiii, lxxix. Curious to say there is no reference to this work in Netter's *Doctrinale*. See Poole, *Dom. Div.* p. xxiii *n*.

[2] We see this in Wyclif's contention that buying and selling is dangerous even for lay Christians (*Civ. Dom.* iii. 311).

into definite 'possession'. An acute lawyer might well have used Wyclif's work to strengthen his devices in conveyancing. Following the view maintained by the Spiritual Franciscans, especially by Marsiglio and Ockham,[1] Wyclif distinguished 'lordship' both from 'right' and 'power' and from 'use'. 'Lordship' is the prerogative of God and differs from the lordship of kings inasmuch as it is never exerted

'mediately through the rule of vassal subjects, since immediately and of Himself He makes, maintains and governs all that which He possesses and helps it to perform its works according to other uses which He requires.'

Moreover—and this again is strictly in accord with feudal ideas—the 'lordship' of God never separates ownership from possession. The creature may have possession, but such possession is always held subject to due service to the lord in chief, i.e. to God, who still continues to exact His dues, for man is but His bailiff or steward. Thus Wyclif works out by a use of feudal ideas the same belief in the duties of property, and the dependence of user upon the discharge of such duties, which modern reformers attempt to reach by other methods. 'Men should be ware that all the goods that they have be goods of their God, and they naked servants of God.'[2]

From these fundamental positions it is an easy transition to the corollary that dominion is dependent on grace, and that mortal sin is a breach of tenure and so 'incurs forfeiture'. In the *de Dominio Divino* this idea is only briefly touched upon as a consequence of the completeness of God's gift to man.[3] The last part of the book that has come down to us—for much seems to be lost [4]—is concerned with the relation of merit and grace. In this Wyclif takes a position contrary to that of Bradwardine. Possession should be the result of grace, for it is the gift of God. Does such possession involve any merit? Wyclif replies that grace is " the antecedent of such deserving ; but the fact that God's help is necessary does not take away

---

[1] *Civ. Dom.* iii. 324 f., and Poole's note *Dom. Div.* 5.
[2] *Dom. Div.* 33, 250, 255. Cf. *Civ. Dom.* ii. 105 ; *Eng. Works*, 284 ; *Sel. Eng. Works*, i. 55.
[3] *Dom. Div.*, 213 f. Cf. *Sel. Eng. Works*, iii. 88.
[4] See *Dom. Div.* 198, 256, which show that both the second and third books are incomplete in all the four Vienna MSS.

from the merit of the man who runs his course aright. The merit is of grace, and the reward is of grace ; but none the less man would deserve nothing unless by the exercise of his own power of volition ". When further inquiry is made " into the relative shares taken by God and man in causing man's merit, it is shown that the operation of God's grace is the principal cause, and that while no one can have merit of works, he can have merit through works of God's grace ".[1]

In his *de Civili Dominio*, Wyclif further developed his doctrine of lordship. This vast work of over a thousand pages is preserved only in a single Vienna manuscript, written, probably, by a Czech student between 1407 and 1410. In spite of its inordinate length and " digressions, meanderings, excursions innumerable ",[2] the treatise has value because of the interest attaching to the ' two truths ' with which it opens : one that no man in mortal sin can hold *dominium* or lordship ; the other that every one in a state of grace has real lordship over the whole universe.[3] Civil lordship can only be ascribed to the wicked by an abuse of language, for such lordship is contrary to the principles of law and of service and is incompatible with the perfection which must belong to all gifts of God. The sinner, in fact, is a conspirator against God who slays God's vassal, namely himself, and so incurs forfeiture. The correlative principle that the righteous is lord of all things really turns on the truth that Christianity supersedes the relation of lord and servant by a universal reciprocity of service. A man is lord just so far as he is the agent of mother church and a servant of his brethren, even though they be bondmen.[4] This universal lordship of the righteous involves the ' Socratic ' doctrine that goods must be held in common, though Wyclif is careful to exclude the community of wives.[5] The present arrangements of society he regards as the result

---

[1] Poole, *Dom. Div.* pp. xxxiii–iv.
[2] Poole, *Civ. Dom.* p. xxi. A characteristic digression is his proof (ii. 201) that Adam must have sinned at the vernal equinox as the opposite of Easter.
[3] *Civ. Dom.* i. cc. 1–14. In *Op. Min.* 239 Wyclif points out a qualification which really takes away all practical value from his theory : a man living in sin may yet have dominion because he is predestinate.
[4] *Civ. Dom.* i. c. xi; ii. 188; iii. 297; cf. *Sel. Eng. Works*, ii. 296, and cf. St. Paul, 1 *Cor.* iii. 21–2.
[5] *Civ. Dom.* i. c. 14.

of sin, as well as contrary to the law of nature;[1] it ought to be exchanged for the simple law of the New Testament, which is sufficient without the assistance of the Canon Law for all the purposes of human life and government.[2] In a digression on the superiority of the life of contemplation to that of action Wyclif emphasizes the grievous results if the cleric takes his active functions as a pretext for secular employments [3]—Wyclif evidently has turned his back on Bruges. In a third division Wyclif discusses whether obedience is due to tyrants. He answers in the affirmative unless by withdrawing the obedience it seems likely that the tyranny can be overthrown.[4] The division ends with an examination of the relative advantages of aristocracy and kingship. He decides in favour of aristocracy, unless one man can be found markedly pre-eminent in virtue. Kingship stands not in human right but in grace, and as such should not pass either by election or heredity.[5] A discussion of the limits within which serfdom and slavery are admissible ends with the rejection of all hereditary slavery.[6]

The most casual reader will recognize that the book is full of dynamite, however careful Wyclif may be to emphasize its purely speculative basis. Wyclif lived in the middle of the Hundred Years' War, and yet maintains that the right of conquest is determined by the righteousness and pure motives of the conqueror.[7] The doctrine that the title of king stands in no human right but in grace [8] had but cold comfort for the rulers of the fourteenth century, as indeed Hus found at the Council of Constance. When the attention of the Emperor Sigismund was drawn to this 'heresy' he replied, not without dignity and cogency, 'John Hus, no one lives without sin '.[9] The Peasants' Revolt was but the application to life of the teaching that the possession of the unrighteous involves theft, and that, all Christians being equal, distinctions of rank must depend on virtue.[10] But the book might have been dismissed as the harmless speculations of a scholar had it not been for Wyclif's application of his principles to the relation of the

---

[1] *Civ. Dom.* i. c. 18 ; ii. 154.
[2] *ib.* i. cc. 17, 44 ; ii. 172, 179.
[3] *ib.* i. cc. 23–5.
[4] *ib.* i. c. 28.
[5] *ib.* i. cc. 26–31.
[6] *ib.* i. cc. 33–4. Cf. *infra*, ii. 241.
[7] *ib.* i. 144, 150 ; ii. 233, 238 f.
[8] *ib.* i. 212 f.
[9] Palacký, *Doc.* 299.
[10] *Civ. Dom.* i. 101, 234.

State to the property of the Church. Almost all the conclusions of Wyclif condemned by Gregory XI in 1377 are found in this section. Wyclif begins by questioning the lawfulness of grants in perpetuity. The title to such grant must rest on the approval of God, and no one has a right to determine that a possession shall be held irrespective of personal merit.[1] From this Wyclif passed to the corollary that if an ecclesiastic habitually abuse his user the secular power should take steps for the deprivation.[2] As such expropriation, one effect of which would be the relief of the people from oppressive taxation,[3] would involve excommunication, Wyclif points out that excommunication, save for strictly spiritual offences, is without effect.[4] This leads Wyclif to dispute the plenitude of power conferred on the successors of St. Peter.[5] Returning to the question of excommunication Wyclif protests against the use of this weapon to secure the payment of tithes. If pronounced at all it should be pronounced by lay folk as part of secular business.[6] He holds that tithes ought to be paid to the clergy as the almoners of the poor, but maintains that if a cleric be notoriously wicked the parishioners may pay to the poor direct or to a committee of laymen on behalf of the poor. As endowments forfeited by abuse could not be revived by a return to grace, it is evident that under certain conditions the whole clergy might be deprived of their possessions.[7] The first book concludes with two long appendices. In the first the Church is defined as the whole body of the predestinate, past, present, and future, whose head and eternal director is Christ,[8] a subject more fully developed two years later in his *de Ecclesia*. The second deals with the limitation of the papal authority. Pope and cardinals alike may err; neither pope nor cardinals are absolutely necessary for the government of the Church. A worldly pope is an heresiarch and should be deprived.[9]

In additional books Wyclif deals with many matters, some irrelevant, others of importance because in them we detect the first indication of teaching that he afterwards developed. One of the most interesting of these digressions is on the limits

[1] *Civ. Dom.* i. cc. 35–6.
[2] *ib.* i. c. 37; also ii. c. 12; ii. 112.
[3] *ib.* iii. 314.
[4] *ib.* i. 307.
[5] *ib.* i. cc. 38–9.
[6] *ib.* i. 355.
[7] *ib.* i. cc. 41–2; iii. 306.
[8] *ib.* i. 358 f.
[9] *ib.* i. c. 43, p. 414; ii. 114; iv. 398, 404.

of a just war. These extra books were almost needless; the subject was exhausted in the first volume. But an unnamed opponent, an Oxford 'Benedictine' who hailed from Ireland,[1] assisted it would seem by some friars—we note the beginning of divergence—including William Woodford,[2] accused Wyclif of blasphemy and heresy. Wyclif, who could never resist the delight of battle, responded with two books reiterating and enlarging his main contentions. In his historical illustrations of expropriation of church property Wyclif cites and commends the action taken against the Templars, William the Conqueror's exactions from monasteries, as for instance Glastonbury, William Rufus' ('Ursus') high-handed spoliations, and ingeniously uses in support of his argument Innocent III's donation of England to John, and Urban V's transfer of Spain from Peter the Cruel to Henry of Trastamare.[3]

The reader will be more satisfied with Wyclif's defence of Simon de Montfort.[4] His puritan outlook is seen in his protest against all luxury in dress, or the giving of dinners.[5] How near he was to his later break with the papacy is evident in his commendation of the deposition of popes by Otto the Great and others, and his approval of the fate of Boniface VIII.[6] One passage is of more than ordinary interest:

'Oh! how happy and fertile' cries Wyclif 'would England be if every parish church had as of yore a saintly rector residing with his family, if every manor had a just lord residing with his wife and children! Then there would not be so much arable land lying fallow and so great a dearth of cattle. The realm would have abundance of every sort of wealth, as well as serfs and artizans. But now there are but hirelings who fret at the civil rule of clergy, naturally abhorring it; who are lazy, indifferent to the tillage of the ground since it is not theirs; who take to theft because of the lack of oversight by a resident squire; who are unbridled in character, and with unrestrained licence squander the wealth of the realm. The clergy,

---

[1] *Civ. Dom.* ii. 1, 33. This cannot therefore be the Franciscan William Woodford as Loserth, *Civ. Dom.* iv. p. 11. I am inclined to think that he was not a 'Benedictine' but the Cistercian, Henry Crump (*infra*, ii. 124). In *Eccles.* 332, where Wyclif also alludes to this controversy, he calls him merely 'quidam doctor'. He there adds to his instances of expropriation recent confiscations of the temporalities of bishops Bateman, Grandisson, and Lyle and Richard's confiscation of alien priories.

[2] *Civ. Dom.* iii. 351; *Op. Min.* 416.
[3] *Civ. Dom.* ii. 4, 34, 47 f. (from Higden). [4] *ib.* ii. 52.
[5] *ib.* ii. 102, 164, 216. See *infra*, ii. 78. [6] *ib.* ii. 117 f.

on their part, rival secular lords in their sumptuous habits, and secular lords seek to outshine the clergy in their style of living and dress, and so the realm suffers manifold pains, the chief cause of which, unless I am mistaken, is the clergy. For if they would teach efficiently in word and deed the law of Christ, as in old times, abuses of this sort would cease. If too the civil tenants owned the temporal wealth there would be an increase in marriages and children —the elements, according to Aristotle, of a republic's growth—and the realm would grow fruitful in wealth.' [1]

Wyclif begins his third book with an attack upon the orders, though not with the vitriol that in later days became constant with him. For the present we pass this by, noting only that Wyclif still defends the right of the friars to beg, though he owns they may beg wrongly. He claims also that the friars differ from the monks ' in wishing more strictly to follow Christ in His poverty ', and that in this the Franciscans show the highest perfection.[2] He then proceeds to refute the arguments of Fitzralph in his *de Questionibus Armenorum* that Christ exercised civil rule, and contends at some length for the complete poverty of Jesus and the apostles.[3] Hence he deduces that the clergy may neither bear civil rule nor hold property except so far as they may hold it for the poor. Even the marriage of the clergy would not interfere with spiritual ministry so much as does the claim to civil lordship.[4] ' The clergy cannot travel by both roads, civil and evangelical ', and the ' universale collegium universitatis (guild) clericorum ought to have all goods in common '. The pope, who has no power to dispense with this rule, should restore the clergy to their primitive freedom by throwing off the burden that Sylvester laid upon him by accepting the Donation of Constantine.[5]

Before we pass away there is one side issue on which a word should be said. A common corollary of Wyclif's main idea, as developed among the people at large, was a lordship founded on the grace of illness. " The sick who in health are *servi*, when visited by the chastening hand of the Almighty, become *domini*, if fortunate enough to gain admission to a hospital." [6] Hence the abounding charity of medieval life, and the number-

---
[1] *Civ. Dom.* ii. 14.   [2] *ib.* iii. 4 f., 12, 57, 350.
[3] *ib.* iii. 10, 51, 54, 60, 100 f., 114, 356 f.
[4] *ib.* iii. 173 f., 193 f., 213, 235 f., 242 f., 254, iv. 385.
[5] *ib.* iii. 251, 253, 333.   [6] *Eng. Hist. Rev.* xvii. 345.

less hospitals ('maison Dieu') the intention of which, it must be confessed, was often better than their unsanitary methods. We mention this to show that Wyclif's idea of dominion founded in grace had some currency in popular thought, as well as affinity with the principles, very differently developed, upon which Hildebrand built up his concept of a theocratic state.[1]

§ 2

We pass to the background of actual politics against which Wyclif's ideal reconstructions were projected. There we shall see the ferment of the hope and unrest to which he appealed, and its issue in increased abuse and corruption. The results of Bruges, added to distress at home, fulfilled the unpopularity of Lancaster. As he had been living abroad for the most part, he could scarcely be held personally responsible. Nevertheless the misgovernment of his minions was laid at his door. It is true that there had been no deliberate design of creating a despotism. But an ill-administered, corrupt government is capable of producing irritation out of all proportion to its intentions. The discontent had been increased by a fourth visitation of the plague, followed by dearth, 1375 being the last of a remarkable series of fourteen dear years. For three years Parliament had not met, in spite of the drain on the nation's resources through the continuance of war. At last an empty exchequer forced the king, at the height of the discontent, to summon Parliament on the 28th December 1375 to meet on the following 12th February. As the duke had not yet returned from his junketings and diplomacy at Bruges, the meeting was prorogued on the 20th January 1376 until the 28th April. By this date Lancaster was back.

On the appointed day the Parliament which has gone down to history with the well-deserved title of 'The Good' was opened by Edward in person. The towns south of the Trent were well represented by forty-four burghers in addition to those from London. Except Newcastle no town in the north sent any members. After the formal opening, on the morrow

---

[1] This is too big a subject to enter into. For proof I refer the student to W. Martens, *Gregor vii* (1894) or C. Mirbt, *Die Publizistik im Zeitalter Gregors vii* (1894).

Knyvet, the chancellor, declared that the reason for their being summoned was the need of a subsidy for the prosecution of the war with France. He ended with exhorting them to be diligent in their business. But the Commons, secure of the support of the Black Prince, who though on his deathbed at Kennington was still the idol of the nation, were in no mood to receive these demands with meekness. On withdrawing from the Painted Chamber to the Chapter House, after first seeking the advice of the bishops, they asked the Lords to appoint a committee to confer with them, as had been done in 1373. The temper of the city was seen in the need for issuing an order prohibiting the sale of armour, nominally to prevent export. The Lords replied by appointing four bishops, four earls, including the earl of March, and four barons. Of the twelve one only, Adam Houghton, was known as a supporter of John of Gaunt. The most powerful of the twelve was Henry Percy, the father of the hero of Chevy Chase, a calculating, ambitious man, whose constant aim was the aggrandizement of his family, but who at the moment was prepared to bring the duke to terms by showing that he could be a formidable foe. The other bishops, Spenser of Norwich and Appleby of Carlisle, were known for their fearless individuality, while Courtenay of London was noted for his life-long hatred of John of Gaunt. In this he was seconded by the earl of March, who, failing Richard, might have had justification for looking upon himself as the heir to the throne, and so dreaded the machinations of the duke. Behind Courtenay we may discern Wykeham, destined soon to pay a heavy price for his enmity to Lancaster.

With ranks thus stiffened the Commons proceeded to elect their 'prolocutor' or 'forespeaker', a word afterwards clipped into the familiar Speaker. They chose Sir Peter de la Mare,[1] the seneschal of the earl of March. This first holder of the then dangerous office was a man whose courage and sacrifices in the cause of parliamentary freedom entitle him to a nation's grateful memory. Addressing the Lords, assembled under Lancaster,

---

[1] *D. N. B.*; also much information as to his estates &c. in *Close Rolls Ed.* xvi. 33; *ib. Ric.* ii. 512, iii. 525; *Pat. Ed.* xv. 353, 438; *Pat. Ric.* i. 459. See also *Reg. Gilbert.* 57–8.

the Speaker in his answer to the demand for a grant dwelt on the vast sums exacted by the ordinary taxes as well as the extraordinary revenues received from ransom of the kings of Scotland and France and the prisoners of Poitiers. He asked what had been done with all this money, and demanded that the guilty parties, 'privy friends of the king', be brought to book, thus employing for the first time "the two-handed engine" of impeachment. Four men were singled out for attack: Richard Lyons, a vintner, the farmer of the 'petty custom', who had levied duties not authorized by Parliament; Lord William Latimer, the keeper of the king's privy purse, constable of Dover castle and warden of the Cinque ports, who was accused of selling two strongholds to the French; John, Lord Neville of Raby, one of the stewards of the king's household, charged with taking up the claims of Crown creditors, especially the tallies, at a discount, and then exacting full payment for himself; and John Pecche, a noted London citizen, formerly mayor and Member of Parliament, one of the ring of victuallers who tried to rule the city in their own interests. On the 26th November 1373 Pecche had obtained a monopoly in London of the sale of sweet wines by retail, and had illegally extorted 3s. 4d. on each tun.

To John of Gaunt these proceedings were wormwood and gall. But the favour of the Black Prince (who sent back indignantly the bribe of £1,000 packed in a barrel labelled sturgeons with which Lyons had sought to secure his own safety) rendered it impossible for him to resist. He was compelled to bow to the storm while Latimer was impeached and imprisoned, Raby fined 8,000 marks, Lyons and Pecche imprisoned and deprived of the freedom of the city. Latimer was not long in ward. He was at once bailed out by a number of lords, including Percy. With the attack of the Commons upon the king's mistress, Alice Perrers,[1] the duke would have more sympathy, for her influence stood in the way of his plans. Among other crimes she was accused of meddling with the administration of justice to secure her own interests. Much

---

[1] In addition to the usual records, *D. N. B.*, Rymer, &c., see *Times Lit. Suppl.* 3 July 1919. There is much information about herself and her husband in the *Close* and *Patent Rolls*. For the extraordinary list of her jewels see Devon, 209–10.

therefore as he disliked what he would deem to be the impertinence of the Commons, he was driven to consent to her banishment from court and the forfeiture of her property, including Moorend in Northamptonshire once leased to Sir John Ypres the king's steward. At this castle, so conveniently close to the royal castle of Rockingham, she had often entertained the king, who, lost to all shame, had dated letters patent from her home. With characteristic care for his own interests the duke secured for himself the grant of her forfeited estates, much of which consisted of real property in the city. Though Alice swore on the Cross of Canterbury to obey the sentence, her banishment was but nominal; nevertheless Edward deemed it wise to appear greatly shocked when informed that she was a married woman. The accusations against her new husband, William de Windsor, ' late the king's lieutenant in Ireland ', were brought overseas in a ' certain coffer ' and read before the council at Westminster.

The Good Parliament was not content with attacking the king's misgovernment. With a thoroughness that must have filled Wyclif with hope it turned its attention to the wrongs of the Church, and in especial to the usurpations of the pope as ' the cause of all the plagues, murrain, famine and poverty of the realm '.[1] This they proved by the contrast between the pope's taxes and the king's. ' There was no prince ' they said ' in Christendom so rich that hath by the fourth part as much treasure as goeth most sinfully out of this realm in the way described.' They complained of the subsidy levied on the clergy, as a result of the Bruges concordat, to maintain the pope's wars in Lombardy. Moreover

' the brokers living in the sinful city of Avignon,[2] for money promote many caitiffs, altogether unlearned and unworthy, to preferments of the value of 1,000 marks by year, whereas a doctor in decrees or a master in divinity must be content with 20 marks; whereby learning decayeth . . . Aliens, enemies to this land, who never saw nor care to see their parishioners, have English livings whereby they bring God's service into contempt and are more injurious to God's Church than the Jews or Saracens '.

[1] For the Good Parliament and the Church see *Rot. Parl.* ii. 336-9, also the confused document in Foxe ii. 786.
[2] The phrase is historic : ' brocours des benefices demorantz en la pecche-rouse cite d'Avenon ' (*Rot. Parl.* ii. 337).

The law of the Church prescribed that livings should be conferred and held in pure alms, without solicitation or payment; and reason and faith demanded that Church endowments should be bestowed for the glory of God and in accordance with the founder's intention, and not upon aliens and enemies. ' God had entrusted the care of the sheep to the Holy Father to be pastured, and not to be shorn.' If lay patrons witnessed the avarice and simony of churchmen, they would learn from their example to sell the offices to which they had the right of collation, to men who would ' devour the people like beasts of prey, just as God was sold to the Jews, who thereupon put Him to death '.

The Good Parliament next fell on the pope's collector,[1] who

' keepeth a great hostel in London, with clerks and officers thereto, as it were a prince's custom-house, transporting thence to the pope twenty thousand marks on an average yearly '.

As a remedy they proposed

' that no foreign proctor or collector do remain in England, on pain of life or limb, and that no Englishman, on the like pains, become collector or proctor to others residing at Rome '.

They added the suggestion

' touching the pope's collector, for that the whole clergy being at his mercy dare not displease him, that Mr. John Strensall,[2] parson of St. Botolph's,[3] living in Holborn in the same house where Sir W. Mirfield used to live, may be sent for to come before the lords and commons of this parliament, who being straightly charged can declare much, for that he lived with the said collector as clerk full five years '.

As a proof how cruelly the sheep were shorn they brought forward a list, by no means complete, of alien non-resident cardinals

' whereof one cardinal is dean of York, another of Salisbury, another of Lincoln, another archdeacon of Canterbury, another archdeacon of Durham, another archdeacon of Suffolk, another archdeacon of York, another prebendary of Thame and Nassington, another prebendary of Bucks.'

The student who takes the trouble to hunt out the names of

---

[1] No doubt Arnold Garnier. See *supra*, p. 220.

[2] See *Pap. Pet.* i. 536; *Cal. Pat.* xv. 64: Licence in March 1371 to cross to Calais taking 100 shillings for expenses and £40 for exchanges.

[3] No record in Hennessy, *Nov. Rep.*

cardinals who held benefices in England,[1] all of whom were aliens and absentees, cannot wonder at the indignation of the Good Parliament, nor at the bitterness with which Wyclif, especially in his later years, attacked them. These ' clerics from over the seas ' were ' betrayers of the king, and robbers of the poor ', against whose exactions it was the duty of the Crown to protect the people.[2] No doubt his indignation was increased by the sense of his own wrong at Lincoln.

The Good Parliament took steps to render more safe the work it had accomplished. With remarkable prescience it discerned that the security for good government lay in the check of Parliament. So it requested that Parliament should meet annually [3] and that the election of the knights should be by the better folk of the shire and not as heretofore on the nomination of the sheriff in the county court. It further attempted to undermine the power of the duke by drawing up a scheme of councillors, ten or twelve in all, by whose advice the king was to act, four of whom at least were to be in constant attendance on the king, though no great business should be undertaken without the consent of all. The members of this council were to be chosen by the Commons—a rough anticipation of the modern Cabinet. If this council, upon which the Duke had no seat,[4] could have maintained the position assigned to it, the political history of England would have been very different. But the times were not yet. The Good Parliament in fact had outlived its power. The death of the Black Prince destroyed its main support; not that this tough, medieval soldier cared for parliamentary liberties or would have hesitated to crush them as mercilessly as he had butchered the citizens of Limoges, but that he dreaded Lancastrian treason against his son. For six years he had been slowly dying. At last he had been carried from his usual house on Fish Street Hill [5] to the more salubrious Kennington, where his palace lay in the midst of a large park. There on the 7th June, realizing that the end

[1] It would not be difficult to supply the missing names in the list of the Good Parliament from Eubel and le Neve.   [2] *Serm.* ii. 407, 415.
[3] *Rot. Parl.* ii. 355. The answer was that annual Parliaments were already statutory.
[4] *Chron. Ang.* 100–1 ; *Rot. Parl.* ii. 322 (which is out of its place), 360 ; and for the names *Chron. Ang.* lxviii.
[5] Stow, *Survey*, i. 216. For Kennington see Besant, *South London*, 98 f. The park had been recently enclosed (*Cal. Pat.* xv. 274, cf. 139).

had come, he made his will, distributed gifts to his servants, and handed over his son to the care of the king. The chamber door was then left open so that all might enter in. Among others came Sir Richard Stury, one of the adherents of Lancaster, whose dismissal from about the king's person the Good Parliament had procured. 'Come, Richard', said the prince, ' come and look on what you have long desired to see.' On Stury protesting, 'God pay you according to your deserts ', the prince replied, ' leave me, and let me see your face no more.' On the next day, Trinity Sunday, ' in the worship of which feast he was wont every year to make the most solemnity that he might '[1] ' about the third hour of the day ' he breathed his last. John Gilbert remained with him to the end, and heard his confession. Whether from illness or design he wished to satisfy the bishop with a mere general assent without repeating the prescribed words. But Gilbert exorcized the evil spirit by sprinkling water on the four corners of the chamber, so that the prince spake out. His final prayer was an invocation of the Trinity. With the last words ' Thanks be to Thee, O God, for all Thy goodness ' the victor of Crecy and Poitiers passed away. Men deemed him ' another Hector ' at

' whose name and fortune of knighthood all men, both Christian and heathen, while he lived and was in good point, wondered much and dread him sore '.

As there was no room on the mound where his ancestors were buried in Westminster Abbey for any other save his father, his body, after lying for four months in state at Westminster, was carried to Canterbury. He had desired to be buried ' in the chapel of Our Lady in the undercroft at a distance of ten feet from the altar ', but public opinion insisted on his burial on the south side of the shrine of St. Thomas. " There he lies as it were in sullen exile and mute protestation against the degeneracy of his house, far from the father whose folly he had vainly tried to correct, and from the son whose doom he might foresee but could not avert."[2] In the following November

---

[1] *Brut*, ii. 330. Wyclif refers to this devotion in *Pol. Works*, ii. 417 ; *Serm.* iv. 11.

[2] Trevelyan, 27 ; C. E. Woodruffe, *Memorials of Canterbury* (1912), 159 f. For his death *Chron. Ang.* 88 f. For his tomb Stothard, 66 f. On 2 October 1383, a grant was made to Canterbury of four fairs yearly ' for his soul ' (*Chart. Rolls*, v. 287).

Richard, his son, was created Prince of Wales, duke of Cornwall, and earl of Chester.

The death of the Black Prince was a disaster. In the sickness and disappointment amid which this great captain ended his days the nation read the story of its own decline. 'With his death the hope of the English perished.' Though the prince could not have averted the evils which were eating out the nation's strength, he might have saved the State from many woes. He was no friend of priests, and would never have played into their hands as did his Lancastrian successors. If he had lived, the teaching of Wyclif, stripped of its extremer elements, might have grown into a national movement, as at one time it seemed in a fair way of becoming. Be this as it may, more certain is the effect of his death on the work of the Good Parliament. John of Gaunt resumed his former power, as the Good Parliament discovered when at the end of the session they waited on Edward at Eltham to hear the answers to their petitions, whose number shows their reforming zeal. Some of the petitions, no doubt, were foolish, as might be expected from an inexperienced assembly. But, wise or foolish, the Commons found to their disgust that the majority were refused, especially those directed against the duke and his associates. When the Commons pleaded that none of those who had been impeached should be pardoned or employed again in the public service, the king replied that 'he would do as seemed good to him'. The Good Parliament, the longest that had yet sat, was then dismissed (July 6). No sooner had the members ridden home than they heard that through the duke's influence—for the king's growing feebleness had left Lancaster supreme—Latimer had been recalled, his fine of 20,000 marks remitted, and himself made one of the executors of the king's will. Lyons and Pecche were released from prison and pardoned their fine, nominally 'at the supplication of certain of the magnates and commonalty of the realm in the last parliament', in reality through the influence of Alice Perrers. Above all, the Cabinet appointed by the Commons, on whose functioning they rested their hopes, had been dissolved. The nobles on it had sold themselves, with lord Percy at their head, to the highest bidder. The only one who resisted, Edmund, earl of March, the Marshal of England, was ordered off to Calais. On his refusal to go, his office was handed over to Percy.[1]

Short work was made of the Good Parliament; all its acts were cancelled and erased. Peter de la Mare, the Speaker, was flung on the 27th November into Nottingham castle. Only with difficulty was he saved from the vengeance of Alice Perrers. The bishops, who had promised in Parliament to excommunicate her if she broke her oath, were powerless—'dumb dogs', as the chronicler calls them—for Courtenay could do nothing against the irresolute Sudbury, and from some of the bishops Alice had borrowed large sums of money which they feared to lose. Moreover, on the 13th October Wykeham, who had taken an active part against Latimer, was cited before Sir William Skipwith, the chief justice of Common Pleas, upon a charge of malversation as chancellor. His temporalities were taken from him [2] and handed over to Richard, the new Prince of Wales (15 March 1377), while he was banished twenty miles from court and ordered to appear for his trial in January. 'So they hunted ye said bishop from place to place both by letters and by writs, so that no man could succour him throughout his diocese.' Nevertheless the work of the Good Parliament survived the annulment of its acts. For that parliament marks " a new period in our parliamentary history, a new stage in the character of the national opposition to the misrule of the Crown. Hitherto the task of resistance had devolved on the baronage "; henceforth the Commons began to take the work into their own hands. How deeply the Parliament had stirred the nation is seen in the new edition which at this time Langland, or some other, brought out of *Piers Plowman*, full of political utterances not found in the original text. The Parliament's resistance to the exactions of Rome enabled Edward even after its dismissal to forbid bulls to be received into the kingdom,[3] and secured for Wyclif a favourable hearing for many of his views. Unfortunately his alliance with John of Gaunt introduced complications which prevented Wyclif from speaking out.

[1] Stubbs, ii. 456 *n.* dates this on 8 May 1377. But he was marshall on 1 Dec. 1376: see *Close Rolls*, xiv. 467; cf. *Cal. Pat.* xvi. 491.
[2] 17 Nov. 1376. The value is given as £1,988 p. a. (Rymer, iii. 1075).
[3] Wilkins, iii. 107-8.

III

THE SUMMIT OF INFLUENCE

§ 1

THE attack of Lancaster upon the Good Parliament was followed up by an alliance with John Wyclif. Politics make strange bed-fellows, and men of opposite opinions find themselves fighting side by side. That Lancaster should seek the services of Wyclif is not strange ; that the Reformer should have allowed himself to be made the tool of a man with whom he had scarcely anything in common is deplorable. The one link between the two was hostility to the power and wealth of the hierarchy. In his theology, such as it was, in his views as to the Eucharist, the papacy, the spiritual powers of the clergy, the nature of orders, and the value of monks and friars, John of Gaunt was one with the men of his times, and had no leanings to the teaching of Wyclif.[1] Throughout his life the duke was the firm friend of monasteries, especially those connected with the Lancastrian estates, though particular circumstances might lead him to a quarrel with some special house. Wyclif on the contrary had already shown an antagonism to the monasteries that was soon to develop into hatred. " Conventional in all things, in none was the duke more conventional than in religious practice ".[2] Wyclif in his old age seems daring even to the advanced thought of to-day. In administrative reform of the hierarchy, such as Wyclif urged, the duke, save for his own purposes, had no belief, at any rate if we may judge by his practice. " The man who possessed the largest ecclesiastical patronage in England had ample opportunity of doing something to remedy the evils of plurality and non-residence. What however is the fact ? The Duke in these matters, as in all others, conformed to the practice of his day ; the Lancastrian household, like the king's government, is

---

[1] The religious opposition of the duke and Wyclif is well brought out by Armitage-Smith, 176–80.

[2] Armitage-Smith, 180.

supported by the very abuses which Wyclif denounced."[1] The chancellor of his duchy was invariably an ecclesiastic, for instance Ralph Erghum, who left his diocese to his vicar-general while attending to his master's business. The duke's treasurers, auditors, receivers, clerks, and higher household officials were all paid in canonries, prebends, benefices for which bulls of grace were obtained from Avignon.[2]

And yet, in spite of all this, it is not difficult to understand the "unholy alliance" of two such opposite men. John of Gaunt was an unprincipled politician—he would probably have considered that the two words were inseparable. A thorough-going opportunist, he saw his chance of using an idealist, who, in common with some other idealists, had his gaze so fixed on his ideal that oftentimes he lost the sense of proportion in the means. Wyclif, on the other hand, had but recently come from the lecture halls of Oxford. He was probably not much better acquainted with the world in which the duke lived than the university don of to-day, who finds himself because of his eminence in science or letters chosen to represent his Alma Mater in Parliament, is acquainted with the squalid byways of the political world. Against the moral character of Wyclif not even his enemies, as archbishop Arundel confessed, could cast a stone; the moral character of John of Gaunt was such that a chancellor of Oxford ascribed his death to his gross immoralities.[3] But this was a phase of the court life of the duke of which Wyclif would know nothing, though it cannot be pleaded that Wyclif would be ignorant of his adultery with Katherine Swynford. Katherine de Roelt,[4] the younger daughter of Sir Payne Roelt, a knight of Hainault, had received charge of John of Gaunt's daughters, and shortly after the death in Gascony of her first husband, Hugh Swynford, in 1372 became the duke's mistress.[5] The scandal was notorious.

---

[1] Armitage-Smith, 173-4.

[2] *Ib.* 175; cf. *Reg. Gaunt*, i. 90; *Pap. Pet.* i. 337, 423, 544; *Pap. Let.* iv. 502.

[3] Gascoigne, 137, on hearsay only. Armitage-Smith, 463, brings forward no rebutting evidence.

[4] *Cal. Pat. Hen. IV*, iv. 324. For Katherine see Kingsford in *D. N. B.* But it is doubtful whether her son, Thomas Swynford (Rymer, viii. 704) murdered Richard II. See Wylie, *Henry IV*, i. 111 f.

[5] So Kingsford in *D. N. B.* l.c.; Armitage-Smith, 462-3, supplies reasons for dating earlier, say in 1371, cf. *ib.* 464.

In 1381 John of Gaunt, in the terror of the Peasants' Revolt, repented of his conduct and withdrew from her company.[1] Not until the 13th January 1396 was she married to the duke at Lincoln,[2] where she was then living. Apart from this Katherine seems to have been a woman of character; at any rate Henry IV in April 1403 openly speaks of her as ' mother '.[3]

As our study of Wyclif's writings has already shown, there were two features in the teaching of the Reformer, the value of which as weapons of party John of Gaunt was not slow to perceive. To Wyclif the secularization of the clergy seemed the great foe against which ' all catholic doctors ' must unite in fight.[4] Accordingly he had demanded that the employment of the clergy in secular business should cease ; ' neither prelates, priests, nor deacons should have secular offices—that is, Chancery, Treasury, Privy Seal, and other such offices in the Exchequer '.[5] In allying himself with the duke to obtain this end Wyclif showed that he was either grossly ignorant of the use that Lancaster made of his ecclesiastical patronage, or else that he had been able to convince himself of the substantial differences "between the case of the man who rose to high ecclesiastical position by keeping the duke's furs and jewels, and the man who rose to the Episcopate by keeping the king's hounds and overseeing his castles ".[6] There were no such refinements in the duke's mind. The principle which inspired his action was clear. He had determined that he would oust the bishops from their places as the chief officers of the Crown, and fill them with creatures of his own. For this purpose Wyclif provided convenient weapons. Wyclif, in writings already published, called on the ' King and witty lords ' to take back by ' process of time ' the endowments of a Church which ' habitually abused them ', that ' the land might be stronger ' and the pressure of taxation lessened. Above all, as Wyclif insisted with wearisome reiteration, by the restoration of the Church to its original poverty, when the priests should live on ' dimes and offerings ', there would be a return to the primitive

---

[1] *Chron. Ang.* 196, 328 ; Walsingham, ii. 42 ; Knighton, ii. 147–8.
[2] *Ann. Ric.* 188.   [3] *Cal. Pat. Hen.* ii. 218.   [4] *Ver. Script.* iii. 163.
[5] Purvey, *Rem.* 2, 154 ; Wyclif, *Blas.* 261. See *supra*, p. 262. In this the lollards had the support of Gascoigne, 21.
[6] Armitage-Smith, 175.

spirituality. About this very time, in addition to the invectives buried in his *de Civili Dominio,* Wyclif published a bitter attack on the prelates. In his *de Daemonio Meridiano,* the date of which would appear to be shortly after the death of the Black Prince, he claims that the prelates and rich clergy by their wealth and worldliness and their consequent neglect of their spiritual duties are sinning against the Holy Trinity as well as ruining the land and robbing the poor of their rights.[1] Nor did Wyclif stand alone. ' Take their lands, ye lords ', called Piers the Plowman ' and let them live by dimes (tithes) '. The duke made Wyclif's scheme of disendowment— ' not robbery but righteous restitution '—peculiarly his own, untrammelled by Wyclif's social aims or spiritual desires, but with far clearer insight into the consequences. He saw his chance of doubling his estates and of gaining over a greedy baronage by the prospect of spoil. So for a few years John of Gaunt and his clique made use of the Reformer and his pen, while Wyclif, either too high-souled to see the selfish aims of his allies, or else so intent on the realization of his ideals that he was willing to avail himself of every weapon that fell into his hands, used their protection to push his doctrines.

Whatever the cause of the alliance, of the fact there can be no doubt. The duke was a man of great ability, and in nothing showed this so much as in his readiness to discover and press into his service the ablest men. Nor should it be forgotten that Wycliffe-on-Tees was in the honor of Richmond, that the duke had been for some years the feudal chief to whom the family of Wyclif would look up. So there may have been local reasons which brought this clever Yorkshireman under the notice of the greatest schemer in Europe. For some years Wyclif had been engaged more or less in the king's service, and there were many opportunities for John of Gaunt to note the value of one who by his career at Oxford as well as by his power of appealing to the people had shown his capacity. The Good Parliament was no sooner dismissed than John of Gaunt, feeling his way to the reversal of its acts, anxious, moreover, to strengthen his position by winning to his side an influential popular leader, on the 22nd September 1376 sent

[1] *Pol. Works,* ii. 417–25.

Alan of Barley with a letter of privy seal to Oxford directing 'Master John Wiclyf, clerk' to appear before the king's council.[1] This seems to have been the beginning of an alliance to which for some years both sides were loyal. The impulsive way in which the alliance began is characteristic of the alliance itself. On the duke's part it was a make-shift expedient; on Wyclif's the grasp of an idealist at an opportunity without due consideration of the loss involved.

We may frankly own that the alliance was a mistake for both parties. If in bringing Wyclif to London Lancaster hoped to win over the support of the people he was mistaken. The hatred of the Londoners for the duke was too deep, their mistrust of his intentions too well-founded, to be lightly laid aside at the behest of Wyclif. While the duke gained little, he consolidated against himself the might of the episcopate, with Courtenay at their head. Moreover the monks, the historians of the times, thought no tale too foul, no treason too incredible, to be ascribed to one who had brought the power of the Crown to the support of an advocate of heresy. In consequence it is somewhat difficult to-day to get a true picture of John of Gaunt. Selfish and unprincipled as we believe him to have been, he was probably a better man than he is represented by the monkish historians. They never forgave him his protection of Wyclif or his attacks on Wykeham. Wyclif on the other hand, by thus allying himself with an unscrupulous politician, lost the support of the people. His movement of reform, which at one time might have become national in scope, became identified with varying cross-currents in politics, and was lowered by its association with the selfish aims of a clique. All that Wyclif gained was the support for a while of the dominant court-party, though even this was lost as soon as it was clear that Wyclif had a deeper aim than the attack upon the wealth of the hierarchy. We may add, to the duke's credit, that, though in later years the alliance was dissolved, he would not allow the Church to take its revenge against his former associate. Through his protection, Wyclif was neither imprisoned nor martyred, but died in peace at Lutterworth.

[1] Devon, 200. Alan received 5s. for this service. 'Barley' is probably the village near Royston.

One other difficulty in this alliance may also be removed. To the reader, looking back on the duke's deeds, it seems inconceivable that Wyclif should have been so out of touch with the work of the Good Parliament that he should have consented to assist in the reversal of its acts. But this is to attribute to Wyclif too great political prescience. From the duke Wyclif would hear nothing of reversals, or of attempts to govern autocratically. Lancaster was too astute to fall into the error that caused the undoing of Richard II. He fell back on an older and more subtle way. Parliaments could be packed and their decisions turned. This was not difficult of accomplishment. What we now call the House of Lords did not really exist; the king summoned to his councils such of the baronage as he felt advisable. As for the Commons, the knights of the shires were nominated at county courts at which few freeholders attended. Contested elections were unknown; the choice was decided by the important men of the county court if not by the sheriff.[1] In one sense " packing " a parliament was so natural a process that it would pass unregarded. By Wyclif and his friends nothing would be noticed that was not customary. All that he would know was that parliament was duly summoned (1 Dec. 1376 [2]). The vast estate of the duke scattered throughout England enabled him to secure that the counties were represented by his friends, retainers, or administrative officers. Lancashire was his; he already held the legal right to nominate its members. Without such sanction he possessed the same power in a score of constituencies. For several parliaments Yorkshire, Derby, Lincoln, Sussex, Kent, Dorset, Wiltshire, and Gloucestershire returned each year an esquire of the duke's retinue, a retainer of his house, a member devoted to his interests or in the pay of the Crown. Of the knights of the shire who had sat in 1376 only eight were returned in 1377.[3] Thus unobtrusively was parliament " packed " by means that Lancaster and his friends would regard as administrative efficiency.

The student, in fact, anxious to do justice to Wyclif's

---

[1] *Eng. Hist. Rev.* v. 154; *Dig. Peer*, i. 329; Pollard, *Evol. Parl.* 111 f.
[2] *Close Rolls*, xiv. 466–7; *Dig. Peer*, iv. 669–71.
[3] *Members*, 193–7; Powell, *Peasants*, 72–3. Cf. *Chron. Ang.* 112 ' pauci qui remanserant '.

position must beware of that great danger to all clear thinking, the reading of the present into the past. The packing of parliament seems to us to-day the crime of crimes. We wonder that the people of the towns did not raise an angry protest, that Wyclif did not show his indignation. All this is to forget that parliament in Wyclif's day was still little more than an ill-defined experiment, in which the House of Commons played but an insignificant part. The future of the institution was hidden from the eyes of all; nor was Wyclif wiser than his age. Democrat though he was, it is not to parliament, least of all the Commons, that he looks for redress of wrong. If he had been reproached he would have replied that he was too anxious to secure results to be able to indulge in dreams or futilities. Like other men in a hurry he chose the longer way. But for this he must not be altogether blamed; parliament itself was largely at fault in its casualness. In Wyclif's day attendance in Parliament, in spite of the wages paid to each member, was looked upon as an irksome duty, from which the fortunate succeeded in obtaining release. It was as much a penalty of position as knighthood became in the fifteenth century. Towns also, which had to find the member's wages, sought every opportunity of escape, and were often successful; though towns which ranked as counties, such as London and later on Bristol, York, Newcastle, Southampton, and Norwich, as well as towns which were equivalent to hundreds, found that their efforts were unavailing.[1] Nor did election for town or county by any means imply attendance, unless there was sufficient inducement of private business or national excitement.

Wyclif's alliance with the duke secured for him for a time the assistance of the friars. Though individual friars may have had cause at Oxford to distrust his reasonings and combat his arguments, nothing as yet had happened to bring the friars and the Reformer into antagonism. At Oxford Wyclif would see the friars at their best, nor, whatever his prejudices, could he have been blind to the part they had played in the intellectual life of the university. We have noted also Wyclif's sympathy with the Franciscan doctrine of evangelical poverty, while his

---

[1] See *Eng. Hist. Rev.* v. 153-4; Pollard, *Evol. Parl.* 154 f.; and for illustrations Rymer, ii. 1063; *Privy Council*, v. 111; *Dig. Peer*, i. 327.

attack upon the wealth of the hierarchy was in complete agreement, theoretically at least, with their tenets.[1] But the friars were the duke's special henchmen. With his usual astuteness he realized the value for his schemes of the assistance of a disciplined army, ceaselessly journeying over the country, which by its public preaching and private confessions secured a great hold on public opinion. Upon all the orders, but especially on his favourite Carmelites, from whose ranks he always chose his confessors, the duke lavished his generosity. In gratitude for his favours, unconscious, possibly, of how far Wyclif would lead them, the friars were willing, at first, to defend the duke's ally in any attack made against him by the seculars.

While Lancaster was thus busy packing his parliament Wyclif, fulfilling his part of the alliance, was engaged in London 'running about from church to church', preaching in such pulpits as were open to him, denouncing in no measured terms the wealth, luxury, and worldliness of the clergy, especially of the episcopate. His alliance with the duke was probably secret as yet,[2] or known only to the few. Wyclif's appeal therefore fell on willing ears. The abuses in the Church against which Wyclif protested had been long apparent; more than half London, not only 'simple citizens' but also from the better classes, openly sympathized with him in his disclosure of corruption, though the evidence of contemporary wills is conclusive that the citizens of substance, though anxious to correct abuses, would not be willing to follow Wyclif in any scheme of church spoliation or evangelical poverty.[3]

Lancaster's packed parliament met on the 27th January 1377, and was opened the next day by Richard, prince of Wales. The members discovered that the ministry had been changed on the eve of their gathering. Adam Houghton, an ally of Lancaster, had been appointed chancellor, and Henry Wakefield bishop of Worcester the treasurer, the duke thus securing for himself if not the silence of the Church, divided counsels

---

[1] Cf. *Chron. Ang.* 116; *infra*, ii. 98.

[2] *Chron. Ang.* 116 states that it was known that he was supported by Lancaster. But this seems improbable, considering that the writer goes on to speak of the help the Londoners gave.

[3] I found this inference on a study of Sharpe, *Wills*, vol. ii, borne out by *Chron. Ang.* 211, Walsingham, i. 380.

among its rulers. Proceedings commenced with a long sermon from Houghton. This, in spite of his protestations of humility, he took care to have recorded on the Rolls. Into this sermon he introduced an eulogy of the duke. Edward, ' a vessel of grace ' who had risen from his sick-bed ' purified from all taint of sin ', had completed his Jubilee. So joyous an event called for liberal subsidies with which to continue the war in France. To sugar the pill Sir Robert Ashton, the chamberlain, followed with an assurance ' that would not lie well in the mouth of a prelate ', that the king was determined to withstand the ' usurpations ' of Rome. Unfortunately the publication a fortnight later (Feb. 15) of the concordat, to which the pope had orally agreed, did not bear out this high claim. The first business of parliament, the election of the Speaker, revealed the changed conditions. Sir Thomas Hungerford of Wiltshire, the duke's seneschal, was elected; the remonstrance of the few at the illegal imprisonment of Sir Peter de la Mare was overborne. The Good Parliament had asked for a committee of peers to be associated with them. John of Gaunt remembered the incident and turned it against the independence of the Commons. Percy, Warwick, and Stafford, former associates of the Commons, who had now been bought over to Lancaster's interests, appeared in the Chapter House to check any tendency to revolt that the lower house might display. In this they were assisted by five other peers and four bishops, the majority of whom—for Courtenay had been carefully excluded—were adherents of the duke, while seven of the twelve had been sureties for Latimer in the last parliament. Under their influence petitions were passed for the restoration of Alice Perrers, of lord Latimer and of the others who had been impeached in the Good Parliament, while a poll-tax was voted of fourpence per head upon every person in the realm, male or female, over the age of fourteen, a tax which bore hardest on the poorest classes.[1]

With no opposition from a muzzled parliament, the duke obtained from the king the grant of two manors for his mistress, Katherine Swynford,[2] and for himself the confirmation of the

[1] *Rot. Parl.* ii. 361 f.; Rymer, iii. 1069 f.; *Chron. Ang.* 113, 130.
[2] *Cal. Pat.* xvi. 433; confirmed, *Pat. Ric.* i. 7.

creation of Lancaster into a county palatine with the same rights as Chester.¹ By this grant John of Gaunt secured a semi-regal jurisdiction, the king merely reserving to himself the parliamentary subsidies, the royal prerogative of pardon, and jurisdiction as a court of supreme appeal ' for correcting errors done or defaults in the courts of the duke '.

§ 2

What Wyclif thought of the doings of Lancaster's puppet parliament and of the levy of the poll-tax we do not know. For that matter he was too busily engaged in his own concerns to have much time for other issues. For the duke, though he could muzzle parliament and secure the services of such bishops as Houghton and Erghum, could not muzzle the Church, and the prelates were infuriated by the attack upon Wykeham. They had also discovered the dangers of Wyclif's views upon endowment and civil jurisdiction. When Convocation met (2 Feb. 1377), Wykeham, though summoned by Courtenay, did not dare to disobey the king's prohibition, so was not in his place. So the bishops refused to proceed to the business of supply until he was restored. Sudbury, in spite of his friendliness with Lancaster, was driven to appeal to the king. Edward, anxious for his subsidy, allowed Wykeham to take his seat.² Encouraged by this success Courtenay determined to push the attack. Lancaster was beyond his reach, but Wyclif, the duke's ally, was vulnerable. At first Sudbury was unwilling to strike. With some of Wyclif's reforms he may have had sympathy, for he was by no means blind to abuses. On his way to Canterbury in 1370, at the time of a Jubilee of Becket, he told a party of pilgrims that the indulgence they sought would be of no avail. His words were received with anger. 'By my soul' retorted an old Kentish knight, Sir Thomas Aldon, ' your life will be ended by a foul death '. As a bishop he was neither non-resident nor neglectful of his

---

¹ Rymer, iii. 1073 (28 Feb. 1377) ; confirmed 10 Nov. 1378 (*Pat. Ric.* i. 284).
² Lowth, 121, 124 ; *Chron. Ang.* 114 f. ; *Reg. Wykeham*, ii. 623 shows that Wykeham was there from Feb. 18 onwards.

duties.¹ But the real power was in stronger hands, who forced him to summon Wyclif to appear before him.

The career of Wyclif's antagonist, William Courtenay, has become part of English history. A brief notice must suffice. The fourth son of Hugh earl of Devon,² connected through his mother Margaret with the royal house, Courtenay was the representative within the Church of the great families which had hitherto ruled England. His sympathies were as his race. For all attempts to alter the old established order in Church or State, and for all innovations in theology or doctrine, Courtenay would have nothing but abhorrence or contempt. In his antagonism to John of Gaunt he represented the resentment of the old nobility against the statecraft of Edward III in creating royal fiefs. But loyal Churchman as he ever proved, Courtenay was no pliant tool of the papacy. When it came to the rights of England he was fully prepared to take a proper stand.

As might be expected, Courtenay's promotion in the Church had been rapid. On the 20th March 1362, when but twenty years of age, he had been given a prebend in York valued at £40. In addition he held other benefices bringing in £134 13s. 4d. a year. In 1367 he had been elected chancellor of Oxford, the first to assert the independence of that honour from the recognition of the bishop of Lincoln. On the 17th August 1369 he was appointed by Urban V to the bishopric of Hereford. As he was only twenty-eight years of age a formal dispensation was necessary. Courtenay was enthroned on the 15th September 1370; but apart from a number of ordinations, many of them connected with Devonshire, made by him on bishop Brantingham's request, his register shows few signs of any activity. For the most part he was an absentee. In spite of his high birth he found considerable difficulty in paying to the curia the firstfruits and other charges, and had to obtain a special dispensation of postponement. From Hereford on the 12th September 1375 he was transferred to London. There he showed his colours by his excommunication at the pope's bidding of the Florentine

---

¹ *Chron. Ang.* 117; *Ang. Sac.* i. 49; *Vict. Co. Essex*, ii. 17; Wilkins, iii. 120.
² For Hugh's will, proved 16 June 1377, see *Reg. Brant.* i. 381–2. He left the bishop, ' mon treshonure fitz ', a buckle of sapphires and pearls.

merchants in the city. For this he had been censured by the Crown. He now entered upon a larger quarrel and determined to put down Wyclif and his teaching.[1]

Wyclif had been cited to appear before the bishops on the afternoon of Thursday, the 19th February 1377.[2] In the week that intervened after the summons was served Lancaster took all the steps necessary for his defence.[3] The duke realized that the attack was as much on himself as on the Reformer. He therefore retained four Oxford friars, one from each order. 'It was not a difficult task' adds the chronicler, 'to compel the friars for they were anxious to assist' one who had 'a natural hatred of the possessioners'. To add authority to their learning Wyclif and the friars 'with incredible pride' were accompanied by the duke himself and by Henry Percy, who had just been appointed the king's marshall. The cathedral was crowded, for the hour was 'a little after noon',[4] and St. Paul's nave was not only the Fop's Ally of the day, but the regular mart and exchange of merchants and lawyers. With difficulty Percy forced a way through the London citizens to the Lady Chapel where the bishops were sitting. Courtenay, protesting against his roughness, declared that he would never have admitted Percy's men if he had known that they would thus behave. Hearing the altercation the duke replied that Percy should discharge his duty.

On reaching the Lady Chapel Percy and the duke seated themselves, and Percy bade Wyclif follow their example. 'Since you have much to reply', he urged, 'you will need the softer seat'. Courtenay, taking the lead out of the hands of Sudbury, protested that the accused must stand, and in spite of the duke, carried his point. Lancaster thereupon uttered threats: he would bring down the pride of all the bishops of

[1] Capes, *Reg. Courtenay* (1913) passim; Eubel, i. 324; *Arch. Jour.* lxxi. 150; *Reg. Grand.* iii. 1260; *Chron. Ang.* 110-11.

[2] For this section see *Chron. Ang.* 117-34 (copied by Foxe, ii. 800), 397-8; Walsingham, i. 325-6. Narratives written before the publication of *Chron. Ang.* are of little value, and, as Lewis 50 f., wrongly dated 1378. Feb. 19 only fell on a Thursday (so the chroniclers) in 1377.

[3] Buddensieg wrongly refers, *Pol. Works*, i. 227 n., to this. But its date is 1383, not 1377 as Buddensieg. It refers to Lancaster's continued shelter of Wyclif. See *infra*, ii. 296.

[4] 'post nonam', not as Lechler 160 'at nine'. There had already been a morning sitting of parliament (Loserth, *Civ. Dom.* iv. p. x n.).

LADY CHAPEL IN OLD ST. PAUL'S

From the engraving by W. Hollar

England; Courtenay must not trust in his parents, for they would have enough to do to take care of themselves. Courtenay answered that his trust was in God. Angered by this dignified retort Lancaster, if we may believe our report, threatened to drag him out by the hair of his head. At this point the assembly broke up in confusion. Courtenay was popular in London, so much so that nine months later (4 Dec. 1378) a letter was sent to the pope by the citizens requesting that Courtenay be not made a cardinal, lest the city should be deprived of his influence, a request renewed in the following April and May.[1] But the break-up of the council was not so much because the Londoners resented this insult to their bishop, or were hostile to Wyclif, or even because of their general hatred of the duke, as because news reached them of an attempt made a few hours before against their liberties. The morning of the trial the king's ministers had introduced into parliament a bill, the object of which was to take the government of London out of the hands of the mayor, and entrust it to a captain chosen by the court. The bill also proposed extending to the city the jurisdiction of the king's marshal, lord Percy, who already had aroused the wrath of the citizens by his imprisonment of a certain Londoner called Prenting.[2] The intention was to revert to the method of former days when kings had punished London by taking it over into their own hands and entrusting its governance to ' improvers '[3]—an early example of the use of words to conceal intention. But as there were now parliaments to be considered, the means employed must be more subtle. So a bill to this effect was entrusted to Percy and to John of Gaunt's younger brother, Thomas of Woodstock, who had recently come of age. On hearing of the outrage the crowd in the cathedral with cries of vengeance broke in upon Lancaster's guard and rescued their bishop, while Wyclif was carried off by his supporters. The devil, adds the chronicler, knew how to save his own. " What Wyclif thought of it all we can never guess. Whether he had wished the duke to accompany him must remain a

[1] Sharpe, *Letter-Book H*, 116–17 ; cf. Walsingham, i. 382.
[2] Nicholas, *Chron. Lond.* 70.
[3] See for 1293 *Chron. Ed. I and II*, i. 102 ; for 1321 *ib.* 291 ; for 1366 Sharpe, *Letter-Book G*, 205 ; Kingsford, *Chron. Lond.* 14 ; and for 1392 *Letter-Book H*, 385–7.

mystery. He does not mention the scene in any of his works, though he speaks much of his later persecutions. In the roaring crowd of infuriated lords, bishops, and citizens he stood silent, and stands silent still." [1]

The next day, as the citizens were considering (probably in the Guildhall, which then existed on the same site as now) [2] what steps should be taken in defence of their liberties, two lords, Sir Guy de Bryan and Walter Fitzwalter, appeared in their assembly. They were both men of considerable influence. Bryan,[3] who came of a South Wales family, had acted for years as king Edward's secretary. He had also served as admiral of the fleet westward.[4] Fitzwalter belonged to one of the most ancient families in England. His ancestor, Robert, had been the leader of the barons in their struggle for the Great Charter. Fitzwalter also claimed to be hereditary standard-bearer to the City ' in fee for the chastilarie which he and his ancestors had by Castle Baynard '.[5] He was also lord of many manors in Essex and East Anglia. As ' chief bannerer ' of London he held ' a great franchise within the city, that is to say that when the mayor will hold a great council he had the right to be summoned '. He now claimed that as he was the leader of the citizens when at war it was his duty to help them. When the two first appeared the citizens could scarcely be restrained from attacking them, for they were known partisans of Lancaster,[6] Fitzwalter, in fact, laying down his life in Lancaster's Castilian crusade ' on the Wednesday before Michelmas ', 1386.[7] Moreover, Fitzwalter's claim for franchises in Castle Baynard had been rebutted by the mayor and council in 1347, and the citizens suspected that his offer was an indirect method of asserting a rejected position.[8] But it turned out that as owners of considerable property in London

---

[1] Trevelyan, 45.   [2] *Eng. Hist. Rev.* iii. 156–7.
[3] For his family see *Collect. Top.* iii. 250 f. See also *supra*, p. 165. For his will, proved in 1386, *ib.* iii. 253. For his monument at Tewkesbury see Stothard, *Mon. Eff.* 73.
[4] *Close Rolls Ed.* xiii. 226 ; *Cal. Pat. Ed.* xv. 104.
[5] For the Fitzwalters see Appendix J.
[6] Sir Guy had been one of the executors of Humphrey de Bohun (proved 16 May 1373), whose heiress married John of Gaunt's son, Henry IV. See Gibbons, 34.
[7] *Cal. Pat.* iii. 287.
[8] Sharpe, *Letter-Book F.* 169 ; Riley, *Mem. Lond.* 236.

their sympathies, at any rate their interests, were with the citizens. So after the two had been duly sworn they were allowed to take their seats and tell their tale. They had come, said Fitzwalter, to warn the council that Percy, anticipating the passage of the bill, had already taken up his duties and imprisoned a man in the marshal's residence. Immediately there was a call to arms and a rush to Percy's house in Aldersgate.[1] The prisoner was released, the stocks to which he had been fastened burnt, while search was made in all the cupboards and cellars for the marshal. Fortunately for Percy he was dining with the duke at the house of Sir John Ypres. Ypres, whose name shows his Flemish origin, was one of London's merchant princes, the steward of the king's household, late controller of his wardrobe,[2] and at one time Constable of the High Peak. He had recently purchased Edward's goodwill by his grant to Alice Perrers of his castle and manor of Moorend in Northamptonshire. On the king's death he was one of his executors.[3] When the news of the riot was brought by one of Lancaster's retinue, Percy and the duke abandoned their dinner—'circumstantes ostreas' adds the monk, thinking of the toothsome bivalves which they could not stay to eat,[4]— the duke barking his shins in his haste, and hurried across the river to Kennington, where they took refuge with the Prince of Wales and his widowed mother, Joan of Kent.

Meanwhile the mob, believing that Lancaster had fled to his own palace, swept out of the city gates to the Savoy, the magnificent residence for a century of the earls of Lancaster.[5] On their way they met a priest who was so foolish as to revile as a traitor Peter de la Mare, who still languished in Notting-

[1] Stow, *Survey*, i. 309; ii. 343. Armitage-Smith, 153 wrongly speaks of the prisoner as in the Marshalsea. But see Stow, ii. 61–2.

[2] *Eng. Hist. Rev.* xxiv. 503 from Feb. 1368 to Nov. 1376.

[3] Rymer, iii. 1080. 'Ypres inn' was in the Vintry (Stow, *Survey*, i. 246–7). The founder of the family came over in 1138. For other details see Dugdale, *Baronage*, i. 612; *Archaeol.* xxii. 261 *n.*; *Dep. Keeper's Rep.* xxxii. 347; *Cal. Pat.* xv. 152, 192; xvi. 296, 399, 477.

[4] *Chron. Ang.* 123; information from a house-porter.

[5] The Savoy was built in 1245 by Peter of Savoy, the uncle of queen Eleanor, who purchased it for her son Edmund, earl of Lancaster. It was burnt in the Peasants' Revolt of 1381 and made into a hospital. See Stow, ii. 92 f.; W. J. Loftie, *Memorials of the Savoy* (1878); *Jour. Brit. Arch. Soc.* (n. s.), iii. 221–31.

ham gaol. Him they beat to death, and would have burnt the Savoy to the ground had not Courtenay, who had hastened after the mob, succeeded in dissuading them. But the duke's retainers, who had formerly swaggered through the streets under the protection of his badge, were glad to escape by tearing away the dangerous collars and hiding them in their sleeves. One knight of his retinue, a Scot by birth, Sir John Swynton,[1] too brave or too proud to hide his allegiance, was mauled by the mob and would have suffered worse had not the mayor delivered him.

The sympathies of Joan, judging from the names of the executors of her will, were with the party of Wyclif.[2] On hearing from Lancaster and Percy of the riot she sent three of her knights to act as mediators. The deputation was skilfully chosen. Sir Aubrey de Vere belonged to a family devoted to Richard's interests.[3] Sir Simon Burley, who in June 1380 was made the young king's tutor, lost his life through his zeal for his master in Richard's struggle for absolute power,[4] while Sir Lewis Clifford was known to have lollard sympathies. The three knights found the task of conciliation difficult. Both sides were very angry. The duke, acting through his brother Thomas of Woodstock, the constable,[5] and Percy, the marshal, had petitioned the king to summon the mayor, Adam Stable and the sheriffs, one of whom was the noted John of Northampton, before the council to answer on the following Monday (Feb. 23) for their conduct. Whether through the mediation of Joan's knights, or because of the dangerous temper of the citizens, at the last moment (Sunday, Feb. 22) the summons was postponed until Saturday, while the mayor

[1] Not 'Thomas' as *Chron. Ang.* 125, nor 'Wynton' as Foxe, ii. 920. On 12 Feb. 1372 he was indentured to the duke 'for peace or war for the term of his life', *Reg. Gaunt*, i. 299; ii. 5.

[2] In A. Strickland, *Queens of England* (1857), i. 599 exaggerated into "a convert of Wyclif". For her will, proved 9 Dec. 1385, see Nicolas, *Test. Vet.* i. 13–15. Among her executors were Clifford, John Clanvowe, Richard Stury, and William Neville, all four suspected of lollardy (*infra*, ii. c. x).

[3] *D. N. B.* In 1393 on the death of his nephew, the duke of Ireland, he became the tenth earl of Oxford (*Rot. Parl.* iii. 304).

[4] *D. N. B.* Beheaded 5 March 1388 (*ib.* iii. 243; Walsingham, ii. 174).

[5] *D. N. B.* Better known as duke of Gloucester. He was constable in right of his wife, Eleanor, the co-heiress of de Bohun. Appointed constable temporarily on 10 June 1376 (*Cal. Pat.* xvi. 279, 339, 355, 408; confirmed, *Pat. Ric.* i. 28).

issued orders for maintaining peace in the City. On the following Friday the summons was again postponed for another week.[1] While parliament and convocation were sitting there was no other option. The citizens were firm : Wykeham and Sir Peter de la Mare must have a fair trial. They added that ' they would have the traitor wherever he was found ', a threat which the duke interpreted to refer to himself. At last pacific counsels prevailed. The bill against the liberties of the City was withdrawn ; a deputation of the citizens, headed, not by the mayor, but by the eminent patriot Sir John Philipot, was graciously received by the king, in spite of the efforts to prevent it of the duke, who pleaded the king's sickness. Edward assured them that so far from desiring to take away their rights ' he was prepared to increase them '. As they retired, the citizens met in the antechamber Lancaster himself. Courteous words were exchanged ; the deputation promised that the guilty should be punished if they could be found, but professed that they could make no definite terms without a further mandate. The leading citizens, anxious to separate themselves from the mob, even took the duke's side when he requested the bishops—for convocation was still sitting—to excommunicate the anonymous authors of the lampoons against him that were posted about the City. After some hesitation, whether due to resentment at the treatment of Wykeham or because they feared the City, the bishops agreed, and the excommunications were duly issued by the duke's henchman, John Gilbert. Here again we might ask what Wyclif thought of the matter, for the use of excommunication for other than spiritual causes was one of the abuses against which no one had thundered more stoutly than himself.

These anonymous excommunications were but the beginning of retaliation. To obtain his subsidy from the clergy Edward had allowed the return of Wykeham. But as soon as convocation—which ' feared the duke more than it feared God '—had voted the poll-tax, the bishops discovered that Lancaster had managed to keep Wykeham's name out of the general amnesty proclaimed in honour of the king's jubilee.[2] On the 2nd March parliament broke up, and the duke was unfettered. The

[1] *Letter-Book H,* 47, 56–7.　　[2] *Rot. Parl.* ii. 364–5 ; *Statutes,* i. 397.

mayor and sheriffs were forced to appear before the king at Sheen. They found Edward propped up in a chair, scarcely able to speak. The civic fathers put in the plea that the insult to the king's son was the work of the apprentices. This was not accepted, and on Saturday the 21st March the mayor, Adam Stable, and the sheriffs were deprived of their posts,[1] and a new mayor elected the same day.[2] The proposal of the duke that as a recompense for the mob's reversal of his arms in Cheapside—the common procedure for condemned traitors— a marble pillar to display the said arms should be erected, 'well and comely metalled, to continue for all time' was not entertained. The new mayor, Sir Nicholas Bembre, a known opponent of Lancaster, organized a procession, nominally in the duke's honour. Great candles were borne, carrying the duke's arms,[3] the usual method of commemorating the dead. The citizens turned the grim jest into a farce by staying at home.

Possibly it was this last insult—or, if we may trust the embittered chronicler, the refusal of the City to make the duke a present of jewels and of 100 tuns of wine as the price of reconciliation—which led the council to carry out on Sunday the 5th June their oft postponed summons to the city officials to appear before them to answer for the riot. 'On which day the mayor, aldermen and certain persons deputed by the commonalty' duly appeared and 'raised a number of exceptions for quashing' the summons. As these were 'not allowed' they asked for a postponement until 'Monday week' that they might 'consider their answer'. Edward was now too ill to continue the struggle, and had already decided on a further postponement until Michaelmas. Before the new date came Edward was dead. As the old man was passing away—he died about 7 p.m. on the 21st June—a new deputation, with Philipot as the spokesman, waited upon the Prince of Wales at Kennington.[4] After condoling with the boy on the approaching decease they recommended the City of London—'your

---

[1] *Chron. Ang.* 131 f.; Rymer, iii. 1076; *Close Rolls*, iv. 486.
[2] *Letter-Book H*, 57, 60-1; Gairdner, *Three Chrons.* 47.
[3] In *Chron. Ang.* 133 the procession is attributed to the king.
[4] *Letter-Book H*, 57; *Close Rolls*, xiv. 556; *Chron. Ang.* 146-50. Walsingham, i. 329-31 (MSS., followed by Armitage-Smith, 186, wrongly read Kingston).

chamber'¹—to the prince's favour, and begged him to assist in securing a reconciliation with Lancaster. The next day Richard sent a message informing the City of his grandfather's death, and assuring them of his good intentions. So a few days later the deputation waited on Richard at Sheen, and there in the presence of the dead king, of Joan the queen-mother, and of many bishops, the reconciliation of Lancaster and the City was completed. In proof thereof, the duke 'kissed each and all' of the deputation 'in presence of the king'. As a further seal, Peter de la Mare was set free from Nottingham castle, Wykeham came back to his own, while Richard the 'Londoners' king'² took up his abode in the Tower for his coronation. The Golden Age would have returned, had not the French on the 29th June taken advantage of the confusion to sack Rye and attack Winchelsea.

§ 3

While the City was thus struggling with the duke and the nation was watching the passing of the Crown, another blow had been struck at Wyclif, this time from Rome itself. Wyclif had been accused at the papal court, probably by some of his Oxford opponents. They had forwarded to the curia about fifty conclusions³ which seemed to them blameworthy. Out of these the pope selected eighteen, and on the 22nd May 1377⁴, in the basilica of S. Maria Maggiore in Rome, Gregory issued a series of bulls against the Reformer.⁵ Gregory either had not been informed of the attempted trial of the Reformer at

---

¹ A common name for London. Cf. Kingsford, *Chron. Lond.* 114, 115; Sharpe, *London*, i. 276-7. Bristol was called the 'Queen's chamber', R. Ricart, *The Maire of Bristowe is Kalendar*, ed. L. T. Smith (1872), 54, 65.

² Sharpe, *op. cit.* i. 212; Walsingham, i. 370; *Chron. Ang.* 149, 200.

³ So *Chron. Ang.*, App. 396.

⁴ Not 30 May as Wood, *Univ.* i. 493; Shirley, *op. cit.*, p. xxviii, who follows a bad reading of ii for xi in *ib.* 244. The date for all was the same 'undecimo Kal. Jun'.

⁵ For these see Walsingham, i. 345-53; *Chron. Ang.* 173-81; Wilkins, iii. 116-18 (who omits those to Oxford and to Edward III); Lewis, 46-9, 254-64; Foxe, iii. 4-7 (who gives the addition that the articles were condemned at Rome by twenty-three cardinals, really a mistaken interpretation of Walsingham, i. 325, that twenty-three conclusions were condemned). In all, the order of the bulls is misleading. *Ziz.* 242-4 gives the Oxford bull, misdated by Netter as 1376 (Shirley's approval, *ib.* 244 *n.* 17, is corrected in his preface, xxviii *n.*). The Oxford bull is partly translated in Wood, *Univ.* i. 494.

St. Paul's, or else his informants had suggested that the failure was due to slackness, as Walsingham hints, on the part of the bishops or of Sudbury himself. Whatever the reason Gregory does not spare his admonitions. ' Now it is plain ', he writes,

' that in that very kingdom which used to produce men endued with a right knowledge of the scriptures, grave, devout champions of the orthodox faith, there are now those who though by their office they ought to be watchmen are yet slothfully negligent, insomuch that the latent motions and open attempts of the enemies are perceived at Rome, situated at a great distance, before they are opposed in England '.

Gregory goes on to state

' that he had heard with much concern on the information of several persons very worthy of credence that John Wyclif rector of Luttelworth [1] professor of divinity—would that he were not a master of errors!—had rashly proceeded to such detestable degree of madness, as not to be afraid to assert, dogmatize, and publicly to preach propositions erroneous and false, contrary to the faith, and that threaten to weaken and overthrow the status of the whole church.'

Gregory therefore forwards a schedule of eighteen [2] erroneous ' propositions and conclusions ', and requires the archbishop and bishop ' or one of them '—a clause added, possibly, to guard against Sudbury's indifference—to inform themselves privately as to whether Wyclif taught such theses. If they found that Wyclif did so,

' they should cause the said John Wyclif to be arrested by our authority and laid in gaol and should endeavour to obtain his confession. This confession, and whatever the said John shall say or write by way of induction or proof of the same propositions, they should transmit to him sealed with their own seals, and disclosed to nobody. Further they should keep the said John in faithful custody in chains until they should receive further orders concerning the matter.'

A second bull, addressed also to Sudbury and Courtenay, contains only a supplement to the principal bull. It states what course must be taken should Wyclif obtain secret intelligence of the threatened process, and save himself by flight from imprisonment. To meet this the two prelates are commissioned

---

[1] So in all the five bulls. In *Chron. Ang.* the spelling is corrected, but not consistently.

[2] In Walsingham, i. 353–5 there are nineteen. But no. 7 should be omitted, as in the *Protestatio* and *Libellus*. See *infra*, p. 311.

to issue at Oxford and elsewhere a citation to Wyclif to present himself in person before Gregory XI within three months.

Historians have not always realized the inwardness of these bulls. They are more than an attack upon Wyclif, or an attempt to come to the rescue of Courtenay. They constitute a deliberate effort to establish in England the papal inquisition. By the law of the land the ecclesiastical courts administered by the bishops had full jurisdiction in all charges of heretical pravity, nor were the secular courts slow to come to their assistance. Gregory here claimed that the jurisdiction should be transferred to himself, that Wyclif should be arrested and imprisoned on a papal warrant, and that his trial should take place at Rome itself. Such a claim was as novel as it was dangerous. If once admitted, the papal inquisition would have secured that recognition in England for which during three centuries it had sought in vain. England in the next two hundred years attempted to crush out heresy, as we see in the later history of the lollards. But the attempt was made by using the ecclesiastical courts and the statute law of the realm, never once by means of the papal inquisition or by papal warrant. Only once did the papal inquisition succeed in establishing itself in England, and that was, by the connivance of Edward II, for the trial of the Templars.[1]

Gregory's attack on Wyclif closely followed an attack he had made on the Waldenses. These humble sectaries, between whom and Wyclif there was no historical link, held doctrines very similar to those professed in later years by Wyclif's followers. Their persecution had been continuous ever since their origin under Peter Waldo of Lyons. But Gregory XI, dissatisfied with the progress made in stamping them out in Provence, Dauphiny, and the Lyonnais, now issued edict after edict. Kings, nobles, and prelates were scolded for their indifference, while a host of friars spread over the land to convert the people. Soon the prisons were so insufficient for the number of captives that Gregory caused new ones to be built at Avignon, Embrun, and Vienne. The expense, 4,000 gold florins, was levied upon negligent bishops, as also the 800

---

[1] Lea, iii. 299 f., and for the trial itself, *ib.* ii. 238–43; *Eng. Hist. Rev.* iii. 149 f.; xxiv. 432–47; *Chron. Ed. I and II*, i. 179–98.

florins a year for the support of the prisoners. But as this proved inadequate to feed the thousands in his dungeons Gregory had final resource to the sale of an indulgence (15 Aug. 1376) so that 'these prisoners shall not starve but shall have time for repentance in the said prisons'.[1] Fresh from these triumphs on the continent, Gregory now turned to crush a more dangerous foe by the use of methods and procedure recognized abroad but illegal in England.

The question of the identity of the accusers of Wyclif has been keenly debated. Foxe considered that it was the English bishops,[2] but if so it were difficult to explain Gregory's castigation of the bishops and his ignorance of Wyclif's trial at St. Paul's. Moreover, in his *Protestatio* Wyclif expressly states that report was sent to Rome 'per pueros'. Lewis[3] argued that the appeal was made by monks and friars. But though Wyclif for some time had been engaged in controversy with the Franciscan, Woodford, his quarrel with the friars had not yet begun; they had stood by his side at St. Paul's, nor is it likely that Woodford would have acted independently of his order. In his *de Ecclesia* Wyclif tells us that suspicion was cast upon 'Thomas Brunton, bishop of Rochester, and his brethren', but in a later sermon he throws the blame for the report of one of the clauses, the fourth, upon a 'canis niger' and his 'whelps'. This clause was misrepresented 'altogether idiotically' and in consequence was condemned.[4] Brunton, it is true, was a Benedictine, but the manuscripts give the name of the reporter as 'Tolstanus' or 'Colstanus', which the commentators give up as unmeaning. We are inclined to regard the words as a corruption of 'Boldon' and to refer to the Benedictine, Uhtred Boldon. We do so the more confidently because Wyclif hints that the appeal was made from Oxford by 'disciples of Antichrist' and a certain 'doctor mixtim theologus'.[5] We are confirmed in this belief when we find that in a third bull directed to Oxford Gregory

---

[1] For this persecution see Lea, ii. 147–56.
[2] Foxe, iii. 4, followed by Lechler, 163; Shirley, *Ziz.* xxvii.
[3] Lewis, 42.
[4] *Eccles*, 354; Walsingham, i. 354; *Ziz.* 247; *Serm.* iii. 189.
[5] Walsingham, i. 357; *Ziz.* 483; *Civ. Dom.* ii. 1. Loserth's idea that it was Woodford (*ib.* iv. p. xi) is a mistake.

'wonders and laments that through a sort of sloth and laziness they have permitted tares to spring up in the glorious field of their university and, what is more pernicious, to grow ripe without applying any care to root them out.'

Gregory therefore warned the university, upon pain of the loss of all their privileges, to guard against the setting forth of erroneous doctrines. He ordered the chancellor to arrest Wyclif and his followers, and to deliver them over to the pope's commissioners, Sudbury and Courtenay.

That the pope or his advisers realized the seriousness of the attempt that they were making to introduce into England the papal inquisition and to secure the arrest of an English subject on a papal writ is shown by the efforts they made to win over the authorities to support their action. In a bull addressed to Sudbury and Courtenay the two prelates are urged to bring the matter before the king, his sons and kindred, before Joan, and the English nobility, by means of 'doctors and men skilled in the Sacred Letters, who are not defiled with these errors, but are sincere and fervent in the faith'. The method they must use is clearly set out. They must convince the authorities that Wyclif's 'Conclusions are not only erroneous with respect to the faith; but that they infer an utter destruction of all polity and government'. Finally a letter was addressed to the king himself. Gregory commends the kingdom over which his majesty ruled as glorious in power and riches but more illustrious for its piety and the defenders of the faith whom it has produced. He urges Edward to give his favour and protection to his commissioners in their prosecution of Wyclif, who is seeking 'to overthrow the status of the whole Church' by teaching identical with the 'opinions and ignorant doctrine of Marsiglio of Padua and John of Jandun [1] of cursed memory' already condemned by John XXII.

A study of Gregory's schedule of Wyclif's errors [2] shows that these 'Conclusions' were taken for the most part, some of

---

[1] In Wood, *Univ.* i. 494 as in the older texts of Walsingham we find 'Gandavo', which Wood, Foxe, iii. 5, translate as 'John of Gaunt of unworthy memory'.

[2] Best studied in Wyclif's *Protestatio* (see *infra*, p. 311) or *Ziz.* 245–57. Short summaries as appended to the bull in Walsingham, i. 353–5; *Chron. Ang.* 181–2.

them word for word, from Wyclif's *de Civili Dominio*.¹ They are concerned with the politics and not the theology of the Church. The grouping is in itself a clever indictment. The first five were intended to impress upon court circles the revolutionary nature of Wyclif's contention that dominion was founded on grace. Four others set forth Wyclif's claim that under certain circumstances the endowments of the Church may be secularized by the lords temporal.² Nine others ³ deal with the limits of church discipline, especially the contention that struck at the heart of the whole ecclesiastical system, that 'it is not possible for a man to be excommunicated unless he has previously excommunicated himself'.⁴ Of equal importance was Wyclif's attack upon the pope's power of the keys, as only valid when it is used ' in conformity with the law of Christ',⁵ while excommunication should be restricted to 'the cause of God' and never be used for obtaining temporal goods and revenues.⁶ Absolution from every sin is within the prerogative of every lawfully ordained priest.⁷ The last thesis, skilfully put at the end and not at the beginning, would seem to the pope the worst: that every ecclesiastic, 'even the Roman pontiff, may be lawfully set right and even impleaded by subjects and laymen'. Wyclif's later defence of this thesis, that it is a necessary consequence of the pope being 'our peccable brother', for whose backsliding into heterodoxy

---

¹ e. g. article 1 from *l.c.* 251 ; 2 and 3 from *l.c.* 252 ; 5 from *l.c.* 253 ; 6 from *l.c.* 267 ; 7 and 8 from *l.c.* 255, 269, 274. Article 4 is in *ib.* 1 where it forms the text for many chapters. Articles 9 and 10 *ib.* 275–6 ; 11 *ib.* 277 ; 12 *ib.* 279 ; 13 is in *ib.* 283 ; 14 and 15 *ib.* 284. The first thesis has often been misinterpreted. It runs as follows ' Totum genus humanum, citra Christum, non habet potestatem simpliciter ordinandi ut Petrus et omne genus suum dominetur politice in perpetuum super mundum '. (As printed in Walsingham, i. 354 there is a misleading semi-colon at ' ordinandi '. Walsingham also reads ' ut Petrus, ut omne '. Comparison should be made with Wyclif's *Protestatio*, Walsingham, i. 357 to obtain the true reading.) Lewis 42 followed by Vaughan and others referred this article to ecclesiastical jurisdiction, understanding ' Petrus et omne genus ' to refer to the apostle and his successors. But to say nothing of using ' genus ' for ' successores ' (Lechler, 166 *n.*), Wyclif often uses ' Petrus ' as well as ' Paulus ' for ' John Doe and Richard Roe ', e. g. *Ver. Script.* i. 128, 328 ; *Dom. Div.* 9. In *Civ. Dom.* i. 39 ' Linus ' is the judge in the imaginary lawsuit of ' Peter ' and ' Paul '. *Civ. Dom.* i. 251 is conclusive for this general sense to be the one here. In Wyclif's *Protestatio* the whole stress is thrown upon ' perpetual political dominion '.

² Articles 6, 7, 17, 18 ; cf. *Civ. Dom.* i. c. 37.
³ Articles 8–16. ⁴ No. 9. ⁵ 15.
⁶ 10, 12, 13 ; cf. *op. cit.* i. 307, 355. ⁷ Article 16.

there is full provision in the *Decretum* of Gratian, would not make the contention sound better.¹

Before Edward could receive the pope's letter he had passed away at Sheen. Richard, his grandson, ' a lad eleven years and fair among men as another Absolom ',² reigned in his stead. Edward's death—possibly in the ' great bed ' purchased in 1370 for £254, whose curtains had recently been ' ornamented ' at a cost of £44 ³—was in keeping with the last years of his life. ' The glory and worship ' of his early years, when ' he passed all men in high joy and blessedness ', had ended in a miserable old age when

' all those joyful and blessed things, good fortune and prosperity, decreased and misshaped. And unfortunate things and unprofitable harms, with many evils, began for to spring and continued long time after '.⁴

Until the end came Edward, ' as if he would live for ever ', continued his frivolous talks with his mistress. Almost his last political act had been to restore the temporalities of his see to Wykeham (June 18).⁵ This might be counted to him for decency had it not been due to the influence of Alice Perrers, with whom Wykeham had come to terms, in spite of Lancaster's opposition.⁶ But in thus treating with the all-powerful mistress Wykeham was only following the example of pope Gregory XI. " Should a bishop be more punctilious than the pope himself ? " ⁷ In his last hours Edward's ' Caesarean ' bishops neglected him. Only one nameless priest urged the dying king

---

¹ Walsingham, i. 362 ; cf. *Civ. Dom.* i. cc. 38–9 ; pp. 414 ; iv. 398, 404.
² Usk, *Chron.* 1, 43.
³ Devon, 192, 207. For his funeral expenses see *Archaeol.* lx. 532.
⁴ Cf. *Chron. Ang.*, App. 401. See the excellent character sketch in *Brut* ii. 333–4.
⁵ *Cal. Pat.* xvi. 483 ; Rymer, iii. 1079 ; *Close Rolls*, xiv. 504.
⁶ *Chron. Ang.* 136–7. The evidence of a writer so favourable to Wykeham seems to me conclusive ; though of course it shocks all good Wykehamists (Lowth, 132). The objection of Trevelyan, 358, that Wykeham would not seek the aid of Alice when the king was dying is pointless, for some time would elapse between his seeking her aid and her securing the grant, especially as Lancaster was opposed. Wykeham and Alice had business dealings as far back as Dec. 1374 (*Times Lit. Suppl.*, 3 July 1919, p. 364).
⁷ Armitage-Smith, 185. On 28 Sept. 1371 Gregory XI wrote to Alice, among others, including Wykeham, on behalf of his brother Roger Beaufort, who was a prisoner in the hands of John Grailly, the captal of Buch (*Pap. Let.* iv. 96).

—for his death seems to have been unexpected—that he should seek forgiveness. His confession was broken by a sob. 'Jesu, have mercy!' cried the king, and became silent. Before all was over Alice Perrers stole the rings from his fingers and slipped away. Many of his jewels had already vanished.[1]

§ 4

As soon as possible the name of the new king was substituted for that of Edward, and the pope's letter presented.[2] But for some time neither king nor archbishop had time to attend to the bulls, much to the disgust of Walsingham. Sudbury and even Courtenay—who, along with Erghum and ten laymen had been formally appointed to be the king's counsellors[3]— were fully aware of the opposition that would be aroused by any attempt to proceed on the lines indicated by the pope. The bishops had already secured one victory, in the formal pardon, soon after the young king's accession, of Wykeham.[4] The times were too critical to start a struggle between Rome and the realm; at any rate Sudbury did nothing and kept back the bull addressed to Oxford university. He could plead the manifold business that a new reign involved, and the need of waiting until after the meeting of parliament. It would be more easy then to discern which way the wind was blowing; in any event there would be ample time for safe action after parliament was dissolved.

Richard's first parliament met at Westminster on the 13th October. It showed at once that it intended to revert to the policy of the Good Parliament. Much in fact had happened to deepen the general disgust. In fear of invasion men were busy everywhere fortifying even such inland cities as Bath and Salisbury. For three months the French had been in possession of the Channel, the isles of Wight and Man overrun, Rye, Hastings, and Rottendean sacked, Gravesend burned. On the Continent much of Gascony had been devastated, while

---

[1] *Chron. Ang.* 142–6; Walsingham, i. 327–9; *Cal. Pat. Ric.* i. 144.
[2] Walsingham, i. 352 *n.* 4, 356.
[3] 20 July; *Cal. Pat.* i. 19; *Rot. Parl.* iii. 386; Rymer, iv. 10.
[4] 31 July 1377. Confirmed at the request of parliament, 4 Dec. 1377, *Rot. Parl.* iii. 387; Rymer, iv. 25; *Cal. Pat.* i. 87.

the English fleet which had been sent to attack the Castilians at Sluys was scattered by the November gales. A petty war on the Scots borders added to the national danger. Money was urgently needed, for the proceeds of the poll-tax had not reached expectations. In his ponderous opening address Sudbury informed the Commons that the government had never been in greater straits. The Commons were not slow to grasp their opportunity. After hearing and applauding a speech from the duke, in which he protested against the rumours insinuating his treason, they chose the duke's victim, Sir Peter de la Mare, to be their Speaker. They then laid before the king three petitions, the third of which—that measures proposed in parliament should not be altered or repealed without the consent of parliament—in reality involved the doctrine of ministerial responsibility.[1] To the granting of this petition the Lords demurred, as trenching on the royal prerogative. But the Commons, pleased with the concession that during the king's minority the officers of state should be chosen by Parliament, gratified also by the promise that Alice Perrers should be brought to justice, voted most liberal supplies. We may note that John of Gaunt, who found it expedient to give evidence against her, was not above putting in his claim for some of the forfeited wealth of the mistress. He received as his spoils a new inn and some houses in the parish of St. Martin the Little in London.[2] Alice took refuge with her husband, who two years later, on the 14th December 1379, was pardoned for 'having harboured her'. Leave was then granted for the two to remain together in the realm as long as they pleased.[3]

Though it would be an exaggeration to say that the parliament was "furiously anti-papal",[4] there were yet two incidents which showed the bishops the need of caution in any measures against Wyclif. Complaints were once more raised against the systematic draining of the country for the benefit of the Roman curia or of aliens by papal provisions and reservations. The income of French clergy alone from English livings was

[1] *Rot. Parl.* iii. 3 f.; *Cal. Pat.* i. 10, 21; *Rot. Scot.* ii. 16; Walsingham, i. 344; Rymer, iv. 26; *Chron. Ang.* 151, 166–7.
[2] *Cal. Pat.* i. 98, 105 on 19 Jan. 1378; *Rot. Parl.* iii. 13 a.
[3] *Cal. Pat.* i. 412.
[4] Trevelyan, 81.

estimated at £10,000 a year.¹ The Commons proposed to put a stop to these usurpations, which violated the concordat between Gregory XI and Edward, by imposing severe penalties upon all persons who should obtain any papal provision, or who should rent from any alien land which was a fief of the English Church. They further proposed that before the next Candlemas (Feb. 2) all foreigners alike, whether monks or seculars, should leave the kingdom, and that during the continuance of the war all their revenues should be applied to the war. The petition, with certain exceptions, was granted, and all aliens were ordered to pass through Dover to Calais. At Dover they were searched to see whether they had any plate or money, except such as was necessary for their expenses.² In order to discover the aliens, including cardinals, in possession of any benefices, and the value of their benefices, a writ from the king dated the 12th December 1377 ordered the bishops to make a full return.³

In connexion with this stoppage of the export of gold the Council [4] asked the advice of Wyclif ' in writing ',

' whether the kingdom of England may lawfully in case of necessity, for its own defence, detain and keep back the treasure of the kingdom that it be not carried away to foreign nations, the pope himself demanding the same under pain of censure and by virtue of obedience '.

This proceeding is the more remarkable when we remember that Gregory's bulls were in the hands of the archbishop. But the need was urgent and overrode all nice considerations. For, as a result of the concordat at Bruges, Arnold Garnier had returned to England,⁵ and in the last two months had exported £4,000 to Italy, the balance of a larger sum, £6,000 in all. Moreover, Wyclif was known by the council already to have entered the fray. He had remembered the oath of Garnier on the 13th February 1372. This Wyclif had recently published,⁶

---

¹ *Rot. Parl.* iii. 19. Lechler, 168, mistakenly says £60,000.
² *Rot. Parl.* iii. 22. Cf. *Cal. Pat.* i. 52 dated 18 Oct.
³ 12 Dec. 1377. See Powell, *Peasants' Rising*, 57 f., and for a fragment, Foxe, ii. 807–10.
⁴ Not the parliament as Lewis, 51.
⁵ 26 April 1375 (*Cal. Pap. Let.* iv. 143 and cf. *ib.* 142, 153); Rymer, iv. 16.
⁶ Printed in Lechler (Ger. ed.), ii. 576–9. Cf. Buddensieg, *Pol. Works*, i. pp. xxx, xlii. Wyclif refers to this oath in *Off. Reg.* 108, where ' gravario ' is

asking also whether there was not an irreconcilable contradiction between it and the permission given to Garnier to collect money for the curia, and ' whether the said collector would not be found perjured before God and man ' ?

Thus requested, Wyclif seized his opportunity and answered the question with a decided affirmative, appealing to three different laws.[1] First, he took his stand upon the *law of nature*, in virtue of which the kingdom of England possesses the power of resistance for its own self-defence. He appealed, secondly, to *the law of the gospel*, according to which all almsgiving (and into this all Church property according to his teaching ultimately resolves itself) in case of necessity ceases of itself to be a duty binding by the law of love. In support of this assertion, Wyclif quoted several strong utterances of ' that most blessed and acute saint ', St. Bernard of Clairvaux, in his *De Consideratione* or memorial to pope Eugene III. Last of all, he appeals to the *law of conscience*, which he explains as the stress that must be laid by kings and governors upon what is due to the national welfare. Our fathers, he claimed, endowed not the Church at large, but the Church in England. If these endowments were diverted, injury would be done to the souls of the donors in purgatory. Moreover, England must be impoverished, and her population decline, while the curia, by the wealth flowing in upon it, would become arrogant and profligate. The enemies of England, by means of her own gold, would be in a position to make her feel their malice, while Englishmen would be laughed at by foreigners for their ' asinine stupidity '. In the second part of his state-paper Wyclif endeavours to remove the apprehension which might arise from the adoption of the measures in question, especially the danger of papal excommunication, as in the recent story of Florence. A curious objection had been raised that if the money remained in England it would lead to an increase of ' petulance,

---

a mistake of the copyists for Garnier. Lechler's date, 1372 (*op. cit.* 138), is impossible, for the paper especially refers to ' our king, in etate juvenili florenti '.

[1] For this state-paper (partly translated in Foxe, iii. 54–6) see *Ziz.* i. 258–71, printed from a MS. in the Bodleian and the Vienna MS. 1337 where it is called *de quest. utrum lic. thesaur. retinere* (Buddensieg, *Pol. Works*, i. xlii, lvi, and for its genuineness, *ib.* i. p. lxxv–vi).

lubricity, and avarice'. Wyclif retorts that this could be met by disendowment. A more interesting reference is to 'the peril that arises from the lack of perseverance in our race'. To meet this the first business must be ' to train our nation in unanimity and constancy'. How much farther his daring would have led Wyclif we know not, for at this point ' silence upon these questions was imposed upon him by our lord the king with the Council of the realm '.[1]

While parliament was still sitting, news of the contents of the papal bulls began to be bruited about, though as yet Sudbury had deemed it prudent to take no steps towards publication. Thomas Brunton, bishop of Rochester,[2] was not so bound by official reticence. In the hearing of many members of parliament[3] he publicly told Wyclif, ' under excitement ', that his Conclusions had been condemned by the curia, and that he, the bishop, had received formal evidence to this effect from the notary of the curia. Wyclif tells us that Brunton's assertion gave great offence. It was deemed to be a slander on the curia and an insult to the king; moreover, it threw suspicion on ' his brethren ', especially on Brunton himself, as the authors of the accusation. Wyclif himself proclaimed that the bull was opposed to English law in ordering the arrest of a subject without conviction of heresy, and in its implication that the king may not punish delinquent clerks by withholding their endowments.

About this time Wyclif was also engaged in controversy with a ' motley doctor ', probably of Oxford, possibly one of those whose accusation of Wyclif to Rome had brought about the papal bulls. The date of this tract[4] is uncertain, but from its tone and outlook, especially its references to the ' hearsay ' knowledge of the bulls[5], we refer it to the early fall of 1377.

[1] For a later protest by Wyclif against the export of gold to the curia see *Pol. Works*, i. 244 (July, 1383).

[2] *Infra*, ii. 256. In Lechler, 131, this is erroneously said to be Thomas Trillek (†1372).

[3] *Eccles.* 354–5. Lechler uses ' in publico parlamento ' (*sic*) as a proof that Wyclif was a member of parliament (*infra*, Appendix J).

[4] In *Ziz.* 481–92. Shirley dates after the *Libellus* and *Protestatio*, for which see *infra*. The first paragraph is repeated in *Ver. Script.* i. 152.

[5] ' ut dicitur ' is in constant use, pointing to the absence of formal publication.

Unlike two later tracts which dealt with the same matter, the *Libellus* and the *Protestatio*, this polemic is more free in style, less systematic in arrangement. The proceedings as yet were too indefinite to drive Wyclif to a formal defence. The tract, whose professed anonymity but thinly veils its author, is remarkable for boldness of tone. Wyclif, leaving Oxford behind him, is already becoming a popular pamphleteer. He calls upon the ' soldiers of Christ, seculars and clerics, and especially the professors of evangelical poverty, the defenders even unto death of the law of God ', to rouse themselves against the claim of the papacy to bind and loose at will. Such a claim makes the pope ' the enemy of the church of Christ, and the worst antichrist '. Though personally polite to the pope, he claims that the pope must be judged by his conformity to the rule of scripture, ' that he live soberly, justly, and piously in evangelical poverty '.

The publication of this tract was the beginning of controversy. On the 28th November parliament was dismissed, and Wyclif returned to Oxford.[1] Freed from this restraint the two commissioners, Sudbury and Courtenay, deemed it no longer imprudent to publish, on the 18th December, Gregory's bulls. A mandate enclosing the bull was served upon the chancellor of Oxford, Adam de Tonworth, by Edmund Stafford.[2] Stafford, afterwards chancellor of England and bishop of Exeter, the second founder of Exeter college at Oxford, was at that time under a vow of pilgrimage to Compostella, from which he did not obtain release until 1414.[3] The mandate called upon the chancellor, assisted by the most learned and orthodox doctors of the university, to ascertain whether Wyclif had taught the theses in question. The result of this inquiry was to be reported in a sealed letter. Furthermore, the chancellor was to cite Wyclif to appear before the commissioners within thirty days at St. Paul's, there to answer concerning the theses. The steps taken by the chancellor in this second issue were to be reported in an open letter. It is worthy of note that though

---

[1] *Rot. Parl.* iii. 29 ; *Eulog. Cont.* iii. 348.

[2] Lewis, 264–5, from Otford. In Wilkins, iii. 123–4 erroneously dated as Dec. 28. For Tonworth see *Snappe*, 330.

[3] Vow made in 1369 ' if his sister recover from illness ' (*Pap. Let.* vi. 439–40). For Stafford see *D.N.B.*

the two commissioners thus tardily published the papal bull they did not dare to carry out its instructions in full. The pope had demanded that Wyclif should be arrested and thrown into prison, there to await the decision of Rome. But not even Courtenay was prepared to go this length with one who stood so high in the confidence of both court and people.

The receipt by the university of the archbishop's mandate and the papal bull placed Oxford in a dilemma. To arrest a subject at the instance of a papal bull was against English law, as Wyclif himself points out. Moreover, it would give additional weapons to the party in the schools that sided with Wyclif. On the other hand the pope threatened to take away the university's privileges, should it prove disobedient to his fiat. The university met the difficulty in characteristic manner :

'So the friends of the said John Wyclif, and John himself, took counsel in the congregation of regents and non-regents that they should not imprison a man of the King of England at the command of the pope, lest they should seem to give the pope lordship and regal authority in England. But since it was needful to do something at the pope's orders, as it seemed to the university on taking counsel, the vice-chancellor,[1] who was a monk, asked Wyclif and ordered him to stay in Black Hall and not to go out because he wished no one else to arrest him. Wyclif agreed to do so because he had sworn to the university to preserve its privileges.'[2]

The archbishop's mandate was similarly dealt with. Wyclif's theses were sent to the masters regent in theology who 'all handed to the chancellor their conclusions'. But instead of sending a sealed report to the commissioners the chancellor 'for all, and by the assent of all, declared publicly in the schools that Wyclif's theses were true though they sounded badly to the ear'. To which Wyclif replied that Catholic truth should not be condemned because of its sound, for 'that would be to confound accident with substance'. More biting was his

---

[1] 'vice-cancellarius', as against Anstey, *Mun. Ac.*, p. x.
[2] *Eulog. Cont.* iii. 348. There were two Black halls at least, one called Great Black hall, opposite Smith Gate, the gate over the Canditch, about the N.W. corner of Hertford college (Wood, *City*, 97, 596 ; Boase, p. xxiv), and the other in Schools Street, swept away in 1736 for the Radcliffe library (Wood, *City*, i. 90 *n*.). This hall belonged to Osney abbey (*ib.* i. 573-4) and so may well have been selected by a vice-chancellor who was a monk as the place where Wyclif should be formally detained. See also Hurst, 113.

later sarcasm that to condemn a truth 'because it sounds bad for sinners and fools would make all Scripture liable to condemnation'.[1]

Before we pass away from the incident of this imprisonment of Wyclif by mutual arrangement, it is of some interest to note the use made of it a few months later by the Crown. One night a courtier from Woodstock came to Oxford and was there insulted by the students, headed by three monks, one from Gloucester, a second from Canterbury, a third from Norwich— as usual these older students were the ringleaders in brawls. They came outside his lodging and sang ' a certain rhyme in English that contained words against the honour of the king ', ending their frolic with a discharge of arrows. On the complaint of the courtier, chancellor, vice-chancellor, and monks were at once summoned to Westminster (22 March 1378) and soundly rated by Houghton, the chancellor of England. ' If ', said he,

' you at Oxford are not able to deal with those who insult the king, it is clear that Oxford cannot be governed by clerks. The king must withdraw its privileges. We depose you from your office.'

The chancellor of the university was not lacking in courage. ' I hold my office ', he replied, ' from both pope and king. The king can take away the part he has conferred, but not rights given by the pope.' ' Very well ', replied the chancellor :

' we deprive you of the king's part, and then you can see what you will be able to make of the pope's part. The king can remove both you and the university from Oxford.'

The chancellor of the university saw that his wisdom lay ' in a spontaneous resignation in convocation ', while the vice-chancellor was thrown into prison on the pretext ' that he had imprisoned John Wyclif at the mandate of the pope '.[2]

Wyclif had been summoned to appear at St. Paul's about the middle of January 1378. It is certain that he did not present himself, nor is there any proof that a court was held.[3] So the summons was changed to a citation to Lambeth. From a work

[1] Walsingham, i. 363 as the close of the *Protestatio*.
[2] *Eulog. Cont.* iii. 348-9 ; Rymer, iv. 32 ; Wilkins, iii. 137 ; and cf. Wyclif, *Eccles.* 355. In place of Toneworth Gilbert was elected and served one year (*Snappe*, 330 ; *Pat. Ric.* i. 302).
[3] Pratt's contrary suggestion, Foxe, iii. 792, is pure surmise.

written by Wyclif shortly after these events we learn the cause of his non-appearance at St. Paul's. He had heard that Sudbury, quoting Scripture for his purpose, had said : 'a little while and ye shall not see me, and again a little while and ye shall see me '. Wyclif professed to believe that the archbishop was plotting his destruction, and that many had been taught, he knew not by whom, that it would be a work of charity ' to put him out of the way by burning, slaughter or other death '.[1] His fears, whether real or not, were exaggerated. Sudbury was not that sort of man. But encouraged, possibly, by his knowledge of the proceedings taken against the vice-chancellor, Wyclif, as we believe, appeared at Lambeth. The exact date of the Lambeth trial is not known ; it must, however, have been a few weeks previous to Lady Day 1378.[2] In this action against Wyclif the bishops were within their rights. But the Crown did not intend to abandon one whose advice they had recently sought. With the sympathy of the government, the Queen-mother, just before the trial began, sent a message, through Sir Lewis Clifford, ordering the bishops to abstain from pronouncing any final judgement concerning the accused, though not contesting their right to hold the court. The trial, thus reduced to a farce—so far at any rate as the papal demand that Wyclif should be sent to Rome—nevertheless proceeded. In defence of his Conclusions Wyclif put in [3] a written statement entitled a *Protestatio*,[4] in which he expounded more fully their meaning. At the same time the citizens of London, probably under the lead of John of Northampton,[5] no longer hindered as at the previous trial from showing their sympathy

[1] *Ver. Script.* i. 374 ; also quoted, not quite accurately, in *Ziz.*, p. xxxiv *n*. Matthew, *Eng. Works*, p. xiv, refers this to a third citation after Lambeth. This seems needless multiplication, nor is a third citation likely considering the death of Gregory.

[2] I have fixed this date from (a) the date of the reference in *Ver. Script.* See *infra*, ii. 4 *n*. (b) Walsingham, i. 356, expressly states that it was before the death of Gregory XI (27 March 1378). Lewis, 54, mistakenly dates in June 1378, though on p. 63 he owns the difficulty of so late a date.

[3] See Walsingham, i. 357 *n*. Shirley, *Ziz.* xxxi *n*. doubts its actual presentation.

[4] Found in Walsingham, i. 357–63, who calls it *Declarationes* ; *Chron. Ang.* 184 f. But Wyclif gives it the title of *Protestatio* in *Ver. Script.* i. 349, from its first words. It is translated in Lewis, 55 f., Foxe, iii. 13 f., and partly in Vaughan, *Mon.* 207 f.

[5] For John of Northampton see *D. N. B.*

with Wyclif by their greater hatred of Lancaster, broke into the archbishop's chapel and with menacing applause of the accused tried to stop the trial.[1]

The commissioners felt that it was useless to proceed. So they contented themselves with prohibiting Wyclif 'from canvassing such theses in schools or sermons because of the scandal thereby given to the laity '.[2] Well might Walsingham pour out his soul in indignation at the impotence of the whole proceedings. When appointed as Gregory's commissioners

' they had declared, in the fulness of their courage, that by no entreaties of men, by no threats or bribes, would they allow themselves to be drawn aside from the line of strict justice in this affair, even if this should involve peril to their lives. But on the very day of hearing, for fear, or because of the wind which blew the reed hither and thither, their words had become smoother than oil, to the public humiliation of their own dignity and to the detriment of the whole Church. Men who had vowed not to bend to the princes and peers of the realm till they had punished the arch-heretic for his extravagances, were seized with such terror at the sight of Sir Lewis Clifford, that one would have supposed that they had no horns; for they became as one that heareth not, and in whose mouth are no reproofs.[3]

Thus it was, adds Walsingham, that the ' slippery hypocrite ', by his written defence of his godless theses, had the better of his judges and escaped, though all his theses were clearly heretical and depraved.[4] Unfortunately also, a few days after the trial Gregory XI passed away and for some time the papacy was too busy with its own troubles to attend to Wyclif, who held up his dead opponent to general reprobation as 'a horrible devil ', an ' abiding heretic ' who had died without showing any signs of penitence for his crimes, his nepotism, and his slaughter of ' many thousands ' in his attempt to regain his temporal dominions.[5]

We have referred to Gregory's citation of Wyclif to appear before him personally ' within three months '. To this at the time Wyclif paid no attention. Secure in the favour of the

[1] Walsingham, i. 356, 363 ; *Chron. Ang.* 183.
[2] Ramsay, *Gen. Lanc.* ii. 118, that they were " condemned ", is too strong.
[3] Walsingham is quoting Ps. xxxviii. 14.
[4] Walsingham, i. 356, 363 ; *Chron. Ang.* 183.
[5] *Eccles.* 366. This estimate of Gregory is not fair, though the Florentine war and the Waldensian persecution are sad blots. Wyclif rightly points to his nepotism. See Mollat-Baluze, i. 430.

Crown he could plead that he could not leave the realm without the royal licence. But though Gregory was dead, the summons still hung over his head. So Wyclif took the opportunity of sending to the new pope a letter of excuse. Few documents from his pen were more skilfully drawn, though it is hard to decide where sincerity ends and sarcasm begins:

'I rejoice to open and declare unto every man the faith that I hold, and especially unto the bishop of Rome: because if as I do suppose it be sound he will most willingly confirm my said faith, or if erroneous amend the same. First I suppose that the gospel of Christ is the heart of the body of God's law ... again I do hold the bishop of Rome, forasmuch as he is the supreme vicar of Christ here on earth, to be most bound of all pilgrims unto that law of the gospel.... Whereupon I do gather out of the heart of the law of the Lord that Christ for the time of his pilgrimage here was a most poor man, abjecting all worldly rule and honour ... hereof I do gather that the pope ought to leave unto the secular power all temporal dominion and thereunto effectually to exhort his whole clergy. Wherefore if I have erred in any of these points I will most humbly submit myself unto correction even by death, if necessity so demand; and if I could labour according to my will or desire in my own person I would humbly present myself before the bishop of Rome; but the Lord hath otherwise visited me, and hath taught me rather to obey God than men.'

Wyclif, who was still persuaded of Urban's good intentions, closed the letter with a personal appeal:

'Since God has given to our pope just evangelical instincts we ought to pray that these be not extinguished by any crafty counsel, and that pope and cardinals be not moved to do anything contrary to the law of God. Wherefore let us pray unto our God that He will so stir up our pope Urban VI as he began that he with his clergy may follow the Lord Jesus Christ in life and manners; and that they may teach the people effectually, and that they, likewise, may faithfully follow them in the same, and let us specially pray that our pope may be preserved from all malign counsel, for we know that a man's foes are they of his household.[1]

Whether Urban ever received or read this letter we cannot tell. Probably not, for greater matters soon engrossed his attention. This summons to Rome crops up more than once in Wyclif's writings. In his *de Servitute Civili*, written about this time, he quotes Gregory's bull and utters his protest. By such means the pope 'can rob the realm of money and men', and may be 'gone to hell' before the summoned arrive. The

[1] For this letter and its date see *infra*, ii. 315 *n*.

man cited may be weak or ill—was Wyclif thinking of himself?
—and yet may be forced to travel by dangerous roads, and in
the pope's own domain be exposed to robbers. The pope may
have nothing against the man except that he has published the
law of God and of the realm. The pope has really no jurisdiction over the body of the king's liegeman, who would do
well therefore ' to stay at home and ask help of the Lord '.[1]

Of the influence of Wyclif at this time with the nation we
have a proof in a revised edition of the *Protestatio*. Netter, to
whom we are indebted for preserving this paper, tells us that
it was published for the parliament. Pictures have been
drawn of the Reformer reading this theological tract before the
astonished knights of the shire, and Lewis fixed the date of the
parliament in question as the 25th April 1378. No parliament
was held at this date, and the parliament at Gloucester in the
following autumn is altogether too late; events came too
thick and fast for a matter dealt with six months before to
continue to be of vital interest. Nor is it possible to consider,
with Bale, that the parliament referred to is the parliament
which met on the 13th October 1377. As we have seen, the
papal bulls had not then been published. Wyclif would not
be so foolish as to stir up strife by assuming a condemnation
not yet made public. We are inclined to think that Netter's
rubric is a mistake; if it means anything it indicates either
that Wyclif in the autumn of 1377, anticipating the publication
of the bulls, composed a tract while parliament was sitting,
in readiness for the event should it occur; or that, after the
publication of the bulls, copies of Wyclif's tract were to be
seen at the Gloucester parliament. In reality this ' libellus '
of Wyclif is but a shortened, popular form of the *Protestatio*.
The fact that the references to the Canon Law which the
Protestatio contains are left out in the *Libellus* would indicate,
were we to believe that it was intended for parliament, that
Wyclif had a just opinion of the legal knowledge of the
Commons. The tract is really an appeal to the general public,
published about the same time as the more theological *Protestatio*.[2]

[1] *Op. Min.*, pp. xxvii, 159-61.
[2] *Ziz.* 245-57; Lewis, 54 *n*. The absence of all reference to the death of

Not content with his *Protestatio* and *Libellus* Wyclif issued about this time a work entitled *The Thirty Three Conclusions on the Poverty of Christ*,[1] ' written not only in Latin but in English as well ', of which, however, only the Latin has survived. ' I do not ', he said,

' seek to evade the papal jurisdiction, nor do I make any secret of my teaching ; else I had not scattered these theses over a great part of England and of Christendom.'

He had forwarded them, along with his letter of excuse for failing to appear personally, to the curia ' by the hands of two bishops '—as usual no names are given for our guidance in this strange affair, and it is useless to guess—for he was anxious for their examination by Rome ' since I believe that it is the head of the Church Militant '.[2] The *Conclusions*, as we may call the work, seems to be a short statement of the argument put forth in the ponderous *de Civili Dominio*, especially in the third book.[3] The work was intended by Wyclif to reach those for whom the larger work was inaccessible. At the same time the tract refers to many points condemned by Gregory XI. These deal chiefly with disendowment on the familiar lines. But in the ninth conclusion Wyclif protests against excommunication for the sake of money or temporal good, and in the eleventh affirms that it is lawful for laymen to judge prelates. He protests against priests giving themselves to secular business. To do so is as when a bailiff calls away men from the important tasks of his master to do his own. In his last conclusion Wyclif lays down that it is ' the duty of kings to defend the evangelical law and diligently to keep it '. This train of thought Wyclif developed very shortly afterwards into his *de Officio Regis*. Owing to the concise form of the *Conclusions*—each thesis sharply stated, then followed up by its proofs from the Bible, the Fathers, and Canon Law—as well as

Gregory or election of Urban forbids a later date. Wyclif was fond of these double publications. See *infra*, ii. 78, 251, 315.

[1] Printed in *Op. Min.* 19–73.

[2] *Ziz.* xxxiii *n.*, *Ver. Script.* i. 349–50. I cannot find any clue in *Patent* or *Close Rolls* for licences for overseas. The bishops may have been suffragans. The only two at all likely to help would be Rede of Chichester or Stretton of Lichfield, the friend of the Black Prince.

[3] Loserth in *Op. Min.*, p. viii. The frequent references to *Civ. Dom.* show that it was later (e. g. p. 21).

from its freedom from extraneous polemic, the work had an extraordinary circulation, seven manuscripts still surviving. Though there is no manuscript in England, one of those at Vienna was written in England and afterwards found its way to Bohemia.[1]

That Wyclif should have forwarded a book to Rome for examination which, in addition to other doctrines, laid down that civil rule is repugnant to the pope's office, that it would be a mortal sin to give goods to support the pope's war, and that rulers may take away property from pope and cardinals if they abuse it,[2] gives an insight into the optimism which prevented Wyclif from seeing the hopelessness of his frontal attack. Possibly he was misled by his success. He had reached the high-water mark of his influence both at the court, the university, and with the people. Three trials or attempted trials by the bishops had ended in failure. A series of prosecutions against those who had obtained papal provisions gave some hope that the government intended at last to deal firmly with this scandal.[3] All things seemed to indicate that Wyclif would succeed in carrying a large measure of his programme of reform. But in reality the movement had no depth of earth. The popular support was not based on real conviction. " Men had not had time to see how far Wyclif was leading them, and were content with the general direction ".[4] But Wyclif was too honest, or too little of a diplomatist, to leave them long in doubt. And then the movement withered away. But all this, as yet, was hidden from Wyclif's eyes.

§ 5

The months immediately following Wyclif's triumph at Lambeth were full of stirring incident. The death of Gregory at Rome had been followed by a disputed election. But before we enter upon the momentous story of the Schism there is an incident in the autumn of 1378 in which for the last time we see Wyclif in alliance with the Crown in his struggle with the

[1] *Op. Min.*, pp. viii–xi.
[2] Ib., 22, 25 (against the Florentines), 37, 39–40.
[3] *Cal. Pat.* i. 303 (10 July 1378) ; i. 308 (25 Oct. 1378).
[4] Trevelyan, 81.

Church. After the autumn of 1378 Wyclif passed from political to theological revolt. Henceforth he fought alone, with all the resources of the Crown, after a brief period of neutrality, at the disposal of the Church. The failure of the expedition to St. Malo in the summer of 1378 and the increase of unpopularity that this brought upon John of Gaunt added also to Wyclif's difficulties.[1]

The incident in question had to do with two English knights, Robert Haulay and John Shakyl who, it would seem, came into the affair as a surety for Haulay.[2] During the campaign of the Black Prince in Castile in 1367 on behalf of Pedro the Cruel, Robert Haulay[3] had captured, at the battle of Najera, a Spanish grandee called the count of Denia.[4] As Denia was of royal blood he belonged by the usages of war to the Black Prince, who, however, had assigned him by deed to the two knights,[5] though retaining some interest in his ransom.[6] Eventually Denia was allowed to return home that he might find the money, the two knights taking his elder son Alphonso as hostage. After some delay Enrique II of Trastamare agreed to find the ransom, 60,000 florins, on condition that Denia's two sons should marry his illegitimate daughters, the advance being considered as their dowry. This arrangement Alphonso declined, and in consequence, ten years later the son was still unredeemed. At last, in August 1377, the money was said to

---

[1] For this expedition see Armitage-Smith, 233–4.

[2] This point, usually missed, is clear from the indenture in *Close Rolls Ed.* xiv. 337–9. The two other sureties for Haulay were Sir Matthew and Sir Richard Redman. They seem to have dropped out.

[3] In the official records always 'Haulay', not 'Hale' as *Chron. Ang.* 207, nor "Haule" as Trevelyan, 87 (Trevelyan's account is inaccurate; Shirley in *Ziz.* xxxv–vi biassed). The name 'Haulay' was common. See *Cal. Pat. Ric.* i. 733; Gibbons, 50; Rymer, iv. 53.

[4] His full title was Alphonso, count of Ribagorza and Denia, marquis of Villena, duke of Gandia, and, later, constable of Castile. He was son of the Infante Pedro and grandson of Jayme II of Aragon (Armitage-Smith, 234). But he is usually called in the English chroniclers 'the earl of Dene' (*Brut*, ii. 335), in Reading, *Chron.* 183 'Doune'. Along with him was captured the noted Du Guesclin (Walsingham, i. 304).

[5] Walsingham, i. 376. The deed was witnessed by John Chandos. For a later deed see *infra*.

[6] So Wyclif, *Eccles.* 142, in his defence of the matter. That Wyclif is correct is seen in the indenture of 14 March 1375, set out in full in *Close Rolls*, xiv. 337–9. The king retained one-third of two-thirds 'first abating therefrom £3,000 for their expenses'. Haulay was to retain the captive or his hostage, first paying the king 2,000 marks.

be ready,¹ and Haulay and Shakyl after long delay were expecting to come into their fortune. To their disgust they found that the government, who had arranged for the release of a certain number of English knights then prisoners in Spain,² demanded the release of the hostage Alphonso as the means for carrying out their plan.

This invasion of private rights seems to have been due to the desire of the government, already committed to a war against Castile, to please the king of Aragon and the count of Foix,³ with both of whom negotiations were pending. Accordingly lord Latimer and Sir Ralph Ferrers lodged a plea in the Marshal's Court that the prisoner was theirs, though ten years had gone by before they made this discovery. Haulay and Shakyl hid their hostage, but the court replied first by a writ ordering him to be produced before the king and council in parliament,⁴ and then, on this proving ineffectual, by bringing the matter before parliament (Nov. 1377).⁵ The House, gratified, possibly, by this rare act of respect, or realizing the importance of the favour of the courts of Aragon and Foix,⁶ ordered the knights to produce their hostage, and on their refusal, apparently before parliament itself, committed Haulay and Shakyl to the Tower for contumacy and for turning their home into a prison.⁷ Efforts were made by parliament to refer the issue to a committee of the council, but without avail.⁸ For nine months the knights refused to disclose where they had hidden the hostage, and at the first opportunity knocked down their jailer, escaped from the Tower, and fled to West-

---

¹ The safe conduct for Denia's representative is dated 4 Aug. 1377 (Rymer, iv. 15).
² So Wyclif. Walsingham, i. 376, says the prisoners were wanted by the duke to further his Castilian schemes.
³ *Eulog. Cont.* iii. 342. Cf. Rymer, iv. 23.
⁴ Dated 28 Oct. 1377 (Rymer, iv. 23).
⁵ *Rot. Parl.* iii. 10. The writ is mentioned as having already been served. This dates the application to parliament as after Oct. 28, but before Nov. 28 when parliament was dissolved.
⁶ Rymer, iv. 23. Negotiations with Aragon began on Oct. 30.
⁷ This should not be called as Shirley in *Ziz.* xxxv " an act of parliament ". Associated with the two knights in the disappearance of the hostage was Sir William Farringdon, who on Dec. 5 was handed over to the custody of Henry Percy (Rymer, iv. 25).
⁸ *Rot. Parl.* iii. 50a. Haulay and Shakyl claimed also 1,100 marks for two Flemish prisoners who had been taken from them.

minster where they took sanctuary. As it was possible that they might escape abroad taking their hostage with them, the court determined on a daring move. On the 11th August 1378 [1] Sir Alan Buxhill, the keeper of the Tower, accompanied by Ferrers came to Westminster with forty soldiers and, after some parley, arrested Shakyl, whom they had enticed by a ruse out of the precincts.[2] Haulay, however, was at mass in the abbey and the priest was reading the Gospel for the day: ' If the goodman of the house had known at what hour the thief would come '. At this moment the soldiers entered the nave, seized the knight and attempted to drag him out of sanctuary. A scuffle followed; Haulay was chased twice round the chancel and at last killed ' beside St. Edward's shrine ', along with one of the sacristans who attempted to save the knight. The soldiers completed their work by flinging Haulay's corpse out of the church.[3]

The outrage at once resolved itself into a struggle between Church and State. The first terror had scarcely subsided when Sudbury roused himself to resolute action. In the presence of five of his suffragans he excommunicated Buxhill, and all those who had aided or abetted the crime,[4] though, with his usual unwillingness to push matters to extremities he added—if the chroniclers can be trusted—a special clause exempting the king, the Queen-mother, and Lancaster. Richard ordered the reading of the excommunication to be stopped—' for to cease of his cursing ' as the chronicler puts it [5]—and the church to be reconsecrated. But to this the abbot, Nicholas Littlington— he who built the present deanery, where his head appears above the entrance, and the greater part of the cloisters—

[1] Nicholas, *Chron. Lond.* 72.
[2] *Eulog. Cont.* iii. 342, with which Wyclif, *Eccles.* 142 is in close agreement. For sanctuaries and their regulation see J. C. Cox, *Sanctuaries and Sanctuary Seekers* (1911), also Cox in *Arch. Jour.* lxviii. 273–99; *Jour. Brit. Arch.* ix. 117–32; xi. 118–39. The Sanctuary at Westminster was not the belfry which stood on the site of the present Middlesex County Hall (as Stanley, *West.* 371, and others suppose), but the whole precincts. See Cox, *op. cit.* 49, and Wyclif, *Eccles.* 244.
[3] Walsingham, i. 377 f. (anti-Lancastrian); *Rot. Parl.* iii. 37; *Eulog. Cont.* iii. 342; *Chron. Ang.* 207–8; and Wyclif, *Eccles.* 142 f. Flete, 136–7 says little.
[4] Wilkins, iii. 132 dated 14 Aug. 1378. *D. N. B.* viii. 105 is thus in error. That the excommunication was sent broadcast is shown by its registration by Arundel at Ely (A. Gibbons, *Ely Episcopal Records*, 1891, p. 394).
[5] Davies, *Eng. Chron.* 2.

refused consent, and all services ceased in the polluted building. When Richard commanded the abbot to appear before him he refused to come, while Courtenay, in spite of the royal orders, read the excommunication every Sunday, Wednesday, and Friday, at St. Paul's Cross, and set to work to stir up the Londoners against the duke. When called to answer before a council at Windsor he failed to appear, nor was he moved by John of Gaunt's threat that he would drag him there ' in spite of the ribald knaves of London '. The prior of the abbey, William Colchester, was away in Avignon at the time of the affray. Thomas Southam, who was with him, advised him on receipt of the news to return at once. He did so, but was forced to ride up to the abbey by devious ways to avoid arrest and violence.[1]

The blame for the whole occurrence has been laid at the door of John of Gaunt,[2] under the plea that it all formed part of the duke's plan for obtaining Castile. How strong was the popular belief to this effect is seen in the elaborate defence of ' my master, the duke ' which Wyclif found it expedient to make, and his protest against the love of scandal which, he maintained, was a sure sign of irreligion. We hold no brief for the duke, and we regret the alliance of Wyclif with so unprincipled a politician. Nevertheless justice demands that we point out that in the outrage at the abbey on the 11th August the duke can have had no share, for he had been away on his expedition to St. Malo for over a month.[3] Wyclif also tells us that John of Gaunt said in his hearing that he desired to retain every privilege which would minister to the good of the monks, or would show pity for fugitives even when charged with treason, unless, indeed, danger to the realm was involved.[4] Moreover, the chroniclers who impute to Lancaster the whole design appeal merely to popular rumour, and at the same time record an alternative rumour that the affair arose from the desire of the court to marry the count to the king's half-sister, Matilda Courtenay.[5] The autumn parliament of 1377, which

[1] E. Pearce, *William de Colchester* (1915), 39–40.
[2] Shirley in *Ziz.* xxxv–vi; Stanley, *West.* 373; *Chron. Ang.* 210–11.
[3] Armitage-Smith, 238. Shirley, *Ziz.* xxxv is wildly inaccurate.
[4] *Eccles.* 266.
[5] Walsingham, i. 376; *Chron. Ang.* 207.

ordered the production of the hostages, was hostile to the duke, and was led by his enemy Sir Peter de la Mare.[1] But Lancaster, though not responsible for its inception, saw the chance of using the incident for his own purposes. As usual this introduced complications. An attack upon the privileges of the Church would have been welcome under most circumstances to the Londoners, who keenly resented the sanctuary rights of St. Martin le Grand, a constant refuge for all thieving apprentices. But their hatred of John of Gaunt, their disgust at his failure in the expedition to St. Malo, was the stronger force. Nor did it make matters easier that at this time Thomas of Woodstock, the faithful adherent of his elder brother, John of Gaunt, had involved himself in a struggle with the City on his own account. How the brawl arose we are not told. The official story is that the men of Cornhill

'made assault upon the servants of the said earl, and beat and wounded them, and pursued them to his hostel and broke and hewed down the doors of the same with axes and other arms, the said earl being then within, and lying on his bed.'

The leader in the fracas had been the master of the mistery of wax chandlers, John Maynard, but Woodstock chose to consider the mayor, Brembre, as officially responsible.[2]

As London was seething with riotous demonstrations, and as the abbey was still closed, for as yet it had not been reconsecrated, parliament was summoned on the 3rd September to meet at St. Peter's, Gloucester, on the 20th October 1378.[3] To prevent possible trouble with the papacy over the violation of sanctuary, permission was given on the 5th October to Arnold Garnier to collect all moneys accustomed to be paid to the church of Rome, thus setting aside Wyclif's arguments and advice.[4] On the appointed day the estates—if we may use a convenient though not strictly accurate phrase—assembled in the guest hall and chapter house of the abbey.[5]

---

[1] *Supra*, p. 267. Cf. Stubbs, ii. 464.
[2] Riley, *Mem. Lond.* 424 f.; Sharpe, *Letter-Book H*, 76.
[3] *Rot. Parl.* iii. 32 f.; *Members*, 199; *Reg. Wykeham*, ii. 599.
[4] *Cal. Pat.* i. 276. See *supra*, p. 303.
[5] For the descriptions of Gloucester which follow see T. D. Fosbroke, *City of Gloucester* (1819); *Arch. Jour.* liv. 77–122; *Valor Eccl.* ii. 409 f.; *Vict. Co. Glos.* ii. 59 f.; *Pat. Ed.* xv. 293; *Pat. Ric.* ii. 22; *Pap. Let.* v. 598–9; W. H. Stevenson, *Records of Gloucester* (1893), 50–1.

Among those present was John Wyclif, who had been summoned to Gloucester for a special purpose. He would be glad to find that one of the members for London was among his adherents, the noted John of Northampton. As there was not sufficient room in the abbey for the court some were lodged at Tewkesbury, and others, no doubt, in the castle at Gloucester. If so we trust that the stench of which such frequent complaint had been made because of the filth thrown near the walls into a place called 'le Barelond' had now been cured—probably there had been a cleaning up for parliament, just as Jerusalem in our day was cleaned up for the late Kaiser. The abbey soon became "more like a fair than a house of religion, and games were played in the cloister garth", for the new abbot, John Bayfield,[1] was "a gentle, simple-minded man", who, no doubt, was powerless to interfere. As a result of the necessary hospitality, the abbey found itself three years later in debt to the extent of 8,000 florins. Part of the debt was due, probably, to the expense of rebuilding the wonderful cloisters, begun by the late abbot, Thomas Horton. These Wyclif would see in their still unfinished state. Wyclif also would hear that the abbey, whose monastic buildings, by a rare exception, were wholly on the north side of the church, lodged 44 monks who needed 200 servants to minister to them. He would remember that the monks were supposed to send three or four of their number 'to study in theology or other lawful faculties at Oxford or other university', but by their own confession this they often found it difficult to do, because of the low standard of scholarship. No doubt as he paced the stately buildings, or gazed at the great hall, but newly finished, with its large 'stew' or tank for keeping fish, and saw all the other evidences of luxury, Wyclif would be confirmed in his prejudice against all 'possessioners'. He would once more ask himself whether the income of 1,700 marks a year was being spent in the best interest of the Church, especially as much of the income came from the appropriation of seventeen wealthy livings.

We wonder if in his moments of leisure Wyclif interested himself in the affairs of Gloucester. If so he would hear how, five years earlier, the citizens had obtained from the king

[1] Bayfield, the precentor, recognized 2 Dec. (*Pat. Ric.* i. 59, 73).

'a certain place in the town called Seintmartynplace, 72 feet long by 24 feet broad, for the purpose of making a tower there to hold a clock to tell the hours of night and day, at an annual rent of 12*d*.'[1]

The citizens would point with pride to their paved streets for which in 1335 a seven years' toll had been granted. One other question we would fain ask. Did the monks, who owed their prosperity to the daring deed of abbot Thoky, when in 1327 he rode to Berkeley and brought back for burial the body of the murdered Edward II, show Wyclif the *Book of the Miracles of Edward, late king of England*, a copy of which at Easter 1395 they sent to Florence as a present to pope Urban VI? If so, what did he think of it? Or did he hear of the scandal at their hospital of St. Bartholomew, where corrodies were sold without licence, and bed-money taken from the poor—'when one of the said poor dies they take his goods and garments except his upper garment'—and where 'pigs and other animals' were driven at will through the wards?[2] But we ask such questions in vain. And yet it was probably the observation of details of this sort that made Wyclif a rebel.

Rumour set down the transfer of parliament to Gloucester to an attempt on the part of John of Gaunt, acting possibly in alliance with Wyclif, to bring in a sweeping measure of confiscation of church property.[3] But if by the transfer the government had hoped for a peaceful session, out of reach of all 'ribald knaves', they were disappointed. The Commons at first refused to grant a subsidy and called for the accounts of the previous year, while the archbishop, in the name of Convocation, demanded satisfaction for the outrage at Westminster. To emphasize the serious nature of the struggle, on

---

[1] For Wyclif's remark 'If a traveller had the sun continuously day and night he would have no need of a costly and treacherous clock', see *Pol. Works*, i. 302. Imagination lingers over 'treacherous'. For the cost £11 7*s*. 4*d*. of a clock set up in 1389 in the steeple of St. Peter's, Barnstaple, see Chanter, ii. 38–9. For repair of a clock at Westminster (£5 0*s*. 10*d*.), see *Privy Council*, iv. 288.

[2] *Pat. Ric.* i. 578 (Oct. 1380). Examples of the abuse of corrodies abound, e. g. *Close Ed.* xiv. 342; *Close Ric.* ii. 418; *Chron. Melsa*, iii. 85; *Reg. Wykeham*, ii. 376, &c. In Arnold, *Chron.* 256–63 there is an undated list of 'the corrodies in all the abbeys of England'.

[3] Walsingham, i. 380. Poole in *Eng. Hist. Rev.* iii. 574 finds confirmation of this in Wyclif, *Eccles.*, cc. 15 and 16, which he considers an expansion of the document Wyclif laid before parliament. Shirley, *Ziz.* xxxvi, speaks of Lancaster's "deeper scheme of revenge".

the 29th October the chancellor, Adam Houghton, resigned; he would be no party to an attack on the privileges of the Church. The court retorted by claiming the right of the king to make the arrest, and pointed out the injury caused to the public weal by the abuse of sanctuary. The privilege of the Church to protect the criminal was not denied, but the case of Haulay and Shakyl, it was urged, was one of debt, for which there were no rights of sanctuary. We are told:

'And on this there came into parliament doctors of theology and civil law, and other clerks on behalf of the king, who in the presence of the lords and all the commons made argument and proof against the prelates on the matter aforesaid by many colourable and strong reasons.'[1]

Among these doctors was John Wyclif, who interrupted the writing of his *de Ecclesia* to lay before parliament a defence of the Crown's action. In his usual strong style he argued that neither God in His omnipotence nor the pope in his sanctity could grant a local exemption from actions for debt.[2] The fugitives, he maintained, were offenders against the law of God and the Church, while Haulay had been the first to pollute the abbey, 'as we are informed',—presumably by drawing his sword in self-defence.[3] So important did Wyclif deem the principles at stake that he incorporated his defence of the Crown in his *de Ecclesia*,[4] the publication of which took place shortly afterwards. To this step he was probably led by his desire to keep the question alive, for parliament had been dissolved and nothing settled. If so, Wyclif scarcely attained his object. In the next parliament, held at Westminster in the spring of 1379,[5] it is true that the right of protection for fraudulent debtors was nominally withdrawn, and sanctuary limited to cases of felony. As a matter of fact the limitation

---

[1] *Rot. Parl.* iii. 35–7; Rymer, iv. 51. Houghton was in difficulties with Urban VI (*ib.* iv. 55).

[2] *Rot. Parl.* iii. 37. Wyclif is not mentioned by name, but the argument is undoubtedly his.

[3] *Eccles.* 150.

[4] *Ib.* 142–274. It still exists at Dublin as an independent treatise called *de Captivo Hispanensi*. See *Eccles.*, pp. xxii–iv. These six chapters were omitted by Hus when he copied Wyclif's work. In *Sel. Eng. Works*, iii. 316–17, we have some brief views of Purvey on the matter.

[5] 25 April–27 May (*Rot. Parl.* iii. 55, 58).

was valueless. The debtor who took sanctuary was summoned at the door of the church once a week for thirty-five days, and if at the end of that time he did not appear judgement went against him by default and his goods, even if given away by collusion, might be seized by his creditors.[1] This proved so ineffectual that Westminster long remained an asylum for debtors who brought with them their creditors' goods. As for other crimes than debt—murder, rape, robbery and the like—the rights—or rather, as Wyclif pointed out, the customs [2]—both of Westminster and other sanctuaries continued until their abolition in 1540.

Before we pass away it is interesting to note that Shakyl, whose tenacity is admiringly dwelt upon by the chroniclers ' that the infamy of his betrayal may shame present and future Englishmen ', gave up his hostage to the Crown in 1379 for lands worth 100 marks per annum and a sum of 500 marks down. The king also agreed to found a chantry for five priests to pray for the souls of Haulay and the sacristan. But the sum was not paid, so Shakyl still possessed his hostage. On the 25th September 1382 arrangements were made by the Crown ' for the better payment ' of the debt, a delightful way, as it turned out, of postponing payment altogether. So Shakyl and seven others removed and concealed his hostage, for which offence on the 5th August 1383 he and his accomplices received full pardon ; as the debt was not yet paid the Crown could do no other. But on the 3rd December 1383 the settlement was once more taken in hand, for Shakyl had appealed to parliament, and in the interval had once more concealed his prisoner. In the upshot he appears to have obtained the huge sum of 20,000 gold francs. After the award was paid, Shakyl's troubles did not end. He had a dispute with Haulay's heir, his sister Matilda, as to the division of the spoils. After some years of litigation the claims were settled by Lancaster, John Gilbert, and others. But on Shakyl's death litigation once more broke out between Shakyl's heirs and Matilda Haulay's heirs. Even as late as July 1409 the case of ' one Alphonso, hostage for a count of Denia ' was still undecided—a story of the delays

---

[1] Walsingham, i. 391-2 ; *Eulog. Cont.* 345-6 ; *Rot. Parl.* iii. 51.
[2] *Eccles.* 223-4 as not founded on Canon Law.

of the law which would have delighted the heart of a medieval Dickens.[1]

Upon this whole subject of sanctuary Wyclif's opinions are of much interest, not merely because of the completeness of his examination but also by reason of his characteristic mixture of arguments. Sometimes he touches a modern note, as when he maintains that the law must be supreme, that there can be no greater crime than any withdrawal from its operation, that exemptions are bad in kind and rarely serve a good purpose.[2] But for the most part he abandons this high ground for the usual medieval logomachies. He claims for the Crown an absolute right of obedience in all matters that are not contrary to God's law, and argues that in this instance the king's command was in accord with Old Testament precedent, instancing Solomon and Joab. But God's law provided no refuge for debtors or criminals; sanctuary is solely for accidental homicide and extends to twenty miles round every church. According to Wyclif, sanctuary for debtors was unheard of before 1351.[3] The claim of Westminster to special rights is subjected to close scrutiny. Privileges are only valid if they are for the good of the people, or if they benefit the grantee upon whose worthiness the privilege depends—here again we see the familiar doctrine of dominion founded on grace. But such benefit is impossible except in the privileges granted by Christ, the highest of which is to be allowed to follow Him in His poverty, a step still open to the Church.[4] The special privilege claimed by the abbey would be a licence to sin, and therefore must be regarded as false and vicious. It would be better if such privileges, with their burden of worldly cares, were abandoned. To turn the Church into a refuge from justice cannot give the monks—'holy men, divorced from the world'—that 'contemplation and rest in the Lord which they need'.[5] Even if the grant by Edgar and the Confessor were proved—Wyclif quotes at length the alleged charters upon

---

[1] Walsingham, i. 411-12; *Chron. Ang.* 241; Rymer, iv. 100; viii. 338, 346; *Pat. Ric.* ii. 166, 302, 339, 377; iv. 318, 324; *Pat. Hen.* i. 524, 548; ii. 315, 385; iv. 100, 391; *Close Rolls Ric.* ii. 487.
[2] *Eccles.* 151, 184, 230.   [3] *Ib.* 145-7, 243, 253.
[4] *Ib.* 148, 168-9, 176, 191, 257.
[5] *Ib.* 149, 175, 234; cf. 237.

which the claim rested[1]—it would be neither founded on Scripture, nor consonant with Canon Law, nor of value for the Church. If made universal it would ruin the realm, for it would allow a hostile army to invade England, take refuge in the abbey, and there prepare for further depredations. This contingency, Wyclif claims, is by no means impossible, considering the three conquests of the land by Britons, Saxons, and Normans, and the raid in the county of Durham in the reign of Edward II.[2] This last, a border brawl rather than a Scots invasion, evidently had made an impression upon the youthful Wyclif.

Wyclif is specially troubled over the excommunication of the king's servants. He owns that the slaughter which took place in the abbey was a great crime. But unjust excommunication, he maintains, is worse than murder—the familiar argument of the Inquisition that the murder of the soul is worse than that of the body—and the current rules regulating intercourse with excommunicated persons are thoroughly bad. The right of the bishop to imprison the excommunicated should be taken away, or should only be allowed after due trial of the accused before the laity. Wyclif concluded his work with the claim that truth is of more weight than custom. But Wyclif made the mistake of mixing up shady politics with what he deemed to be 'truth'. He would have done better if he had restricted himself to exposing the abuses which arose from the right of sanctuary. He could then have claimed that he was but developing a policy that a few years previously had commended itself to pope Urban V when he deprived his cardinals of the sanctuary privileges previously enjoyed by their palaces.[3]

---

[1] *Eccles.* 205–6. These charters are spurious. They were generally accepted, e. g. by Stow, *Survey*, ii. 111.
[2] *Eccles.* 149, 151, 175, 205–6, 218, 224. *Supra*, p. 49.
[3] *Ib.* 155–7, 268, 271 ; *Eng. Hist. Rev.* iii. 574.

APPENDIXES TO VOL. I

APPENDIX A

THE MEANING OF LOLLARD

As this word occurs so frequently the reader may be glad to know its real meaning. The original meaning would appear to be a wandering 'praise-God', 'chanter' or 'canter'. Cf. Ducange (quoting Hocsemius, 1309): 'Quidam hypocritae gyrovagi qui lollardi sive Deum-laudantes vocabantur per Hannoniam et Brabantiam quasdam mulieres nobiles deceperunt.' He adds that Trithemius, s. a. 1315, says 'ita appellatos a Gualtero Lolhardo, Germano quodam', an idea at one time extensively held, e. g. Birckbeck, *Prot. Evidence*, ii. 86, who makes the name Raynard Lollard, a Franciscan. The probable derivation is from O. Dut. *lollen* or *lullen*, to sing, cf. *lollaerd*, a mumbler of prayers, a word applied to the Beghards (*N. E. D.*, which considers it originally applied to the Alexian fraternity, also called 'lollebroeders', who looked after poor sick). The word was designedly confused with M. E. *loller*, a loafer. Cf. *P. Plow*, C. vi. 2, 'lollars of London', x. 213–18, and *Brut* ii. 551. By a pun this was derived from the Lat. *lolia*, tares, cf. 'Lollardi sunt zizania' (*Pol. Poems*, i. 232) and the title *Fasciculus Zizaniorum*. Both uses are united in Chaucer, 'I smelle a lollere in the wynde ... who wolde sprengen cokkel in our clene corn' (*Ship. Prol.* 11). Other uses added to the confusion, e. g. *Piers Plow*, B. xii. 191, xv. 131, 'to be lolled up', i. e. to be hung; and cf. Purvey, 'The most blessed loller that ever shall be was our Lord Jesus, for our sins lolling on the rood tree' (Deanesly, 274). The earliest university use in England seems to have been in 1382 by Crump (*Ziz.* 312). In 1387 the word is officially used by bishop Wakefield (Wilkins, iii. 202). The earliest use of the English form given in *N. E. D.* is in 1415. Cf. also Skeat, *P. Plow*, C. vi. 2 *n*. I may add that 'lollardy' seems a trifle earlier (Gower, 1390) than 'lollardry' (1414). Both were used. See further in *N. E. D.*

APPENDIX B

LUTHER AND HUS

For the understanding of the judgements of later centuries on the relation of Wyclif and Hus I give details of the early printed editions of Hus, especially of Luther's contribution.

According to Palacký, *Doc.*, p. viii, the first printed edition of the writings of Hus was a quarto brought out at Prague in 1502. This seems doubtful; no record of it is in either Panzer, *Annales Typographici*, or in Graesse, *Trésor de Livres Rares*. The first two printed works of Hus in the Brit. Mus. are (i) *de Causa Boemica*. No date, author, or printer. In reality, a short abbreviation of the *de Ecclesia*, and probably printed about the same time as (ii) *Liber Egregi US* (sic) *de Unitate Ecclesiae*. Really the same text as the above. No place or printer given, but, according to Graesse, by J. Schoeffer at Mainz. Dated as 1520. In 1525 there followed, from Strassburg (so Graesse; date, place, not given in the work), *Johannis Hus Opuscula*, ed. Otho Brunfels, with a dedication to 'Martin Luther, Apostle of Christ'. Practically very little of this volume is by Hus (see my *Age of Hus*, App. H). It was printed from MSS. in the possession of Hutten, and by its mistakes has profoundly influenced later editors. Bound up with this copy in the Brit. Mus. is a very rare *Processus Consistorialis Martyris Jo. Hus cum correspondentia legis Gratiae, et de Victoria Christi*, from the library of Hutten, with curious woodcuts. The work is mentioned in Panzer (p. 425), but no indication of author, date, or place. Perhaps Strassburg, about 1525. The same may be said of the *Epistola liiii*. (sic) *Nobilium Moraviae pro defensione J. Hus*, one date-limit of which is given by an interesting *Epistola familiaris adulescentis cujusdam Constantiensis ad consobrinum*, written from Constance '16 Kal. Jan. 1524', i. e. 17 Dec. 1524. In Nov. 1536 there was printed at Wittenberg, by Joseph Klug, *Tres Epistolae Sanctissimi Martyris J. Hussii e carcere Constant. ad Boemos scriptae*, with a preface by Luther. 'Has epistolas', says Luther, 'Boemica lingua scriptas *curavi* mihi Latine reddi.' In reality it contains not three, but four epistles, viz. Nos. 85, 83, 71, and 86, in Palacký, *Doc*. It also contains the *Epistle of the Lords of Bohemia and Moravia*, sent on '2 Sept. 1416', with their seals; a mistake for 2 Sept. 1415. See *ib*. 580. Luther knew no Czech, but does not tell us who did his translation. In 1537 Hans Lufft brought out a larger *Epistolae Quaedam Piissimae et Eruditissimae J. Hus*, with a characteristic preface by Luther. Luther's editing is worse than indifferent. The circumstances which led him thus twice within a few months to publish Hus's letters are given by his note: 'ut Theologi ad quodcumque concilium accessuri, tyrannide judicum Constantiensis concilii admoniti cautiores sint.' Luther was expecting a similar Council, convoked for Mantua, which met at Trent

LUTHER AND HUS

in 1542. This volume contains also Mladenowic's *Relatio*, of the details of Hus's death, sadly botched. Unfortunately it is the basis of most subsequent writers.

In 1558 there was brought out at Nuremberg the anonymous *Historia et Monumenta J. Hus et Hieronymi Pragensis*. This work contains the *Epistolae Piissimae*, Brunfels' *J. Hus Opuscula*, Mladenowic's *Relatio* in the corrupted form, as well as many letters, works, &c. It contains all the mistakes and misleading documents of the works it incorporates. Marginal notes have been added at the side, which oftentimes exaggerate tendencies. This work, or the edition of 1715, was the basis of all study until Höfler and Palacký. It is still indispensable. The general effect of all this literature was to hide Wyclif and exalt Hus. As Wyclif's works were still unprinted this was easy.

APPENDIX C

WYCLIF'S ENGLISH WORKS

It is difficult to decide which of the English Works printed by Arnold and Matthew should be assigned to Wyclif and which were the production of his disciples. Wyclif never refers to them at all, and the two English Bibles have problems of their own and cannot help us (*infra*, ii. c. 5). But we may assume that the *Sermons* were his, including the translations they contain of Gospels and Epistles. See Wyclif's own declaration, quoted *infra*, ii. p. 208. These have a forceful style of their own which the reader soon recognizes. Nor can the translations of the Gospels and Epistles be separated from the rest and regarded (as Jones, *op. cit.*, *infra*) as the hack-work of disciples. The style is too good and uniform for this. Moreover, they are assigned to Wyclif by Netter in *Doct.* ii. c. 86. iii. c. 66, though this will not shut out occasional help or editing by Purvey (*infra*, ii. 309). We may assume that mere hack-work, e. g. translations from Latin originals of his tracts, would be left to a disciple, possibly Purvey. This will rule out *de Officio Pastorali* (*Eng. Works*, 405-7; cf. *infra*, ii. 329; the English version closely follows the Latin, but both works contain sections not in the other, and the English is more vehement than the Latin), *Confession* (*ib.* 325), *Of Dominion* (*ib.* 282 f. Matthew disagrees in both cases), *Five Questions on Love* (*Sel. Eng. Works*,

iii. 183 f. ; original Latin in *Op. Min.* 8–10). Lechler, 495, thinks this last was an early tract and that the English was the original. But the reference to studying the English Bible precludes this, and the translator expressly tells us that he finds it ' hard to tell truly in English '. But the *de Blasphemia contra Fratres* (*Sel. Eng. Works*, iii. 402 f.) is a totally different work from the Latin *de Blasphemia*.

On the ground of a style different from that in the *Sermons* E. D. Jones (*Anglia*, xxx. 261 f.) would rule out also *Of the Leaven of the Pharisees* (*Eng. Works*, 1 f. Matthew owns " monotonous and poor "), *Of Prelates* (*ib.* 52 f. Matthew agrees), and more doubtfully *Of Clerks Possessioners* (*ib.* 114 f. Matthew agrees), *How Men ought to obey Prelates* (*ib.* 28 f. Matthew thinks it is " the work of some poor clergyman who spoke from the bitterness of his personal experience "), *The Office of Curates* (*ib.* 141 f. Matthew agrees), *The Order of Priesthood* (*ib.* 164 f. Matthew writes : " If by Wyclif it must be one of the earliest of his tracts "), *Three Things Destroy this World* (*ib.* 180 f.), *The Clergy may not hold Property* (*ib.* 359 f. Matthew agrees), *How Satan and his Children turn Works of Mercy upside down* (*ib.* 209 f. Matthew says, " in Wyclif's worst style, if indeed his "), and *Faith, Hope, and Charity* (*Eng. Works*, 346 f.). On linguistic grounds we also rule out *An Apology for Lollard Doctrine*, which was written after 1408 in a north-midland dialect. See *The Lantern of Light*, E. E. T. S., 1917, p. xvii. The *Apology* was printed by the unfortunate J. H. Todd for the Camden Soc. 1842 and assigned by him to Wyclif. Its style and contents are heavy and unlike Wyclif's. There are also some tracts written in a Western dialect which Wyclif never uses. These contain words found in *Piers Plowman* and have the same love of alliteration, e. g. ' But yet Belial brolles blabur ', &c. (*Sel. Eng. Works*, iii. 238). Certain words in them are found in Hereford's translation of the Old Testament (*infra*, ii. 160), but not in Wyclif's writings (Jones, *Anglia*, xxx. 266–7). We thus rule out *Lincolniensis* (*Sel. Eng. Works*, iii. 230–2), *Vita Sacerdotum* (*ib.* iii. 233 f.), *On the Seven Deadly Sins* (*ib.* iii. 119 f. ; Arnold also doubtful ; written after 1383, see *l. c.* p. 141). These we assign to Hereford or Aston.

To Purvey we would assign *The Fifty Heresies and Errors of Friars* (*ib.* iii. 366 f., also very imperfectly in T. James, *Two Short Treatises against the Begging Friars*, 1608, and R. Vaughan, *Tracts and Treatises of Wycliffe*, 1845). Arnold assigned it to the lollard ex-friar Pattishull. Pattishull was a rogue (see *infra*, ii. 140 *n.*). The lists in Bale, i. 510, *Index*, 322, of his supposed works are quite untrustworthy and show confusion with both Peter Payne and Kilmington. (Leland, *Com*. 384, is confused and inaccurate.) In Bale, i. 452; *Index Script*. 271, this *Fifty Heresies* is attributed to Wyclif under the title *de Fratrum Nequitiis*. On internal evidence—absence of usual, fierce polemics on the Eucharist, absence of bitterness against the Blackfriars' council, reference to the friars' attempts to burn Poor Priests and 'the gospels of Christ written in English' (*ib*. iii. 393)—we assign to a later date than Wyclif (cf. *infra*, ii. 326, and Deanesly, 399). If this work is by Purvey, then the striking similarities of language and thought lead us to assign also to Purvey *The Great Sentence of the Curse Expounded* (*Sel. Eng. Works*, iii. 267 f.; not in Bale). The absence of all Eucharistic controversy is the more remarkable as the work was written while Spenser's Crusade was in progress (*ib*. 329, i. e. in 1383), especially also as there is reference to the Earthquake (*ib*. 313). We also assign to Purvey the exceedingly bitter *Of the Leaven of the Pharisees* (*Eng. Works*, 1–27).

From this critical survey it is evident that the major part of Matthew's *Eng. Works* disappears, as also much that Arnold accepted. But the reader should remember that the writings are genuine enough so far as matter goes; the voice is the voice of Wyclif though the hand is not always his. We must remember that if Wyclif dictated the scribe would pen it in his own dialect. To Wyclif we may definitely assign *de Papa* (*Eng. Works*, 460 f.), *The Seven Werkys of Mercy*, which, however, has some northern features, *The Ten Commandments, Ave Maria, Wedded Men and Wives, The Church and her Members* (all in *Sel. Eng. Works*, iii)—this, possibly, the very last tract he wrote—together with some others, including several political pieces to which reference is made in this work. For internal reasons *On the Twenty-Five Points* (*ib*. iii. 454 f.) must be assigned to Wyclif's followers, for it was composed before the death of Urban VI in 1389, and after the opening of Parliament in Feb. 1388 (see *infra*, ii. 388). The work meets one by one the accusations against the Poor Priests. The *Speculum Vitae Christianae* must also be rejected, for articles 1, 7 are from a manual of religious instruction written in English in 1387 (see Arnold, iii. p. vi). The so-called Tennison Wyclif tracts, purchased for the Brit. Mus. in 1361, are also to be excluded, except *Wedded Men*, which exists also at Corpus Coll. Camb. Two Tennison tracts, *The Seven Sacraments* and *The Seven Vertues*, are by John Gaytrig, a fragment of his sermon of Shrift; see Horstmann,

i. 104 (8); Paues, *op. cit.* (1902), p. lxxi *n.*; Wells, 348. The foolish *Last Age of the Church* (*supra*, p. 14) should never have been printed as Wyclif's. For the *Wycket*, see *infra*, ii. 39 *n.* Miss Deanesly has printed Wyclif's *The Holy Prophet David saith* in her *Lollard Bible*, 445 f. See also *supra*, i. 14.

APPENDIX D

WYCLIF'S PHILOSOPHICAL AND EARLY THEOLOGICAL WRITINGS

THE genuineness of these and other Latin works is beyond dispute. Four important catalogues of Wyclif's Latin works are found in a Vienna *MS.*, and printed in *Pol. Works*, i. pp. lix–lxxxiv.

Many of the works have been wrongly dated, e. g. Harris, in his *de Ben. Incarn.*, p. viii, gives 1367 for this work, i. e., as he argues, four years after the doctorate. There is here a double error (*supra*, p. 203). Dziewicki (*Ente.* p. viii) dates the philosophical works as between 1363 and 1367, on the idea that Wyclif took his doctorate about 1363, and that these works are post-doctorate. This reasoning would really fling all these works after 1372. The date of the *de Ente* would seem to be determined as shortly after his disappointment at Canterbury. See the vague references to his lost benefice in *ib.* 32, 126. An early date is also posited by its few references to Church abuses, e. g. *ib.* 269-70, which again may be connected with his disappointment. But in his *Misc. Phil.* i. p. v, Dziewicki dates " in the first years of his mastership at Balliol ". According to Wyclif's own statement (*ib.* 106) he was not yet forty years of age, but that unfortunately gives us no exact date. Of the early theological works we are able to date the *Ben. Incarn.*, for we are told that it was written ' super sententias ' (see the heading of the Oriel MS., dating from about 1400, in which we find 42s. given on 18 April 1454 for ' Wyclyff super sententias ' ; *op. cit.* pp. xv, xx). It was thus Wyclif's treatise as a ' sententiary ', possibly his ' principium ', and therefore written about 1370 (*supra*, p. 97).

We add a few notes on the separate works.

The *de Ente* is a vast treatise in two books, each with six tractates, of which the *de Ente Praedicamentali* (Book I, div. 5) and the *de Tempore* (divs. 6 and 7) have often been regarded as separate works.

When the *Summa* was published the *de Ente* was made the first book. In it Wyclif deals with the difficulties involved in his theory of Universal Being as a predicate common to ourselves and God, finitely in our case, infinitely with God, but which yet binds the universe together in unity and harmony. The second book deals with the relations between God's intellections and volitions.

The *de Logica* was written in the interval between his bachelor's and doctor's degree in divinity. This is clear from comparing *Logica*, iii. 137, with Woodford's account of Wyclif's development (*infra*, ii. 34). But it would seem to be based on disputations held before he had begun the course (*ib.* iii. 74, ' I leave this to the theologians '), but was touched up and edited in 1383 (*ib.* iii. 183), though the alterations were slight, as we see from the absence of all eucharistic comment. The work is of interest because of its full exposition of Wyclif's realism in his explanation of time and space. I am inclined to think that Wyclif's views would fit in better with Einstein than with Newton.

One of Wyclif's earliest scholastic writings is his *de Universalibus* (in *Misc. Phil.*) written as one of the exercises for his master's degree. Proof of this is seen in his acceptance of accidents without subjects (*ib.* ii. 78). In *ib.* ii. 85, 137 he speaks of writing ' satis pueraliter ', and refers to the ' dean of the faculty '. In *ib.* ii. 152-6 we have an extract from one of his hearer's note-books written when Wyclif had obtained his master's degree. See *Addenda*.

At Stockholm among the five treatises copied out by Hus (see *supra*, p. 17) there is one *Replicacio de Universalibus*, purporting to be by Wyclif, which is pure nominalism, except that one of the persons in the dialogue called ' reverend Master ' asserts realism against the author. The ' master ' in question may be Wyclif, and the tract an account of a controversy between Wyclif and a nominalist (Dziewicki in *Misc. Phil.* i. pp. lxiii f.). This is better than to assume that Wyclif began his career as a nominalist.

In the *de Compositione Hominis* the number of quotations average four a page. The immaturity of treatment, in spite of keen argument and occasional eloquence (e. g. p. 8, ' the human intellect is created on the horizon of eternity '), point to a period before Wyclif had become quite sure of himself or had sufficiently digested his material into a whole. Sometimes in fact we have only " a conglomeration of mutually destructive ideas ", leading its editor, Dr. Beer, to regard the book in its present form as rather notes written down by some scholar from the master's lectures than a mature treatise (*ib.* pp. xiv–xv). Beer claims that p. 53, l. 19 could have no meaning except as spoken to an audience in a lecture-room. In spite of the constant appeal to the Bible (*ib.* 3), and of the claim of the author—probably inserted when the *Summa* was formed, for it has no relevance to the succeeding argument—that the book leads up to the treatise *de Dominio* (inasmuch as we cannot know how man serves or rules unless we know the double nature in which service and dominion meet in man), the work should be dated about the close of his master's degree. This surmise is strengthened by the absence of all references to the *Sentences* as well as by the use of the technical term ' Soc ' (i. e. Socrates) for A or B (*ib.* 99). The interest of the treatise, evinced by the number of manuscripts, may be accounted for by the discussions some sixty years earlier on the same theme, and the condemnations issued by archbishops Kilwardby and Peckham to which Wyclif refers (*op. cit.* p. 74. See *supra*, p. 105). The work is an attempt to harmonize Aristotelian psychology as interpreted by Avicenna with Christian doctrine and the psychology of St. Augustine.

Wyclif's *de Ente Praedicamentali*, written after his *de Universalibus* (see his reference on p. 3), in its present form is unfinished, possibly because of manuscript defect (Beer, *Ente Praed.* pp. xii, xv). In this work Wyclif closely follows the plan of the *Organon* and shows the influence of Fitzralph and Bradwardine, as well as of Grosseteste's *Commentaria in libros Posteriorum Aristotelis*. Though the theme is the nature of the categories, the work is closely related to Wyclif's later theological opinions. In the discussion of Time, for instance, we can see that Wyclif, when he should come to examine Transubstantiation, would be driven into antagonism to annihilation, if only because he maintained that time was an eternal present in the cognition of God, incapable of increase or diminution (*ib.* 199). The theme of the work is not every man's meat, so we are not surprised that at the end of the first chapter a wearied Czech scribe should exclaim, ' Dear God, help me to finish this work as quickly as possible '. The book is almost unredeemed by human notes. ' Serfs ', writes Wyclif, ' are a sort of cattle of their lords ', but the remark, so different from Wyclif's real opinions, is merely an illustration in a logical argument (*ib.* 67). Much space is devoted to the question whether action and passion are identical (cc. 9 ff.). From this the transition is natural to the action of God. God, ' the circle Whose centre is everywhere and Whose circumference is nowhere ' (*ib.* 151 ; cf. *Eccl.* 100), is the First Cause of all predicaments; everything predicable is but the creature of God, to whom all positive actions must be referred (*ib.* 131 f.). In consequence Wyclif is driven to deny the reality of evil. Evil is a defect or privation which exists only as an entity in intellect.

Wyclif's *Quaestiones XIII* (printed in *Ente. Praed.* 224 ff.) is a collection of heterogeneous matters under an argumentative form. The last was a discussion with an unnamed 'master' and may have formed part of his academic course. The early date of the work is shown by Wyclif's belief in the possible annihilation of the bread (*ib.* 232). The discussion of Free Will shows Wyclif's close following of Anselm's *de Libero Arbitrio* (in Migne, clviii). Wyclif's earnest nature breaks through the bonds of the scholastic method when he points out that a will that has once left righteousness can only recover it by God's help, that to stray from righteousness is worse than suicide, and that in restoring righteousness to the will God works a greater miracle than in raising the dead (*ib.* 268). His discussion of Creation shows his indebtedness to Plato, read in Augustine. As regards riches, Wyclif points out that want thereof helps more to virtuous life, and that a state of innocence would be a state of communism (*ib.* 268). But no attempt is made to apply the doctrine to the endowments of the Church. This is another mark of early date, if indeed the work be Wyclif's.

APPENDIX E

WYCLIF'S QUOTATIONS FROM RARE WRITERS

WYCLIF sometimes quotes from sources almost unknown by modern scholars. We must not assume that he had read all these writers any more than he had read the Arab commentators. Many of the quotations were taken from the commonplace books of the age. But in our ignorance of the then contents of Oxford libraries we cannot dogmatize. Had Wyclif, for instance, read the *Aphorisms* of the schoolman, Urso (*Comp. Hom.* 71; *Ent. Praed.* 38; *Trial.* 87)? Copies of the writings of Urso (thirteenth century) both in the Bodleian and New College (Coxe, 67) show that Urso was not unknown at Oxford. For Wyclif's supposed quotations (*Ver. Script.* i. 52 *n.*) from John of Paris († 1306) see *infra*, App. K. Another Dominican to whom Wyclif acknowledges his indebtedness was John Januensis de Balbis, who flourished about 1280, and whose grammatical works—a *Prosodia*—as well as his *Catholicon* or lexicon, were in great demand, as is shown by their being among the earliest works to be printed (*Ver. Script.* i. 74; *Civ. Dom.* iv. 425). See also *infra*, Appendix K.

In addition to Averroës and Avicenna Wyclif makes occasional reference to ' Haly Aben Ragel ' (*Quaest. Log.* 298), i. e. 'Ali ibn 'Abû-r-Rijâl aš Šaibani, whose work on Ptolemy's *Centum Verbum* was printed at Venice in 1484; ' Algazel ' (*Quaest. Log.* 298; *Misc. Phil.* i. 91, 183), i. e. Muhammad ibn Muhammad al Gazalli, on whom see either Carra de Vaux, *Gazzali* (1902), or Mandonnet, *Siger de Brabant*, pt. 2, whose works were printed at Venice in 1506; Avicebron, i. e. Salomon ibn Gabirol, a Spanish Jew poet and philosopher (Ueberweg, i. 424), whose chief work was the *Fons Vitae* (*de Ente Praed.* 37; *Misc. Phil.* i. 178), a favourite with Duns Scotus (Ueberweg, i. 453); and ' Albumazar ', i. e. Abu Nasr Alfarabi, *de Judiciis Astrorum*, taken from ' Ypocrates ' (*Serm.* ii. 382; *Op. Evang.* i. 82, ii. 194). Wyclif also refers (*Ver. Script.* i. 78 *n.*) to Caelius Sedulius, an Irish poet who flourished about 430, but his reference cannot now be traced. Nearer his own time was Cardinal John Halgrin († 1238) of Abbeville, archbishop of Besançon, patriarch of Constantinople (Eubel, i. 6, 38, 213), whose *Sermones* he mentions with approbation (*Ver. Script.* i. 90). Other writers, now mere names, to whom Wyclif refers are Haimo, bishop of Halberstadt (*Serm.* iii. 4), who died 27 March 853, for whose *Homilies* a countess of Anjou once gave 200 sheep, five quarters of wheat, and five of rye (Gasquet, *Monastic Life in the Middle Ages*, p. 102). A curious reference is to a writer called ' one of the twenty-four philosophers ' (*Ente Praed.* 151; *Eccles.* 100; *Dom. Div.* 84). This *Liber xxiv Philosophorum* has been printed by Denifle in *Archiv.* ii. 427 f. ' Dionysius the Areopagite ', whom Wyclif often quotes (*Pot. Pap.* 54, 276, 277; *Ver. Script.* iii. 158), was one of the most potent mystical forces in the Middle Ages. His works translated in the early years of the ninth century by John Scotus Eriugena had universal repute (see my *Christian Thought*, 153 f.). Wyclif also seems to have dipped into the Qur'ân in the Latin translation made in 1153 by the order of Peter, abbot of Cluny. See the remarkable reference in *Ver. Script.* i. 254, with Nöldeke's learned note, and cf. *ib.* i. 265-6. To Muhammad and the wide extent of the Saracen conquests he makes frequent references which show his interest. That Wyclif should talk of Muhammad's ' forgeries ' was natural to his age.

APPENDIX F

PETER'S PENCE

THE sole authority for dating this withholding of Peter's Pence in 1365 (*supra*, p. 218) is Reading, 163-4, nor is it entered in *Rot. Parl.* Stubbs, ii. 435, following Barnes, 670, *Brut* ii. 316, assigned to 1366 (*supra*, p. 219), but the dates in *Brut* for this period are all a year out. From *Brut* it passed, with same date, to Higden, viii. 525, Fabyan, 477. The decision was probably not formal but administrative, and in 1370 the whole sum due for 1365 was paid over (*Trans. Hist. Soc.* xv. 226 f.). There was great delay in 1372 in payment, and on 2 May 1373 the archdeaconries of Winchester and Surrey were sequestrated for the sum owing, £17 6s. 8d. (*Reg. Wykeham*, ii. 191). In 1377 when the question of payment was raised the answer was that no change should be made; see *Rot. Parl.* iii. 21 (84). Payments were generally in arrears, e. g. at Hereford in 1380, five years in arrears (*Reg. Gilbert*, 8). For the history of Peter's Pence in England, see O. Jensen in *Trans. Hist. Soc.* xv. 178-247, or in brief Tait's note in Reading, *Chron.* 323. If we may judge from a return of the diocese of Worcester in 1302 the cost of collecting Peter's Pence was out of all proportion to its receipts. Out of £34 2s. 7½d. the pope only received £10 5s. 0d. (*Sed. Vac. Worc.* 33-4), a sum which seems to have been fixed (*Trans. Hist. Soc.* xv. 206, 223, 228). The bishops in fact made a profit out of the collection, retaining all above the fixed 300 marks (*ib.* 184), while delaying payment of the rest (see Clement V's threats in March 1313, *Pap. Let.* ii. 117, 443). The total papal receipts for the kingdom appear to have been £199 6s. 8d., if we may judge from a letter of Pope Gregory X in 1272 (*Reg. Giffard*, ii. 57), and cf. Jensen, *op. cit.* 186, who shows that this was the sum originally paid in 855 by Æthelwulf. But the Welsh dioceses and Durham are not included in this return. John XXII, characteristically, made an effort to prevent the collectors retaining so much of the tax (*Pap. Let.* ii. 443).

APPENDIX G

JOHN'S TRIBUTE AND ITS PAYMENT

JOHN'S surrender was made on 13 May 1212 at Dover; the yearly tribute—700 marks for England, 300 for Ireland (cf. Wyclif, *Op. Min.* 424; *Civ. Dom.* iii. 100; and cf. *supra*, p. 218 f.)—was offered on 15 May, and accepted 6 July (Rymer, i. 111-12; Migne, *Op. Innocent.* iii. 881; James, *MSS. Corp.* ii. 369, for a fourteenth-century MS.). The Isle of Man was included on 22 Sept. 1219 (*Pap. Let.* i. 69). In consequence of his action king John narrowly missed becoming a saint! In Nov. 1252 Innocent IV granted one year and forty days remission of penance to those 'penitents who assist in rebuilding the cathedral of Worcester, in which lies the body of king John' (*Pap. Let.* i. 282). Payment of this tribute was made most irregularly. There are receipts for payment in 1233 and 1257 (Devon, 35, 512). It would appear to have been paid in 1259 (*Pap. Let.* i. 380); in 1261 (*ib.* i. 423). In 1266 it was obtained by means of a financial shuffle with the king (*ib.* i. 424). In 1278 an attempt was made by Edward I to hand over the payment to certain monasteries, but Nicholas III would have nothing to do with this attempt to escape humiliation, and Edward accordingly paid it (*ib.* i. 455, 475), as also in 1282 (*ib.* i. 477). Another attempt of Edward I in 1292 to hand over the payment to certain churches was also refused (*ib.* i. 557). In consequence no payment was made by Edward after 1290 (*ib.* i. 598). There was a demand for 24,000 marks arrears as well as for renewal of homage and oath of fealty in April and May 1317 (*ib.* ii. 128; Theiner, 193). But the cess for 1317 itself seems to have been paid (*Trans. Hist. Soc.* xv. 188; cf. *Pap. Let.* ii. 140). There is a receipt for payment in June 1320 (*ib.* ii. 206). In 1329 an arrangement was made to pay arrears in instalments (*Trans. Hist. Soc.* xv. 220). The receipt for 1333, to which the pope alludes (Raynaldi, xxvi. 116), was a receipt of 1,000 marks for 1330 and 500 for 1331 (Rymer, iv. 428, 563; *Pap. Let.* ii. 495).

APPENDIX H

JOHN SHEPPEY

JOHN was the son of a certain Jordan of Sheppey, a village in Leicestershire, who in 1340, along with another John of Sheppey, loaned £200 to Edward III (*Pat. Ed.* xvi. 504). His grandfather, Lawrence of Sheppey, was a wealthy Coventry burgher who founded a chantry in the church of St. Michael [T. Sharp, *Hist. of Coventry*, ed. W. G. Fretton (1871), 35; *Pat. Ric.* ii. 242, iii. 315]. This chantry, in April 1383 and Nov. 1390, John Sheppey further endowed ' for the good estate of the said John, for his soul after death, and for the souls of the said Lawrence, Jordan and others '. His connexion with Coventry is also seen in his petition on 15 Aug. 1378 for protection against the burghers of Coventry. As a result ' four of the better sort of every mistery ' were ordered to give security for their good behaviour (*Pat. Ric.* i. 306). Sheppey's promotions had been rapid and continuous (*Pap. Pet.* i. 398, 400, 401; *Pap. Let.* iv. 50, 59). On 25 Feb. 1368 he was appointed by Wykeham chancellor of Winchester, and on 19 April 1369 was present as an official at the ceremony in the chapel of Lambeth when Wykeham ' placed the pallium round the neck ' of the new archbishop, Wittlesey, and administered to him the oath of fealty to Rome. In the Convocation of May 1373 Sheppey acted as Wykeham's deputy (*Reg. Wykeham*, ii. 24, 83-4, 192, 301), an appointment which would bring him under the notice of the authorities, and so account for his selection as a member of the deputation to Avignon. On his return he was chosen one of the parties to settle a dispute at St. Augustine's, Bristol, and drew up an agreement between the convent and the abbot. (For this very interesting document with details of knives to be mended yearly, &c., see *Reg. Sed. Vac. Worc.* 318-20.) In Oct. 1376 he was granted a pension of £50 per annum until a benefice ' without cure ' of the value of 100 marks could be provided for him (*Pat. Ed.* xvi. 259, 365; *Pat. Ric.* i. 338). In 1378 he was appointed Dean of Lincoln after a struggle with Richard Ravenser, the elect of the Chapter (*Pat. Ed.* xvi. 156). In 1394 the dean, his clerks, and servants, of whom nineteen are mentioned by name, committed ' trespasses, misprisions and contempts ' in cathedral and city in a struggle with his canons, into which Arundel was instructed to inquire, but to Sheppey's disgust could not find the time (*Pat. Ric.* v. 410, vi. 69). The affair was not settled in the dean's favour until March 1405; see *Pap. Let.* ii. 520, 529; v. 460; vi. 30; Bradshaw, *Statutes Linc. Cath.* iii. 249–57. He died in 1412 (Le Neve, ii. 33; *Vict. Co. Linc.* ii. 95).

APPENDIX I

WAS WYCLIF A MEMBER OF PARLIAMENT?

I. THE relations of the clergy to Parliament are somewhat complicated, and their discussion would take us too far afield. They may be studied in Wake. From 1283 onwards Convocation had included two proctors from each diocese to represent the inferior clergy. In 1295 Edward I had summoned these clergy-representatives to Parliament, but all his efforts to induce the lower clergy to take a real part in Parliament were met by stubborn and successful resistance, and were not repeated after 1314. See Makower, 203–6, especially *n.* 23; also Stubbs, ii. 96, 130, 210, 427, 629. Stubbs, however, inclines to the view that Thomas Haxey (1397), a canon of Lincoln, Lichfield, Howden, Southwell, and afterwards of York, Ripon, and Salisbury (*Pap. Let.* iv. 395), was really a member of Parliament, an idea rejected by Pollard, *Evol. Parl.* 74 *n.* But if he was in the Parliament he was probably proctor for the Earl of Nottingham (Stubbs, ii. 516, 624). Haxey, we note, was for many years one of Richard's clerks (*Close Ric.* iii. 226, *passim*). Bishops also had their proctors. When in Nov. 1395 Ralph Erghum was excused all further attendance in parliament or council ' because too old and too weak ' it was expressly provided that he should have ' by his letters patent proctors thereat to agree to what shall be ordained at the said parliaments ' (*Pat. Ric.* v. 635, and cf. *Reg. Brant.*, *passim*).

II. We have already given (*supra*, p. 237 f.) the reasons for our rejection of Wyclif's supposed membership of parliament. Matthew (*Eng. Works*, p. vii) thinks some support for Lechler's view (largely founded on *Eccl.* 354, which he takes as signifying that Wyclif was a member of Parliament in 1377, and therefore, possibly, of earlier parliaments) is to be found in Lewis, 365, or the better text in *Op. Min.* 424 : ' Si autem ego talia assererem contra regnum nostrum, olim fuissent in parlamento (*sic*) dominorum Anglie ventilata.' But this seems only a claim that all Wyclif's arguments for disendowment had been canvassed in parliament. Rashdall, ii. 519 n., suggests that Wyclif may possibly have been one of the members for the university, though he owns that there is no record of such return, and that the university members did not begin until James I. He draws attention to a writ in Ayliffe, ii, App., p. lxxxviii of 28 Ed. I, requiring the chancellor to send to parliament 'quatuor vel quinque de discretioribus et in jure scripto magis expertos universitatis predictu'. The practice, as Rashdall owns, was not kept up because of the new relations (*supra*) of the (clerical) convocation to parliament. Oxford may possibly have been represented in the convocation. In 1408 we read 'in concilio cleri celebrato Londiniis, assistentibus doctoribus universitatum, tractatum est de obedientia papae subtrahendis vel non subtrahendis' (Walsingham, *Ypodigma Neustriae*, in Rolls Series 424-5). But this was really a provincial council (Wake, 347).

APPENDIX J

THE FITZWALTERS

STOW, *Survey*, ii. 60-5, corrected in Kingsford's notes, ii. 278-9 (cf. *Eng. Hist. Rev.* xix. 707-11), gives the history of the family, their tenure of Baynard's Castle, and the ceremonies connected with the 'bannerer's' rights and duties in time of war—'which banner shall be guiles, the image of St. Paul gold, the face, hands, feet and sword of silver'. He was entitled to £20 in money, and a horse worth £20. In 1383 our Fitzwalter was admiral of the northern fleet (*Pat. Ric.* ii. 256). For details of his will see *ib.* iii. 287; *Close Ric.* iii. 213. After his death trouble arose over a transaction between himself and Alice Perrers for £1,000 for the castle of Egremont (*ib.* iii. 309). On 13 Nov. 1389 an annuity was granted to his widow (*Privy Counc.* i. 14, corrected by *ib.* i. p. xiv). The original Baynard's Castle on the site of the Blackfriars was sold by the Fitzwalters in 1275 to found the friary, and the castle was shifted east (Stow, *Survey*, i. 68; cf. *Eng. Hist. Rev.* xvii. 485-6). The male line of the Fitzwalters became extinct in 1432. For further details of this important family see G. E. C. (new ed.) v. 709 ff.

APPENDIX K

WYCLIF'S DEBT TO WILLIAM OF PÉRAULT

THE discovery of Wyclif's great indebtedness to one obscure writer has been made by Dr. Loserth in his *Johann von Wiclif und Guilelmus Peraldus* (Vienna, 1916). Owing to the war this tractate did not obtain in England the recognition it deserved. Wyclif constantly cites a writer whom he calls ' Parisiensis ', e. g. *Ver. Sac. Script.* i. 52, 125 ; *Sim.* 8 ; *Op. Evang.* iii. 37, 222 ; *Serm.* i. 364, iii. 20 ; *Eng. Works*, 399 ; cf. Tissington in *Ziz.* 165. The identity of this ' Parisiensis ' has long been a difficulty. He has usually been taken to be John of Paris (*supra* i. 355), or John Gerson (Shirley in *Ziz.* 165 n.), or Peter Cantor (Matthew in *Eng. Works*, 529), or ignored. Loserth has now shown that we have here one of the inevitable Wyclif doubles, and that ' Parisiensis ' as used by Wyclif refers to two different people, both called William, and both Dominicans. The one—born at Pérault near Vienne, hence *Peraldus*—entered the Dominican convent at Lyons and thence to Paris. His works were printed in 1512. The date of birth and death alike are unknown. For a full account of his writings with MSS. see Quétif, i. 131–6. The other, William of Auvergne, became bishop of Paris (10 April 1228–30 March 1248, see Eubel, i. 410). To Peraldus Wyclif is especially indebted, and has incorporated many sections of his *Summa Virtutum ac Vitiorum*. With his usual industry Loserth has tracked these down, and printed the parallel passages. In addition to those mentioned above Wyclif's indebtedness in his *de Mandatis* (cc. 26–9), the first volume of Wyclif's *Summa*, should be specially noted. Wyclif seems also to have been acquainted with the *de Eruditione Principis* of Peraldus (see Loserth, pp. 25–6, or Quétif, *loc. cit*.). Of the *Sermones* of Peraldus, long attributed to Aquinas (Quétif), Wyclif had no knowledge save in so far as they are in the *Summa* (Loserth, 27 f.). It is interesting to note that Peraldus is one of the sources from which Wyclif obtained his phrase ' Lex Dei ' for the Scriptures (Loserth, 36 ; Peraldus, *Summa*, 82 f. ; and see *infra*, ii. 153. See also Addenda).

It would appear also that Wyclif quotes from the other ' Parisiensis ', bishop William, whose work *de Fide et Legibus* came under Wyclif's notice (Loserth, 77 f.). It would be interesting to know whether the MS. Wyclif used of Peraldus still survives.

www.ingramcontent.com/pod-product-compliance
Lightning Source LLC
Chambersburg PA
CBHW061421300426
44114CB00015B/2019